D0006978

the Daily God™ Book

A YEAR OF LISTENING FOR GOD

Erin Keeley Marshall

TYNDALE HOUSE PUBLISHERS, INC.
CAROL STREAM, ILLINOIS

Dear Emily,
Congratulations on your baptism.
We are so honored to be able to witness your journey of faith. It is always very refreshing to see a young person w/such a strong connection of their faith.
God Bless,
Ramon A Devise

Visit Tyndale's exciting Web site at www.tyndale.com

The Daily God Book: A Year of Listening for God

Designed by Mark Anthony Lane II

Edited by Erin Gwynne

Library of Congress Cataloging-in-Publication Data

Marshall, Erin Keeley, date.
The daily God book : a year of listening for God / Erin Keeley Marshall.
p. cm.
Includes index.
ISBN 978-1-4143-1606-2 (hardcover)
1. Devotional calendars. I. Title.
BV4811.M329 2009
242'.2—dc22 2009005469

Printed in the United States of America

15 14 13 12 11 10 09
7 6 5 4 3 2 1

TO DAD AND MOM. Thank you for the legacy of faith and love. You made a very special home for our family. You're treasures to me. I love you!

GOD'S WORDS TO YOU

If you could hear God speak audibly to you, what would you hope he'd say? Your answer might change from day to day as you react to life's challenges. Some days you might want his reassurance that he's still in control. Other days your heart might crave a reminder of his strength. And then there are the days when you just want to curl up in his arms and hear that he loves you no matter what.

The Bible is called God's Word for a reason. It contains essential, life-giving messages from the heart of God to us—to *you*. But it's easy to get so caught up in the language and history and ancient names that the words seem locked in the past. When that happens, it's tough to feel an intimate connection with the One who created you and wants to share himself through the Bible.

The Daily God Book brings God's Word to you in a format that builds the habit of hearing Scripture as God intended: as his letter of love to you. Each day begins with a quotation based on a suggested Bible reading, written as if God were sitting next to you. A brief follow-up explains how you can apply that portion of Scripture to your life today, and a prayerful response prompts further conversation with the Lord. Finally, a related quote or set of lyrics caps off the day.

This year, take your moments with your Creator to fresh depths with *The Daily God Book*, a resource that's sure to beckon you back for years to come.

"I create worlds of promise from nothing."

Then God said, "Let there be light." . . . And evening passed and morning came.

GENESIS 1:3, 5

Early morning darkness blankets the sky, a velvety whisper of good-bye to the previous day. At the horizon, a sliver of light yawns upward. Minutes pass. The sliver widens, unable to hold back the gush of color. A bird twitters, inviting a chorus of welcome to the display. The sun flexes its rays, and the hush of night gives way to the new day's authority.

Welcome to a fresh start.

Do you ever think of each sunrise as God's reminder that he was and is and always will be the Lover of new beginnings? How amazing that the One who made this world from nothing sends us a daily message that he still is in the art of creating.

His creative details are universal, yes. But they are utterly personal as well. He made the earth round so every person anywhere on it can receive his promise of morning every twenty-four hours. His planning inspires awe, each detail orchestrated to reveal himself to us, his creations.

He invites you to look for him in your world. Listen for his voice, his whispers of love and guidance, in the coming year. Invite him to create something new in you. Anticipate his presence, and rest in his Son's light on the road ahead.

No matter what last year held, no matter what *yesterday* held, this day is new. Fresh. Uncluttered by mistakes and chaos and full of potential.

God is in this day, speaking to you now.

Let the past hush behind you; look and listen for your Maker who sends his love with the rise of the sun.

He will be here for tomorrow as well, and for all the tomorrows of this year.

TALK TO HIM

"Lord, create in me new landscapes of faith, new eyes to look for you this year."

If you begin to live life looking for the God that is all around you,
every moment becomes a prayer.
FRANK BIANCO

January 2 GENESIS 1:26-31

"I put my hope in you."

Then God said, "Let us make human beings in our image, to be like us." GENESIS 1:26

Hope. It's about looking forward, seeing beyond the here and now, and anticipating the future. Hope pulls the joys of the future into the present because it believes there's more to come, and it doesn't wait to celebrate.

God is all about hope. He is full of hopes and dreams for us. We can see it right there in the first chapter of his Word. He created an ideal environment to sustain us because he intended a future for us. Since he made us in his image, he created us to reflect his hope-filled character.

Even before God created us and placed his image in us, he knew we were headed for disaster. We're sinners, and sin is an enemy of hope. However, God also knew himself. He *is* hope, which means he reigns over every trouble that threatens us as well as every sin we commit. He is our ever-present reason to celebrate.

Consider these truths as you approach your day.

Will your attitudes, words, and actions reveal a confidence that God will continue to be God? Not just in the Garden of Eden, not just in Sally Somebody's life—but in your life. And not just today, but tomorrow, next month, and years from now.

Circumstances are never the real killers of hope. The death of hope lies in forgetting to focus on the One whose image you bear.

You can celebrate today, no matter what your current circumstances look like. Life often hurts—and you may not experience the answers or provisions right now—but God promises you a hope-filled future in him.

TALK TO HIM

"Lord, please help me reflect your character today to a world that needs hope."

We were made for God. . . . When we see the face of God
we shall know that we have always known it.
C. S. LEWIS

"I am pleased with you because you are mine."

Then God looked over all he had made, and he saw that it was very good! GENESIS 1:31

God created a good, good, good, good, good, good world. He said so six times in chapter 1 and finished with a resounding "Very good!" after he made human beings.

Then chapter 2 takes a unique spin, interesting in its own right and easy to overlook at first glance. God spent extra time with the masterpiece of his creation: the first person, Adam. He spoke directly to Adam, communicating the first words of relationship and giving him purposeful work to do and boundaries of safety to help Adam thrive.

God was pleased with everything in his creation and took pride in what he made. He invited Adam to share the joy by enlisting him to name all the animals God himself cherished.

Notice that?

Adam had an assignment that he could dive into or avoid, succeed at or fail. However, before Adam even had the opportunity to prove himself through his actions, he already had God's approval simply because he was part of God's very good handiwork.

Adam belonged to God. He did not have to, and in fact *could not,* earn God's love.

Nothing has changed through the generations. For all the technological advancements we've made, all the higher-thinking psychology we boast in this "enlightened" age, we look pretty much the same to God as Adam did way back when. Try as we might—and too often do—we simply cannot impress him. How freeing! Some might call that reality unfair or arrogant on God's part, because we want to be impressive. But consider a sobering alternative: We are at God's mercy. Without him, we would not be here at all, and we certainly would not have the option of choosing to be with him forever. God is the only Being with the right to an ego—and how graciously he handles his supremacy.

God does not ask you to prove yourself. Not today. Not ever. You already have his thumbs-up.

Simply be his.

TALK TO HIM

"Father, thank you for making me yours. Please help me to find wholeness in you, not in my own efforts."

God is not in need of anything,
but all things are in need of him.
MARCUS ARISTIDES

January 4 GENESIS 2:8–3:10

"You will find beauty and freedom in my ways."

The LORD *God warned him.* GENESIS 2:16

Why is our natural instinct to balk at rules? We tell children rules are for their good, but then we picket and protest laws we think limit our rights. Remember loathing the infamous parental phrase "Because I said so" and promising to never utter it? We don't like feeling controlled. It's in our nature to want what we want, and we typically want both the first and final say about our freedoms. But that's a problem when it comes to God's rules, and the reason may surprise you: Our definition of freedom is far too limiting compared to his.

Picture the scene. God created Adam and placed him in a lush garden full of breathtaking scenery and mouthwatering delicacies, precious resources and flowing waterways. Eden was a veritable heaven on earth, and it was all for Adam and his descendants, including us. Surely Adam and Eve couldn't want for anything.

God did set one boundary. They were not to eat the fruit from one special tree. Far from being a killjoy, God set that guideline in place so Adam and Eve could enjoy *more* life. Obey, and they'd thrive in free and open communication with their Maker. Disobey, and they'd lose freedom. Of course, they did what any of us would have done eventually and indeed have done in our own ways: They stepped outside of God's safety net by choosing their will instead of his. And they paid dearly for it. Their sin locked them out of the utopia God had given them. We're still paying for it today.

Some things in life are simply "because God said so." That will never change, and what a wonderful thing that is!

No doubt you're facing a decision. You are free to choose to follow God or take an alternate route. What will your choice cost you or someone else? Will you free your grip on your will and trust God's boundaries for you?

TALK TO HIM

"God, thank you for the freedom you offer. Please don't let me be satisfied with anything less."

Freedom is not an unlimited license, an unlimited
choice, or an unlimited opportunity.
Freedom is first of all a responsibility before
the God from whom we come.
ALAN KEYES

"I provided the solution to your need before you knew you had one."

"He will strike your head, and you will strike his heel." GENESIS 3:15

Think of your current greatest need. Money? Healing? Time? We toss around the concept of need, often confusing the vital ones with desires that belong on a wish list—until we face a genuine necessity. Sometimes doing without feels overwhelming.

Since the Garden of Eden, amid the plethora of the world's needs, our greatest need has always been for God to save us from ourselves. Imagine being Adam or Eve. In all of humankind, they were the only ones who ever experienced the *complete absence of need.* They had it all—for a while, anyway.

Now imagine the shock of losing it all. Not just Eden's abundance, but an unhindered relationship with God—gone in an instant. Really, none of us can understand the extremity of their loss because we've never lived in a sinless world. We don't know what it's like to have eternal life and lose it. Consider the new and foreign emotions that bombarded them: Desperation. Terror. Shame. Disgrace.

God, however, was not caught off guard by their sin. Before he created the world, he knew he'd pay the highest price to save us. He set the solution in motion before time began. Then he assured us of his provision by spelling out his solution in the above verse, in which he warned Satan of a battle Satan was guaranteed to lose. Satan's future attack on Jesus, Eve's offspring, would be a nip to Jesus' heel compared to the fatal blow Jesus would deliver to Satan's head. This verse predicts provision for our eternal need and, thus, for every other insufficiency.

God knew the solution because he *is* the solution.

He sees your need today, just as he sees those you'll face every tomorrow until your final moments on earth. Better still, he knows how he'll meet each one.

TALK TO HIM

"Thank you for knowing my needs, God! Please keep me in awe of your sufficiency."

O unexampled love! O all-redeeming grace!
How swiftly didst thou move to save a fallen race!
CHARLES WESLEY,
"LET EARTH AND HEAVEN AGREE"

January 6 GENESIS 5:1-32

"I have cared for your family from the beginning of time, and I still have you covered."

This is the written account of the descendants of Adam. GENESIS 5:1

Most of us tend to skim the genealogies in God's Word. After all, what do all those multisyllabic names have to do with us here and now?

The names take on new meaning, however, when we realize that God knew the actual persons behind them, their strengths and weaknesses, fears and dreams. He knew their childhood traumas and adult failures, and he knew how their family history helped shape them to influence the following generations across the pages of time until today.

The Bible's genealogies illustrate God's faithfulness through the ages. His planning and care for his people long ago serve as anchors of faith for us. Those ancient men and women are part of your family history. In fact, if the list picked up where the writer ended, your name eventually would be included.

Our relationships with our families typically are fraught with emotions, running the gamut from love to anger to regret to loyalty. Sometimes those relationships leave a great deal to be desired. We tend to give and receive the best and worst in the relationships closest to us. That's part of being human on this earth. We love each other the best we can, but the strongest human commitment is not beyond the threats of individual imperfections and trying circumstances. Even in a lifelong relationship, life on earth eventually ends, and someone is left behind.

But God stands up to the test of time. Just as he loved and healed and disciplined and guided those parents and children, and all the grandchildren and great-grandchildren of biblical genealogies, he still watches over you and yours.

Whatever family issues you're dealing with, trust God to be faithful now, as he always has been. No matter how dried up the roots of your family tree, your faith will invite heavenly nourishment to the soil.

Ask God to use your branch of the tree to bring healing to future generations in your family and beyond.

TALK TO HIM

"Thank you for your faithfulness, God. Help me to trust you to care for those who mean so much to me."

The more we depend on God, the more dependable we find He is.

CLIFF RICHARD

"When life floods around you, it still fits in my hand."

As the waters rose higher and higher above the ground, the boat floated safely on the surface. GENESIS 7:18

In 2005, Hurricane Katrina annihilated Louisiana's coast and left a city in ruin. Hundreds lost their lives in New Orleans and its outlying regions; thousands more mourned the loss of loved ones, homes, and belongings. Grief reverberated across the world as survivors faced starting over with nothing.

It's difficult enough to hear about horrors of a flood on the radio, but it is still more heartwrenching to see the devastation on television, where pain-filled faces register emotions we can't really begin to touch. To experience such loss firsthand is difficult for most of us to comprehend.

That is, until we realize pain is pain, something no one escapes. Life, like water, is a blessing that can overtake us with little to no warning. It was no secret that New Orleans was below sea level. Its citizens had built levees to hold back the unpredictable ocean outside their doors. But their efforts proved futile when those levees broke.

We may not live on a floodplain, but we will face times when life dares to drown us. Problems may pummel us, leaving us gasping for relief from circumstances that seem determined to destroy us.

God is the only levee that will hold no matter what. He holds you as you face life's storms in his palm, and he won't let the waters overflow the boundaries of his hand. You might feel as if you've sunk to the bottom, but if you look up through the murkiness, you'll discover the waves haven't overtaken him. They never will.

Those who seek God wholeheartedly will experience his strength in the midst of whatever shakes up their world. God will provide in his way and time, and he'll see you safely to his destination for you when you rely on him.

Like Noah and his family during history's most disastrous flood, you can float safely within God's grasp.

Trust him to be your unbreachable Levee.

TALK TO HIM

"God, you know what worries me. Help me see clearly that I'm safe in your hand."

God be prais'd, that to believing souls gives light in darkness, comfort in despair.

WILLIAM SHAKESPEARE

January 8 GENESIS 8:1-22

"I am holding you in the silence."

God remembered Noah. GENESIS 8:1

Yesterday's devotion revealed that God is a strong levee when life reaches flood stage. Trusting his protection brings peace and hope.

But what about when life in survival mode seems never ending? Knowing we're in God's care doesn't eliminate daily weariness when struggles don't abate and the journey appears to be endless.

What then?

God blessed Noah by saving him. But the blessing came with its own challenges and heartaches. It couldn't have been easy to endure decades of ridicule from friends and neighbors, even much-loved relatives, whom Noah knew would die at God's hand. During each hour spent building the ark, he likely thought about God's character. As he anticipated the coming storm, surely he battled a few storms within himself.

Do you think a few fears crossed his mind? After all, he had never seen rain. How about grief? The screams of dying people and animals likely lingered in his memory. Noah had God's promise that his family would survive, but how much would they have to withstand, and for how long? Noah chose to rest in God's faithfulness. As a result, God led him on a unique journey and showed Noah new heights of his provision.

Other than instructing Noah to board the boat, there's no record of God speaking to Noah from the time he told Noah to build the boat until over 120 years later, when he told Noah to leave it. God might have talked with Noah during those years, but maybe he truly was silent.

You might know the storm of God's silence. As he did with Noah, God won't remain silent forever. Feel the relief of verse 15 from three simple words: "Then God said." After God's cleansing of the earth and his refining of Noah, he spoke.

Silent or not, God will carry you until the waters recede and he eases you onto a stable resting place. He still reveals his faithfulness to those who listen for him.

TALK TO HIM

"God, I need to hear from you. Please reassure me that you're in the quiet."

Come ye yourselves apart and rest awhile;
Weary, I know it, of the press and throng,
Wipe from your brow the sweat and dust of toil,
And in My quiet strength again be strong.

EDWARD H. BICKERSTETH JR., "COME YE YOURSELVES APART"

"Look for signs of me in your world."

"I have placed my rainbow in the clouds." GENESIS 9:13

Do you ever long for a sign from God? The direct approach—like a neon light, a highway billboard, or even a "We interrupt this broadcast"? Anything that helps us to know what he's telling us. Anything to quell our anxious search for guidance.

Believe it or not, God sends us signs all the time. He makes himself obvious through his Spirit's nudges when we pray and read the Bible, with peace that assures us, in the wonders of creation, through godly leaders, and in countless other ways.

Whether we notice him depends on how attuned to him we remain. It's one thing to think about him vaguely now and then; it's a whole other habit to actively look for him to communicate. He has a personal language with each of his children, unique between him and that person. We can hear and be encouraged by his work in others' lives, but eventually that excitement won't be enough. We need to experience him for ourselves.

Keeping in touch with him requires our sensitive effort—a discipline we often forgo in the rush of our days. He'd probably love to shake us to get our attention because he knows we'd function better if we'd listen for him more closely.

Noah not only listened *to* God, but he listened *for* God. He proactively pursued God. We saw evidence of that in Genesis 8 when he repeatedly sent a dove to see whether God had dried the land. It was his way of saying, "God, let me know when and where to land this ship."

And in Genesis 9, we see God giving him—and us—another sign. Rainbows aren't a haphazard reaction to rain. Every time we see one, God is communicating. He's reminding himself and us that he'll never again destroy the earth with a flood. But rainbows also remind us that God is as present and mightily involved with us as he was with Noah. And he wants us to search earnestly for him as Noah did.

Never doubt; he will guide you. But maybe he's waiting for a sign from you that you're looking for him.

TALK TO HIM

"God, what a wonder that you show yourself to me. Please remind me to look for you today."

People see God every day, they just don't recognize him.

PEARL BAILEY

January 10 GENESIS 15:1-21

"My plans for you are beyond your dreams."

"Look up into the sky and count the stars if you can." GENESIS 15:5

The sky is a mesmerizing place. Its limitless boundaries send our daydreams soaring. We can only wonder what's beyond our imagination. But the sky can be as intimidating as it is intriguing. What's really out there?

We might ask the same about the future because, like the sky, its unknowns both thrill and terrify us.

When God gave Abram a vision of the future, he began by calming Abram's fears. Then God delivered the news. Abram was in for a future full of God's protection and reward. Like the unmatchable Artist he is, God illustrated his promises for Abram's future by telling Abram to look up at the sky. But counting the stars was beyond Abram's ability. Similar to his future, numbering the stars was too much to comprehend.

Our futures are like the sky too. So much potential, yet so much we can't get our brains around. God loves you with the intensity he showed Abram. He's a bigger dreamer than you are, and your dreams for yourself can't measure up to his for you. The question today is, Will your faith in him rise to meet his dreams?

God counted Abram as righteous because Abram took God at his word. It sounded ludicrous to Abram to think he could father a child at his age. But God said it would happen, and one ancient man of faith chose to live in the security of that promise. That decision marked Abram's life, a decision of faith we read about thousands of years later.

Our trust in God is a big deal to him. Giving in to doubt is the easy road, particularly when it comes to situations that appear impossible to us. But it's also the road of regret and settling for less than the best. Faith requires courage. But one decision to trust God can affect your future in ways you can't comprehend from your earthly vantage point today.

Choose to believe that God's dreams for you are as limitless as the sky.

TALK TO HIM

"Lord, I trust you with my dreams. Please give me courage to let your dreams lift me above fear."

God's gifts put man's best dreams to shame.

ELIZABETH BARRETT BROWNING

"A relationship with me will change you forever."

"What's more, I am changing your name." GENESIS 17:5

If you could have more, what would that more include? More money, time, friends, patience, love, peace, fun . . . whatever? Most of us can compile a lengthy list of whatever could make us more content.

God gave Abram plenty of more, including promises he'd never granted anyone else. He guaranteed Abram a line of descendants, plus land and a nation of his own. Imagine handing down that heritage to your children and grandchildren. What more could Abram desire?

Well, God had more in store. He redefined Abram's identity with a new name, Abraham, that symbolized the way God changed him. Those changes impacted everyone in Abraham's life, from his family and household to the surrounding nations whose land God would take and give to Abraham's descendants.

We cannot be in relationship with God without him changing us. Those close to us may notice changes as God reworks our character, redefines our priorities, and possibly even redirects our path.

Part of God's "more" will involve unexpected changes. Some may be easy to accept, such as peace. But other changes might require letting go of something in order to give God first place. Abraham had to release his culture and his past to move forward in God's plan. He let go of good, comfortable things to give God room to bring in more—to bring in the best.

Everything God does is to clear out what's less to give us more of himself. Your identity as his won't leave you the same. But you're safe inside the more he has for you. Release to him everything less, let him change you as he knows best, and he'll leave his fingerprint on you and on generations after you.

TALK TO HIM

"Thank you for being the God of more. Please help me not to settle for anything less."

When I saw others straining toward God, I did not understand it, for though I may have had him less than they did, there was no one blocking the way between him and me, and I could reach his heart easily. It is up to him, after all, to have us, our part consists of almost solely in letting him grasp us.

RAINER MARIA RILKE

January 12 GENESIS 18:16–19:29

"I accomplish great things through your prayers for others."

God had listened to Abraham's request and kept Lot safe. GENESIS 19:29

It's tough to accept our inability to change someone else.

We may worry some over our own problems, but when it comes to someone we care about, our worry can skyrocket because we face a greater lack of control over the situation. Our concern may revolve around an issue someone wants to take responsibility for but can't, or it may be rooted in someone's foolishness. We want to fix things, but many times we feel powerless to make a difference.

Abraham faced this dilemma with his nephew Lot. Lot was a "righteous man" who was sick of the corruption around him (see 2 Peter 2:7), but he made some destructive decisions.

Lot had planted his family in a bad situation. We cringe at his attitudes, actions, and hesitation to act when the danger seemed obvious. God sent angels to warn him repeatedly, but Lot needed multiple nudges to push him out of harm's way.

As his uncle, Abraham may have felt a mixture of responsibility, concern, love, frustration, and anger. Scripture offers no evidence that Abraham nagged, coerced, harped on, manipulated, or beat Lot over the head with words to get him to wake up. All we see is Abraham taking his concerns for Lot straight to God.

Knowing that God hears and responds to prayer, Abraham became bold on Lot's behalf. With a humble attitude that acknowledged God's power and authority, Abraham took the serious issue to his Lord and relied upon God's mercy.

And as he always does, God listened. Not only did God listen patiently as Abraham stepped up his requests, but God moved and saved and rescued in response. Imagine the story's outcome had Abraham not prayed for Lot.

Who needs your prayers? Do you believe God will honor your concerns for others who may or may not know they need help? Take a faith step today and pray with renewed vision and faith for someone else. Your prayers may be the catalyst God uses for change.

TALK TO HIM

"Thank you, Lord, for caring even more about my loved one's needs than I do. Help me to trust you to show your power and mercy on his or her behalf."

Are you wrinkled with burden? Come to God for a faith lift.

AUTHOR UNKNOWN

"You will know my greatest blessings when you give everything to me."

"—all because you have obeyed me." GENESIS 22:18

Why do we cringe at having to obey? Unless we remove ourselves from structured society, we're subject to authority such as police officers, governments, and bosses. Actually, even if we became hermits, we'd have to answer to God. Contrary to what some people believe, he still has ultimate say over our lives.

Obedience sometimes draws negative feelings from us. But what if we were to view the whole concept from God's viewpoint?

Consider the most crucial test of obedience Abraham faced, and ask yourself how he was able to give up what was most precious to him. God knew what his command would cost Abraham. Notice verse 2: "Take your son, your only son—yes, Isaac, whom you love so much." It's as if God stressed how much he was requiring of Abraham.

Verse 5 suggests something about Abraham's faith, which explains how he could pay such a price to obey God. In giving to God everything most precious to him, Abraham was assured of receiving God's best in return. "The boy and I will travel a little farther. We will worship there, and then we will come right back." At that point, Abraham didn't know how God would resolve things, but he knew God wouldn't command something of him without having something better in store. Abraham acted on his trust that God would honor his obedience.

Our everything means a lot to God. He wants it all. He deserves it all. He doesn't take lightly the cost to us. However, he knows his return offer when we obey him. And he knows the trade-off is so much better.

How would things have turned out if Abraham had behaved indecisively or disobeyed God? We don't know this side of eternity. But consider that each obedience or disobedience affects more than ourselves.

Today, God is writing another page in your story. Will it include how he blessed you for giving him your all?

TALK TO HIM

"God, letting go of what's precious to me is frightening when I don't consider that I'm giving everything to you. Help me to trust that seeing you work outweighs the cost of obedience."

Be god or let God.

AUTHOR UNKNOWN

January 14 GENESIS 24:1-27

"When you go about your daily business of love, you'll be amazed by my work through you."

"I'll draw water for your camels, too, until they have had enough to drink." GENESIS 24:19

Rebekah's day began like any other. Routine. Run-of-the-mill. Utterly unassuming.

She steadied the jug on her shoulder and walked for the umpteenth time to the well. While her sandals scuffed the path, she could have mulled over a conversation with her mother or a friend's troubles. Maybe she prayed or thought about the chores left to do. Whatever the case, there was certainly nothing extraordinary about that day . . . or so she thought.

Someone once commented how easily we walk into the miracles of our lives. How true for Rebekah. She had no idea whom she'd meet at the path's end, no clue she was about to be an answer to someone's prayer. She simply approached her morning with a generous attitude that pleased God. As a result, she was ready to respond to someone's need. By making herself available and investing time to care, she left a lasting impression we read about generations later.

Her offer to water the camels was no small gesture, given that each animal could guzzle twenty-five gallons. And Abraham was no pauper. He was a man of means who likely sent numerous camels with his servant to win over a bride for his son. Rebekah's generosity takes on new proportions when those factors are considered. Her kind gesture could have taken hours from her day. But in giving of herself, Rebekah showed she valued people over her agenda.

How will you approach today? Will your actions invite God to work through you? We stifle God's Spirit when we don't show his love. If we're too busy to go the extra mile, then maybe our schedules need revising.

Leave room in your day—and your attitude—for God's interruptions. You may be surprised at what he does when you show love and leave the rest to him.

TALK TO HIM

"I want this ordinary day to be different, Father. I know you want to work through me. Arrange my moments for your purposes, and help me stay available to others."

Every action in our lives touches on some chord that will vibrate in eternity.

EDWIN H. CHAPIN

"I work behind the scenes to bring out the best for you."

"Before I had finished praying in my heart, I saw Rebekah coming out with her water jug on her shoulder." GENESIS 24:45

What do you think God is doing right now? Admittedly, it's a somewhat crazy question. After all, God's abilities to multitask make ours laughable. To narrow it down, what do you think he's doing in your life right now? Is he at work in that particular situation weighing on your heart?

Abraham's servant had a burden. His master had entrusted him with the weighty task of choosing a wife for Isaac, Abraham's beloved son who would inherit God's promise of a nation, a land, and descendants beyond counting. It was more than enough responsibility to assume on one's own behalf, but handling the situation for someone else would've left most of us a tad uneasy about the mission's success.

Fortunately, Abraham picked his servant well. The servant knew the job was too much to accomplish on his own, so he handed the problem to God. And God took care of it by setting his answer in motion even before the servant had finished praying.

God is the Master of behind-the-scenes work, not just in stories from biblical history, but in your life. Today, right now, there's no telling how God is moving people and circumstances on your behalf. He wants you to be like Abraham's servant, asking and believing that he'll answer you, attuned to notice when he does.

He knows what answers you're waiting for, which ones you need immediately, and how he will provide. Will you be bold and move forward, despite how overwhelming the task seems? God isn't overwhelmed, so you can rest your heart about it.

Give your concern to God, and picture him working behind the scenes. Then plan to be wowed by how he provides.

TALK TO HIM

"Lord, although this task seems too much for me, I know you're working. Thank you for not leaving it all up to me. Help my heart to rest even as I actively watch for you to work."

Trouble and perplexity drive me to prayer and prayer drives away perplexity and trouble.

PHILIPP MELANCHTHON

January 16 GENESIS 28:10-22

"Anywhere you meet with me becomes a holy place."

"What an awesome place this is! It is none other than the house of God, the very gateway to heaven!" GENESIS 28:17

Ever feel that life works against your desire to talk with God? You want to spend time with him, but responsibilities intrude on your best intentions. You can hardly keep up with family and friends and work and errands and kids and church activities and . . . big sigh. It's tiring. Although many of our distractions are worthwhile and necessary, it's easy to feel like it's them against any sort of meaningful spiritual life.

How nice it would be to have stretches of focused time for prayer and worship, hidden away from other demands! But most often that isn't our everyday reality. Instead, we settle for sentence prayers on the go as we scurry from one task to the next. Where's the quiet in our quiet times? Today's reading offers hope.

Jacob, Isaac's son and Abraham's grandson, discovered that an ordinary place could become holy with God's presence. He experienced a life-changing worship time in the rustic environment of a campsite away from home.

God can turn the most insubstantial place and the most insignificant moment into an environment of intimate worship. Anywhere he is becomes a holy setting, the house of God, the very gateway to heaven.

That means your vehicle, office, bedroom, kitchen counter, or even the grocery store aisle can be a spiritual sanctuary in the briefest moments you have to send up a prayer or hum a worship tune.

We need to make time for church and corporate worship, but we also need to view the other 167 hours of the week as opportunities for private conversations with our heavenly Father, however scattered they may become. Witness God's holiness right now, right where you are. Don't miss him because you long for more time or a more ideal environment.

This moment is awesome simply because God is present.

TALK TO HIM

"Thank you, Lord, for here and now. Please don't let me miss you in the whirlwind around me."

Every happening, great and small, is a parable whereby God speaks to us, and the art of life is to get the message.

MALCOLM MUGGERIDGE

"Your struggles will reveal ugliness or develop godliness."

"I have struggled hard with my sister, and I'm winning!" GENESIS 30:8

These sisters got a raw deal. Because of their father's deceit, they married the same man. This was unfortunate for Leah because that man, Jacob, didn't love her. It was unfortunate for Rachel because she had to share her true love with her own sibling.

Although God gave Leah several sons, she still craved Jacob's love; Rachel, on the other hand, had her husband's love but remained barren for many years. Neither sister had what she wanted, and disappointment took its toll.

We can't know all they went through each day, but we can relate on some level to disappointment. How many of us would have done better in Rachel's or Leah's place? We all have our private hurts, and we haven't always shown fabulous character when circumstances left us wanting. God doesn't expect us to be perfect, but he does want us to learn to lean on him. Oftentimes he uses our low points to show us himself in ways we might not see when life feels okay. Our job is not to miss those growth lessons.

Even though Rachel was a beautiful woman, jealousy did not look good on her. And who knows how a beautiful nature could have enhanced plain Leah's appeal to her husband? Keeping in mind what God says about true beauty and life-changing love, we can imagine their lives could have gone differently (see 1 Samuel 16:7; Mark 7:20-23; Romans 8:28; Colossians 3:14; James 3:15-16). God could have turned a rotten situation into something beautiful for both women.

God did give Leah and Rachel an incredible gift: They were the mothers of his twelve tribes of chosen people, the Israelites. Although they lived with great responsibility and great heartaches, their lives were special to almighty God.

Yours is too.

No matter what God allows you to experience, he wants to deepen your faith in him. The journey often carries pain. That's growth. Don't waste that pain, but let him sift and refine your character.

Fight him, and watch ugliness fester. Or lean into him, and let him develop godliness in you.

TALK TO HIM

"Lord, please soften my heart and strengthen my faith as you use my hurts to develop your beauty in me."

Beauty . . . is the shadow of God on the universe.

GABRIELA MISTRAL

January 18 GENESIS 39:1-23

"When you put me first, I will take care of your reputation."

The L*ORD made Joseph a favorite with the prison warden.* GENESIS 39:21

Some things never change. Take, for instance, the fact that life is messy. Yesterday's reading revolved around the woes of two sisters who found themselves in a painful situation because of someone else's actions. Today's passage bears similarities.

Joseph was the long-awaited answer to the prayers of his mother, Rachel. Her firstborn, he no doubt held a coveted place in her heart as well as in that of his father, Jacob. He was his father's favorite, and his brothers resented him for it. In fact, Joseph suffered greatly because of his brothers' jealousy. Looks like sibling rivalry didn't end with Mom and Aunt Leah.

But one key difference shows itself in his life. Joseph allowed God to create something beautiful from his problems, and it made all the difference. As a result, Joseph's character grew, and he experienced God's power to restore deep brokenness.

It's one thing to pay for our own mistakes, but when we're doing everything we think is right and we still suffer, our sense of justice cries out to be rectified. That was Joseph's life for many years. After his brothers sold him into Egyptian slavery, Joseph continued to see his once-promising future destroyed over and over again. His riches to rags to riches story reads like a roller-coaster ride of being falsely accused, spending time in prison, earning respect again, getting knocked down, and finally seeing God restore his reputation in a way he never could have anticipated.

Instead of giving in to bitterness, Joseph left room for God to work. As a result, God wove his character into Joseph and used him to save a nation. Joseph put God first, and God took care of his reputation.

Let God work through the messiness in your world, and watch him make your life into something of beauty—no matter how circumstances threaten to undo you.

TALK TO HIM

"Lord, you are trustworthy to handle my reputation. I know it even when life seems to shout otherwise. Please help me live for your reputation above my own."

Don't pray to escape trouble. Don't pray to be comfortable in your emotions. Pray to do the will of God in every situation. Nothing else is worth praying for.

SAMUEL M. SHOEMAKER

"I want to show my power through you."

"It is beyond my power to do this," Joseph replied. "But God can tell you what it means and set you at ease." GENESIS 41:16

What are your limitations worth to you? We'd do anything to shed whatever holds us back, but those weaknesses are priceless to God. In fact, one of faith's great paradoxes revolves around our imperfections.

We tend to view our weaknesses as liabilities, but they are assets when we hand them over to God. The quirks and characteristics we've battled for years—perhaps a physical or mental challenge, an emotional struggle, a financial hardship, or even pain at someone else's hand—are opportunities for God to show himself strong in us.

Joseph struggled with numerous limitations, including relationship heartaches and financial and social hardships that arrived on his doorstep through the wicked acts of others. His youthful dreams were shattered repeatedly. While his brothers and childhood friends enjoyed independent lives, he sat in prison, unjustly accused, probably wondering if life would ever improve. Was a slave's fate all he had to look forward to? In his own strength, Joseph was powerless to change his situation.

However, God used Joseph's humbling, even humiliating, circumstances to impact a life devoted to God. He empowered Joseph to interpret dreams—a skill beyond human ability. Although Joseph knew God had unlimited power, he was able to experience God Almighty in a unique way. Anyone who has tasted God's power over a human limitation can attest to the life-changing awe it inspires. Scripture clues us in to Joseph's reaction later on in Genesis 50:20, where we see that his own faith was bolstered through all he endured.

The fact is, God enriched Joseph's life through his hardships—a tough reality that's full of such grace.

God can turn a worst-case scenario into an anchor of faith. Ask God to use your frustrating limitations for his mighty purposes. You never know how he'll answer, but be assured he will.

TALK TO HIM

"Lord, I'm so tired of these things that hold me back. Please turn them to strengths by showing me more of yourself through them. In faith, I thank you ahead of time for your answers."

Faith is the strength by which a shattered world shall emerge into the light.

HELEN KELLER

January 20 GENESIS 41:37-57

"I will not forget you."

"God has made me fruitful in this land of my grief." GENESIS 41:52

Finally . . . The word draws a sigh of relief. There's nothing like finally getting something you've waited for, finally saying good-bye to a difficult season of life, or finally experiencing God's answer to prayer.

Being human, Joseph experienced moments when he likely wondered if God had forgotten him, or if God could have been more sympathetic to his trials. Chances are his human nature rebelled at being thrown down again whenever he started to get back on his feet. Dirty prison walls stood impenetrable as days dragged by with no promise from above that he ever would be free.

But God did rescue and restore in his way and time, and he gave Joseph personal understanding of the power of finally.

Maybe you feel stuck in a prison of circumstances you can't control, and you question how long you'll have to wait for God to answer. Maybe the doubts are growing faster than your faith is overcoming them. You question whether God forgot you, and you wonder if there's something more you can do to get his attention.

Although we chafe at having to wait, the process builds appreciation for whatever we long for. Waiting stretches our faith, too, by challenging us to live by God's promise that he won't forget us (see Isaiah 44:21; 49:15).

Set your mind against questioning whether God has forgotten you. He has not. He not only sees your hurts, but he feels them with you. Expect him to free you. Whether he changes circumstances or changes you is up to him, but either way you can look forward to his freedom when you trust him.

Just like he finally brought Joseph's story full circle, he will complete what he has begun in you.

TALK TO HIM

"Lord, you're very quiet these days, and it feels as if you've lost track of me. Please help me hold on to your promise that you won't forget me."

Let God's promises shine on your problems.

CORRIE TEN BOOM

"I can heal your relationships."

"God has sent me ahead of you to keep you and your families alive and to preserve many survivors." GENESIS 45:7

God is not only a creator of new things; he is a restorer of old things, such as relationships that have gone sour. Any of those lurking like skeletons in your life's closet?

The past few days, we have focused on Joseph and his ruined relationships with his brothers. Genesis gives a lot of detail about Joseph's years away from home, but we don't learn much about his brothers. Imagine what their lives were like between handing him over to the slave traders and ending up on his doorstep, asking for help during the famine. Were they eaten by remorse? Did he cross their minds much? Did they ever talk about him?

Human relationships are bound to encounter storms because of our different temperaments and our innate selfishness. Even our best intentions fail at times.

But there's hope for relationships that have deteriorated—that is, deteriorated from a human perspective. No problem is unresolvable from God's viewpoint. If someone crosses your mind as you read this, take heart that God can restore any relationship. Joseph was dead in his brothers' minds. As far as they knew, there was zero hope of reconciling. And Joseph likely thought his connections to his childhood family were as dead and buried as his father, Jacob, thought he was.

Yet God had big plans for wonderful healing.

Although you can't see what God has in store for a hurting relationship, you can ask him what you can do to begin the healing process. Prayer may be your only option. But prayer may be exactly what is needed while God works in both of you. Whether or not the relationship is restored, at least you can experience God's healing and rely on him to take care of the other person as well.

TALK TO HIM

"God, only you can see inside our hearts, and only you can make something beautiful from our messes. Please heal in your perfect way."

If you were going to die soon and had only one phone call you could make, who would you call and what would you say? And why are you waiting?

STEPHEN LEVINE

January 22 GENESIS 50:14-21

"I am more powerful than anyone who intends to harm you."

"You intended to harm me, but God intended it all for good." GENESIS 50:20

Sometimes keeping up with the news is exhausting. It's hard enough to hear about atrocities happening to others, but if evil ever hits home personally, life is never the same. Security becomes a lost luxury, a figment of a past trampled by someone bent on destruction. The feeling of being violated doesn't pass quickly, if ever.

The Bible contains countless reminders of sin's devastation on our world. Its stories involve human beings who lived and dreamed, related to each other and to God, and experienced joy and pain as we do. The human condition hasn't changed much over the course of history.

Imagine the heartbreak Joseph felt over his brothers' betrayal. They didn't just throw a few punches for revenge and call it even. They sold him to foreign traders, destroying his dreams and breaking their father's heart. The terror, confusion, and loneliness had to be overwhelming for Joseph as he was ruthlessly dragged away from the security of his childhood home.

But God saw Joseph and remained with him. As he was then, God is still aware of everything that goes on in this world he created. It grieves him deeply to see the environment he lovingly fashioned battered into a place that doesn't offer the safety and peace he originally intended. He sees every horror and catches every tear, and he longs to make everything right. But he waits to do away with evil to give more people time to turn to him.

God has a plan for this world and for your life that remains in place despite how the world may try to destroy it. No harm can overpower his goodness or his love for you.

Evil is a temporary part of life, but God is eternal. He will have the final say.

TALK TO HIM

"Lord, I get scared when I realize how fragile life is. Please remind me that you hold me close and won't allow anything to hurt me that you won't use for good. Thank you for the lasting security I have in you."

There is much in the world to make us afraid. There is much more in our faith to make us unafraid.

FREDERICK W. CROPP

"I am pleased by your courageous faith."

Because the midwives feared God, they refused to obey the king's orders. EXODUS 1:17

Times were beyond difficult for the Israelites of Moses' day. Year after year they slaved under a ruthless Pharaoh. With fear at an all-time high and no human rescuer in sight, it was time for each person to act in faith that God would be greater than their fears.

Fortunately, several courageous people acted with do-or-die trust that God, not any human, was ultimately in control. Their names have gone down in history as people who dared to buck the system in order to obey God.

Shiphrah and Puah boldly refused to follow Pharaoh's murderous orders. Moses' mother acted with courageous faith when she dared to hide him, sticking to her belief that God had special plans for her little son. Then his sister boldly approached Pharaoh's daughter, who eventually raised Moses.

Had those midwives and Moses' family not taken many risks to live by faith, Moses wouldn't have grown up to lead their nation out of the very slavery that instilled fear and threatened their faith in the first place. Instead of giving in to human fear, they exemplified a fear of God, the One who really held the power over their circumstances—and over Pharaoh.

The faith of a few changed the course of history. Faith still holds that power today.

Acting on faith in God will never disappoint us because God blesses obedient trust in him. Faith carries risk only when the object of that faith is undependable, so faith in our supremely dependable God is a sure thing. The courage part comes in when we choose to move forward with him, believing in his matchless power.

If you aren't facing a situation that requires courageous faith, it's only a matter of time until one presents itself. Deciding now to be a bold believer in God will make it easier to follow through when the time comes.

Your faithful actions will make a difference. Act on that conviction, and watch God provide.

TALK TO HIM

"Lord, I need courage. Please remind me of your faithfulness, and help me focus on your power instead of on the trouble that threatens my trust in you."

He does not believe who does not live according to his belief.

THOMAS FULLER

January 24 EXODUS 2:23–3:10

"I will respond to you."

God heard their groaning, and he remembered his covenant promise. EXODUS 2:24

No one likes the silent treatment. In fact, sometimes silence sounds deafening.

God's silence reverberated through the Israelites' homes as they groaned from their slavery. Why didn't he answer? They'd suffered for so long, but God still said nothing.

And then, finally, he did.

Far away from the Israelites' plight, God spoke to Moses, setting the stage for an incredible rescue plan. And as God is known to do, he responded in a unique way. His burning-bush conversation with Moses still serves as a reminder that God is a responder. He always hears, and he always answers (see Isaiah 65:24). In fact, he wants us to expect him to respond to us (see James 1:5-6).

But when we enclose our expectations of him in a box and set a timer, we're saying to him, "I trust you, God, if you answer in this way and by that time." That strategy invites doubt and suffocates faith. God is more interested in our growth than in our comfort, and he doesn't often do things our way. That reality may be difficult to accept when we hear silence from heaven, but God does everything for our good when we're committed to him.

God isn't uncaring in his silence. He aches with us even while he knows that sending the answer too soon would diminish the quality of his provision. Silence often promotes deeper thought and richer faith. He knows when time and quiet are needed to fit us and our circumstances for his finished answer.

Sometimes he stretches our faith muscles, or he uses our faith to build someone else's. Sometimes he waits while we get through the fretting and fuming and come to turn our attention back to him.

If you've put your expectations of God's answers in a box where doubt has festered, release them to him. There's room to breathe when you don't try to close him in.

Know that he'll respond in his perfectly creative way and time, and rest in renewed faith.

TALK TO HIM

"God, I choose to trust you in this confusing silence. Please help me trust that you're listening and moving, and help me find refuge in you in the quiet."

You can hear the footsteps of God when silence reigns in the mind.

SRI SATHYA SAI BABA

"I Am Who I Am, and I Am more than enough."

"Who makes a person's mouth? Who decides whether people speak or do not speak, hear or do not hear, see or do not see? Is it not I, the LORD?" EXODUS 4:11

Have you ever noticed that confidence breeds confidence? In other words, people who exude confidence tend to build our trust in them too.

It's one thing to hear other people say that God is more powerful than anything or anyone, that he knows all and sees all, and that he is completely in control. But we gain an entirely greater confidence from hearing him say those things of himself.

We all battle doubts and fears and weaknesses throughout life—throughout each day, actually. But God never does. Never. In fact, he never has experienced a moment of doubt, and he never will.

Has that truth embedded itself in you yet?

Because he knows his character and his power, he knows there's no room or reason for doubting himself. And so he says confidently, "I Am Who I Am." No ifs, ands, or buts. No wavering or questioning. Just pure and simple truth.

Moses faced a crisis of faith when God appointed him to lead the Israelites out of Egypt. The only thing Moses felt confident about was his own inability to accomplish the task. So God reminded him who was in charge. "I AM WHO I AM . . . Yahweh, the God of your ancestors. . . . This is my eternal name, my name to remember for all generations" (Exodus 3:14-15).

When you struggle to keep your faith going, do you hear God whisper his own name to you? Listen closely, because he's saying it. "I Am Who I Am. In this situation, in this battle, I am Yahweh. I Am your God. Remember today."

Take confidence in God's self-confidence. He is incapable of failing you because his character is faithfulness.

Trust him to be more than enough for you, as he knows full well he is.

TALK TO HIM

"What a relief to know that you are sure of yourself, Lord. Please forgive my doubts, and grow my confidence in you until it matches your own."

This is how humans are: we question all our beliefs, except for the ones we really believe, and those we never think to question.

ORSON SCOTT CARD

January 26 EXODUS 5:1–6:13

"I will pick up the pieces of your hope."

Moses told the people of Israel what the LORD had said, but they refused to listen anymore. They had become too discouraged. EXODUS 6:9

The Israelites were understandably discouraged. Their situation was desperate. They had had enough, but things continued to get worse. They needed God, but they had grown too tired to hope, lest it disappoint them again. So in their pain, they shut their ears and hearts.

God knows we struggle to keep trusting, or hoping, when life bottoms out and seems to stay there. The Israelites had been humbled and humiliated, mistreated and abused. They knew the burn of shame and the power it has to reduce one's inner fight.

Maybe you've experienced brokenness that left you at the end of the end of the end of yourself. You've been tempted to shut down to protect yourself from more blows that bring despair and shame. When the hope you once held gradually has been beaten to a morsel, sometimes it seems more worthwhile to drop-kick it out of sight for good.

Thankfully, that morsel is never out of God's sight. His twenty-twenty vision of your life doesn't miss a single thing. Even if you've abandoned your last bits of hope, he's already picking up the pieces and rebuilding them, just as he did for the Israelites.

Isaiah 49:23 says, "Those who trust in me will never be put to shame." The New International Version words it as "Those who hope in me will not be disappointed."

When circumstances threaten to destroy your hope, the one thing that can save it is to keep it based on God. Looking around at shattered circumstances only weakens you further. But focusing on him, looking for his face, will give you the strength for one more step. And that's all he asks of you—one more step of hope in him.

Hold him to his word that hope in him will not disappoint you, and risk one more step today.

TALK TO HIM

"Lord, I feel too worn out to risk hoping again. All I can do is collapse at your feet and ask for refreshment to endure today. Please grant me strength to trust your faithfulness at this moment."

When the world says, "Give up,"
Hope whispers, "Try it one more time."
AUTHOR UNKNOWN

"Remember the times I protected you; they are anchors for your faith."

"This is a day to remember." EXODUS 12:14

Welcome to a great day for your faith! There's no better time for a refresher course about the safety features of your faith—namely, its anchors. If you weren't aware you possessed them, today is even more exciting for you.

The times God works in your life are anchors for your faith because experiencing his faithfulness solidifies that faith and holds it securely amid the waves and tumults of life. When a storm hits, a well-anchored faith in God will be fit to weather the turbulence.

God commanded the Israelites to remind themselves on a regular basis of how he brought them out of Egypt. Although he had many blessings in store, he knew their faith would need bolstering countless times in their future. So important was anchoring their faith that he made this command into an official law.

What anchors do you have? You may recall favorite Scriptures or memories of God working on your behalf. Or maybe you've established traditions or celebrations as reminders that your heavenly Father still holds you securely.

No one's life of faith is free from storms. Sure, he takes us through seasons of smooth sailing and lets us rest in peaceful harbors. However, he also allows us to go through seasons when the wind blows fiercely and life feels like turmoil day after day. Those times are when we need our sturdy anchors.

Just as your relationship with God is unique, he'll mold your faith anchors to fit your journey, readying you for the next patch of uneasy water.

Ask him to bring to mind when he has come through for you. Save your list where you'll find it when something tests the sureness of your faith. Then thank God for his anchors of the past and the new anchors he's bringing your way.

TALK TO HIM

"Thank you, God, for giving me unique anchors of faith in you. Please keep me aware of all the ways you continue to prove yourself faithful."

Far out on the desolate billow
The sailor sails the sea,
Alone with the night and the tempest,
Where countless dangers be;
Yet never alone is the Christian,
Who lives by faith and prayer.

ROSSITER W. RAYMOND, "FAR OUT ON THE DESOLATE BILLOW"

January 28 EXODUS 13:17-22

"My detours are for your good."

God did not lead them along the main road . . . even though that was the shortest route.

EXODUS 13:17

The Israelites had one goal: to get out of Egypt, and fast. They wanted to get to the land God had promised them, and they felt exhausted and irritable from having to wait so long. When God finally gave the moving orders and they set out on the road to freedom, most likely they wanted the most direct route to getting resettled. No wasting time.

How often do you feel unsettled by a circumstance that causes you to reset your time frame yet again? A friend or family member suddenly needs you for something, the boss puts one more file in your in-box, or the doctor says you're not quite healed yet. Life can seem like the filler between interruptions and detours. It's easy to get irritable when something messes with our agenda.

However, God doesn't view the road as we do because he has a bigger vision in mind than getting us from one goal to the next in the quickest time possible. His detours are only for our good. He may want to grow our patience or our willingness to prioritize people above the to-do list. Or he might be protecting us from an unforeseen problem our headstrong pushiness might be steering us toward.

God took the Israelites on a roundabout route through the wilderness to protect them from the Philistines nearby. By hiding them off the main road, God spared them from their enemies and their own tendency to change their minds. Their journey took longer, but he knew a battle might be the Israelites' undoing. His detour showed his mercy.

It takes creative trust not to get bent out of shape when we feel like we're wasting time on God's side roads. But if and when you face a detour today, remind yourself that the life God gives you includes detours. A simple change of perspective can make a huge difference in how much you enjoy the journey.

TALK TO HIM

"Lord, I expect a detour or several today. Thank you ahead of time for your mercy in them. Please use them to grow me as you want."

Establishing goals is all right if you don't let them deprive you of interesting detours.

DOUG LARSON

"I will fight for you. Rest and watch."

"The LORD himself will fight for you. Just stay calm." EXODUS 14:14

The earth vibrated under the Israelites' sandals, pulsing terror into their fractured nerves. On the horizon, thousands of trained soldiers in swift chariots closed the gap with each beat of their horses' hooves. After many years bent under Egyptian abuse, the Israelites were getting a taste of what freedom looked like. But barely beyond the borders of their captivity, they realized their enemies had decided not to free them after all. In their current condition, they were no match for such a threat.

The Israelites feared the Egyptians, and for good reason. But God had begun this adventure by calling them out of Egypt, and Moses urged the people to turn their fear into faith that God would rescue them.

Fear is universal; we've all experienced it. But fear can also be very personal. What triggers one person's fight-or-flight instinct may not faze someone else. Suppose you face your worst-case scenario, and you feel fear that freezes you in a panicked state of reaction or nonaction, neither of which puts you in a position of strength. Learning to turn your fight-or-flight toward the Lord focuses you on the One with the perfect battle plan ready.

God knew Moses was ready to trust him instead of panic. Like Moses, our job when we face fear can be simplified to two strategies. First of all, trust God's control. Second, stay calm to hear God's direction. From that position of spiritual strength, we can hear God say to *wait* or *move.*

Even when we sense him saying *go,* that go is couched in the understanding that we're moving within his overarching strength. For his followers, there is always an element of standing still—in other words, remaining calm—and watching him fight for us. Resting in faith that he is acting on our behalf is far from passive. It involves listening and heeding and seeking his wisdom in prayer.

In order to rest in God's fight for you, turn your flight to him.

TALK TO HIM

"Lord, you know my fears, and you know you're greater. Please help me to calmly stand and face them in your strength."

Fear is the needle that pierces us that it may carry a thread to bind us to heaven.

JAMES HASTINGS

January 30 EXODUS 16:1-15

"Look for me and see that I will provide for you."

"Then you will know that I am the Lord *your God."* EXODUS 16:12

What does it take for you to see God's hand in your life? Some people need repeated convincing.

The Israelites often were a doubtful bunch in their wilderness wandering. No matter how many times God proved he was with them, they continued to question his presence, even his goodness. They needed reminders to look up at the cloud where God's glory hovered over them, a constant sign that he hadn't abandoned them. It's no wonder they pushed his patience many times.

One of the reasons we tend to push God's patience is because we're more focused on our circumstances, or what we wish God would do, than we are tuned in to him, simply for the sake of being close to him. As with the Israelites, God wants us to want him more than we want his answers. He knows that our needs will be met by his person more than by his provisions. It may sound strange or improbable to us, but it is his truth.

The Israelites could have saved themselves heartache and worry if they had spent their energy fixing their eyes on God instead of looking around at their troubles and feeding off each other's complaints.

When you keep your gaze on God, in essence you're letting him lift you above your earthly cares to a secure seat in his hand. From that vantage point, you have a much clearer view of all that his hand is doing for you. Problems don't necessarily go away, but it's easier to keep trusting when you're resting in his grip than when you're floundering for answers among a world whose gaze isn't directed on him.

Pour out your concerns to God; he wants to hear from you. But express your heart from a position of trust rather than from one of worry or complaint. He'll listen to you either way, but you'll save your spiritual energy when you stay focused on him, knowing that he will provide.

TALK TO HIM

"Thank you, God, for never leaving me. Please help me to look to you and refuse to let my gaze flicker back to my problems."

Nothing touches our lives but it is God Himself speaking.
Do we discern His hand or only mere occurrence?
OSWALD CHAMBERS

"Don't take for granted my gift of rest."

"The Sabbath is the Lord's *gift to you."* EXODUS 16:29

Know anything significant about the number 60? How about 1,440? 10,080?

They tell you how many minutes you have: 60 minutes in an hour, 1,440 minutes in a day, and 10,080 minutes in a week. That's quite a cacophony of ticks on the clock.

If you were to categorize those minutes based on how you spend them, do you know what you'd discover? If you're like most stressed-out people, chances are you'd end up wishing for more of those 60-second intervals to get more done. Time is a precious commodity, but it isn't something we can ever have more of than what God grants us.

Fortunately, God knew what he was doing when he created the 60-minute hour, the 1,440-minute day, and the 10,080-minute week. He knew they would be more than enough time for us to finish the tasks he asks us to tackle. In fact, he wants us to set aside a portion to do nothing but rest.

Although Moses' era is ancient history, we have more in common with those Israelites than we may think. They struggled to take God seriously, too, when he said Sabbath rest was for their good. Instead of taking time off to recuperate and refresh, they viewed those hours as a chance to get more done. The funny thing is, their extra efforts proved futile. For all their foraging for extra manna on the Sabbath, they were rewarded with nothing. God had provided for their needs over the previous six weekdays so they'd be free to rest on the seventh.

You may have work or other responsibilities on Sundays. If that's the case, you're not off the hook. You may just need to be a bit more creative about reserving time for R & R.

Rest is not laziness; it is extremely purposeful. Your spiritual, physical, mental, emotional, relational, and even financial health depends on it. By investing 1,440 minutes each week in rest, you'll be amazed at your productivity and well-being during the remaining 8,640 minutes God gives you.

TALK TO HIM

"Thank you, Lord, for rest. Please help me to value your reasons for rest, and show me that your time frame can increase my usefulness for you."

Take rest; a field that has rested gives a bountiful crop.

OVID

February 1 EXODUS 17:8-16

"I put people in your life to help you stay strong."

They stood on each side of Moses, holding up his hands. So his hands held steady until sunset. EXODUS 17:12

Close your eyes and let your mind flip through the faces of people in your life—those who grace the picture frames and photo albums in your home, the ones who fill the offices at work and the sanctuary at church. How about acquaintances like the postal carrier, the clerk at the dry cleaner, or the staff at your child's school?

If you were to list all the people you see on a regular basis, you'd probably be amazed at how long that would take.

It's no coincidence that each one of them is in your life, or that you're in theirs. Whether our roles in each other's lives seem minor to us, we never know how God may use us to help another person. Life is full of everyday heroes. Sometimes those heroes are close to us; other times they may be complete strangers. After all, consider the news stories of strangers helping someone in a life-threatening emergency. Being at the perfect place and time might seem cliché to us, but God is behind those moments. What a gracious gift he gives us through the strength and care of others!

Moses and Joshua experienced the opportunity to lean on others, literally. Arms raised is a sign of victory, but Moses couldn't be victorious against the Amalekites without the help of Aaron and Hur. And without Moses' raised arms, Joshua wouldn't have successfully led the Israelites on the battlefield.

We often feel humbled by our need for others. Sometimes our individualist natures resist help. What a tragedy that is!

The people you encounter today are there by God's design, gifts from his heavenly storehouse of blessings. Do you see each one through eyes of gratitude?

TALK TO HIM

"Lord, please help me notice people with fresh insight today. Alert my ears to spoken needs, and awaken my heart to unspoken ones. Thank you for your gift of other people."

"Independence" . . . [is] middle-class blasphemy. We are all dependent on one another, every soul of us on earth.

GEORGE BERNARD SHAW

"I did not equip you to do it all alone."

"What are you really accomplishing here? Why are you trying to do all this alone?"

EXODUS 18:14

What is it about ourselves that wants to play the hero, the one who gets it done when it seems no one else can? It's a timeless ambition. Moses fell prey to the misconception that it was all up to him when he tried to be everyone's fix-it guy.

Thankfully, he had a wise father-in-law who called him on his methods before they led to burnout. Jethro had years more life experience than Moses and knew the importance of valuing other people's skills and leaving room for others to lend a hand. Moses was operating in survival mode. If he didn't share some of the responsibility, not only would he wear himself out, but he'd be useless to anyone he tried to help.

God didn't wire us to handle everything on our own. But sometimes we pride ourselves on striving for the top position, or we get so used to meeting other people's needs that we lose perspective on how busy and overworked we've become. The idea that it's easier to do something ourselves than to train someone else weakens long-term success because it's founded on the false notion that we'll be around forever.

The term *team player* has become a catchphrase these days, but it's an old, old concept. God created us to need and care for each other. He doesn't want us to stifle anyone else's unique abilities, insights, and perspectives. Romans 12:4-5 says, "Just as our bodies have many parts and each part has a special function, so it is with [us]. We are many parts of one body, and we all belong to each other."

Whose contribution might we deny if we don't give someone else a chance?

TALK TO HIM

"Lord, please stop me in my rush to handle things myself. Remind me that my time on earth is limited, and part of my role is to prepare others to take over when I need to stop."

Do not commit the error, common among the young, of assuming that if you cannot save the whole of mankind you have failed.

JAN DE HARTOG

February 3 EXODUS 20:1-17

"I have the right to expect your obedience."

"I am the Lord *your God, who rescued you from the land of Egypt, the place of your slavery."*

EXODUS 20:2

For all our talk about team players, our society still tends to balk at authority. We value our individualism to the point of becoming put off by following someone else. We wear the word *obedience* like a chain, wishing to roam free of its burden.

We've got it backward.

Before he listed his Ten Commandments, God established his authority to place those rules in our lives. By reminding the Israelites that he was the One who rescued them from slavery, he also let them know his rules weren't another form of slavery. The commandments were really about freedom, if only they'd view them through his perspective.

Rules given only to establish someone's control naturally invite rebellion. We don't enjoy being controlled. However, God has nothing to prove, so he has no need to place meaningless boundaries around us. He doesn't create commandments to prove his control. Therefore, we can trust that the ones he puts in place are for our good, whether or not we understand his reasoning.

As God, he has the right to expect our obedience. Yet he is a gentleman about it, giving us the choice to obey him. That kind of leadership invites instead of demanding that we abide by his standards. There will always be consequences for disobedience, but the option is still ours. His motivation is love, not spite or a craving for power. In the process of establishing his rightful place as our Lord, he wants to spare us from facing negative consequences.

View obedience to him as a blessing and a privilege, and live protected by his sheltering authority.

TALK TO HIM

"Almighty God. Heavenly Father. King of kings. All names that show me your right to call the shots in my life. Thank you for the protection your authority offers me. Please help me offer you my obedience today, which you rightfully deserve."

There are two freedoms—the false, where a man is free to do what he likes; the true, where he is free to do what he ought.

CHARLES KINGSLEY

"Don't toy with a little disobedience."

"You must not . . . imitate their evil practices." EXODUS 23:24

The only consistent thing about trends is their fickleness. Just when you think you've updated your life with the latest fashions, fads, and electronic gadgets, something new hits the market.

Detoxifying the body has entered mainstream consciousness in recent years, although it's been more than a fad for health gurus who have followed this practice longer than the rest of us. Tune in to many cable channels, and you're likely to hear a celebrity touting the praises of their favorite digestive-detox plan.

Just as our bodies collect toxins that need flushing through natural or assisted means, our souls can store up toxins when we don't filter out the junk of the world. God loves purity, and he gave some guidelines about remaining pure and toxin free in a corrupt world that scoffs at his holiness.

Long ago he warned the Israelites about the dangers of becoming involved with the neighboring pagan nations that he would slowly drive from the land he intended to give his people. He left no room for compromise because he's well aware of our tendency to run toward things that look good to our eyes but aren't necessarily good for our souls. He knows the power of one look, one touch, one moment's hesitation; each pause in our decision to obey is welcoming a little toxin into our system.

To really get a picture of how serious he is about not compromising his standards, ask yourself whether you'd eat a bowl of chili if you saw someone toss in a teaspoon of raw sewage. A bowl of steaming, scrumptious chili on a cold day . . . yum! Could the whole thing really be tainted by just a little slime?

That's the picture of our hearts and minds when we toy with just a little disobedience.

TALK TO HIM

"Lord, impress on my mind the importance of turning immediately from behaviors and beliefs that don't reflect your purity. Thank you for wanting only the best for me. Please help me see wholehearted obedience to you as the only path toward your best."

The doors we open and close each day decide the lives we live.

FLORA WHITTEMORE

February 5 EXODUS 31:1-11

"I uniquely fit you for my work."

"I have filled him with the Spirit of God, giving him great wisdom, ability, and expertise."
EXODUS 31:3

What a thrill and an honor for Bezalel and Oholiab to be chosen by God as master craftsmen in charge of building his Tabernacle, the place where his people would worship, then to be filled with his Spirit and fitted with unique wisdom and skills to get the work done precisely how God envisioned it. If only we all could be so fortunate. . . .

Then again, we are.

You know that talent of yours? The one others have said seems to come so naturally to you? Maybe it is something you wouldn't even consider a skill at first glance. It could simply be a character quality such as a calming presence, a giving nature, or a knack for making others feel welcome.

You didn't come by any of those wonderful assets by accident. They're signs of God's hand at work in you, readying you to serve him and others in a special way he designed.

How easily we lose sight of our own uniqueness. You're one of a kind, a priceless masterpiece. That might sound cliché, but let it sink in before you move on with your day. No one can touch others' lives exactly as you can. God molded your quirks and idiosyncrasies for something bigger than yourself. Your life is purposeful, whether or not you feel like it is today.

You're on this earth for God's greater plan, a plan that extends into eternity. Instead of viewing life as merely passing time, grab hold of God's gifts to you and let him use you for something remarkable. He may touch one life through you, or he may change the world.

Either way, you'll bless others—and be blessed, too—when you ask him to fill you with his Spirit and put you to use for whatever he intends.

TALK TO HIM

"God, please remind me that my life is your design, and my unique qualities have a purpose for you. Thank you for fitting me for something unlike what you plan for anyone else. Please help me to not be shortsighted and miss it."

What we are is God's gift to us. What we become is our gift to God.
ELEANOR POWELL

"I am your Savior."

"O Israel, these are the gods who brought you out of the land of Egypt." EXODUS 32:4

"What!?" Stop and listen to the sound of appalled astonishment God must have felt when his people credited a gold cow with saving them from Egyptian slavery. After all he had done for them, how closely he had aligned himself to them, they couldn't manage more than a gold earring's worth of loyalty toward him. The utter gall!

It's a good thing people aren't like that today.

Except, somehow this story makes the skin itch if you pause to think about it. Then it hits a bit too close to home for comfort.

We're really not so different from the Israelites in our loyalty toward God. We're just as easily distracted by creature comforts and convenient antidotes to boredom. And we're just as quick to take credit or pass credit to someone else for what God alone has accomplished.

Those Israelites. It's so easy to criticize them, so easy to relate to them. If only they'd applied more of their stubborn hardheadedness to their faith, maybe their faith wouldn't have been so flimsy. How would their journey have been improved by an unwavering loyalty to God? He alone had rescued them from the Egyptians. Not some gold cow, not some human leader, not some magical potion. God alone.

Even before he sent his Son, Jesus, as the Savior from our sins, God had carried the role of Savior in many other ways. Today, if we would only focus every doubt on one thought—God is Savior—how much deeper our faith would extend.

Do you believe that God is your Savior? Is that belief merely an afterthought, or does it set the course of your day, affecting every thought and action?

TALK TO HIM

"Lord, thank you for saving me from more than I could know. Please reveal where I may be putting my loyalty other than with you. You alone deserve credit for being my Savior."

Savior, while my heart is tender, I would yield that heart to Thee;
All my powers to Thee surrender, Thine and only Thine to be.
May this solemn consecration never once forgotten be;
Let it know no revocation, registered and confirmed by Thee.
JOHN BURTON JR., "SAVIOR, WHILE MY HEART IS TENDER"

February 7 EXODUS 33:12–34:10

"I will guide you and show you more of myself."

"Let me know your ways so I may understand you more fully." EXODUS 33:13

Of all our requests of God, perhaps the one he loves best is when someone asks him for more of himself. Everything he does, all his answers to prayer, are foremost to show his holy character. He loves a heartfelt request for more of him instead of for more "stuff" on our behalf. Would you want to be appreciated as the one who doles out perks and provisions more than for being who you are? You'd end up feeling used. Why would it be any different for God?

God promised to grant Moses' request for his presence with the people because Moses acknowledged the people's primary need for God himself to be with them. The rescue from Egypt and the manna God provided were wonderful gifts, but the people first needed to know the wonders of who their God was and is—his characteristics as almighty Lord, yet intimate Savior.

The gift of God's presence is so precious because he doesn't have to give us the time of day, yet he wants to spend time with us. He continues to woo us with his love, his goodness, his faithfulness, his mercy, and many other qualities that invite us to love him in return. When he shows himself uniquely to someone, that person glimpses eternity.

God's presence is the greatest gift you could ever hope for, the greatest one available. As he promised Moses, God will tuck you into a safe place and keep you covered by his presence (see Exodus 33:22). Enjoy being safe in his hand today.

TALK TO HIM

"Lord, sometimes I think I start to understand how precious your gift of you is. But God, please awaken me to even more of you today."

There is a place of comfort sweet, near to the heart of God.
A place where we our Savior meet, near to the heart of God.
There is a place of full release, near to the heart of God.
A place where all is joy and peace, near to the heart of God.

CLELAND B. MCAFEE, "NEAR TO THE HEART OF GOD"

"Let your first thoughts be of me."

The people continued to bring additional gifts each morning. EXODUS 36:3

Think back to your waking moments this morning. Recall the tidbits of thought that tiptoed into your consciousness as the sun yawned over the horizon. Did you notice the early morning chill in the room? the sheets warmed by sleep? the quiet that permeated? Maybe you enjoyed a peaceful few minutes with God. Before the day's rush hit or the sun's rays dried the ground, maybe your thoughts turned heavenward.

For all their mistakes, the early Israelites sometimes got it right. Like when it came to contributing to building the Tabernacle. They began each morning with excitement about being able to give more to God that day. It was as if they couldn't get enough of giving back to him. What a way to approach life!

By ordering their daily habits around God, they gave him the worship he deserves, and they also built their community and enjoyed being part of something that stretched them beyond their own concerns. They discovered unique ways they could give, and they saw God bless their talents. Their lives held meaning that extended into eternal realms, the fortification of God's home.

We have very little to give to the supreme Giver on our own merits, but all he really wants is our devotion and time. When we offer those, he can steer us in the best direction and bring maximum good from the energy he gives us.

Train your mind to give God your first moments, and he'll set you up for a day fit for your King and a heritage of worshiping him.

TALK TO HIM

"Thank you for the morning, Lord. Please plant your thoughts within me so I wake up on the right track for the day."

One thought I have, my ample creed, so deep it is and broad,
And equal to my every need—it is the thought of God.
Each morn unfolds some fresh surprise, I feast at life's full board;
And rising in my inner skies shines forth the thought of God.
My rest by night, my strength by day O blessèd thought of God.

FREDERICK L. HOSMER, "THE THOUGHT OF GOD"

February 9 EXODUS 40:1-38

"Finish the work I give you."

At last Moses finished the work. EXODUS 40:33

Ah, the joys of a job well done! Knowing you dotted each *i* and crossed each *t*. Feeling the satisfaction of no regrets, nothing left hanging over your head. Draws a sigh of relief, doesn't it?

Moses likely felt all that when he put the finishing touches on his God-given to-do list for the Tabernacle. It was a weighty assignment, and although many people contributed, Moses was the final human authority to make sure everything was completed to his Boss's satisfaction.

It's interesting that God's special cloud of leading didn't cover the Tabernacle and the Lord's glory didn't fill it until everything was complete.

There's a lesson here for us.

Sometimes it's tempting to scrimp on the details of a task because we're bored or worn out from it, or impatient to move on to the next thing. When we've been at a job long enough, we often start glossing over the fine tuning that makes the difference between good enough and excellent. But God wants excellence from us.

If they hadn't seen the project through to completion, Moses and the Israelites would have missed out on God showing his full presence in and through their work. They wouldn't have known their own feeling of accomplishment, much less God's pleasure over their job done well. They also would have missed out on years of communicating with him through the Tabernacle and his closest guidance for the remainder of their journey.

We never know how God may use the work he gives us now and into the future. If we don't complete our tasks with the quality and passion he instills in us, we may never come to understand the extent of blessing he wants to bring to us and to others.

Whatever your work today, keep in mind that God is in it, and he will surely bless your efforts when you apply his kind of excellence to the final *i* and *t*.

TALK TO HIM

"Lord, teach me about your excellence today. Please give me the energy and passion to complete each project for you."

Perseverance is the hard work you do after you get
tired of doing the hard work you already did.
NEWT GINGRICH

"I love receiving your best."

"It is a special gift, a pleasing aroma to the LORD." LEVITICUS 2:2

Say you receive an invitation to a party honoring someone special, a true VIP. This person already has power, prestige, and all the perks money can buy. The pressure is on to bring the ideal gift, something that shows this person's importance.

You riffle through your cupboards and find a half-eaten box of cereal. That'll be great for starters. But this person deserves more, so you head to the linen closet, where you spot that set of rainbow-colored towels. They're only a year old, but they've never been exactly what you've wanted. So into the bag they go. You're doing great, but you think you should do more. You hem and haw a few minutes, then suddenly it hits you. The pièce de résistance to really spice up your offering. Back to the kitchen, you yank a soggy tea bag from your mug and drop it into a plastic bag before depositing it with your other gifts. You're all set. Not just one gift, but bunches of loot sure to impress the guest of honor.

By now you're either scowling or laughing. Who would have the nerve to give such "treasures" to anyone?

But that's the kind of message we send to God when we give him less than our best. Everything we have we receive as gifts from him. He doesn't expect us to offer him riches we don't have, but from the wealth of love he's given us, he wants the best of our hearts, minds, and motivations to show genuine gratitude for his worth.

He impressed upon the Israelites the importance of offering only their best to him, and the message holds true for us.

Would you give anything less to the Lord of the universe, the Creator of the world, the King of kings? Would you give anything less to the most precious Friend you could hope to find? He is one and the same, and he loves receiving your best.

TALK TO HIM

"God, you are worthy of more than I can give, but I offer you my best. Thank you for accepting those gifts, even though I'd love to give you much more."

God waits to win back his own flowers as gifts from man's hands.

RABINDRANATH TAGORE

February 11 LEVITICUS 10:1-7

"I take leadership very seriously."

"You have been anointed with the LORD's anointing oil." LEVITICUS 10:7

Assuming a leadership position doesn't necessarily equal being a quality leader. A leader may have title, privileges, and responsibilities, but lack what it takes to be a solid guide.

God showed two Old Testament priests how serious he is about those who lead. Nadab and Abihu learned the high price leaders pay when they don't follow God's ways. Called to set a godly example for the Israelite nation, they chose not to do things according to God's directions. As a result, God made them examples of the consequences of opposing him.

Many places throughout the Bible detail guidelines for leaders; they're held to a higher standard because of their impact on others. Unfortunately, a list of good and bad leaders in personal, work, spiritual, and public life likely will reveal more names on the negative side.

While it's easy to pick apart authority figures, it's important to balance criticism with understanding the need to improve our own leadership impact. Whether we ask for it or reject it, each of us influences someone else. From young children to friends to those we mentor to subordinates at work, people constantly observe us. We have to keep our heads straight and our hearts focused on God as our own leader because stress, temptation, and questionable ethics can destroy leadership potential when our guard is down.

As far as the Bible says, only God watched Nadab and Abihu perform their duties. But God is the observer who counts the most because our behind-the-scenes lives determine our true worth as authorities.

Some of the best leaders never asked for the job, but qualities like patience, integrity, discernment, wisdom, and compassion show clearly in a life well lived. Ask God to help you develop the lasting qualities of a good leader, and commit to leading his way even when it seems no one is watching.

TALK TO HIM

"Lord, please help me not to assume leadership attention without assuming leadership responsibilities. Please help me follow your example of integrity and compassion so I'll set the right example for those who may be watching."

Nothing so conclusively proves [one's] ability to lead others as what [one] does from day to day to lead [oneself].

THOMAS J. WATSON

"My holiness does not mix with impurity."

"Through this process, he will purify the Most Holy Place." LEVITICUS 16:16

Some things are nonnegotiable with God, and holiness is one of them. We may struggle to understand its importance because God may seem unmerciful in expecting faulty humans to be holy like him. But the truth is, he can't accept us as we are. Our sinfulness makes us the oil that won't mix with the pure water that he is.

Back in Old Testament times, the people had to endure rigorous purification processes and repeated animal sacrifices to pay for their sins. God showed his grace through that plan of covering for the people's wrongs. But since Jesus died in our place, we're now covered forever by his greater grace and acceptable to God. Instead of priests purifying the Most Holy Place in the Tabernacle, Jesus, our Most High Priest, purifies our hearts.

Have you viewed your heart as God's Most Holy Place? If you've accepted Jesus as Savior, that's exactly what your heart is to God—a precious place of purity where he dwells. God protected his Most Holy Place when it was located in the Tabernacle, and now his Holy Spirit protects your heart for himself.

Consider the impact of God's Spirit living within you. Consider the extent of his protection:

His presence is constantly with you.
His love is forever filling you.
His grace is always ready to forgive you.
His character is consistently working in you.
His holiness is eternally marking you as his child.

As God's Most Holy Place, your heart is being purified as he refines it to resemble his own. Your life is a story of grace that you'll see to fulfillment when you meet your Savior someday.

View today's moments as more opportunities to make him feel at home in your life.

TALK TO HIM

"Lord, please help me remember that my heart is a sacred place where you want to live comfortably. Thank you for making your home in me."

Purer in heart, O God, help me to be;
Until Thy holy face one day I see:
Keep me from secret sin,
Reign Thou my soul within;
Purer in heart, help me to be.

FANNIE E. DAVISON, "PURER IN HEART, O GOD"

February 13 LEVITICUS 18:1-5, 24-30; 19:1-37

"My rules bring you life and health."

"If you obey my decrees and my regulations, you will find life through them. I am the Lord."

LEVITICUS 18:5

Oh how we don't like rules! The idea of being restrained by dos and confined by don'ts leaves us fidgeting and figuring out a fast way to buck the system. We're like kids. In fact, how many of us as children groaned when we heard our parents say, "Rules are good for you"? After all, we're sure we know what's best for ourselves.

However, God had another idea about his people's wisdom to act in their own best interests. The book of Leviticus is known for containing rules and regulations, many of which make sense to us, as well as others that leave us struggling to understand why God went to such extremes. Surely meat was still good three days after it was sacrificed.

Or not.

We humans are wild cards, and no one knows it better than God. Left to our know-how, we often go with the impulse of the moment, and when it comes to learning from mistakes, we often have short-term memories. Add our tendency to let our emotions rule, and we have ingredients that stir up a batch of trouble large enough to sicken a life, like bad meat.

We may know enough to get by without too much trouble, but having knowledge isn't the same as possessing consistent willpower. Therefore, God laid out his standards to protect us from ourselves and from each other.

Like children, we may not enjoy being under authority. But a humble attitude that acknowledges God's right to govern us will keep us within his protection. Only then can we enjoy the bountiful spread of blessings he offers. His rules whet our appetites for more of his goodness and keep us from living off the meager consequences of our unhealthy decisions.

Savor the benefits of living by his rules.

TALK TO HIM

"Lord, please help me treasure your rules. Help me to remember that you put them in place because you treasure me."

Even when we know what is right, too often we fail to act.
More often we grab greedily for the day, letting tomorrow
bring what it will, putting off the unpleasant and unpopular.

BERNARD M. BARUCH

"I will establish your family legacy."

"Each tribe of Israel will camp in a designated area with its own family banner."

NUMBERS 1:52

We all need to belong, to experience the comforting sense that we're part of something larger than ourselves. We need independence, but people don't thrive in perpetual loneliness because God created us for himself and each other.

Within their nation, the Israelites enjoyed the identity of being God's chosen people. But they found further belonging within their separate tribes. By establishing tribes, God helped the people govern and experience deeper loyalty and unity than they may have felt as individuals among an entire nation. And by directing each tribe to set up camp in a unique place under a banner heralding their spot in the world, God gave them somewhere to belong and a sense of pride and protection within their families. No doubt the people ran into difficulties with each other; deepest hurts often come from within families. Still, God made his point that family is important.

The family you were born into may be a tightly knit group whose members love each other deeply and support each other through life's challenges. Or your family may be in turmoil. Either way, God cares about all of you. He makes no mistakes, and that goes for placing you together.

You have a unique opportunity to impact your relatives and make a difference for them. You have a role in deepening and strengthening your God-given family legacy. Through prayer and looking out for their best interests, you can invite God's life-changing love to the sheltering banner that identifies your family as a solid place to belong.

Will you care for the ones he chose for you?

TALK TO HIM

"Lord, you know my family's potential, and you know our struggles. Please soften us toward one another, and heal and grow us as you know best."

Most of us would give our own life for the survival of a family member, yet we lead our daily life too often as if we take our family for granted.

PAUL PEARSHALL

February 15 NUMBERS 3:1-39

"I invite you to come close to me."

Anyone other than a priest or Levite who went too near the sanctuary was to be put to death.
NUMBERS 3:38

Did you receive your invitation today? Maybe a better question would be, Did you know Someone sent you one? It's nice to be remembered and welcomed by someone. But when that person is almighty God, the Commander of earth and heaven, the value of a daily invitation can't be measured.

He didn't always let people come close to him. During Old Testament days, only the high priest was allowed to enter the Tabernacle's Most Holy Place, and only once a year. Commoners weren't allowed near such sacred ground under penalty of death.

However, Jesus' death on our behalf changed that, and we live in the age of grace and warm welcomes from God. Not only does he tolerate us, but he cherishes time with us.

He craves time with us. How many of us crave time with him? Sure, we get warm feelings about being close to him—when the mood hits. But we're spoiled knowing that he'll be there whenever we choose to "bless" him with our presence. Even with the best of intentions to make him our number-one priority, we still get distracted by the all-important items on our agendas. As if he doesn't have a to-do list longer than we could fathom! He doesn't need our time, but he wants it. And he knows we need that time with him.

Today, spend a few moments sharing your heart and quieting your spirit with him. That time is sacred, something people thousands of years ago couldn't enjoy. Yet it's yours anytime you want it.

Will you respond to his invitation and join him?

TALK TO HIM

"Lord, to think that you want to spend time with me is beyond understanding. Please broaden my mind to grasp the gift of your presence, and quiet my heart so I'm more in tune to you."

We are at this moment as close to God as we choose to be.
JOHN OSWALD SANDERS

"Look for my guidance, and don't move ahead or lag behind me."

They traveled and camped at the LORD's command wherever he told them to go.

NUMBERS 9:18

God's timing is perfect for you. Depending on how much you believe it, that truth can change your day.

One common struggle most of us have when trying to follow God is trusting his timing. More often than not, our time frame doesn't match his, and more often than not, we wish he would move faster.

Consider his reasoning for moving the Israelites on each leg of their wilderness journey. Sometimes he rested them in one place overnight; other times he kept them stationary for much longer. They had no way to predict his next move, but certainly anyone attuned to him noticed that his calls to go and stop came at ideal times. He knew when they needed rest, when they needed the discipline of waiting on him, and when they needed to take action even if they didn't feel like it. His daytime cloud and nighttime pillar of fire were clear signals from him regarding his perfect timing for them.

We may not have such visible direction on a daily basis, but those who know God as Lord do have the greater benefit of his Spirit living within them. It takes conscious focus and seeking him to hear his Spirit's leading voice, but he speaks to us now as much as he spoke to the ancient Israelites.

However, distance wreaks havoc on our powers of hearing, and it's difficult to hear him when we don't remain in step with him. Whatever his timing for the issues in your life, stay in tune with him so you don't rush ahead or fall behind. Whether today is a stay-put day or a move-on day is up to God. Watch and listen for him, and in his perfect time he'll reveal his next move.

TALK TO HIM

"Lord, please make your guidance obvious to me. I know you want me to see you, so please help me wait on you and move with you."

Before me, even as behind, God is, and all is well.

JOHN GREENLEAF WHITTIER

February 17 NUMBERS 11:1-23, 31-35

"Don't try to force me to comply with you."

"Has my arm lost its power? Now you will see whether or not my word comes true!"

NUMBERS 11:23

Here we go again. More gripes and groans from the Israelite nation as they wandered in the wilderness.

It's easy to criticize them, but we're so much like them! We think we know what we want. We think we know what's best. But many times we have it wrong.

You would think that, after observing God's working in countless lives, plus reading story after story in the Bible about how he provided for his people, we would willingly wait on him. We would trust him through life's hardships, and we would enjoy peace and soul-satisfying rest within his care.

You would think.

But we humans can be pretty dense. We're easily worn down by our desires for more comforts. When we're hurting, our self-interests tend to rule our stamina, narrowing our vision of God. We start to crack under pressure, and those cracks let in doubts about his character, his interest in us, and his goodness.

That's when we become dangerous to ourselves.

We rationalize our complaints and tell ourselves that he is God; he can take our venting and fuming. Our passion builds, but instead of leaning into God so he can strengthen our faith, we turn on him and beg for what we're sure will fix our circumstances.

The Israelites were sure they wanted meat to eat. Their complaints built into a fervor, and their desire grew into obsession. They needed meat. Their passion twisted itself in their minds, making them view the horrific days of slavery as preferable to the challenges of their journey with God into freedom. Eventually God complied with them and taught them a painful lesson about pushing for their will over his.

Whatever your deepest desire, lean into God for strength instead of pushing against him to get what you want. Then you're sure to get what he knows you need.

TALK TO HIM

"Lord, please plant in my mind an image of me leaning into you instead of forcing my will against yours. You are God today, just as you have been for thousands of years."

There are two kinds of people: those who say to God, "Thy will be done,"
and those to whom God says, "All right, then, have it your way."

C. S. LEWIS

"*When you take me at my word, you won't need to fear.*"

"They are only helpless prey to us! They have no protection, but the LORD is with us!"

NUMBERS 14:9

Fear. A small word with an enormous intimidation factor. Capable of rendering us powerless, it grips and paralyzes like a famished snake. You would think that we'd run from its coils, but sometimes its powers seem hypnotic, tempting us, drawing us into its lair, trapping and suffocating our energy.

The Israelites of old knew this kind of fear. They knew what it was to be held captive by its force. As fear often does, it caught them off guard at a key moment when they needed to decide on a plan of action.

They were on the brink of finally experiencing God's promises come true. The land he offered them lay before them, a bountiful, beautiful home of their own. Yet the opportunity involved frightening unknowns. Would they take him at his word, or would they become victims of their anxieties? They gave in to the thrust of fear, worked themselves into a panic, and became fear's prey instead of its victor.

This kind of fear is not from God. He created us to be victorious, to trust his strength, and to live with confidence in his ability to carry us through dangerous territory.

Life is not safe. Each day we face more threats than we realize from natural sources, as well as from our supernatural predator, Satan. But God, like an undefeatable hunter, destroys fear before it destroys us, his cherished children. Fear holds no power when he is present. He invites us to rebel against fear and enjoy his protection and empowerment.

When you face a circumstance that looms over you, choose victory by trusting God to help you. Stick closely to his side, and live within his protection.

He has you covered today. Shed your fear and trust him.

TALK TO HIM

"Father God, thank you for understanding my fears, and thank you for being stronger. I can't defeat fear in my strength, so please help me believe that you will see me through the frightening unknowns."

He who fears something gives it power over him.

MOORISH PROVERB

February 19 NUMBERS 14:10-25

"Your faith and obedience ensure that you receive my perfect plans for you."

"Please, Lord, prove that your power is as great as you have claimed." NUMBERS 14:17

At the heart of our anxieties, don't we want to know more than anything that God is as powerful as he claims? Once we're sure of him, we can rest.

Sometimes, though, God expects us to remember his faithfulness without begging him for more signs that he will be enough again. Mature faith chooses to be faithful to what we know is true of him.

Imagine spending years proving your love for someone, but never gaining that person's trust. Eventually you would weary of their lack of faith. God feels the same when we constantly ask for another sign before we'll take him at his word. Exasperated by the Israelites' continued disloyalty, he said to Moses, "How long will these people treat me with contempt? Will they never believe me, even after all the miraculous signs I have done among them?" (Numbers 14:11). It's shocking to read that chronic doubts about God's character show contempt for his ways.

The Israelites' lack of obedient faith cost a generation the joy of his perfect plans for them. They had one life to trust him, but they wasted it and paid dearly.

God will remain true to himself, which means he will be trustworthy. Part of trusting him requires that we choose to believe in his unchanging goodness and love no matter what circumstances or other people tell us. Trust takes practice, but that's how we know him better.

Today is full of decisive moments that affect your experience of his perfect plans for you. Will you trust him to be God again, same as he always has been, same as he will be for eternity?

TALK TO HIM

"Lord, you are trustworthy. I know this even when my feelings waver. Please help me trust you again, knowing that you will be you."

> *Faith . . . is the art of holding on to things your reason has once accepted, in spite of your changing moods. . . . Unless you teach your moods "where they get off," you can never be . . . a sound Christian, . . . but just a creature dithering to and fro.*
>
> C. S. LEWIS

February 20

"Nothing can stand in the way of my purposes."

Then the LORD gave the donkey the ability to speak. NUMBERS 22:28

Very few absolutes exist in this world, although laws of nature may argue otherwise. Nature's laws say that some things are possible and others are not. For instance, science tells us animals do not speak. However, God is not limited by science. Animals talk if he wants them to.

The story of Balaam and the donkey reveals a couple of things. First of all, God has a sense of humor. What a comical scene to see a regular old donkey park itself in the road and talk back to Balaam! We may have watched such things in kids' movies, but not in real life. Well, this experience truly happened, and it changed Balaam's life.

Secondly, the story shows us that God will have his way. King Balak of Moab tried to manipulate circumstances to protect his interests. Determined to make it impossible for the Israelites to defeat him, he hired Balaam to put a curse on them. Yet God was still God, and his determination to protect his people literally stopped the plans of these men in their tracks.

Try as we might to force our will over situations and people, we will not succeed when God stops us. He is the only absolute, and his decisions stand against anything and anyone who tries to threaten them.

Knowing God will have his way is comforting when we're standing with him, but not for those who want their own way.

No matter what, he will be God. Will you see that as a good thing today?

TALK TO HIM

"Lord, too often I notice myself pushing my desires instead of letting you be God. Thank you for not leaving the truth of the matter up to me—you are God no matter what. Please help me stand with you and not get in your way."

Your mind works very simply: you are either trying to find out what are God's laws in order to follow them; or you are trying to outsmart Him.

MARTIN H. FISCHER

February 21 NUMBERS 27:12-23

"Pray for those who will take over your work."

"Give them someone who will guide them wherever they go and will lead them."

NUMBERS 27:17

What tasks fill your days? You know, the job that forces you to stop hitting the snooze button and get out of bed every morning?

Whether you enjoy it or not, your work leaves a lasting impression on someone. No one works in a vacuum, no matter how isolated some jobs may feel at times. The very necessity of a task says that someone is influenced by what you do.

But what will your efforts amount to after you're gone? Who will carry on what you've either begun or taken over from your predecessor?

Moses knew his time was coming to an end as the Israelites' leader. He also knew they needed a godly person to guide them and help them stay on God's path. As part of his resignation process, Moses asked God to provide the right person to come after him.

He set a good example about finishing well. He made his share of mistakes in his career, but he left his leadership role with godly class. Instead of waving good-bye with a "See ya later, folks. I'm outta here," Moses considered commissioning his replacement as part of his role. His attitude of responsibility served the people well, because God picked Joshua next.

God fits you for purposeful work, and his penchant for long-term planning (think "eternity") draws the conclusion that he wants longevity to characterize your good efforts. Therefore, if he wants your work to continue, he has someone in mind to take over where you leave off.

Consider the aspects of what you do, and offer those details to the Lord. Keep your eyes open to individuals in your circle who could use a prayer of preparation for their future. Then trust that God has the future of your work in good hands.

TALK TO HIM

"Thank you, Lord, for creating me for meaningful work. Please help me see what I do through your eyes, and open mine to the person you have in mind to carry it on after me."

Do not hire a man who does your work for money,
but him who does it for love of it.

HENRY DAVID THOREAU

"Remember how I cared for you in the past."

"Be careful never to forget what you yourself have seen. Do not let these memories escape from your mind as long as you live! And be sure to pass them on to your children and grandchildren." DEUTERONOMY 4:9

Why did God create us with memories? God isn't one to do things haphazardly, or to be surprised that something turned out the way it did. It stands to reason, then, that he created our memories for a purpose.

Moses urged the Israelites to use their God-given memories to help them stay close to God in the future as he had been close to them throughout their past. Before Moses left his role as their leader, he took them on a refresher tour through their memories to deepen their obedience to God.

What a plethora of experiences to choose from—the ups, downs, highs, and lows of being God's chosen people. Their experiences reminded them of mistakes and tough times, yes, but even more of God's graciousness to see them through everything.

Not every memory is pleasant. In fact, many can be horribly painful. However, remembering God's mercy that brought you this far develops courage to trust him again. God never forgets a moment of your life. Your memories are tucked away safely with him. Thank him for the joyful ones, trust him to heal the hurtful ones, and commit to him the ones yet to be created.

Most importantly, ask him to develop in you a garden to hold reminders of his love for you. Water them daily by spending time with him in prayer and through his Word so the memories of his voice will overflow on a consistent basis.

Remember: He does not forget you. He wants to spend eternity with you. He paid the high price of his Son's life to ensure that you can create precious, eternal memories with him.

Remember him.

TALK TO HIM

"Heavenly Father, please free me from the memories that hold me prisoner, and bless me with memories of how you've carried me this far. Help me remember that you never will forget me."

To look backward for a while is to refresh the eye, to restore it, and to render it the more fit for its prime function of looking forward.

MARGARET FAIRLESS BARBER

February 23 DEUTERONOMY 6:1-25

"I want my truths to fill your home and impact future generations."

"Repeat them again and again to your children. Talk about them when you are at home."
DEUTERONOMY 6:7

Surely you've heard the saying "Repetition is the mother of learning." Wherever it came from, it shows the timelessness of how we humans gain knowledge and understanding. What we see and hear time and again becomes part of our subconscious that sticks with us for the long term.

That longevity explains, at least in part, why the atmosphere in our homes has such far-reaching impact on us. Repetitious daily home life provides countless learning opportunities, both planned and spontaneous. There's a reason parenting quotes such as "Because I said so" have become clichés. They have been repeated so often that they're second nature.

When the Israelites were about to settle in their land, God gave them instructions through Moses for their new phase of life. God wanted to instill his values in their future generations from the get-go, so he told them to establish positive habits in their homes.

Home was to be a place where his truth reigned, where it was spoken of continually as part of everyday life. God knew consistency would pay off when future generations would think back on their early days and recall lessons learned. Those remembrances would serve as catalysts for developing spiritual maturity as adults. As a result, his ways would be passed down through the people's line of descendants, preserving his laws.

Just as God was interested in the early Israelites' home atmosphere, he cares about what goes on in our homes. Whether your home is filled with your own children or you welcome guests into it, the place you live is a primary way God intends for you to influence others.

Does your home speak to others about God's love?

TALK TO HIM

"Lord, thank you for creating the concept of home, a place intended for safety, security, and growth. Please dwell in mine, and let me be a positive influence in the lives of all who walk through the door."

Home ought to be our clearinghouse, the place from which we go forth lessoned and disciplined, and ready for life.

KATHLEEN NORRIS

"Don't forget me in the midst of your good life."

"He did all this so you would never say to yourself, 'I have achieved this wealth with my own strength and energy.'" DEUTERONOMY 8:17

Have you ever felt humbled by a gift? Maybe it was so special that you didn't think you deserved it.

God reminded the Israelites of his gifts to help them remember that the good things of life come from him. They had come a long way since leaving Egypt, geographically and spiritually, and they wouldn't have made it without God. After surviving a great deal and experiencing his repeated discipline, his people were on the brink of the good life—a condition that carries hidden dangers for the spiritually unaware.

We think of the rough spots of life as times when we need God most, and in many ways that's true. However, if we're not aware of the pitfalls in seasons of blessing, we could end up in dangerous territory of another kind: spiritual blindness to God as our provider. When we lose sight of him because other blessings pile up around us, we place ourselves in a precarious position.

We long for prosperity, health, loving relationships, and time to enjoy them. Those times are wonderful. May we have more of them, Lord willing. But if we don't credit God for them, we put on blinders that keep us from seeing him in the midst of his blessings. We end up craving the gifts more than the Giver.

There's something achingly precious about being in the center of difficulty that lets us know we need the Lord. That clarification is a gift we don't often ask for, one we don't often find when life feels smooth.

By all means, soak up God's blessings. He intends them for your enjoyment. But ask him to humble your heart and open your eyes to him more than to what he does for you.

Don't let other gifts cause you to miss the gift of him.

TALK TO HIM

"Lord, I'm not a fan of tough times, but I know you have hidden gifts for me in them. Please keep me humble to maintain my focus on you instead of on what I'd like from you."

Prosperity is not without many fears and distastes,
and adversity is not without comforts and hopes.
FRANCIS BACON

February 25 DEUTERONOMY 14:22-29

"Give to me a portion of what I've given you."

"You must set aside a tithe. . . . Doing this will teach you always to fear the LORD *your God."*
DEUTERONOMY 14:22-23

In addition to asking God to keep us humble during prosperous times, another way we stay on track with him is by acknowledging that everything he gives us still belongs to him. Therefore, he deserves our best in return for what he has provided for us.

Do you practice tithing—giving the first part, the best part, of your earnings to God? Just as important, do you understand why God originally commanded tithes from his people? According to today's reading, God's purpose for tithing was to instill the people with respect for him.

You may know the verse from Job that says, "The LORD gave me what I had, and the LORD has taken it away. Praise the name of the LORD!" (Job 1:21). That is the respect, otherwise known as fear of the Lord, referred to in today's verse.

Everything we have really isn't ours; it's God's. Our first impulse upon realizing our poverty might be to feel surprised or disappointed. However, consider this truth another way. If all we have belongs to God, we are freed from worrying about losing it. We can't lose what's never truly ours. No use grasping for material perks that can't go with us into eternity.

Since we're surrounded by what we think of as ours, we're challenged to maintain a healthy fear of God. That's where tithing comes in. Tithing our best serves as a regular reminder to keep God's perspective about the stuff of this world.

Think about what you cherish. Would you offer it back to God if he asked? Would you offer it without waiting for him to ask?

TALK TO HIM

"Thank you, God, for the reminder that I own nothing; it's all yours. And thank you for the freedom of poverty and the greater riches I have in a relationship with you."

We are all of us from birth to death guests at a table which we did not spread.
The sun, the earth, love, friends, our very breath are parts of the banquet. . . .
Shall we think of the day as a chance to come nearer to our Host, and
to find out something of Him who has fed us so long?
REBECCA HARDING DAVIS

"Beware of 'truths' other than mine."

"You may wonder, 'How will we know whether or not a prophecy is from the Lord*?'"*

DEUTERONOMY 18:21

How good are you at spotting a lie? Sometimes it depends on the liar; other times it depends on the believability of what is being promoted as truth.

Unfortunately, sometimes an idea can seem so logical that it seems true. It sounds too good not to be true. Sometimes a theory holds a nugget of sense, making it easier to believe that it's right.

God's Word warns us repeatedly to be on guard for people who preach non-truths. Why would God say so much about false teachers? Surely once we've heard his standards, we won't be vulnerable to believing ideas that go against them, right?

Maybe. Maybe not.

If someone's message is obviously wrong, we're not likely to fall for it. The lies that cause the most harm are the ones that seem right. They're tougher to spot and are more powerful in luring us from God's best.

God maintains certain nonnegotiables that will never change, the main one—that he is the only God, and he has the authority to determine truth. He provides the wisdom to discern right from wrong. To know whether a "truth" lines up with him, we must compare it to the Bible.

The world is full of misconceptions and twisted truths from people who either don't like how God does things or haven't searched his Word for the real truth. Society says people should be free to create their own right and wrong. But God didn't create different truths for different people. For those who think his standards are stifling, it might come as a surprise that God's truths are always freeing because they point the way to him, the One with all authority.

Sticking with his truths enriches our lives instead of crippling us. His truths are sources of strength, endurance, purity, and holiness for those who embrace them.

Dig into his Word, and discover the freedom he offers you.

TALK TO HIM

"Lord, thank you for being the Author of truth, and thank you for giving me a mind to process your message. Please give me wisdom and clear thinking to recognize non-truths."

"You will know the truth, and the truth will set you free."

JOHN 8:32

February 27 DEUTERONOMY 30:1-20

"I offer you life, but you must choose to take it."

"Today I have given you the choice between life and death, between blessings and curses."
DEUTERONOMY 30:19

Who in their right mind would choose curses and death over blessings and life when given the choice and literally asked to opt for the better way? Yet that's exactly what countless people have done since shortly after God breathed life into Adam.

Human beings, as a collective group, don't take God seriously. We're busy with life, and we view God as someone to deal with later, if we must at all. Another reason people don't take him seriously is because his Old Testament principles might seem outdated for our "advanced" culture. But the Israelites who heard his original command to choose life got it fresh and new from God through Moses. They struggled with the same temptations we do that kept them from consistently following God, yet they certainly couldn't plead the excuse that it only applied to former generations.

Maybe ignoring our choice about life and death relates to our innate faultiness. As sinners, we're more apt to choose the harmful, destructive option rather than God's way of life, which we often view as stifling.

Sad to say, one day people will discover how seriously God should be taken. But the window of opportunity to choose him will be closed.

You may have made the ultimate choice to follow him, but what about the daily decisions of obedience to him? They might be your challenges today. Each of those seemingly minor choices to live by his standards affects the quality of your life on earth, as well as your eternal blessings. Will you go for the blessings of choosing him today?

TALK TO HIM
"Lord, thank you for the option to choose you instead of destruction. Please help me grow in godliness to keep choosing you in the little things."

Life is the time to serve the Lord,
The time to ensure the great reward;
And while the lamp holds out to burn,
The vilest sinner may return.
Life is the hour that God has given
To 'scape from hell and fly to Heav'n;
The day of grace, and mortals may
Secure the blessings of the day.

ISAAC WATTS, "LIFE IS THE TIME TO SERVE THE LORD"

"Strength and courage come from trusting me."

"The LORD your God will personally go ahead of you. He will neither fail you nor abandon you." DEUTERONOMY 31:6

Would your life be different if you never feared anything? Most of us would answer yes to that question, because the earth is full of reasons to feel anxious and sometimes even terrorized. None of us are immune to fear, whether internal or external. We might shudder at the thought of a chronic illness, losing a loved one, or being victimized by terrorism. It seems as if there's no place of guaranteed safety. Fear puts a hitch in life, and when it's allowed its way, it can keep us from our full potential.

God understands. No one knows the power of evil as he does. He has seen it all. Yet there's hope because no one knows his power as he does. And his power is altogether greater than evil. God sees every wicked scheme Satan and his followers twist up, and one day we'll know the extent he went to time and again to save us from threats we had no idea existed.

God goes before you today, from where you are now into every situation you're headed toward. You'll never be alone, so relax and take the moments as they come, knowing God already has met each one and tamed the dangers for you. He does this because your soul is precious to him. True, he may allow pain in your life. But if you're tempted to doubt his goodness, trust that he loves you enough to experience the hurt, and he won't waste it.

Take courage from his strength. He's been leading his people successfully for a very long time, and he won't abandon you. Face those fears today, but instead of seeing them, see the face of your heavenly Father, who is already there, standing between you and whatever troubles you.

TALK TO HIM

"Father, please ease my fears through a greater view of you as my protective Daddy. Thank you for being stronger than any threat."

As true as God's own promise stands,
Not earth nor hell with all their bands
Against us shall prevail;
The Lord shall mock them from His throne;
God is with us; we are His own;
Our victory cannot fail!

TRANSLATED BY CATHERINE WINKWORTH, "FEAR NOT, O LITTLE FLOCK"

March 1 JOSHUA 2:1-24; 6:22-25

"Faith in me requires action on your part."

"I know the L*ORD has given you this land."* JOSHUA 2:9

Do you know what is inspiring about this story? The fact that Rahab and the two Israelite spies took a frightening situation and turned fear on its head. Even though they knew victory was theirs because God had picked the land for the Israelites, they still could have cowered in terror because of the uncertain path to victory. Their confident actions revealed their faith, a key element of living a vital Christian life.

It is easy to say that faith requires action, but it is not always easy to, well, to act. That is when the rubber meets the road and we find out whether our faith really is faith or merely a case of wannabe trust.

Rahab and the spies showed they truly believed that God is the "supreme God of the heavens above and the earth below" (Joshua 2:11), with the authority to thwart their enemies and hand over land if he chose. If they had not moved forward in faith, only God knows what they—and generations after them—would have missed.

What do your actions reveal about your confidence in God? That is what faith is, really—confidence that God will be who he claims to be and do what he promises to do.

You can probably think of a situation that requires a step of faith on your part. Will you play it safe and miss out on God's best, or will you make the move and discover what God has in store next?

TALK TO HIM

"Lord, it's hard to trust at times. Yet I don't want to miss what you have planned. Please draw others to you when they see me put my confidence in you."

By faith the people passed through the sea as on dry land,
And faith was why the walls of Jericho just could not stand.
Though they are gone, they speak this word:
That without faith, none can please the Lord.
God therefore was not ashamed to be named as their Lord;
For they believed that He was real and would their faith reward.
Oh, give me faith to trust Your Word,
That by my life I may please You, Lord.

SUSAN H. PETERSON, "FAITH MEANS WE'RE SURE"

"Your actions always affect others."

"Get up! Why are you lying on your face like this? Israel has sinned and broken my covenant!"

JOSHUA 7:10-11

If only temptation had perfect hindsight. . . .

How many sins might we avoid? God warns us to be on guard against giving in to sin, but oftentimes we do not pause long enough to consider those warnings that could spare us. Then we act shocked when the consequences hurt.

God had little tolerance for Joshua's grief over the Israelites' defeat because they expected victory regardless of disobeying him. That sort of attitude takes advantage of God's mercy and naturally does not sit well with him.

If Achan could have seen the consequences of giving in to temptation, he might have shown more restraint instead of stealing the plunder from their victory. Just look at the carnage his one decision left in its shadow—dozens of warriors killed, his entire family wiped out, all because he had to have a robe and some silver and gold.

Temptation does in fact have perfect hindsight, and it always sees the same result clearly: Sin never ends well, and it always affects others. Achan's family paid directly for his wrongs, but all who cared about them felt the painful loss of those lives.

The next time you face temptation, keep in mind what it will look like from hindsight. It will not be a pretty picture. Are you willing to subject people you care about, people who care about you, to the effects of a wrong decision?

TALK TO HIM

"Lord, you know sin is never worth committing, but sometimes the temptation is so strong it clouds my vision. Please get my attention and remind me of the value of hindsight before I create pain for myself and the people I love."

When the gospel trumpet sounds,
When I think how grace abounds,
When I feel sweet peace within,
Then I'd rather die than sin.
When the cross I view by faith,
Sin is madness, poison, death;
Tempt me not, 'tis all in vain,
Sure I ne'er can yield again.

JOHN NEWTON, "SIN, WHEN VIEWED BY SCRIPTURE LIGHT"

March 3 JOSHUA 14:6-15

"When you are old and gray, I will still be working in your life."

"As you can see, the Lord *has kept me alive and well as he promised."* JOSHUA 14:10

God is a God of the long term. What huge comfort that truth offers to those who follow him.

We live in a fast-paced, impatient world that bores easily and gives up too soon when difficulties arise. We hit the stop button early on the microwave because it takes too long; we have fast-food restaurants every quarter mile because we have no time to sit over a family dinner. We even have drive-through divorces because we can't wait to move on once we become bored with our family.

Imagine if God operated like that. Heaven forbid he ever becomes bored with us or gives up on including us in his eternity. If that were the case, our future would be hopeless, our present worthless. With no future, we wouldn't bother seeking God. We would have no use for motivation or goals, nor would we feel any desire to make the world a better place. Crime and chaos would reign, searing a path of destruction and horror across the globe. God's long-term care for us gives us hope for what's to come, but it also shines over the present.

Just as God continued to work faithfully in Caleb's life, he won't be finished working in you until the end of your days here on earth. Therefore, you can thrive in the knowledge that he will be the same God in forty years as he is right now. He doesn't forget your history, and he will never grow bored with you.

He gave his Son for you, so he has a lot invested in you. He must love you hugely. One of the joys of aging is an ever-deepening relationship with him, so go ahead and dream of life with him years into the future. Get excited about knowing him better with each passing day.

He's pretty excited about you.

TALK TO HIM

"Lord, it boggles my mind that you get excited about me. Thank you for being with me now and for the rest of my life. Please show me more of yourself so I keep growing in excitement about you."

I know not what the future holds, but I know who holds the future.

AUTHOR UNKNOWN

"Take care to cling to me, to love me, and to believe me."

"Cling tightly to the LORD your God as you have done until now. . . . Be very careful to love the LORD your God. . . . Deep in your hearts you know that every promise of the LORD your God has come true." JOSHUA 23:8, 11, 14

Parting words are powerful words, perhaps because of their finality, perhaps because of the emotions surrounding good-byes. Whatever the reason, we tend to listen when we know we might not hear from someone again.

Likewise, if we are the one leaving, we choose our parting words carefully, communicating information we don't want people to miss. Helpful information suddenly becomes extra valuable; valuable information becomes critical.

Joshua had led his people well, and through his parting words he attempted to show them how to finish well. As he closed in on the end of his life, he urged the Israelites to take care of their individual relationships with God.

It's easy to go through the motions of obeying God, doing what's right, and avoiding sins. But there's additional depth involved in taking care in everything we do. Taking care requires more thought, more effort, and more investment—a step above the ordinary. Our daily routines are commonplace to us; we can accomplish much of our normal responsibilities with haphazard effort. But our own relationship with God deserves special attention if we want it to remain vibrant and life changing.

To guard against communication with God becoming run-of-the-mill, we need to heed Joshua's timeless advice to cling to the Lord, to love him, and to believe what he tells us. Living by those standards invites God to permeate every nook and cranny so in all of life we are centered around him.

Then when it is our time to say good-bye, we will have a lifetime of powerful parting words to share with those who come after us.

TALK TO HIM

"Lord, I know every sentence of your Word holds powerful parting words from you to me. Please help me to listen closely, cling to you, love your message, and believe its truth."

The future lies before you, like paths of pure white snow.
Be careful how you tread it, for every step will show.
AUTHOR UNKNOWN

March 5 JOSHUA 24:1-33

"Consider the spiritual atmosphere you set for your family."

"But as for me and my family, we will serve the Lord." JOSHUA 24:15

Some words raise our curiosity by their very existence. For example, the word *but* in verse 15 begs the question, *But* what?

Joshua spoke those words to the Israelites in his farewell speech. Everything about him, including his family life, was noticed by all. Oftentimes the most telling qualities about a leader can be seen in the quality of their home life. Sad to say, home and family tend to be especially vulnerable to negative influences when care isn't taken to protect them.

Joshua's question-raising *but* refers to his resolve to keep his family pointed toward God. He knew temptations would be strong in drawing people to serve other gods. They would be so powerful, in fact, that people would naturally choose the wrong way. Therein lies the importance of that little word *but*.

Through that word, it's as if Joshua were telling the people, "Look, we're going to be inundated with things that pull us from God, but my family and I will fight to keep God number one." His words carry ironclad determination and thoughtful commitment.

Like Joshua, we have a choice about whom we invite our family to serve. What we put our energy and time into reveals whom we serve. A bank account, a demanding boss, or a crazy schedule can take the form of gods when we prioritize them to our spiritual detriment.

The good news is we have an opportunity every day to choose God again.

We can neglect to place God's spiritual guard over our loved ones, or we can set the example of making God our ultimate leader to follow.

Choose today whom you will serve.

TALK TO HIM

"God, please help me realize that I'm serving other gods when I let other interests take your place. I want my home to raise others' curiosity about you."

Praise in the common words I speak,
Life's common looks and tones,
In fellowship in hearth and board
With my belovèd ones;
Not in the temple crowd alone
Where holy voices chime,
But in the silent paths of earth,
The quiet rooms of time.

HORATIUS BONAR, "FILL THOU MY LIFE"

"Consider whether you really want your way or mine."

"But you disobeyed my command. . . . So now I declare that I will no longer drive out the people living in your land." JUDGES 2:2-3

He warned them and warned them again. But they wanted what they wanted, and eventually God gave it to them. Only thing was, then they didn't want it so badly.

Those Israelites of old were a stubborn lot, not unlike us. We're sure we know what will make us happy, but our desires become like blinders when they don't match up with what God knows we need.

God told the Israelites to destroy the pagan nations' altars as protection against corruption by ungodly lifestyles. When they didn't, God basically said, "Alright, you asked for it. I am not going to help you if you fight me all the way." He let them get cozy with people whose habits would cause them misery and distance them from him.

Sometimes we insist on learning things the hard way. In allowing us room to make mistakes, God also allows us space to hurt ourselves and him as we selfishly run down the shortsighted path.

Yet we have a daily reminder at our fingertips if we'll learn from the failures and successes of these and other biblical characters. We serve the same God they did, and his ways never change. Neither does his mercy, which sometimes lets us go our own way until we learn that he knows better.

Consider whether or not your desires line up with God's. If not, are they worth separating yourself from the One who knows what's best for you and loves you enough to help you reach his goals? Be sure, because he just might give you what you want.

TALK TO HIM

"Thank you, Lord, for desiring things better than anything I could dream up myself. Please protect me from my shortsighted tendency to get off track from you."

I could not do without Thee,
I cannot stand alone,
I have no strength or goodness,
No wisdom of my own;
But Thou, beloved Savior,
Art all in all to me,
And weakness will be power
If leaning hard on Thee.

FRANCES R. HAVERGAL, "I COULD NOT DO WITHOUT THEE"

March 7 JUDGES 4:1-24

"I have given you a circle of influence to lead."

Deborah, the wife of Lappidoth, was a prophet who was judging Israel at that time.

JUDGES 4:4

There's a program on the Animal Planet network called *Meerkat Manor* that chronicles the lives and times of the Whiskers, a family of small meerkats in Africa. Quite the communal group, these critters follow their fearless leader and mom, Flower. Don't be fooled by her size; Flower is a bundle of authority in a twelve-inch body.

God's miraculous designs in nature extend to the ranks of influence in even the smallest communities. Just as he created his various creatures to need each other, he instilled in humans the power to influence one another.

The Old Testament judge Deborah had a large circle of influence. As the only female judge mentioned in Judges, Deborah might seem a rare fit for the role. However, God isn't necessarily interested in growing run-of-the-mill people to impact others. He creates each of us with a unique part to play, a part no one else is perfectly suited to accomplish.

Whom do you influence? Just by breathing and functioning in the world, you touch other lives. Besides friends and family, how about the grocery store checker? the postal worker? the furnace repairman? Your world is larger than you may imagine. Even if you don't communicate with many people in one day, you surely cross paths with numerous individuals over a month or a year.

What impression do you leave on them? Does your smile and the atmosphere you bring into a room invite others to know God better? It doesn't take much to give someone a taste of God's love—a luxury that can be in short supply in the days of many.

Open your eyes and broaden your heart's view of your environment. God can orchestrate your comings and goings to intersect with people as he desires, even if the opportunity seems unusual or you don't feel very influential.

Don't miss your chance to bless and be blessed.

TALK TO HIM

"Lord, I often overlook opportunities to shine your love. Please deepen my sensitivity to notice others who could use a smile or a word of encouragement."

Every individual has a place to fill in the world and is important in some respect whether he chooses to be so or not.

NATHANIEL HAWTHORNE

"When I ask you to do something, remember that I see you as capable in my strength."

"Mighty hero, the LORD is with you! . . . Go with the strength you have. . . . I am sending you!"
JUDGES 6:12, 14

Imagine if God appeared at work and told you he's sending you into battle to rescue your country . . . oh, and you're the leader. Even if you're military trained, it would raise your blood pressure.

That's what happened to Gideon. One minute he was threshing wheat; the next he was a "mighty hero." Sometimes he gets a bad rap for questioning God, but even if Gideon's motivations were wrong, it's tough to criticize him much for responding as most of us would. He was possibly the least likely and least qualified for the job.

However, God looked beyond that and thrust him into a role that forced Gideon to let go and trust. God basically told Gideon he had all the strength he'd need, because he really didn't need his own power. The success would be God's achievement, accomplished in God's strength.

When God asks any of us to take on a challenging task, even a bigger-than-life one, he never doubts our capabilities when we rely on him to get us to his goal. He never asks or expects us to be God. That's a job reserved for him. Ours is to trust and keep in step with him.

Challenging assignments actually provide fresh opportunities to experience God's ability in immeasurable ways. It's one thing to trust him with the same old daily stuff. All that can become routine. However, there's nothing quite like a seemingly impossible request from him to launch us to higher levels of faith and courage despite fears.

Why not be bold and ask him to meet you on your "threshing floor" with a brand-new reason to grow your relationship with him. It might seem like a high risk, but then again, with God so sure of his own capabilities, there really are no risks when we rely on him.

TALK TO HIM

"Lord, I'm often not sure of myself, but I am growing more sure of you day by day. Please challenge my faith to grow. Thank you for the nudges forward."

Faith enables persons to be persons because it lets God be God.
CARTER LINDBERG

March 9 JUDGES 7:1-25

"Boost others' faith by showing them your confidence in me."

"Get up! For the LORD has given you victory over the Midianite hordes!" JUDGES 7:15

What a change in Gideon! However shakily he began, we can't fault the guy for not giving his faith a chance to grow. Here we see him not only moving forward, excitedly taking God at his word, but we also see him empowering his soldiers.

His faith still wasn't perfect. Verses 10 and 11 show God giving him the option to double-check his fears. Yet even with his rookie faith, Gideon's growing trust instilled confidence in the soldiers regarding God's ability to bring them successfully through the struggle.

What an encouragement to know that we don't have to get it just right before we can be effective! In fact, 2 Corinthians 12:9-10 tells us that our weaknesses actually become strong forces for revealing God's power. Imagine that . . . our weaknesses are often the very qualities that point others to God. Take a moment to realize how profound that truth is. Strengths are strengths, but weaknesses can be strengths too.

Perhaps Gideon discovered the way to this strength by giving his faith the opportunity to grow. Perhaps that's an important lesson we all need to grasp. Instead of sitting on his faith, he stood and let it raise him higher and closer to God. As a result, he became the mighty hero God called him to be.

Your faith will always be stronger than that of some, weaker than that of others. God knows exactly what he wants to do through you right here and now.

Stifled faith becomes stagnant, and stagnant faith soon rots away to nothing. Faith was created to grow and flourish. Will you give yours a chance to climb toward the heavens?

TALK TO HIM

"Thank you, Father God, for having a purpose for my weaknesses. I'm glad to know they can be good for something because so often they drain me. Please grow my faith by using my weaknesses to show your power to others."

> *The sense in which a Christian leaves it to God is that he puts all his trust in Christ: trusts that Christ will somehow share with him the perfect human obedience which He carried out from His birth to crucifixion: that Christ will make the man more like Himself and, in a sense, make good his deficiencies.*
>
> C. S. LEWIS

"I am pleased when you don't seek praise for yourself."

After Abimelech had ruled over Israel for three years, God sent a spirit that stirred up trouble between Abimelech and the leading citizens of Shechem, and they revolted.

JUDGES 9:22-23

You have to love a good irony. Abimelech's life illustrates a great one: Self-centered living ends up centering trouble on self.

The guy was bad, bad, bad. In his quest for power, he killed all but one of his seventy half brothers, sparing the one only because that brother escaped. He seemed to have a god complex and in essence worshiped himself.

God let Abimelech gain ground for a while, but then he simplified Abimelech's complex—no one gets to be God except God. No one else can handle the job. Ultimately, not many would want it, either, because of the Abimelechs God has to deal with.

We're all tempted at times to promote ourselves too much. We love feeling admired. But when a desire for recognition takes over, it turns on others and ultimately on oneself.

Most of us will hardly approach the extremes that Abimelech did, but that doesn't negate the seed of self-centeredness common to everyone. A part of us would love to be revered, idolized to some degree, and seen as the best.

Yet we have no right to that attitude, just as Abimelech didn't have a right to steal the throne. In essence, when we seek credit that belongs to God, we're attempting to rob his throne. When we do that, we're creating a list of people we hurt. That list always includes our own name, sometimes hidden between the lines, but there nonetheless. When we insist on taking the throne, we alienate ourselves from God and others and trap ourselves in a world of distorted views and twisted priorities.

Who is on the throne of your life?

TALK TO HIM

"Thank you, Lord, for not letting me dethrone you. Please keep me from fooling myself into thinking that's possible. I want you on the throne of my life, where you belong."

The words "I am" are potent words; be careful what you hitch them to.
The thing you're claiming has a way of reaching back and claiming you.

A. L. KITSELMAN

March 11 JUDGES 14:1-20

"Beware of settling for what looks good at the expense of what's best."

But Samson told his father, "Get her for me! She looks good to me." JUDGES 14:3

Ah, Samson, the poster boy for impulsive living. Mr. Live-for-the-Moment. A guy of short-range goals and shortsighted passions, Samson was most interested in what was convenient for Samson. He had to learn the hard way many times over. Even then, it's questionable whether he took to heart the consequences of his haphazard approach to life.

Driven by shallow attraction instead of deep love, Samson insisted on marrying a pagan woman, and a Philistine at that. Considering the long-running hatred between the Philistines and the Israelites, it's no wonder that his parents questioned their son's judgment. Yet Samson went for what appealed to him at the present, with little to no consideration for any best-case scenario God had waiting for him. Waiting was not Samson's style.

Like Samson, we would be wise to learn to wait. If we never grow our ability to say no to a whim, we don't allow time for better sense to kick in. That's when regrets develop, and a life full of regrets feels more rotten by the year—as Samson discovered. His impulsive decisions led him deeper into trouble the longer he lived, until eventually they ruined him. He never knew what he missed from God because he kept interfering.

You will face many good options each day. But you would be wise to pause. Pauses let God "interfere" before we make messes of our lives.

Let God interfere with his best for you today. That is one decision with no regrets.

TALK TO HIM

"Lord, thank you for helping me live above regrets I could cause myself. Please help me to pause to consider whether something is merely good or your ultimate best."

Know that when you seek anything of your own, you will never find God, because you do not seek God purely. You are seeking something along with God, and you are acting just as if you were to make a candle out of God in order to look for something with it. Once one finds the things one is looking for, one throws the candle away.

MEISTER ECKHART

"Live today with the character you want to be remembered for."

There were about 3,000 men and women on the roof who were watching as Samson amused them. JUDGES 16:27

What a tragedy that someone with such potential would be remembered as a joke! Samson was set apart for God even before he entered the world, but he didn't live up to all he had going for him. He is noted for incredible physical strength. Unfortunately, he also gained a reputation for his many weaknesses in character. Tales of his fierceness in battle draw gasps of amazement, but they lose their impact to impress in light of his inability to act like a hero of godliness and integrity.

His last hurrah of knocking down the temple pillars, while a superhuman feat, was sadly pathetic. Instead of standing victorious before the enemy Philistines, Samson emerged in chains, blind. Although he couldn't see the faces of those who laughed at his defeat, his inner eyes likely were opened to see clearly the foolish decisions he had made that led him to that sorry end when his enemies used him for amusement.

For someone with his arrogance, no doubt Samson had hoped to be remembered more respectfully. Yet his life is a long list of what-ifs. What if he had made wiser decisions? What if he had obeyed God? What if he had avoided that relationship or refused to let his pride dominate?

So much potential; so much heartache.

Each decision you make builds or chips away at your reputation. Could those who know you—even someone you might call an enemy—recall times when you didn't act with integrity?

Your character today impacts your future. Avoid the Samson-style what-ifs, and live today the way you want to be remembered.

TALK TO HIM

"Father, you see the things I do as well as the things I almost do—actions that please you and some that don't. Help me to show others the character you are building in me."

Reputation comes over one from without; character grows up from within. . . .
Reputation is made in a moment; character is built in a lifetime. . . .
Reputation is what men say about you on your tombstone;
character is what angels say about you before the throne of God.
WILLIAM HERSEY DAVIS

March 13 JUDGES 18:1-31

"When I'm not the focus of your worship, expect eventual chaos."

"You've taken away all the gods I have made . . . and I have nothing left!" JUDGES 18:24

Do Micah's words "all the gods I have made" strike you as odd? Shouldn't a "god" suggest power and authority, instill confidence, and inspire reverence and awe?

How lame is a god that must be created and can be taken away by human whim? What is the point in worshiping something so passive? Yet that's what Micah chose to worship instead of the true God who has always existed and never was created by anyone. He does the creating, thank you very much, Micah.

How sad that, once Micah's powerless gods were stolen, he had nothing left. No almighty deity to trust in, no sure rock to lean on, no hope for the future, no Lord to praise. When Micah's spiritual focus became skewed and he failed to focus on God as the One to worship, events grew chaotic. He wasn't alone in his decline; the spiritual corruption extended throughout Israelite society, including the priesthood. Before long, they were attacking peaceful towns in a selfish drive to take over.

This story illustrates our tendency toward disorder and ungodliness. There is no indication that the people of Laish, the town the Israelites attacked, practiced idolatry or worshiped God. But it's certain that the Israelites weren't a positive spiritual influence. God told his people to attack certain towns to destroy idolatry and establish peace and godliness, but in this case the Israelites brought only destruction.

When our worship drifts from the Lord, the decline shows throughout our lives. Little by little, distractions weaken our resolve to put God first. Regular worship serves its primary purpose of giving God the glory and honor he deserves, and it reminds us to train our eyes consistently on him. It's the only way to combat the pull away from him.

Who are you looking for today?

TALK TO HIM

"Lord, when distractions attract my attention, please guide my focus back to you. Help me to fight for godliness, which brings peace instead of chaos."

None else but Thee, for evermore,
One, All, we dread, believe, adore:
Great Earth and Heaven shall have their day
And worn and old shall pass away,
But Thou remainest, on Thy throne
Eternal, changeless, and alone!

SAMUEL J. STONE, "NONE ELSE BUT THEE, FOR EVERMORE"

"Beware the desire to blame others for your sin."

The Levite took hold of his concubine and pushed her out the door. JUDGES 19:25

Today's reading is a heartbreaker. Not only because of the horror suffered by the concubine, but also because someone who should have stood up for her aided in her murder and then refused to take responsibility for his part in the crime.

We typically have no trouble recognizing someone else's wrongs, but when it comes to our own, we tend to brush off the bad stuff in favor of viewing ourselves as justified for questionable or outright wrong actions.

Just what was the Levite upset about? Nothing in the text leads us to believe he cared much at all for his concubine. Like a coward, he tossed her out on the street to be beaten and raped all night and then compounded his wicked behavior by demanding that she get up as she lay dead on the doorstep.

When he cut up her body and sent the pieces to the Israelite tribes, we have to think he felt the crime was committed against him instead of the woman he helped abuse. The Levite's actions say a great deal about the brutality of sin and its power to blind the sinner.

Before we pat ourselves on the back because we would never do something so heinous, let's remember that God views all sins as reprehensible. We all tend to justify our actions because they feel right to us. Yet sin is sin. Keep in mind that sin ultimately brings death, and where there's death, someone suffers.

The least we can do is have the courage to face the truth rather than play the coward by trying to escape the guilt.

TALK TO HIM

"Father, it's humbling to think that you see my sins for what they are. Even when I try to ignore their existence, you know the truth. Please help me live in the world of your truth instead of the world of lies I try to pass off as truth."

Choice of attention—to pay attention to this and ignore that—is to the inner life what choice of action is to the outer. In both cases, a man is responsible for his choice and must accept the consequences, whatever they may be.

W. H. AUDEN

March 15 RUTH 1:1-22

"Consider the costs of connecting with someone else's pain—and how I reward loyalty."

"Things are far more bitter for me than for you." RUTH 1:13

It is intriguing to note that the book of Ruth begins as Naomi's story. Ruth's mother-in-law is actually the main character in chapter 1. Naomi had been dealt the tough blows of losing her husband and two sons, leaving her a widow with no support. Back then, her situation usually meant financial ruin. Add that burden to her devastating emotional losses, and Naomi faced a bleak future. Pain soaked the atmosphere around her.

We don't like pain. We don't even like connecting ourselves with someone else's hurt because it clouds our otherwise sunny lives. Pain is an interruption, an unwanted guest that stays too long, no matter how quickly it leaves. We don't like our own pain, and we tend to avoid getting too deeply involved with other people's, lest we get sucked into something we can't tactfully back away from if it becomes too much.

Ruth, however, modeled a higher way. Instead of shying away from Naomi's sorrow, she aligned herself with it—at the same time dealing with her own grief of widowhood. She chose the way of pain out of loyalty and love for her husband's mother, picking a difficult future for herself because her life was about more than herself. She understood and practiced what it means to live for others.

It's difficult for us to fully comprehend the sacrifices Ruth made. We can hop on a plane to visit faraway family, and our finances aren't limited by gender or marital status. Ruth truly gave up everything to help Naomi. And God blessed her with a second family and the honor of being an ancestor of Jesus.

Today will bring choices of whether to care deeply for others going through hard times. Are you willing to invest yourself in someone else's pain? Consider the rewards God has in store for those who make the sacrifices of loyalty and love.

TALK TO HIM

"Father God, sometimes showing loyalty seems too costly, especially when it requires taking on someone else's heartaches and feeling them as if they were mine. But God, your way isn't always easy. Help me to choose right over easy."

Loyalty in time of need is possibly one of the noblest of victories.

HONORÉ DE BALZAC

"I offer you relief from the exhaustion of life."

"What have I done to deserve such kindness?" RUTH 2:10

When was the last time you felt exhausted? Right now? When we hear someone say they feel exhausted, sleep is the first solution we consider. Maybe sleep is the answer, but weariness can encompass more than a mere shortage of shut-eye. We end up worn out for many reasons, including stress, emotional trauma, working too hard, working too little, change, loneliness, or sickness.

Ruth probably knew how soul-wearying exhaustion felt. She had experienced all of those causes of tiredness. After losing her husband, she traveled to a foreign land and worked long hours in the hot sun to provide food for herself and her mother-in-law. Her circumstances certainly qualified as highly stressful, full of change and heartache and more than her share of backbreaking work.

The book of Ruth gives us every indication that she handled her burdens like a trouper, but still, all that stress would take its toll on anyone. In all probability Ruth craved relief. In fact, she acknowledged that Boaz's kindness comforted her (see verses 10 and 13).

Fatigue leaves us hungry for anything that soothes. God understands this about us, which is why he sent Boaz to Ruth. It is also why he offers us comfort. He may allow difficult circumstances to linger, but he never leaves us without himself as our relief. His comfort arrives in various ways, but it is always available. His presence is our greatest relief, our most powerful antidote for exhaustion.

Your current difficulty carries a blessing in disguise because it offers you the opportunity to experience God's relief in whatever creative form he sends it. Ruth had no idea when she went out to the field that day how mightily God would care for her, but he showed her that his provision was exactly fit for her need.

It will be for yours as well.

TALK TO HIM

"God, I'm worn out. I feel like I have nothing left to give except this simple request for your relief. Thank you in advance for your provision."

Rest of the weary, joy of the sad,
Hope of the dreary, light of the glad;
Home of the stranger, strength to the end,
Refuge from danger, Savior and Friend!

JOHN S. B. MONSELL, "REST OF THE WEARY"

March 17 RUTH 4:1-22

"Your quiet and humble life will speak volumes to others."

"And may the LORD give you descendants." RUTH 4:12

"And may the LORD give you descendants." That brief sentiment carried enormous importance for a humble man named Boaz who lived quietly, yet impacted the world through his generosity.

Boaz was a man of integrity and compassion. Before he even met Ruth, he had noticed her needs as she gathered grain. Then Boaz met those needs without fanfare or drawing attention to himself. And as second in line as her family redeemer, Boaz could have opted not to marry her, as her nearer relative had done. But Boaz shared high character qualities with Ruth. He did the noble thing and brought her home as his wife, securing the women's future and producing a son whom Naomi would consider her own.

Boaz made many personal sacrifices in what seems to be a quiet, gentle way that didn't seek recognition, but earned it regardless.

People noticed and respected him for his character. "We are witnesses!" they called out before showering down prayers for prosperity, including countless descendants who would follow his good name. God answered those prayers and sent our Savior through humble Boaz.

Boaz's life proves that we don't need to worry about gaining admiration for ourselves because God is watching out for our reputations. Our job is to live well and to honor him with our everyday actions and words, making others' needs a top priority.

We don't have to shout our presence to make an impact. Many times the quiet, humble life is the one heard best.

TALK TO HIM

"Thank you, Lord, for examples of gentle godliness that lives humbly and trusts you with the events of life. Please help me to be such a gift and example to others."

Humility does not mean thinking less of yourself than of other people,
nor does it mean having a low opinion of your own gifts. It
means freedom from thinking about yourself at all.

WILLIAM TEMPLE

"Someone's bad behavior toward you is not an excuse for bad behavior from you."

Year after year it was the same—Peninnah would taunt Hannah. 1 SAMUEL 1:7

Peninnah was no peach. She was the type of woman who never seemed to mature past the middle-school taunting years. Her adolescent ridicule of sweet Hannah grates on our nerves probably as much as it reduced Hannah to tears.

Haven't we all encountered someone like her? Or maybe a better question would be, Haven't we all been like her at one time or another? As shameful as it is, we would all have to admit to less-than-stellar behavior toward others on occasion. No one is exempt from that one. Sometimes we excuse ourselves because the other person started it (adolescent reasoning again), but that response doesn't go very far with the Lord.

Some might think Hannah's response is maddening because she gave in to tears instead of defending herself or launching a retaliatory verbal assault on Peninnah. Those people could argue, and argue well, that Peninnah deserved it. However, returning Peninnah's bad behavior would only make Hannah deserving of additional trouble.

Instead of being reactors when we are mistreated, God expects us to be pro-actors, meaning we are to proactively stick to a higher, better standard. If we change our behavior standards based on other people's conduct, we will become wishy-washy and weak very quickly.

Hannah's quiet responses might not have gained her points according to Peninnah's ethics, but they earned the respect of the Lord. She showed character worthy of being the mother of Samuel, one of Israel's great priests.

The next time someone treats you poorly, prove by your response that you live by a higher way.

TALK TO HIM

"Lord, it's so hard to keep myself from striking back at someone who I think deserves it. Please help me to show the level of class that Hannah did."

The ultimate measure of a man is not where he stands in moments of comfort, but where he stands at times of challenge and controversy.

MARTIN LUTHER KING JR.

March 19 1 SAMUEL 1:19-28

"Are you willing to give my gifts to you back to me?"

"Now I am giving him to the LORD, and he will belong to the LORD his whole life."

1 SAMUEL 1:28

Some people have lots of class. The only problem is, it is all low.

Not Hannah. She was loaded with class of the highest sort. When she made a promise, she stuck to it no matter what. That is why, when the Lord answered her request for a child, she willingly gave little Samuel back to God in keeping with her commitment made before he was born.

It's one thing to make a promise like hers before having the long-awaited answer to prayer in hand. But once we have what we've wanted so badly, once we have a taste of the sweetness of God's gift, would most of us exhibit a similar level of class to give our beloved desire back to him? What if that desire is your dream job? your soul mate? your health? your loved one's health?

Releasing our best dreams to God with the sincerity that desires him above all else is no easy surrender. It requires a transfer of passion from the dream to the Lord, with the conviction that he is the greatest dream we could have, and he is worth sacrificing all other hopes if he asks for them.

But that kind of surrender also expects that God will more than make up for losses we experience from living for him.

Who holds ownership of your dreams? You or God? Keep in mind that God is a class act, and he has only your best interests at heart, no matter what difficult requests he might ask of you. Following his lead with class won't always be a simple matter, but it carries great rewards and abundant peace that are your gifts forever when you offer all his other gifts back to him.

TALK TO HIM

"Heavenly Father, I tend to hold tightly to the good things in my life, fooling myself into believing they belong to me instead of to you. Please help me to surrender to you all that matters most to me, knowing that you are the greatest gift I could hope for."

All to Jesus, I surrender;
All to Him I freely give;
I will ever love and trust Him,
In His presence daily live.

JUDSON W. VAN DEVENTER, "I SURRENDER ALL"

1 SAMUEL 3:1-21 March 20

"Are you listening for my message to you?"

Samuel replied, "Speak, your servant is listening." 1 SAMUEL 3:10

Do you always recognize God speaking to you? If so, you're in a minority. Many people recognize him sometimes, even often, but always is a rarity. Not to say it can't be done; it absolutely can. It's just that learning to recognize God's voice takes practice, even for Bible heroes like Samuel. Even his mentor, Eli the priest, didn't catch on immediately that God was calling to Samuel.

Although hearing God is a learned process for most of us, it is completely possible for anyone. The only requirement aside from practice is a heart that wants to know him enough to stay consistently tuned in to him . . . and that is what sets the minority apart from the rest. Most people either don't care about him or don't care enough about him to stay close enough to hear his quiet call.

He often speaks to us at unexpected moments, such as when he spoke to Samuel in the middle of the night. That habit of his is actually helpful for us, because most of our days don't allow hours on end to sit still waiting to hear from him. He can catch our attention when we're driving or sitting in front of a computer or preparing supper. We don't need hours every day to stay close to him, but we do need to stay attentive so we don't miss him.

The point is to keep your heart pointed in God's direction. Of course, get alone with him when you can, when other distractions won't muddy his message to you. But don't wait for those rare occasions. Listen up right now. He surely has something important to tell you. Look how one message one night changed Samuel's life, as well as many other lives.

Who knows what he has to say to you?

You can, actually.

TALK TO HIM

"Lord, please quiet me in the midst of the busyness hollering in my world. Please help me hear you more and more often until I hear you always."

Hark! there comes a whisper
Stealing on thine ear:
'Tis the Savior calling,
Soft, soft and clear.

FANNY CROSBY, "HARK! THERE COMES A WHISPER"

March 21 1 SAMUEL 4:1-11

"Do you trust my power as much as my enemies do?"

"This is a disaster! We have never had to face anything like this before! Help!"

1 SAMUEL 4:7-8

If only the Philistines had saving faith in God's power instead of fearful faith. . . .

It might seem surprising, but God's enemies have a great deal of faith in him—sometimes more than his own followers, although that's due to our weakness, not his.

The problem with his enemies' confidence is, of course, that it opposes him. Satan and his forces believe wholeheartedly that God is all-powerful, all-knowing, and the ultimate authority over them. But instead of finding joy in that truth, they scoff at him and do their utmost to keep the souls God loves from trusting him.

The Philistines knew they couldn't match God's power, much less defeat it. They also knew the Israelites were his chosen nation and, as such, had the Lord of Heaven's armies backing their every move. There was no chance the Philistines—or anyone, for that matter—could win a victory against that kind of might. They were so convinced about his authority that they panicked.

Did the Israelites trust their own God that much?

Do you?

Imagine what a powerful force the Philistines' faith would have been had they turned to God instead of fighting against him. If only they had seen his truth instead of living for their idols and worthless gods. If only.

If only God's people today would believe in him every bit as strongly as his enemies still do. What a force we would be.

If only.

TALK TO HIM

"Lord, it's humbling to think of the times my faith in you falters, when I know your enemies tremble at your name because they are so convinced of you. Please grow me as a faith warrior who never doubts you."

A mighty fortress is our God, a bulwark never failing;
Our helper He, amid the flood of mortal ills prevailing: . . .
And though this world, with devils filled, should threaten to undo us,
We will not fear, for God hath willed His truth to triumph through us.

MARTIN LUTHER, "A MIGHTY FORTRESS IS OUR GOD"

"I choose you to obey me above all other authorities."

"Even so, we still want a king." 1 SAMUEL 8:19

In asking for a king, the people of Israel were about to discover the truth of the phrase "Don't know what you've got till it's gone." They didn't understand the privilege God granted by choosing them as his own people. When they asked for a human king so they could be like other nations, they rejected the greatest gain anyone could hope for.

God set them apart to give them himself, but they viewed being chosen by him as a burden instead of an unprecedented blessing.

God warned them; Samuel warned them. But they refused to accept what was best for them. Why would someone—much less many someones—want to be ruled by an imperfect, selfish human rather than the generous, gracious Lord? It makes no sense. Their choice defies wisdom and logic, but so do many of ours.

Their mistake is common. If we could see what God has in store for us, the perks of this life wouldn't appear so perky. Day after day we are swamped by earthly ethics that don't measure up to God's, and we follow them as if they have authority. We make the world's attitudes our kings.

God's best comes only to those who refuse to be fooled by lesser enticements. There are many wonderful qualities about life on earth. But when earth's abundance takes a bigger role than God does, we place ourselves in a position to miss his abundance. We risk missing out on more of him.

Let God maintain his rightful kingship in your life. Welcome being set apart as his own, and you will guard against being misled by mediocre authorities.

TALK TO HIM

"Lord, please make me aware of attitudes of this world that I've allowed to become kings over me. I want to follow your standards. Thank you for being the ideal authority."

O thank the Lord, the Lord of love;
O thank the God all gods above;
O thank the mighty King of kings,
Whose arm hath done such wondrous things. . . .
Who thought on us amidst our woes,
And rescued us from all our foes;
Who daily feeds each living thing;
O thank the Heav'n's Almighty King.

"KING OF KINGS," ADAPTED FROM PSALM 136

March 23 1 SAMUEL 12:1-25

"I keep my word to you for the sake of my name."

"The LORD will not abandon his people, because that would dishonor his great name."
1 SAMUEL 12:22

A person's word is a great determiner of reputation. When someone's reputation is questioned, faithfulness to one's own word can argue powerfully for or against the validity of any doubts.

Unfortunately, God's reputation is often wrongly questioned. In fact, he could be voted the One most likely to be unfairly accused. Very often he is not known to have a wonderful reputation because so many people speak against him. Although everything he does is for the ultimate good of humanity, it is quite the challenge to get many folks to believe him since our shortsighted view of what is good for us differs so frequently from his perfect one.

Fortunately, his commitment to keep his word speaks far more powerfully in his favor than any lies that shout against him. He never has nor ever will be untrue to his word.

Even though God's reputation is questioned and maligned every day, his name is never truly at stake. People may choose to hold a negative view of him, but he never doubts who he is, what he's about, or how he works. He always will be true to his name and his character, which explains why Samuel could confidently reassure the Israelites that God would not abandon them.

Which of God's promises are you clinging to today? Because he takes his name seriously, you can too. In fact, he expects you to rely on him to be true to himself, and thus, true to you. Take his name seriously. He certainly does. With that confidence, move forward in faith that he will make good on every promise he makes to you.

TALK TO HIM

"Lord, it gives me such relief to know that I can rely on you to be you today, tomorrow, and forever. Thank you for being true to your holy name."

Standing on the promises of Christ my King,
Through eternal ages let His praises ring,
Glory in the highest, I will shout and sing,
Standing on the promises of God.

R. KELSO CARTER, "STANDING ON THE PROMISES OF GOD"

"I give you wisdom and good sense when you follow me with all your heart."

"My father has made trouble for us all!" 1 SAMUEL 14:29

Saul, Saul, Saul. Speaking of names, his draws a big sigh and a weary head shake for all his impulsive actions. What a chariotload of trouble he got his men into with one rash command!

King Saul isn't known for his good wisdom and sense because most times he didn't exhibit those qualities. And the reason he didn't is because he sought God's direction only when it suited him, and then only as an afterthought. His inconsistency and self-absorption created a heap of havoc that he compounded with more unreliable behavior.

He pushed his men to exhaustion, tried to make amends for their sin to avoid God's punishment, then wanted to drive them hard again all night. He listened long enough to hear a priest's suggestion to ask God's opinion, then became confused by God's silence. He nearly killed his son, then called off his army and let the enemy return home . . . phew, all in a day's work. His tornado approach left him in a swirl of confusion. It isn't the picture of godly good sense or wise leadership.

Two by-products of living God's way include receiving his wisdom and sense, characteristics sure to bring unlimited benefits, most notably his approval. Really, his followers should be known for their intelligent decisions because we have his perfectly intelligent Holy Spirit within, imparting his wisdom and discernment.

It's pretty easy to get ourselves into plenty of predicaments, like King Saul created for himself and others. But as usual, God has a better way if we'll turn our impulses in his direction and let his wisdom guide us.

TALK TO HIM

"Lord, please help me live by one primary impulse—that is, to look to you as my first course of action in every decision. Then please show me the peaceful lifestyle that results from seeking your wisdom."

The astute mind behind is the Mind of God, not human wisdom at all. We give credit to human wisdom when we should give credit to the Divine guidance of God through childlike people who were foolish enough to trust God's wisdom and the supernatural equipment of God.

OSWALD CHAMBERS

March 25 1 SAMUEL 15:10-35

"True repentance is more than being sorry you got caught."

"I know I have sinned. But please, at least honor me before the elders of my people and before Israel." 1 SAMUEL 15:30

King Saul never seemed to get it right spiritually. He knew the words to say, but his heart was divided, and it showed.

A person can hide mixed motivations for only so long. Eventually the truth comes out, as Saul discovered when Samuel told him God was sorry he had ever made Saul king. Samuel seemed more grieved than Saul—at least for the right reason, which is that God was disappointed. Saul seemed more concerned about what others would think than repentant over his sins against God.

Saul showed classic signs of being sorry he got caught. Sure, he acknowledged his sin, but there is no indication in Scripture that he was a changed man. Some of his worst crimes were yet to come as he felt his monarchy threatened by God's newly appointed king, young David.

God is about more than words. He wants to see lives turned around when we come face-to-face with the reality of our errors. Think over those "little" sins that seem harmless. Swearing? Speeding? Stretching the truth? Maybe you find yourself apologizing to God for the same mess-ups, but repetitious "I'm sorry's" don't mean much if you don't shed the bad habit.

Consider how honorable the state of your heart is before God. Would he be pleased with your core motives? If those motives don't center around honoring him, then it might be time for a motivation modification to rid your spiritual life of mixed motivations that interfere with true repentance.

TALK TO HIM

"Lord, it's time again for a cleanup of my motivations. Please impress on my heart the spiritual depth that genuinely grieves when I sin and lives to honor you."

When the Holy Spirit rouses a man's conscience and brings him into the presence of God, it is not his relationship with men that bothers him, but his relationship with God. . . . Repentance always brings a man to this point: I have sinned. The surest sign that God is at work is when a man says that and means it. Anything less than this is remorse for having made blunders, the reflex action of disgust at himself.

OSWALD CHAMBERS

"When I look at your heart, I want to see someone who studies mine."

"But the Lord *looks at the heart."* 1 SAMUEL 16:7

Verse 7 is often focused on for its message about not placing too much value on outward beauty. That message is important, but there's more to the verse. The major point begins with the little contrasting word *but.* With it, God clears up a big difference between his visual acuity and ours. We judge by what we see on the outside, but God sees what really matters: the heart. The state of our hearts is the heart of the verse.

God isn't saying don't be pretty. After all, David was no ugly duckling; verse 12 says, "He was dark and handsome, with beautiful eyes." God simply wants us to put our energy into enhancing the beauty of our character, growing a heart that looks like his. When God looked at David, he saw someone with a character patterned after his own. David's godliness could have developed only one way, by studying his heavenly Father's heart.

You may know someone who exudes God's grace and love. Those are highly attractive qualities that do not begin on the surface. That kind of refinement is rare and unforgettable, and it comes only from patterning our hearts after God's. Beautiful character that reflects God's loving Spirit glows throughout a person's being. High character like that grows stronger over the years; at the same time, outward looks lose their vitality.

David had the beautiful heart of someone who made knowing God a learning process. When God looks at your heart, the image of himself should be clearer every day.

TALK TO HIM

"Heavenly Father, the times I stop to take a good look at your beauty, I am in awe. I want what you have, and I'm thankful you want it for me, too. Please help me to study you well, but more importantly, help the beauty of those lessons to show through my countenance."

Live out Thy life within me, in all things have Thy way!
I, the transparent medium, Thy glory to display.
FRANCES R. HAVERGAL, "LIVE OUT THY LIFE WITHIN ME"

March 27 1 SAMUEL 17:1-51

"The giants you face are miniscule to me."

"The LORD rescues his people. . . . This is the LORD's battle." 1 SAMUEL 17:47

Topic of the day . . . giants. Or should we say GIANTS? Those larger-than-life fear instigators that attack as health problems, job insecurities, relationship disasters, and grown-up bullies, to name a few. We all have them, and they're all ugly. Mean, too.

But let's cut them down to size: God is bigger and he is on your side.

With that truth, young David trusted God to turn a small pebble into a guided attack missile and won an impressive victory.

What were God's thoughts as he watched the weak but innocent devastate the powerful but wicked? Did he look at David and say, "That's my boy"? Did he grieve the carnage Goliath had caused? Did he rejoice with the angels over another victory against evil? Perhaps he did all those things, because he certainly cared about David as the young man faced the giant.

Now take a moment to wonder what God thinks of your giants. God sees and cares deeply about you in the midst of them. He wants them defeated, and he is not scared of them. He knows that he will destroy them someday, and he knows precisely how and when.

He is also convinced about the courage you should feel knowing he is on your side. You don't have to know how he will win your battles—most likely his solution will be creative. All you need to know is that your Giant fights for you, and all you need to do is let him be himself because he'll always be bigger than any problem.

When it comes to giants, it's not a case of you are small, they are big. Really, it's that they are small, and God is big.

Your God.

Your Giant.

Give him the blessing of watching you trust him.

TALK TO HIM

"Thank you, Lord, for being a gigantic force against problems that tower over me but are miniscule to you. Please be my Giant again today."

In the midst of battle be thou not dismayed,
Tho' the pow'rs of darkness 'gainst thee are arrayed.
God, thy Strength, is with thee, causing thee to stand,
Heaven's allied armies wait at thy command.

LEILA N. MORRIS, "VICTORY ALL THE TIME"

⊱ ✿ ⊰

"You are not bound by mistakes in your family history."

"May the LORD *be with you as he used to be with my father."* 1 SAMUEL 20:13

Sadness must have filled Jonathan's voice as he spoke verse 13 to David. Sadness, regret, and remorse. Maybe even some shame. No doubt he grew up idolizing his father, the king. But somewhere along the way, King Saul fell off the proverbial pedestal. Surely the fact that the God who "used to be" with his father was no longer had put a daily damper on Jonathan's heart.

There's no pain quite like a parent failing a child in a significant way, especially when that child, young or old, remembers better times for family pride and unity. Sometimes we grieve what we once had more than what we don't know we missed.

We all have ghosts in our family history because there is pain in every family. We wish for picture-perfect families where everyone is loved and accepted, but none of us can have that because that situation requires perfect people. However, we don't need to remain in bondage to our ancestors' mistakes.

Yes, we suffer consequences of our parents' sins. It's the reality of life. Exodus 20:5 says, "I lay the sins of the parents upon their children; the entire family is affected—even children in the third and fourth generations of those who reject me."

However, you can be the generation that loves the Lord and changes the course of history. In turning to God wholeheartedly and trusting him to heal your family, you can make a crucial difference for your descendants. Even if you don't have descendants of your own, your Christlike love can model God's healing to another family.

Through you, God can transform what "used to be" into what "will be."

TALK TO HIM

"Lord, you know my hurts because of family baggage. I'm tired of carrying on the tradition of pain. Please use me to transform bad patterns into rich history for those who come after me."

To put the world right in order, we must first put the nation in order; to put the nation in order, we must first put the family in order; to put the family in order, we must first cultivate our personal life; we must first set our hearts right.

CONFUCIUS

March 29 1 SAMUEL 24:1-22

"Exhibit the shocking virtue of mercy."

"The LORD placed you at my mercy." 1 SAMUEL 24:10

Mercy is shocking. Since Creation, the King of mercy has baffled the hardest of hearts because everything about mercy flies in the face of a world burdened by vengeance.

To our minds, mercy seems wrong. We want an even score. We want justice. In our compulsive way, we hang on for a reckoning. But our idea of justice shortchanges God's bigger definition of it, which somehow allows room for reformed offenders to escape what they deserve.

David understood mercy. He had every opportunity to rid himself of the pest that was King Saul. Yet he spared Saul's life and went so far as to show the king respect, calling him father and lord.

Why did he do it? Saul certainly didn't deserve such kindness. By resisting the urge to approach justice from a human definition, David extended his own inconveniences and continued to put his life at risk. David shocked Saul with mercy, which left a far more indelible impression on Saul, Saul's troops, and David's own men than killing him would have done.

Mercy typically exists at critical junctures when right meets wrong, when we either give it life or suffocate its healing powers. Mercy costs the giver, and it might appear impossibly painful at first. But it actually soothes as no vengeance could hope to do.

Mercy doesn't make sense to us. The world looks at it as a flimsy excuse for weakness, but with its iron-strong spine and tender hands, mercy is a powerhouse, rare in its ability to comfort those on both sides.

Anyone can dole out justice, but offering mercy requires a heart committed to God's way of doing things.

Give someone a shocker today by extending the power of mercy. Who knows? You might need it more.

TALK TO HIM

"Lord, mercy catches me off guard with its humbling power. Sometimes I don't want to offer it, even knowing how merciful you've been to me. Please help me see the power of mercy as you do."

Who will not mercie unto others show, How can he mercie ever hope to have?

EDMUND SPENSER

March 30

"Choose wisely when aligning yourself with others."

"Thank God for your good sense!" 1 SAMUEL 25:33

Even before he was officially king, David found himself in situations that drew fire, no matter how graciously he acted. Some enemies based their hatred on the position instead of the man. Others simply were rotten souls.

Take Nabal, for instance. His wife, Abigail, definitely was his better half. He, on the other hand, made no good contributions to their marriage.

Without realizing the trouble he was walking into, David attempted to connect with Nabal by asking for hospitality. To David's surprise, Nabal insulted him past the point of ignoring. Not a wise choice.

The story did a 180 when Abigail entered the picture. She understood the trouble her husband had led them into and saved the day with character, good sense, and a level of class that attracted David to her. Abigail gently encouraged David to reconsider how attacking Nabal would hinder David's own relationship with God.

The alliances we make, personal and professional, either move us forward or trip us up spiritually, even through matters that don't seem spiritually based. We will meet plenty of Nabals over the course of life, but the Abigails are more rare. Very few relationships embody a lifetime's worth of depth and growth potential. Someone God places in our life with the fortitude and good judgment to talk sense into us when we need it is someone worth cherishing.

Do the people closest to you motivate you to take your relationship with God seriously? Do they do so gently, without dumping loads of guilt on you? Do you do the same for them?

When you align yourself with healthy people, you set yourself up to go far, bolstered not only by the sense God grants you as his follower, but also by the sense he gives to others close to you.

TALK TO HIM

"Lord, like David, I can't always foresee who is safe and who isn't. Please grow good sense and discernment in me. Provide me with an Abigail or two who will set me straight when I need it, and please help me to be an Abigail for those I care about."

Blessed influence of one true loving human soul on another.

GEORGE ELIOT

March 31 1 SAMUEL 30:1-31

"The way you treat people reflects your gratitude toward me."

"Don't be selfish with what the L*ORD has given us."* 1 SAMUEL 30:23

A grateful heart speaks a language all its own, a rare blend of mercy and graciousness, forgiveness and gentleness. A grateful heart makes time to imagine life in someone else's world because quite often it can recall how it felt to do without. Because it remembers being in need, or that it easily could be there in the future, it extends its concern beyond its own troubles to others, looking for ways to ease burdens and soothe hurts. A heart of gratitude beats more powerfully for others, having been tenderized through its own difficulties.

David understood the tenderness of a grateful heart because he had one beating inside him. As heir to Israel's throne, David was the target of King Saul's jealousy, a position not many would envy because it meant running for his life, hiding out, doing without.

As difficult as David's circumstances often were, they afforded him countless opportunities to experience God's saving power, which grew his gratitude toward the Lord he served. That gratitude led him to treat others with the same care God had shown him. He learned the language of gratefulness through hardship, which gave him the desire to act graciously toward his soldiers, who stayed back instead of helping retrieve their families and possessions.

Each day we either grow gratitude or nurture selfishness. Circumstances do not determine which one—we do. Whether we realize it or not, every time we deal with others we speak for or against our gratitude toward all God has done for us.

Despite the situation that threatens to drag you down, you can decide to be grateful. Translate that language of gratitude into caring for others, and watch yourself be surrounded in an environment of friends who speak as God does.

TALK TO HIM

"Lord, you've shown me another unexpected benefit that you offer through my hard times. You are a surprising God, and I am grateful for you. Please help me speak the gracious language of gratitude to others."

A thankful heart is not only the greatest virtue,
but the parent of all the other virtues.
MARCUS TULLIUS CICERO

⊱ ✿ ⊰

"Loving me with abandon frees you from bitterness."

But as the Ark of the LORD entered the City of David, Michal, the daughter of Saul, looked down from her window. 2 SAMUEL 6:16

Michal had a problem, and it didn't start with David. Although we aren't given details about what triggered her hostility toward her husband, it's enough to know she allowed it to interfere with her joy in the Lord.

It was a big day for Israel. The Ark of the Lord was on its way back into Jerusalem, a cause for celebration for all who loved God. Verse 15 says David and all the people took part in the celebration.

But then, like an abrupt scene change in a movie, the picture cuts to a window high up in the palace, where King David's wife Michal looked down on the celebration. The story takes on an instant tone of gloom.

If all the people were celebrating, why was she holed up in her room? It seems her venom must have been toward God to some degree; otherwise, surely she could have overlooked her anger toward David in lieu of the greater joy surrounding the Ark's return.

Her inability to abandon bitterness kept her from loving God with abandon. Or quite possibly it was the other way around, and her unwillingness to love God freely kept her bitterness going strong. Either way, bitterness and loving God wholeheartedly do not mix.

When God's Spirit fills a person with his love, he leaves no room for harboring grudges or nurturing anger. At some point, a person's love will either grow cold or bitterness will get cleaned out by the freeing effect of God's presence.

Every step you take in bitterness pushes you on an uphill climb toward a closed-off tower that holds you prisoner like Michal.

Let go of it, and revel in the freedom of loving with abandon.

TALK TO HIM

"Bitterness, anger, hostility. Lord, I've felt them all. Please clean me up and help me live and love freely in you."

Whenever evil befalls us, we ought to ask ourselves, after the first suffering,
how we can turn it into good. So shall we take occasion, from
one bitter root, to raise perhaps many flowers.

JAMES HENRY LEIGH HUNT

April 2 2 SAMUEL 7:18-29

"At the height of success, don't forget me."

"How great you are, O Sovereign Lord! There is no one like you." 2 SAMUEL 7:22

Ahh, where to begin? This passage reads like a cooling breeze of gratitude.

It's no secret that it's easy to relegate God to a corner of our lives when things are looking bright, in contrast to the tough times when we're well aware of how much we need him.

Yet, in the middle of a season of huge blessing, King David went on and on in his grateful praise for God's care—and not just his care, but his personhood. At the height of good times, David remembered to worship God for who he is, praise him for what he does, focus on honoring his name, thank him for how he provides, and lastly, ask him for ongoing sustenance.

David gave far more than a cursory "Thanks for the great stuff, God; please bring on more." He engaged with his Maker and invested time and thought in remembering God's history of providing and blessing David and the Israelite people.

When you give someone a gift, isn't one of the best perks seeing happiness light up the recipient's face? The more joy we bring someone, the more joy we feel.

God feels the same about his gifts to us. He doesn't give in order to coerce gratitude from us; he loves being gracious. But of course he also loves to see us receive graciously, which means making the effort to show sincere thankfulness.

What can you thank him for? Express your feelings about him, his gifts, his honor, and why you can't help but worship him. The more tuned in to him you remain, the more you'll feel gratitude.

TALK TO HIM

"Thank you, Lord, for home and family, work and service, for answered prayer and opportunities for faith. Thank you also for tough times and lessons learned. Please grow me in good times as well, and help me stay tuned in to you."

Thanks to God for my Redeemer,
Thanks for all Thou dost provide!
Thanks for times now but a memory,
Thanks for Jesus by my side!
Thanks for pleasant, balmy springtime,
Thanks for dark and stormy fall!
Thanks for tears by now forgotten,
Thanks for peace within my soul!

AUGUST L. STORM, "THANKS TO GOD"

"Remember your commitments; I do."

"I intend to show kindness to you because of my promise." 2 SAMUEL 9:7

Do you ever find it easy to make commitments and then not follow through? Here are a few that commonly get misfiled to the back vault of our memory bank:

"I'll get right on that."

"I'll be praying."

"I promise I won't tell."

"I'll slow down, Officer."

Those quick promises might not appear to be a big deal; in fact, they roll off our tongues before we realize we've committed ourselves.

When David promised his friend Jonathan that he would treat Jonathan's family well, he couldn't have foreseen what that would involve. But he had the presence of mind to remember years later what he had sworn to his friend. There was no one around to call David on whether he kept his word or not, but it didn't matter. He was a man of his word. Period.

When he made a commitment, he acted on it, and God used David's faithful follow-through to improve someone else's life.

Are you the type of person who does what you say you'll do, regardless of who may or may not remember your words?

Many things remain between you and God, and many times no one on earth will call you on your promises. However, consider all that is at stake. Every time you make good on something you say, you're defending the power of your word. Suppose someday your reputation really is on the line; others may come to your defense, but there's no greater advocate for your reliability than your past record. That speaks for itself, no matter what words come out of your mouth.

Defend your words by following through on them.

TALK TO HIM

"Lord, those little failures seem so innocent when I forget to follow through. But Father, please help me build a strong defense for my word by keeping it in the little things."

It is not the oath that makes us believe the man, but the man the oath.

AESCHYLUS

April 4 2 SAMUEL 11:1–12:12

"When you speak truth, follow my lead and count on my wisdom and courage."

So the LORD sent Nathan the prophet. 2 SAMUEL 12:1

God had a tough task to assign, one that required courage, wisdom, and tact. The job? To speak truth to someone who might not want to hear it, confront that person about their own horrific sin, and do it in such a way as to encourage repentance instead of rebellion.

Oh, and by the way, the person who needed confronting happened to be the king who, by the way again, could send the messenger to his death with one word.

Fun, fun, fun. And you thought your workday was rough.

Nathan the prophet was God's choice to call King David to account for adultery and the murder of Bathsheba's husband. When he was a young boy, surely Nathan never dreamed of being in such a position, but somewhere along the way he developed the character, strength, and godliness to handle such responsibility.

God's truth does not accuse for the sake of making someone feel bad. It wisely seeks to clean up wrongs in order to set someone on the right path. It desires to make things better, not to use a person's guilt as a weapon against him or her.

Nathan obviously had the wherewithal to follow God's wisdom, and he drew courage from having God's truth on his side. Instead of accusing David outright, Nathan led David to defend truth, thus letting the king accuse himself. Nathan took this creative approach in God's strength, and ultimately, a nation benefited from his wise actions.

Anyone can speak the truth, but with a helping of godly insight, you can have the courage that Nathan had to use truth as a building block for healing instead of as a weapon for destruction.

TALK TO HIM

"Lord, truth can be just as difficult to speak as it is to hear. Please guide me and grant me courage when I need to stand up for your truth. Show me helpful ways to approach it with others."

Speaking the truth wisely requires one brain and one mouth,
not two hands and a club.
ANONYMOUS

"If you are truly sorry, accept my consequences willingly."

Then David got up from the ground. . . . He went to the Tabernacle and worshiped the Lord.

2 SAMUEL 12:20

Yesterday's reading focused on being a wise speaker of truth. Now for the flip side. What kind of truth receiver are you?

David turned out to be a great one.

Receiving tough truth about our own wrongs often reveals more about us than the wrongs themselves. For instance, if all we knew about David is that he stole a man's wife and plotted the man's murder, we'd be quick to nail his kingly hide to the wall. Yet his humble acceptance of God's consequences makes us pause before delivering the hammer blow.

It's no trite statement that God is a God of second chances. He sees our sins, and he hates them. But he offers us the opportunity to let him clean us up. We live and breathe and find our hope for eternity in God's second chances. Those second chances often don't eliminate the consequences of our actions, but true repentance accepts the penalty as a necessary step of moving beyond the sin and moving forward with God.

What if David foolishly had rejected God and refused to seek forgiveness? In addition to being guilty of adultery and murder, he'd still have to deal with losing his son—God's consequence for David's sin—plus he'd carry the burden of the wall he had erected between God and himself.

We all sin. It's the unfortunate reality of being human. But God does not desire for us to stay bound to our sins.

Receive his truth willingly, and let him move you closer to himself.

TALK TO HIM

"God, I understand the statement that 'truth hurts,' yet I know I need to deal with your truth about my sin on a daily basis. Please help me listen willingly."

The Holy Spirit will locate the one impregnable thing in you,
but He cannot budge it unless you are willing to let Him.

OSWALD CHAMBERS

April 6 2 SAMUEL 16:5-14

"Will you still trust me when your reputation is on the line?"

"Perhaps the L*ORD will see that I am being wronged and will bless me because of these curses today."* 2 SAMUEL 16:12

Why do we care what other people think of us?

Every now and then you meet someone with the uncanny ability to brush off negative comments about themselves. As for the rest of us, no matter how old or successful we appear, we're still vulnerable to hits against our reputation. Once in a while the hurt sneaks up and tweaks our self-esteem, leaving us perplexed about how to protect our good name, wondering if others believe the bad stuff.

King David was no stranger to rumors or heckling. It must have felt invasive to face accusations from strangers like Shimei, who didn't know him but based his opinion of him on hearsay.

To combat Shimei's negativity, David chose the quiet way. A wise military strategist, he was capable of fighting back. But he knew that sometimes the best way to tame the enemy is to refuse to engage in battle. David didn't combat Shimei but let the man level all the verbal assaults he wanted.

Sometimes fighting back only provides more ammo for the accuser. David was accused of stealing the throne; he certainly wasn't going to respond with violence and give people reason to believe the lies. Perhaps he knew that Shimei's tirades would reveal more about Shimei than about David, as accusations often do.

David released his reputation into God's hands and made his life about God's reputation instead of his own. If someone wanted to diss him, so be it. God knew the truth; as long as David was living for God, no one's words could thwart what God accomplished through David.

There always will be someone who doesn't like you, for good reason or no reason. Don't give them cause to back up their feelings. Your reputation is on the line only with God, so look to him to clear things up when it matters, and continue quietly with your business.

TALK TO HIM

"God, sometimes I struggle to overlook rude comments. But Father, please remind me that truth remains with you, as does my reputation. Thank you for that freedom."

The way to gain a good reputation is to endeavor to be what you desire to appear.

SOCRATES

"Invest in the honor of your descendants."

"For my sake, deal gently with young Absalom." 2 SAMUEL 18:5

King David's words in verse 5 are loaded with melancholy. It tears up a parent's heart when a child rebels, but knowing as David did that Absalom's hatred toward him stemmed from David's own disobedience must have twisted the emotional dagger in David's heart.

Back when David sinned with Bathsheba and manipulated her husband's death, Nathan the prophet delivered news that David's sons would rebel as punishment for their father's sins.

So that explains Absalom.

David may have been a brilliant leader in many ways, but his nation and his family endured his mistakes as well. The son he had with Bathsheba died, and Absalom took another brunt of David's punishment. David still loved his son desperately, and however wrong they were, Absalom's actions resulted from consequences that David brought on him.

Thousands of years have passed, but even over the passage of time and half a world's distance, this father's regret is palpable here and now. David's most important success stories did not occur within his family. For all his investment in his people's future, the hearts most precious to him suffered.

Absalom wasn't known for honor, and he certainly didn't die honorably. David had to live with the fact that, had he not committed adultery and murder, Absalom wouldn't have carried the weight of his father's wrongs. Yes, Absalom was responsible for his own actions. However, his life was needlessly tainted by his father's sin. Who knows what honor Absalom could have brought to his family had David protected the honor of his descendants by avoiding sin?

You invest every day in the honor of those who come after you, whether your own children or others you influence. Based on this moment, will you be able to look back without regrets? You haven't lived your final moment yet, so there's still time to invest well.

TALK TO HIM

"Lord, you've invested much in me so I can invest in others. Please remind me to care for the character of those who come after me by living right today."

Make me a channel of blessing today,
Make me a channel of blessing, I pray;
My life possessing, my service blessing,
Make me a channel of blessing today.

HARPER G. SMYTH, "MAKE ME A CHANNEL OF BLESSING"

April 8 1 KINGS 1:1-53

"Your service to me begins with responsibilities to your family."

"Adonijah has made himself king, and my lord the king does not even know about it."

1 KINGS 1:18

What was King David thinking? Apparently not much about guiding his young son Adonijah.

Another sad story in David's family had Adonijah's name written at the top of it. Somewhere along the way, Adonijah, another of David's boys, got it in his head that he was all that and then some. Like his older brother Absalom, Adonijah had quite the arrogant nature. Wealthy, powerful, and handsome, with the world by the tail, those two did all they could to spin it around with themselves at the center.

Perhaps they learned not to focus on their family responsibilities from their father, who had never trained them. Verse 6 of this chapter says that David never disciplined Adonijah, not even to question the boy's actions. It's no surprise that Adonijah rebelled against authority because David failed to establish who was in charge at home.

His focus on his job as king caused David to lose touch with his family. Even though his national responsibilities were enormous, he also was raising up the next generation of leaders to ensure not only his family's future, but the future of the nation he worked so hard to make great.

His failures at home had repercussions on the entire nation of Israel. If we could hear his voice of experience, it very well might warn us about prioritizing service to family first.

TALK TO HIM

"Lord, the pull toward responsibilities away from home is very strong. I forget that all my work to help others must start with the precious souls you have placed closest to me. Please help me love them first through my words, actions, and time."

The strength of a nation derives from the integrity of the home.

CONFUCIUS

"Though I cannot be contained, I choose to live within those who are mine."

"May you watch over this Temple night and day, this place where you have said, 'My name will be there.'" 1 KINGS 8:29

It was quite a day for King Solomon and the Israelites when he made this prayer to dedicate the new Temple. It was a masterpiece, fashioned by God's intricate design, formed to his exact specifications, and birthed for his purposes. For those Israelites, the consecration of the Temple was the pinnacle of years of hard work and yearning to welcome God home, for no place could match the place where God dwells.

Imagine their excitement if they had understood that someday God would choose to live within human beings—his masterpieces, fashioned by his intricate design, formed to his exact specifications, and birthed for his purposes.

Do you get excited about being his temple? If you're his follower, then you are a consecrated dwelling place of the God of the universe. By his choice, he fills those who commit their lives to him with his own Spirit, the same unmatchable Holy Spirit whose glory appeared only once a year and only to the high priest in the Most Holy Place.

If you know him as Savior, you are his Most Holy Place, and he's accessible to you 24-7. Do you welcome him into your life, into the most secret depths of your soul, to live and move and work? Do you throw open the doors and invite him to take free reign, to settle as he pleases, and rearrange you as he knows best?

Hospitality toward the King of kings and Lord of lords is a serious matter, but what a privilege it is to live with him, what a pleasure beyond words!

As you ask him to make himself more at home in your life, your relationship with him will shine his glory to the world and create a haven of joyful rest within your spirit.

TALK TO HIM

"Heavenly Father, please be more than a houseguest in me. I invite you to set up home; rearrange me in whatever way is necessary to make me a sanctuary for your glory."

Make your home in me, Lord, a place where you keep your
most cherished emotions and your treasured secrets.
ANONYMOUS

April 10 1 KINGS 11:1-13

"You are always one decision from staying close to me or drifting away from me."

He refused to follow the L*ORD* *completely.* 1 KINGS 11:6

The development of any new habit has a tipping point. That one decision to change, the one moment when it's all or nothing, when you're in or out.

King Solomon reached a tipping point in his relationship with God when he first crossed the forbidden line and worshiped his foreign wives' false gods.

Then again, maybe his tipping point was when he allowed their idols into his home. Or was it the first time he married a pagan woman? How about the first time he gave one of those women more than a passing glance, when it became difficult to resist the attraction?

God warned him not to marry them because they'd turn his heart from the Lord. Sure enough, somewhere along the way Solomon's heart grew complacent; then he drifted farther and farther from a close walk with God. He traded his godly passion for worldly ones, and his heart paid dearly.

Actually, his family and even his whole nation suffered from that first moment of weakness when Solomon hesitated in his pursuit of God. His hesitation snowballed, and soon he had welcomed seven hundred wives and three hundred concubines, who negatively influenced his spiritual health.

Digest that for a minute. One thousand. No moderation whatsoever.

Once we reach our tipping point, it becomes increasingly difficult to climb out of the hole we dig for ourselves. It's like losing weight—so much easier not to put on extra pounds in the first place than it is to shed them.

One decision on its own might not have many repercussions. However, no decision we make is really isolated from the next one. We're always either moving toward God or away from him.

Make your next move a good one.

TALK TO HIM

"Father, you see the decisions headed my way. Please prepare me to make wise choices, remembering that each one helps or hinders my focus on you."

A man's judgment is best when he can forget himself and any reputation he may have acquired and can concentrate wholly on making the right decisions.

ADM. RAYMOND A. SPRUANCE

"When life storms around you, listen for my whisper."

"What are you doing here?" 1 KINGS 19:13

During a tough season of life, the one-word question, Why? lodges itself at the forefront of our thoughts. Not much turns our questions toward God like a tornado of confusing circumstances.

The first gust of trouble steals our breath. When we recover from the initial shock, we head for a comfortable shelter for our emotions, whether that's home or church, with family or friends. As the storm batters our world, its gales rattle our perspective like sleet against a window, the whys keeping time with its staccato beat.

We might hear silence in answer to our questions. Or if we listen closely, we might hear a whisper.

Elijah heard God's whisper as he sought shelter from the storm of Jezebel and Ahab. We can assume he wondered why he was stuck in the middle of the chaos, running for his life from Jezebel's murderous whirlwind. God's whisper came in the form of a question, namely the question, What?

"What are you doing here, Elijah?"

What was God's goal in responding with a question? There could be any number of reasons, but maybe God wanted to steady his servant with a fundamental reevaluation of Elijah's purpose. In asking what Elijah was doing there, God refocused Elijah on his greater purpose, a purpose that brought meaning to the difficult season. Knowing our purpose strengthens us to keep going. It drives our anchor of faith deeper so we'll have power to stand tall against many forces.

What are you doing with this life I've given you? What are you about? What are you going to become through the challenges I allow you to face? All are questions God may pose to you during your own storms as reminders that he must be your Captain if you intend to make it intact through the turbulence.

Try expanding your why into "Why don't you grow me through this, Lord?" and see what he whispers back to you.

TALK TO HIM

"I wonder sometimes if you tire of my questions, Lord. But I trust that you'll answer in your perfect way. I love to hear your voice, Father. I'm listening now."

Prayer is less about changing the world than it is about changing ourselves.

DAVID J. WOLPE

April 12 1 KINGS 21:1-29

"The world seems swallowed by evil, but I have the final say."

"So, my enemy, you have found me!" 1 KINGS 21:20

Every now and then a news story slaps us hard with the reality of evil. When it does, we're shaken, even haunted, by the heinous acts God's creations commit against each other. Evil has enveloped this world, but there is hope. God wins, along with all his followers.

In the prophet Elijah's day, Queen Jezebel was as bad as they come. She had no qualms about murdering when it suited her. She even went so far as to use the false cover of prayer and fasting as a tease tactic to get Naboth to think he was being honored. Jezebel was an arrogant finger in God's face if there ever was one.

Although he couldn't get much worse, her husband, Ahab, wasn't much better. With taunting words, he registered surprise at Elijah's confrontation. "So, my enemy, you have found me!" With one statement, he clarified his position as God's opposition. Elijah represented God and all that is good and pure, a stark contrast to Ahab and Jezebel's wickedness.

Ironically, Satan will someday utter his final jeering words to God, but then he will be done. Destroyed forever. Perhaps those words will be "So, my enemy, you have found me."

Ahab and Jezebel did not defeat God. No enemy of God's has ever defeated him, and none ever will. Neither Satan nor any of his evil forces will escape God. Our mighty Lord will have the final say over the world's problems as well as over the issues that specifically distress you. That's a guarantee you can take into eternity.

TALK TO HIM

"Lord, I'm so weary of evil, yet I know you must be even more ready to put an end to it. Thank you for being the Victor, and for inviting me to join you in your eternal victory."

Victory is nigh! yes, victory is nigh!
Shout with voice triumphant to the vaulted sky;
Victory is nigh! yes, victory is nigh!
We will win the battle for the King on high.
Shouting loud hosannas as we onward go,
With determination sin to overthrow;
Satan's hosts are trembling, foes before us fly,
For victory is nigh, yes, victory is nigh.

F. H. SHAUL, "VICTORY IS NIGH"

"Respect your mentors; I wish to work through you where I left off with them."

"Please let me inherit a double share of your spirit and become your successor."

2 KINGS 2:9

Elisha could not get enough. He couldn't soak up enough training from his mentor, Elijah. With the humility of a man who counted their minutes together as treasures, Elisha wouldn't let Elijah out of his sight. Each reminder from other people that Elijah's days on earth were numbered pushed Elisha to insist on remaining with Elijah, holding on to every last speck of insight he could glean. But finally it was Elijah's time to go.

Do you have people you consider to be mentors? Anyone whose insights you'd feel somewhat lost without? If so, count yourself blessed by the Lord. You've inherited someone's lifetime of wisdom to grow on, an entire set of experiences that no doubt include things you'll face yourself, examples to follow or avoid, depending on the lessons they provide. Those mentors also will have gone through things you'll never face that will offer you broader wisdom for life.

Our time with our mentors and trainers is limited as well. We may move on in this lifetime, or we may be separated until heaven. Either way, we won't have them around forever on this earth.

Listen well to those who have gone before you. God has brought you together for a reason, not the least of which is to raise you up to carry on where they finished. Will you be ready for the job when your time comes?

Then will you be ready to pass on your lifetime of insights to an Elisha God sends your way?

TALK TO HIM

"Lord, thank you for the Elijahs in my life. Please help me be a wise Elisha and soak up every moment you give me with them. Then, Father, please prepare me to be an Elijah for someone else."

There are two ways of spreading light: to be the candle or the mirror that reflects it.

EDITH WHARTON

April 14 2 KINGS 4:1-7

"Your place of emptiness is my opportunity to fill you."

Her sons kept bringing jars to her, and she filled one after another. 2 KINGS 4:5

The end of your rope is a scary place. If you've ever made it that far, you know it isn't a point you'd like to visit again.

The poor widow in this brief story was very familiar with hers. Without a lot of detail, just the simple facts, the writer lays out the circumstances.

She was the wife of a deceased prophet, a man who feared the Lord. However, when he died, so did her source of income. Add to that burden the terrifying possibility of losing her sons to slavery, and it's obvious this was a family in crisis. Like the woman's empty house, her spirit gradually emptied of hope. But before giving up completely, she sought out Elisha. Most likely she had no idea how he could help, much less confidence that he could at all. What sustainable income could he twist from one jar of oil?

Well, none actually. But his God on the other hand? No problem.

The story's brevity adds power to its message. Without fanfare or crowds flocking to watch the show, God met one of his children at her most dire need and quietly provided more than she knew to ask for. How incredibly beautiful!

God's provision is beautiful every time. When he meets us at our point of need, he fills us up, he does not scrimp, he leaves no doubt that he is the Source, and he supplies more than just temporary appeasement. As he continued filling the widow's jars with sustainable nourishment, his refreshment for our every need is meant to carry us through the trouble.

God is already waiting for you at the end of your rope. He will not leave you hanging; he will provide, and it will be beautiful.

TALK TO HIM

"Father, I'm scared. This place I'm in seems so insecure, but I choose to trust in your security. I know you will provide for me here and carry me through. Thank you, Lord, for the opportunity to experience you filling me up."

To Thee, O God most merciful,
My thankful song I raise;
My Might, my strong, secure Abode,
I will proclaim Thy praise.

AUTHOR UNKNOWN, "PROTECT AND SAVE ME, O MY GOD"

"When you struggle with loss, know that I have more in store for your good."

"Don't deceive me and get my hopes up." 2 KINGS 4:16

Think back to the last loss you experienced. The memory may still evoke tender emotions. Maybe you feel your heart clench while tears spring to your eyes. Or maybe instead of weeping, you shut down that place inside yourself that dares to feel because the negative emotions are too much to bear.

The losses we endure hurt like bruises on our hope. There's something about losing someone or something of value that sets us on edge for the next possible hit. Our guard goes up lest our hopes rise too high, because the higher we let them go, the farther they have to fall, and the harder they may crash.

There's no denying the risk involved in hope. Disappointment is part of life. But there is a way to insure our hopes. When we put them in God, he guarantees we won't be disappointed (see Isaiah 49:23, NIV).

You might argue that God doesn't always answer as we prefer. True. However, when our hope ultimately is in his person rather than his answers, we know that in the end he'll come through in his perfect way. We may face loss—again, that's part of life. Yet we'll never lose him.

He brought the woman from Shunem's son back to life, a miracle that showed her his power and presence and the fact that he always has more good in store for those who please him. No matter how he moves in your life, he always has more good for you if you continue trusting him. The path likely won't be as you'd plan it, but it will be the best one for the whole picture of your life.

If you know the Lord as Savior and King, then you always have reason to hope. Always, always, always. Let that reality carry your hopes to heaven's heights; God will not let them crash.

TALK TO HIM

"Lord, I can hope because of you. My life begins and ends in you, and I trust that you have good ahead for me beyond the hurts. Thank you for being exactly what my hope needs."

Hope is the feeling you have that the feeling you have isn't permanent.

JEAN KERR

April 16 2 KINGS 18:1-37

"I expect my enemies to belittle your faith in me; I also expect you to hold strong in that faith."

"So what makes you think that the LORD *can rescue Jerusalem from me?"* 2 KINGS 18:35

The world has never lacked for thugs, and King Sennacherib knew a great one. His chief of staff seemed to revel in mocking not only the Israelite king Hezekiah but, more seriously, the people's faith in God. At first he saved his fists for the battlefield, choosing instead to pack the punch of his speech with intimidating and derogatory words as his initial forms of ammunition to keep the Israelites under Sennacherib's power. You can almost hear the sneer in his tone as he ridiculed the Israelites' belief and said that God not only wouldn't, but couldn't, save them from Sennacherib's assault.

He would almost be convincing if it weren't for the utter godlessness in his argument. He and Sennacherib were obvious enemies of the Israelite nation, but they made the death-sentence error of being enemies of the Almighty who, incidentally, had chosen the Israelites as his own people. Any Israelite who held strong to God's promise to care for them if they'd obey him would have God's power to withstand mockery and abuse from enemies.

Trying to belittle God's name only reveals one's own smallness, as those who stand against God will discover. His name is far too great to be belittled. On the flip side, holding strong to your beliefs that God will see you through will strengthen any measure of faith you already have, compounding it each time you decide to remain true to him.

God expects his enemies to mock him and to ridicule you in their ignorance. However, he also expects that his followers will act on what they say they believe.

Hold on to that bit of faith you have, and watch it grow as you see God cut his mockers' belittling words down to size.

TALK TO HIM

"Almighty God . . . I have to stop right there and consider your name. Almighty. Your name alone establishes your power. Please help me to stay true to you, and grow my faith as I trust you again today."

Faith is building on what you know is here, so you can reach what you know is there.

CULLEN HIGHTOWER

"Prayer should be your first plan of action in crisis, not your final act of desperation."

"You alone are God of all the kingdoms of the earth." 2 KINGS 19:15

King Hezekiah understood one crucial bit of information that made him a good king. He knew God was it. Not just it, but IT. Everything that happened to the nation of Israel had to go through God's hands; every step they took depended on God's sufficiency. There was no substitute.

Not then.

Not now.

Not ever.

Hezekiah got it. Three times in prayer he emphasized one thing through his use of the word *alone*. God alone is God of all the kingdoms. He alone created the universe. He alone is God.

What else do we need to know? This life on earth is ever so brief and ever so complicated; but for the rest of eternity those who know God will experience his incomparable aloneness. He is God alone. All of life comes back to one thing: almighty God.

Given that fact, it doesn't make sense to turn anywhere else in crisis. If God is it, then why should we look anywhere besides him as our first source of help, direction, and comfort?

If Hezekiah hadn't taken his need to God, he would have missed God's plan of attack, namely, that God would "move against" the Assyrian king. Hezekiah spared both himself and his people huge grief and confusion trying to figure things out on his own. Instead, he received access to the whole picture because he tapped into God's wisdom.

Prayer is our greatest resource and highest privilege. We may not understand its power until we try it a few times, but what better time than the present, and what more important need than the one you're struggling with right now?

TALK TO HIM

"Father God, I don't understand how prayer works, but thank you for hearing my words and seeing the hidden things of my heart. Please help me grow my prayer life, and let me know you're listening."

Pray on, pray on, O trusting heart,
Let not thy courage fail;
But take thy Savior at His word,
And know thou shalt prevail.

FANNY CROSBY, "BALM IN SECRET PRAYER"

April 18 2 KINGS 20:1-21

"Each day I give you is a gift, so live with purpose for my glory, not your own profit."

"I will defend this city for my own honor." 2 KINGS 20:6

Can you have too much of a good thing? How about food? money? work? time off? attention? sunny days? rainy ones? relationships? Probably any of those things could become excessive without moderation. Too much abundance can take up so much of our energy that we lose sight of the world outside our environment. We can lose a healthy perspective on who provides those blessings if we're too wrapped up in them—sort of a can't-see-God-for-the-perks lifestyle.

King Hezekiah was one of the few good kings in the Old Testament, but he still made mistakes. One of his errors seems to have grown from his abundant wealth. The luxuries of palace living and the attention to him as king might have jaded his view of whom it really belonged to, because apparently he was plenty happy to show off everything he owned. He didn't leave out a single lavish room or a square foot of royal countryside (verse 13).

God gifted Hezekiah with more than most people will ever have, yet it appears that once those possessions transferred from God's storehouse to Hezekiah's palace, the king lost sight of the source. Contrast the Lord's words in verse 6 with King Hezekiah's in verse 15. Notice anything odd about the ownership? God said he would defend the city for his honor; but then Hezekiah paraded visitors through the palace and showed them his royal treasuries.

Who owns your possessions? Better yet, who owns your purpose and your priorities? When God gives you a gift, consider offering it back to him for his glory.

TALK TO HIM

"I sometimes get confused about your ownership of my life, Lord. Please help me remember that everything I am and everything I have comes through your generosity. I give myself and my lifestyle to you for your glory, not mine."

Give of your best to the Master;
Give Him first place in your heart.
Give Him first place in your service;
Consecrate every part.
Give, and to you will be given;
God His beloved Son gave.
Gratefully seeking to serve Him,
Give Him the best that you have.

HOWARD B. GROSE, "GIVE OF YOUR BEST TO THE MASTER"

"My Word is for your growth; are you letting it change you?"

When the king heard what was written in the Book of the Law, he tore his clothes in despair.
2 KINGS 22:11

Walk into any bookstore these days, and you'll notice a self-help section that promotes healthy change, from overcoming addictions to finding true love to discovering the perfect diet. Many of those books provide helpful information and encourage real change in readers' habits.

Yet no book can match the Bible's life-changing message. There's something about God being its author that sets the Bible apart from anything humans could write. That something is the Holy Spirit living and breathing God's life into us through his Word.

The Bible is the only document written by God; it includes everything we need to make deep soul changes, not just in our habits but in our very identity. Because its words are empowered by God's Spirit, the Bible creates change whenever it is read.

Change often is painful, especially when it comes to transforming who we are. King Josiah knew this pain well when he discovered the Book of the Law, God's Word as it had been compiled thus far. He knew the nation needed to reform their actions and obey God's Word, and he knew those changes must begin with him.

God wrote his Book to change us, most significantly to clean out our sinfulness and replace it with godly purity. Anyone who desires the same thing only needs to soak up God's messages in his Word, asking his Spirit's help to understand them.

When you open his Word, you'll never be the same. The parts of your character that drain you? You and God can deal with them together. That habit you can't seem to quit? He will address that in his Word.

Change is good. Without forward-moving growth, you'll end up going backward. Open up the Bible, and ask God to carry you forward with him.

TALK TO HIM

"Lord God, I know your changes in me are for my good. But change hurts. Please show me what changes you want to make in me through your Word."

Word of the Father, O light from on high,
Wonderful book, wonderful book,
Guide to our glorious home in the sky,
Wonderful book of life.

LIZZIE DEARMOND, "WONDERFUL BOOK"

April 20 1 CHRONICLES 11:1-9

"I rule heaven's armies, and I can handle the pressures you face."

David became more and more powerful, because the LORD *of Heaven's Armies was with him.*

1 CHRONICLES 11:9

Civilization has witnessed some impressive armies. One of those belonged to King David. Even before he was their king, his people acknowledged his military success.

When he finally became king officially, he sought a commander for his armies. It was a smart strategy; his soldiers needed a strong leader if they were to continue battling enemy forces, defending their own, and protecting their authority when necessary.

The buck stops with the commander. His word is law, and what he says goes. Military folks know this so deeply that it becomes part of their blood. When God calls himself the Lord of Heaven's Armies, he holds out to us an immeasurable source of protection and authority. We can either run to him and live willingly under the shelter of his rule, or we can take sides against him until one day we have no choice but to yield to his sovereignty.

One thing we humans ought to keep in mind when making such a crucial decision is that God not only is on the good side—he *is* the good side. The King of kings, Lord of lords, Commander of commanders. The buck ultimately stops with him. What he says goes. Eventually there will be no bad side because his armies will defeat it once and for all.

Your God fearlessly handles the pressures of battle as he leads his armies in heaven. Certainly he can direct and protect you here on earth in the pressures you face. Take him into the battle with you, shield yourself under his guard, and trust him to lead you through the fray.

TALK TO HIM

"I love knowing you are Lord of Heaven's Armies, and right now I can't imagine a better reason for peace than knowing you are Lord in this battle of my life. I am hiding under your protection; please be my shield and safety."

O the glorious victory!
Jesus slain awakes again,
Triumphs over Calvary,
And the wiles of men!
Jesus now the risen King
Is alive forevermore!
Earth and Heaven tribute sing—
And hail Him Conqueror!

S. C. KIRK, "THE CONQUEROR"

"Be a leader people love to follow, a leader devoted to me."

They were all eager to see David become king instead of Saul, just as the LORD had promised. 1 CHRONICLES 12:23

What makes a leader who is devoted to God stand apart from other leaders?

Leaders are a dime a dozen. Anyone can take charge; that's the easy part. Few can lead well. While it's true that leaders occasionally have to use some muscle—mental, emotional, physical, whatever the context calls for—leading is more than pulling, pushing, coercing, manipulating, or forcing. True leading is inspiring. It respects and wants the best for its followers, so it beckons and invites, encourages and motivates, builds up and trains its learners to go further still.

Looking through the long list of David's chosen men, it's apparent that many different personalities blended into this mix of warriors. However, they were all in agreement that David was the one to get on board with. With single-minded purpose, they pursued him as their new king (verse 38). Undoubtedly they felt empowered by David, who wisely delegated areas of responsibility, a move that instilled his confidence in them and bolstered their desire to serve well (verse 18). They knew from his track record that David didn't make decisions in his own wisdom, but sought God's direction—a key habit of a godly leader. He had proven to them that his goal was larger than his own interests.

Godly leadership brings a sigh of relief, as the Israelites experienced when David finally took the throne after Saul's death. Godly leadership also boosts people's hope for the future, because God's man or woman brings the Holy Spirit's peace and prosperity to the job (verse 18). Order and unity flourish, even when disagreements inevitably come up. A godly leader is a joy to follow.

Whether you're leading at the head of the pack or by setting an example of following well, be the kind of leader God would choose.

TALK TO HIM

"Thank you, Father, for setting an example of leading humbly and with integrity. Please show me my area of influence, and help me lead for the good of others and with your big picture in mind, not my agenda."

A leader is a dealer in hope.

NAPOLEON BONAPARTE

April 22 1 CHRONICLES 17:1-15

"No matter where you come from, I have beautiful plans for the rest of your story."

"I took you from tending sheep in the pasture and selected you to be the leader of my people Israel." 1 CHRONICLES 17:7

For anyone who has ever felt small or overlooked—like minor news in a top-story world—God is the best news around. Actually the best news, period. He has always found delight in taking unknowns and making headline successes of their lives.

King David is just one example. His headline could read many ways. How about "Shepherd Boy Makes It Big"? "Country Boy Takes Over Palace Duty"? "Stone Slinger Sings Psalms from Throne"?

God excels at creating beautiful stories with people's lives. Yours is no exception.

Far from leaving us trapped by the limitations, mistakes, and even the sins of our pasts, God wants to use those events to shape us into people suited for his specific plans for us.

No one has your experiences. No one has your heartaches. No one has grown exactly as you have through them. And because of them, no one else can go exactly where God wants to take you from here.

Your history does not define you. What you think of as hindrances to your future God sees as opportunities to make an even greater difference in your life and to send a greater message to the world about his goodness and power.

God chose a shepherd boy to be king in the line of his Son, Jesus, our Savior. Regardless of whether you came from the lap of luxury or from the wrong side of the tracks, God has a wonderful story to tell through you.

Your beginning was only a blank page, far from the whole story. Let God have the keyboard and write the rest of your life.

It's sure to be a page-turner.

TALK TO HIM

"Lord, there are parts of my past that bother me, even though I've tried to release them to you. Please heal the areas that need it, reform the broken parts, and piece together a story that shows others your skills at authoring a beautiful life."

Author of life divine . . .
Preserve the life Thyself hast given,
And feed and train us up for Heav'n.
JOHN WESLEY, "AUTHOR OF LIFE DIVINE"

"What is following me costing you?"

"I will not present burnt offerings that have cost me nothing!" 1 CHRONICLES 21:24

What is your faith worth? Could you ever put a price on it? If you could interview a few of the martyrs who chose faith in God over life on earth, what do you think their answers would be?

Here's food for thought: If you aren't willing to die for your faith, is it really faith or merely a wishful desire for the real thing?

That might hit a little close for comfort, but any unease you feel about that question could indicate your dissatisfaction at not having the courageous answer more readily available. There is hope for growth! If you didn't care at all, the question wouldn't bother you.

Most of us won't have our faith tested to the life-or-death extreme, but real faith on any level is guaranteed to cost something. Living wholly for God will mean giving up certain things of this world that don't fit with his standards.

But living wholly for God also involves a desire to love him sacrificially in response to the huge sacrifices he has made for us. His love for us makes us want to give back to him. King David couldn't fathom giving cheaply to God after all God had done for him, knowing all God deserved.

So what is your faith worth to you? It was worth it to God to give his Son in your place. Your faith is highly cherished by your Creator and Savior, almighty God. Following him does come at a cost, but what a precious privilege it is to pay!

TALK TO HIM

"Lord, I owe you so much—more than I can truly fathom with my shortsighted human mind. Please grow my faith to give wholeheartedly back to you."

A faith that lasts for eternity is worth the cost of an earthly life.

ANONYMOUS

April 24 1 CHRONICLES 28:1-10

"Does your life inspire others to religion and rules or relationship with me?"

"Learn to know the God of your ancestors intimately." 1 CHRONICLES 28:9

If you were to ask random people what comes to mind when they hear the word *religion*, what would you guess many would answer?

Faith? Intolerance? God?

Sadly, for all its good qualities, religion carries a negative connotation for a large part of the world's population. It's no wonder, considering the atrocities committed in the name of religion. In many ways, religious people have given religion a bad rap.

The next question for the masses: Would it surprise you to know that God didn't create religion? There's a fact to stump a few.

God created humans for relationship with him, not as puppets subject to a plethora of rules for his own entertainment. He isn't into power plays; he has nothing to prove.

King David, in his speech to prepare his son Solomon for the throne, charged his officials to obey God's commands. Then in an intimate gesture, he spoke directly to Solomon and encouraged him to learn to know his Lord. So personal. So edifying from a father's heart to his son. Rules are important, but David passed on the legacy of a relationship with his heavenly Father and King to his beloved son.

Do you see the significance? In speaking of such a personal relationship with God, David got personal with his son. One father's heart speaking as his heavenly Father's heart had spoken to him.

Instead of thinking of God and cringing over the idea of narrow religious rules, warm to the idea that God wants a relationship with you. The joy of a relationship with God your Creator—there's something to take to the masses.

TALK TO HIM

"Heavenly Father, I can't believe you want a relationship with me—and not just me, but with each of us on earth. Please use our relationship to inspire others to want to know you despite the faults of human-organized religion."

God, who needs nothing, loves into existence wholly superfluous creatures in order that he may love and perfect them.

C. S. LEWIS

"Discover the joys of generosity."

"Everything we have has come from you, and we give you only what you first gave us!"
1 CHRONICLES 29:14

Taking the idea of relationship further, we see King David's love for his heavenly Father through his attitude about giving.

David set the pace for giving abundantly to the Temple of the God he adored (verse 11) by donating all of his own private treasures of gold and silver. Before David could understand the joys of generosity, he learned to love his Maker, the One who showed David the freedom of giving. The intimacy in David's praise reveals his closeness with his Lord, and his understanding of God's love freed him to give back everything that only appeared to be his. All David had came from God, and all he had still ultimately belonged to God because he himself belonged to God. David looked at his life as the passing shadow it was, and he knew he had no reason to hold on to blessings that were never truly his.

We tend to hold more tightly to what we can see. If we're wrapped up too much in this life, then it's no surprise if we hesitate to show generosity. But God gives with abandon, no holding back. He has nothing to lose because it's all his. When we realize he offers his entire Kingdom to those who belong to him, giving becomes much more simple, yet profound. In giving back to him, we're really moving the blessings he gives us to a different part of the life we share with him. It sounds pretty good—and simple—but it still has a selfish bent to it. The profound part comes when we continue falling more in love with God until finally we realize we'd give everything to him regardless of whether we get anything in return.

That's when we tap into the full joy that he feels when he gives to us.

TALK TO HIM

"Lord, you are the Giver who makes givers out of takers. Thank you for showing me the unexpected joys of learning to give as you do. Please show me what I still may be holding back from you."

The manner of giving is worth more than the gift.
PIERRE CORNEILLE

April 26 2 CHRONICLES 1:1-17

"What do you ask of me?"

"O LORD God, please continue to keep your promise to David my father, for you have made me king over a people as numerous as the dust of the earth!" 2 CHRONICLES 1:9

It is interesting how David's and Solomon's lives show the connection between relationships and generosity. Now as 2 Chronicles opens, it flows the theme of giving into a lesson about asking for higher gifts from God. Actually, it begins with a question from God.

God asked Solomon the dream question anyone would love to hear: "What do you want?" (verse 7). Then God follows it by committing to give Solomon whatever he requests. What an opportunity! Where would a person begin?

Solomon kept it simple. First he asked God to keep his promise to David so his line would remain on the throne forever. Then Solomon went a step further. Realizing the hefty responsibility he had been born into, he looked to the God who had given his family such high privilege and asked for wisdom to help him lead God's people. God put him on the throne; God would help him all the way.

Notice the focus of Solomon's desire. Even though he could have treated God as a deified genie, he kept himself grounded and asked for what was already in line with the path God had chosen for him.

God does new things in our lives from time to time, but sometimes it's best to keep things simple and ask for more of him right where we are. Your here-and-now life can always benefit from more of his wisdom and faithfulness.

Asking for more of God's presence is always a higher request than asking him to change situations. He created you for a relationship with himself, so go ahead and raise the bar on your requests. Take your desire for him higher, and he'll lift you up to greater closeness with him.

TALK TO HIM

"Thank you, Lord, for giving of yourself. Please give me more of you here and now, and continue providing what I need to finish the job you created me to do."

Print Thine image, pure and holy,
On my heart, O Lord of Grace;
So that nothing, high or lowly,
Thy blest likeness can efface.

THOMAS H. KINGO, "PRINT THINE IMAGE, PURE AND HOLY"

"Let me awe you every day."

They fell face down on the ground and worshiped and praised the LORD.

2 CHRONICLES 7:3

It's springtime. Can you feel it in the air? Trees budding, flowers blooming, grass greening after long months of winter. Maybe you've plotted your flower beds already and are waiting for prime planting time so you can get your hands in the soil and create something beautiful. Colors, heights, growing needs, annuals, perennials . . . so many options to choose from. Maybe a few perennials mixed with bunches of annuals. Why fill the beds with varieties you may be tired of next year?

Choosing spring flowers doesn't hold eternal importance, but when it comes to the bigger issues of life, most people become trapped by an annual-oriented focus. We live in a world that constantly demands the biggest, brightest, next best thing. We get bored quickly with the status quo, in part because the perks of this earth are not all we're created to hope for. We're created for eternity; deep down we crave the longevity of a forever relationship with our Maker, who formed us from the same soil we work every spring and who breathed life into us.

Each spring he awes us with his newness, but behind the budding nature, he still is the same God he was when he amazed the people with fire from heaven that burned up their offerings. Year after year he keeps the universe in order. Day after day he holds us in his palm.

He is Lord of little moments as well as earth-moving events. Everything he does—as well as who he is—is mighty enough to instill awe in us for the rest of eternity.

Does he awe you still?

TALK TO HIM

"Almighty God, what a wonder you are! I'm amazed today when I think about your huge hand that runs the universe yet wipes the tear of every child across the earth. Please keep me tuned in to you so I never lose the sense of awe you constantly inspire."

This world is loveless—but above
What wondrous boundlessness of love!
The King of Glory stoops to me
My spirit's life and strength to be.

MATTHIAS LOY, "AN AWE-FULL MYSTERY IS HERE"

April 28 2 CHRONICLES 9:1-12

"Does the real you match the perceived you?"

"Everything I heard in my country about your achievements and wisdom is true!"
2 CHRONICLES 9:5

When people know something of your reputation before meeting you, would they be pleasantly surprised, a little disappointed, or fairly satisfied by how the real you compares with what they've heard?

What if they could see the really real you that doesn't often show itself—you know, those sides of your personality that you try to cover? We all have them. The less-than-gracious thoughts we don't voice about others . . . the not-so-lovely sentiments we utter to rude drivers when we're alone in the car . . . the selfish motivations we try to hide even from ourselves.

Because of his high visibility, King Solomon no doubt was talked about a lot. But as with any celebrity, the majority of the world knew Solomon only by hearsay.

When the Queen of Sheba finally met him in person, she was pleasantly surprised to find that the real man matched the image portrayed. In fact, he was more than she expected, and his authentic person spoke so clearly of God that she—a foreigner to the Israelite faith—was moved to praise God.

Being real instills confidence and respect in others because they know what they're getting with you. They don't need to worry about being backstabbed or manipulated. When others know the real you, they can take you at your word, and they know where they stand with you.

You have twenty-four hours every day to be you. Will you waste your breath trying to portray someone you weren't created to be, or will you fill your time with the genuine deal?

TALK TO HIM

"Lord, I'm so glad you are exactly as you portray yourself. Please wake me up to ways I try to be someone I'm not. Please help me be a what-you-see-is-what-you-get person who people can feel sure about."

The world has enough phoniness. Be the real thing.
ANONYMOUS

"Your faith in me is your mightiest weapon and your guaranteed victory."

"Help us, O Lord our God, for we trust in you alone." 2 CHRONICLES 14:11

Everyone loves a good upset. There is nothing quite like the satisfaction of an underdog coming from behind and beating the top seed.

God must love a good underdog victory, because he certainly excels at empowering the weak to achieve success. Just look at what he did with King Asa's army against the million-strong force of the Ethiopians. Anyone would guess that the Ethiopians had those Israelites beat, hands down.

But they would be wrong if they didn't stop to consider a critical point: God was backing Asa's troops, and there is no such thing as an underdog when God is involved.

Asa's mightiest weapon was not a high number of men. It was one God, God alone. The Bible leaves no room for doubt that God didn't just lead Asa—he did the defeating. He destroyed the enemy, and Asa's men carried off the plunder of God's victory.

Our victories are always God's, and they are extra sweet because he knows no underdogs among his followers. His followers make up the winning team, regardless of numbers or skill.

Despite whatever weaknesses or limitations you perceive in yourself, you always have the unbeatable strategy of faith.

Unbeatable.

What will you do with your victorious life?

TALK TO HIM

"God, I am small on my own but unbeatable with you. Please keep my heart on your team, and use me mightily for your success."

Shout your freedom ev'rywhere,
His eternal peace declare,
Victory, victory.
Let us sing it here below,
In the face of ev'ry foe,
Victory, victory.

BARNEY E. WARREN, "VICTORY"

April 30 2 CHRONICLES 15:1-19

"My peace in you attracts others to you."

Many from Israel had moved to Judah during Asa's reign when they saw that the L*ORD* *his God was with him.* 2 CHRONICLES 15:9

Have you ever noticed a similarity shared by the people you're naturally drawn to? Maybe you enjoy a good sense of humor or a reliable character. Maybe gentler souls appeal to you more than boisterous personalities. Or maybe confidence in others pulls you to them.

We're all different in what moves us toward others, but peace is one quality that works like a magnet all the time.

It's well known that opposites attract, so it makes sense that God's peace looks so attractive in a world severely depleted of it. Peace speaks powerfully without necessarily using words, and it lights a person's face with a brightness that seems inexplicable to anyone without firsthand experience of it. Just look at how people flocked to Judah during Asa's reign simply because his obedience to God brought peace to the land.

We want peace. We need peace. But we can't find it outside of God because the lasting kind comes only from him.

King Asa's decision to obey God wholeheartedly, no wavering, was the key factor in the peace his kingdom enjoyed. Obedience is still the defining point today, which explains why our society as a whole is in such shortage of peace. True God-followers are few and far between.

There's nothing more appealing or more lasting than the effects of peace on a worn-out world. If you're in need of a peace perk, take a look at how wholehearted your relationship with God is these days. When your countenance is marked by peace, others will notice it as surely as you'll feel it.

TALK TO HIM

"Peace that passes understanding . . . I've heard that somewhere, God. I need more of it. Please show me if I'm not following you wholeheartedly, and please grant me more of your peace, which attracts others to you shining through me."

Peace, like a river, flows from a higher Source and refreshes everything in its path.

ANONYMOUS

"Knowing my eye is on you will cause you to either rebel or rest."

The eyes of the Lord *search the whole earth in order to strengthen those whose hearts are fully committed to him.* 2 CHRONICLES 16:9

Asa's story is troublesome. It seems he deliberately exchanged God's peace for sickness, unrest, and anger. This king who began so well, who saw the Lord defeat a million enemy warriors, later reacted badly to being held accountable for sin.

His first error was making a treaty with the king of Aram instead of trusting God. As a consequence, his people would be at war from then on.

But instead of taking the humble route and repenting, in his unhappiness, Asa threw a tantrum and oppressed his own people. He stuck up his nose at God and threw away decades of faithfully listening to God. Even a serious disease didn't soften his heart. His story is nuttier still because he had experienced God's goodness for many years; it wasn't as if he didn't know what his bad choices were causing him to miss out on.

Before we toss stones at Asa, it's good to remember that we're all one decision away from moving toward God or distancing ourselves from him. Our failures can do crazy things to our pride and humanness, as Asa's reaction to discipline illustrates. It's as if he hated getting his hand slapped, knowing God saw his messed-up heart behind his actions.

Knowing God has his eye on us will bring us peace if we are seeking him wholeheartedly. However, if we harbor stubborn rebellion against him, we're bound to feel uneasy at the thought that he's watching us.

When you think of God's eyes on you, what emotions surface? Comfort? Anxiety? Guilt? Joy? Your answer reveals something about your heart's commitment to God.

TALK TO HIM

"Lord God, I want to be fully committed to you, but it makes me uneasy to think that I could toss aside our close relationship through one rebellious decision. Please guard my heart for you, and warn me when I am tempted to wander."

Arm me with jealous care,
As in Thy sight to live;
And O Thy servant, Lord, prepare
A strict account to give!

CHARLES WESLEY, "A CHARGE TO KEEP I HAVE"

May 2 2 CHRONICLES 20:1-30

"If you could see how I move the very moment you seek me . . ."

At the very moment they began to sing and give praise, the LORD caused . . .

2 CHRONICLES 20:22

When it comes to taking God at his word, there's believing and then there's *believing*. The second sort moves beyond lip service and shows itself in action.

King Jehoshaphat set the tone for acting in faith on God's promise of victory by calling for a parade of thanksgiving to God before their upcoming battle. Given how he led his people in praising God between the promise and its fulfillment, it's apparent that they truly took the Lord at his word. These folks got it right. They started the victory dance before the fight had even begun. Now that's faith!

God said he'd be with them in the battle, as he promises us. Yet we often worry anyway until we see that he really keeps his word. If our outlook doesn't change, do we really trust him?

One way to boost your faith is to imagine God taking immediate action in response to your prayers. If you've never wondered what goes on in his throne room when prayers arrive there, dwelling on it can be a great faith booster. God moves in faithful love at the moment you share your concern with him. Sometimes his answer may seem delayed, but not because of inaction on his part. He tunes his ear to you immediately.

Look closely at verse 24. Jehoshaphat and his people couldn't see with physical eyes that their enemies were fighting among themselves until those three armies had destroyed each other. But it didn't matter because their eyes of faith had already seen the victory they believed God would hand them.

When you believe your heavenly Father acts at the very moment you call to him, your eyes of faith have the ability to "see" his promises come to fruition before they actually do. Based on your countenance and actions, would those around you guess that you truly believe him?

TALK TO HIM

"Thank you, God, for keeping your promises. I depend on them, and I believe you when you say you'll hear and answer every prayer."

All I have seen teaches me to trust the Creator for all I have not seen.

RALPH WALDO EMERSON

"Are you safe or toxic to the family I gave you?"

She began to destroy the rest of Judah's royal family. 2 CHRONICLES 22:10

Every family has pain. There is no way around it, because every family is made up of faulty humans. Few families, however, have a member as toxic as Judah's notorious queen mother Athaliah.

Ruthless, heartless, merciless—her motto seemed to revolve around the concept of less is more. Fewer family members meant more power for her, so she killed them off. Not even the little ones were safe around her.

Although Athaliah is an extreme example, she makes us think about whether we bring healing or destruction to the ones closest to us. It doesn't take horrible treatment to cause harm; we can chip away at someone's self-esteem without realizing it through little negative comments, impatient body language, or nitpicking what we perceive as faults.

On the other hand, we can bring healing to the ones we care about through encouraging words, understanding expressions, and compassionate responses. Fortunately for baby Joash, his aunt Jehosheba proved to be a much safer person in their family. She dedicated herself to hiding him safely in the Temple for six years while evil Athaliah ruled. She was a true support for him and built into him a legacy of security and healing that he could learn from and pass on to his descendants as well as to the people he would later rule.

We all need a cheerleader in our corner, someone like Jehosheba who believes in us and stubbornly fights for our best—and we all have the power to be that person for someone else. What greater privilege than to do that for those God chose as your family? Beware of the toxic buildup of your words and actions; make a point to be a safe person for the precious souls God places in your life.

TALK TO HIM

"Father God, when stress and busyness take over, sometimes I lose sight of reasons to appreciate my family. Please help me give them my best, remembering that everything I do and say either hurts or heals them."

Oh, the comfort—the inexpressible comfort of feeling safe with a person.

DINAH MULOCK CRAIK

May 4 2 CHRONICLES 24:1-14

"My temple is in you, and together we strengthen and restore you to my original design."

They restored the Temple of God according to its original design and strengthened it.

2 CHRONICLES 24:13

Scar tissue is one of God's fascinating, yet overlooked, details of creation. It's remarkable. A scar is made of tough skin, much tougher in most cases than the original, tender skin that was traumatized. Isn't it just like God to turn something that was once broken into something of greater strength?

He did that with his broken Temple during the days of King Joash. During previous years when wicked Queen Athaliah reigned, her followers abused God's home with their idolatry. When Joash took the throne, he called for godly reforms and renovations of the Temple, which needed serious healing from the scars it had endured from God's enemies.

Fast-forward to now, when God's people are his temple, and see a correlation between the restoration of the Old Testament Temple and the human temples of today.

If you have accepted God's salvation through Jesus, then his Spirit lives in you, making your body God's temple. Whatever scars of your past may hide inside you, God wants to work a restoration in you for the rest of your life. Like the men in charge of the Old Testament Temple's renovation, he will steadily rebuild your broken parts so you will be stronger than ever.

We all have scars from the pains of life, even as God's touch is healing us to extents we can only imagine. We may be tempted to cover up our scars, but there is something beautiful about a scar that sensitive eyes can appreciate: Its presence speaks of victory and renewal, strength and endurance—characteristics of people who love the Lord.

Wear your scars well, trusting that your Savior continues his restoration process in you.

TALK TO HIM

"Lord, you're my healer. I love that about you. I need that about you. Please use my scars to remind me that you aren't finished making something beautiful out of me."

Heal us, Emmanuel, here we are
We wait to feel Thy touch;
Deep wounded souls to Thee repair,
And Savior, we are such.

WILLIAM COWPER, "HEAL US, EMMANUEL"

"I created you to be strong, and it pleases me to see you work hard."

"There is a power far greater on our side!" 2 CHRONICLES 32:7

Big jobs call for courageous people. Life is a big job. Fortunately, we have a bigger God who provides all the courage we need to tackle the responsibilities he gives us, however large they appear to be.

The Bible is filled with stories that seem larger than life, yet they're every bit as real as the situations we live through today. Case in point: the story of King Hezekiah fortifying the wall and working to save Jerusalem from the Assyrians. Instead of cowering under the enemy's threat—an enormous, teeth-baring, growling threat—Hezekiah put his God-given strength into action.

Picture the scene. . . . Hearing the pounding of an approaching army, the king calls for action. Organize a work crew! Cut off the enemy's water source! Fix the broken wall! Build a second wall! Construct the towers! Reinforce the terraces! You over there—gather the people at the city gate! People—be strong and courageous! Don't be afraid or discouraged! God will fight for us!

King Hezekiah reacted as a victorious prince of the King of the universe, full of courage and, more importantly, faith that their Defender would fight for them.

God promised to show up when we need him, and he always keeps his promises. Yet he takes additional pride in us when we approach our battles with a victorious outlook. Cowering countenances don't belong on his people. We don't wear them well; in fact, we have no business assuming a defeatist mentality because we are created for victory. Sure, we may lose a battle every now and then. But the ultimate victory of life is ours through God's Spirit in us.

Call yourself to action as Hezekiah did and rely on God's strength. He will show up in your battle as he always has done for his people.

TALK TO HIM

"Thank you, Father, for not expecting me to handle my struggles alone. As your victorious child, I want to make you proud by approaching life with courage from you."

Work as if you were to live a hundred years; pray as if you were to die tomorrow.

BENJAMIN FRANKLIN

May 6 2 CHRONICLES 34:1-11

"You may not have chosen me when you were young, but you still have today to make a difference."

While he was still young, Josiah began to seek the God of his ancestor David.

2 CHRONICLES 34:3

How long have you known the Lord? Or should the question be, Do you know him yet?

Depending on the current spiritual state of your heart, that question could either make you very comfortable or very uncomfortable. However, let's not shy away from such a crucial query. We each have only one lifetime to choose him or not, and none of us are getting any younger. Amen if you've chosen to follow him. Amen hallelujah if you chose him when you were young with all those years ahead to pattern your life around him.

King Josiah chose God early on when he had a lot of time to make a powerful impact, and God used him mightily. The Temple needed renovating again, and the land and people once more needed cleansing from idolatry. Obviously, Josiah was God's man for the job, with a faith that grew along with him in his role as king.

Yet if he had wanted to, God just as easily could have used someone with a newer faith.

If it took you longer to turn to him—or if you weren't introduced to him until later in life—you may carry regrets about time you think was wasted, spiritually speaking. If that is the case, don't be discouraged. If you're reading this, you obviously aren't done living. Only God knows right now how he can use those preliminary years for his upcoming purposes.

He will use your specific story of faith to draw someone else to him. Count on it, and move forward into the rest of your future with him.

TALK TO HIM

"Lord, I wish I had known you sooner. How different my life may have been. But God, I praise you for finding me at all! Please show me where you would like us to go together from here. I am yours to use for however long you give me on earth."

Spared to see another year,
Let Thy blessing meet us here. . . .
Make this year a time of love!

JOHN NEWTON, "TIME, BY MOMENTS, STEALS AWAY"

"I am supremely patient, and I have unique ways of getting your attention."

They scoffed at the prophets until the LORD's anger could no longer be restrained and nothing could be done. 2 CHRONICLES 36:16

It's a good thing for us that God is in charge of the world, instead of some human. There is no way any human being could show enough patience to deal with all our junk. We would end up destroying each other, and then ourselves, if it weren't for God's tempering hand.

We can be stubborn souls. Although God is incredibly patient, sometimes he sends tough lessons to get our attention. We see this over and over in the lives of the ancient Israelites and their rotation of kings. It's not that God runs out of patience; he has as much as he'll ever need. He just knows when we resist teachability and require a different approach. Many times that different approach isn't too fun. For the Israelites, it often meant defeat by an enemy nation.

When we're heading away from God, our tendency is to get even more aggravated (and aggravating) when we feel his discipline. Yet we have it all wrong when we respond negatively. His discipline proves his compassion. He would rather we suffer consequences on this earth than lose us for eternity. What immense mercy his discipline is! He knows just how tough the lesson needs to be, based on the condition of our hearts, and he always wants our restoration, not our destruction.

If he were to ignore the times we stray, or if we could see the results of our disobedience ahead of time, we would beg for his discipline. We would long for him to set us straight before we make a mess of our lives and before we hurt others.

Be grateful for his warnings and for his discipline. They are his unique methods of mercy toward those he loves.

TALK TO HIM

"Lord, you are creative, right down to how you urge me to stay close to you. Please change my stubborn heart, and help me pay attention to your warnings so I don't have to learn the hard way."

The very true beginning of her [wisdom] is the desire of discipline;
and the care of discipline is love.
WISDOM OF SOLOMON 6:17

May 8 EZRA 1:1-11

"After a dark season, I will send refreshment and help you start again."

He stirred the heart of Cyrus. . . . Then God stirred the hearts of the priests and Levites and the leaders of the tribes. EZRA 1:1, 5

As spring warms the air and the ground thaws from a frigid winter, the days lengthen, bringing more sunshine to chase away the long hours of darkness.

One sign of summer's approach will show up any evening now: fireflies. What simple delight they offer the world each night! Their flicker gives hope by offering a bit of light to the sunset-washed landscape, as if reassuring us, "No worries, world. We will be around to light up the darkness until the sun returns tomorrow."

It's just like God to send us hope through the little details of everyday life—the power of a firefly. Who knew?

None of us enjoy a dreary season of life when circumstances confuse us, or when our situation feels desolate, cold, and dark. Those seasons are a part of life, though, and they teach us to appreciate the sparks of light God sends our way. As he stirs the fireflies in late spring, he stirs his people's hearts with refreshment.

When King Cyrus came to power after the Israelites had spent seventy years in exile, God stirred the heart of the new monarch to allow the people to return and rebuild the Temple in Jerusalem. Then he stirred the hearts of the Israelite leaders to take the king up on his offer. New times had arrived, and God promised refreshment.

God is amazing at creating new beginnings to refresh us after difficult seasons. He may use other people or a tiny firefly to "lighten" our burdens and to show us he is still with us.

Look for him to stir your soul with his creative refreshment, and anticipate a new season ahead for you.

TALK TO HIM

"I need your refreshment now, Lord. I can't see you for the dark, but I will keep looking for glimpses of your light to show me the way. Thank you for the hope of a new beginning."

However long the night, the dawn will break.

AFRICAN PROVERB

"Take time to celebrate my work in you."

When the builders completed the foundation of the LORD's Temple, the priests put on their robes and took their places to blow their trumpets. And the Levites, descendants of Asaph, clashed their cymbals to praise the LORD. EZRA 3:10

A new day had dawned for the Israelites. Their energy was building over the reality of a restored Temple. God had brought them through a lot, and their excitement was palpable as they saw his new beginning for them take shape. Once they laid the foundation, it was time for a celebration to signify their renewed commitment to worship God.

When we take time to celebrate God's work in our lives, we are not only acknowledging his faithfulness, but we are also planting memories in our minds of our commitment to continue with him. We also teach the next generation to find joy in worshiping God for who he is as we praise him for what he does.

Sure, there was a lot more to do before the Temple was complete, but those Israelites couldn't keep their enthusiasm bottled up. There is something precious about rejoicing over what God has done, what he is doing, and what he has yet to do. All three reasons provide a whole perspective of gratitude for God's consistent care.

If he is Lord of your days, give him a little more of your time by celebrating your past, present, and future with him. Then take the memory of your joy with you into tomorrow, knowing full well that the God you rejoiced over today will remain solid and true forever.

Your times are in his hand, so celebrate them!

TALK TO HIM

"Lord, if anyone has reason to celebrate, it's those who belong to you. You give us a secure future, as well as healing from the past and restoration in the present. Let's celebrate together all that you have in store."

There are two ways to live your life. One is as though nothing is a miracle. The other is as though everything is.
ALBERT EINSTEIN

May 10 EZRA 4:1–5:5

"Refuse to be discouraged by those who oppose you because of me."

Because their God was watching over them, the leaders of the Jews were not prevented from building until a report was sent to Darius and he returned his decision. EZRA 5:5

No matter how awesome a goal, there will always be a bummer man (or woman), someone who drags down your enthusiasm intentionally or through passive negativity otherwise known as indifference.

When it comes to enthusiasm about God things, expect naysayers to creep from the shadows and try to put the kibosh on your excitement. Without the eternal hope of God, the world can't remain positive against the negative influence of Satan's forces.

When the Israelites were moving forward on the Temple restoration, their enemies worked hard to stop them. Motivated by fear of the Israelites' God—the obvious source of the nation's successes—the enemy leaders manipulated the situation to discourage the Israelites from continuing.

Discouragement could have reigned through the building process. However, God's prophets refused to give in to frustration. God was the one their enemies were rejecting. But because God had stirred the Israelites to rebuild in the first place, obviously he had a plan for accomplishing such an undertaking. With their eyes on the goal, the Israelites continued the construction. God was in charge. He would see his work to completion.

Even if someone hasn't actively opposed you because of your faith, you probably can recall receiving a blank stare or a knowing look that told you someone belittled your beliefs. Satan uses discouragement not only to halt our progress with God, but also to cripple our emotions, making it difficult to see from God's perspective. Before you face opposition to your faith, determine to brush off the claws of discouragement.

If you belong to God, then you are his temple. He is still in charge of his temple restoration. Don't waste time on discouragement when there is beautiful work to be done in you.

TALK TO HIM

"Lord, I get weary of feeling like the odd one out around people who don't know you and don't care to meet you. Please help me stay focused on my goal of knowing you more, and grow me strong against discouragement."

'Tis the set of the soul that determines the goal
And not the storm and the strife.
ELLA WHEELER WILCOX

"I want you to be so in tune with me that the things that break my heart break yours."

When I heard this, I tore my cloak and my shirt, pulled hair from my head and beard, and sat down utterly shocked. EZRA 9:3

What breaks your heart? Child abuse? War? Adultery? Sins don't necessarily have to be committed directly against us before we can feel their heartbreaking power. In fact, sometimes we hurt more over someone else's pain because we didn't (or couldn't) do something to prevent it. We hate to see good people suffer.

Ezra the prophet felt the pain his people caused God through their sin of intermarrying against God's command. Ezra's grief is unique because it was based on God's pain. His wrenching response raises a valuable question for us: Do we hurt over the things that hurt our God?

God is a God of big emotions. Big love. Big humility. Big jealousy. Naturally, then, we can assume he also feels pain to a big degree. But how often do we stop to consider the hurts we level on him when we fail to obey him? More likely than not, we rarely consider his heart when we're tempted to sin. We'd rather not get caught, and we'd definitely prefer to avoid uncomfortable consequences. But is our motivation not to sin ever primarily rooted in not wanting to hurt God?

Sin breaks God's heart. In our relationship with him, as we grow to be more like him, we should expect our hearts to become more tenderized to the issues that cause him pain. As we develop his heart in us, our passion for his purity will increase, and our hearts will break from the wounds he takes on our behalf. Yet in that brokenness, we are empowered to guard his causes in a world that constantly works against him.

Thank him for opening your eyes to his broken heart, and determine to be a healing person on his behalf.

TALK TO HIM

"Father God, I'm sorry for forgetting that I cause you pain when I sin. The very thought breaks my heart because I love you and don't want to hurt you—especially knowing how much you love me. Please help my life to bring healing in your world instead of more hurt."

Let us do something beautiful for God.

MOTHER TERESA

May 12 EZRA 10:1-44

"Open your eyes to areas of your heart that I want to change."

"Yes, you are right; we must do as you say!" EZRA 10:12

You can lead a horse to water, but you can't make him drink. You can point out the errors of someone's ways, but you can't change a heart. It would probably be a lot easier to force a horse to drink than to change a human heart. Our hearts are stubborn creatures, bent on doing our own thing whether it's good for us or anyone else.

Some preliminary work has to be done before our hearts can change. We first need to hear that we've done wrong, and then we need to accept it. Finally, we need to commit to do things differently before we actually begin to move in the right direction. Those are some significant changes to make before visible change really takes place. Seeing and accepting our failures are perhaps the two toughest steps in the process because a rebel heart often wants to remain rebellious.

For all their sins of intermarrying with pagan nations, the Israelites did well to turn their hearts back to God when they, along with the prophet Ezra, understood the depth of their wrongs. With eyes opened, they grieved for how they'd messed up their lives. Then they took action to rid themselves of sin. As a result, they made changes that pleased God and moved them back to him.

No matter how much you love God, you're in the same boat of humanness as everyone else since the first sin in the Garden of Eden. Those who have accepted Christ as Savior still sin and need forgiveness and change in their lives. Every now and then we all need our eyes opened to ways God wants to heal, grow, and purify our hearts. When he opens yours, keep yourself tuned to his voice, and thank him for not letting you continue on a path that doesn't lead straight to him.

TALK TO HIM

"God, sometimes I'm blinded to areas that I need to work on. Please open my eyes wider so I can see myself as you do, and open my heart to welcome your changing influence."

Confession of our faults is the next thing to innocence.

PUBLILIUS SYRUS, MAXIM 1060

"True success is directly related to the depth of your prayer life."

For days I mourned, fasted, and prayed to the God of heaven. . . . "Listen to the prayers of those of us who delight in honoring you. Please grant me success today." NEHEMIAH 1:4, 11

Nehemiah was a get-it-done guy. When he took action, he began with prayer, an odd choice by many people's thinking. To those who don't know better, prayer can seem passive, as if the person praying expects God to do all the work.

But true prayer is the most powerful first step we could ever take because prayer puts us in touch with our power source and aligns us on a successful track. Prayer expects God to do all the work we cannot do ourselves, and it doesn't apologize for recognizing its need for God. In fact, the Bible expects us to pray always, and to pray always anticipating God to respond to us (see Philippians 4:6; James 1:6). Nehemiah knew his success depended on God. Much more was at stake than Nehemiah could handle on his own, so naturally his prayers were filled with intensity and heartfelt longing for God to move.

Passionate, balanced prayer pours out our deepest impulses while recognizing that our preliminary role as doers for God requires us to find out first what God would have us do. Prayer seeks. Prayer desires. Prayer expects. God created that form of communication, and he wants us to put it to use. He wouldn't tell us to pray if it served no purpose or if he wasn't the mighty force behind it.

When you talk with your Savior, go deep as Nehemiah did. His passionate prayers of faith moved God's hand to help the people successfully rebuild the wall. Discover what successes God wants to lead you toward.

TALK TO HIM

"Lord, you are the God of success. Please show me through our communication what your definition of success involves for me, and help me put my heart and soul into staying close to you in prayer."

Orare est laborare, laborare est orare [To pray is to work, to work is to pray].
ANCIENT MOTTO OF THE BENEDICTINE ORDER

May 14 NEHEMIAH 2:1-20

"If fear holds you back, we need to deal with it together."

The king granted these requests, because the gracious hand of God was on me.

NEHEMIAH 2:8

As kids, most of us played on a seesaw a time or two. Up and down we went, steadying our weight with that of the person on the opposite end, pushing off the ground with our toes—a simple balancing act, but one that required a firm grip on the handle so we wouldn't teeter and topple off.

Fun times at recess . . . until the playground bully showed up. Fear prickled our spine at that ferocious face, and we knew something not-so-pleasant was about to go down. Sure enough, with a grunt, a shove, and no room for discussion, he (or she!) demanded a turn.

Like the bullies of elementary school, fear is a great "unsteadier." Nehemiah felt fear's force when he told the king why he felt so troubled. He knew kings of that day could be grown-up bullies, and the thought didn't help his courage. Fortunately, Nehemiah had a greater source of courage. His trust in God kept him from toppling from his steady perch in God's hand, high above his trouble on earth.

Although bullies of all ages still roam the world, God is like the playground monitor. Our Savior settles the score with those who threaten us. If we have been bumped and bruised, he helps us to stand, cleans us up, and assures us everything will be okay because he is nearby. He raises his people to a secure place, resettles us, and nudges us back in motion. Plus, he lets us know the bullies will answer to him when "recess" is over.

Because Nehemiah didn't let fear hold him back, he didn't cheat himself of the joy of experiencing God's protection and empowerment.

Don't let fear hold you back today. Go for life with the enthusiasm of a confident child of God, knowing the Great Steadier is on constant watch over you.

TALK TO HIM

"Father God, when fear threatens to knock down my courage, please remind me that I am still your child. Thank you for watching me and helping me deal with my fears."

In a world filled with causes for worry and anxiety . . . we need the peace of God standing guard over our hearts and minds.

JERRY MCCANT

"Remember your purpose."

"Remember the Lord, who is great and glorious, and fight for your brothers, your sons, your daughters, your wives, and your homes!" NEHEMIAH 4:14

What keeps a person going when life presses mercilessly? You've heard stories of people living through inhumane conditions, mistreated and stressed to the hilt. It's a wonder many people make it through extreme hardships.

One key source of strength must be their sense of purpose. Hanging on to a goal bigger than their present conditions brings hope.

For the Israelites of Nehemiah's day, rebuilding the wall required stubborn tenacity, as well as a consistent, focused vision of their ultimate goal. Remembering their purpose helped them withstand threats from enemies, weariness, long hours, tough conditions, and back-breaking work. Building that wall would have been difficult if surrounding circumstances were ideal, but imagine the additional strain of having a workforce cut in half while the other half stood guard. Imagine each worker using only one hand while the other gripped a weapon poised for defense. Most people wouldn't endure with all that working against them . . . except of course when they remembered why they needed to work so hard.

When we know our purpose, we arm ourselves with a weapon against discouragement. The purpose of a purpose is to keep us moving from our present conditions toward a greater goal.

Antagonists would love nothing more than to see us fail. When we live for God, we inherit instant enemies who are highly motivated to destroy our work for him. But sticking with God's purpose for us arms us with every defense we need to finish the task he gives us.

God created us for the greatest purpose of bringing glory to him. Ultimately, everything we fight for comes back to that. Remember the purpose of your purpose, and keep moving forward with your eyes on God's big picture for you.

TALK TO HIM

"Lord, you know the extents to which people have gone to accomplish incredible feats through your strength. They stuck to a purpose that helped them through pain. Please help me keep sight of your purposes for me so I can succeed in the challenges you allow me to face."

This is the true joy in life, being used for a purpose
recognized by yourself as a mighty one.
GEORGE BERNARD SHAW

May 16 NEHEMIAH 6:1-19

"Use opposition to anchor your determination."

They were just trying to intimidate us, imagining that they could discourage us and stop the work. So I continued the work with even greater determination. NEHEMIAH 6:9

God does not give up on us, and he does not want his children to bail on the work he gives us to do. He created us in his image, and nothing about him says to us, "Give up. You'll never make it." Not by a long shot.

God is a finisher, and he values that characteristic in his people. However, he also is supremely compassionate about the challenges that work against us, as well as our human limitations. His enemies automatically are ours, and while they're no match for him, we're vulnerable to their incessant attacks. Fortunately, being created in his image means that we have a dose of his tenacity. He is, after all, a very determined God—he puts up with us, doesn't he?

The Israelites who rebuilt the wall must have made him smile with their refusal to give in to their enemies' intimidation. Children of God are created to be overcomers, and those builders actually turned negatives into positives by using others' animosity against them as catalysts for their own strength. They translated that energy into greater determination to stick to their purpose.

As a Christian, you will never run out of opposition to your faith, not until God destroys his enemies forever. But you're an overcomer by nature of the Holy Spirit in you. You were reborn spiritually to succeed at God's plan for you, regardless of whatever works against you.

Make your eventual victory even sweeter by growing stronger through opposition, and use those negatives as anchors to hold your faith fast. Beat the opposition at its own game, and claim the life of victory that God is helping you to construct.

TALK TO HIM

"How amazing, Lord, that you created me to soar above anything that opposes you. Please help me push past the negatives, seeing them as faith strengtheners."

We are made strong by what we overcome.

JOHN BURROUGHS

NEHEMIAH 12:27-43 **May 17**

"Take time to celebrate my goodness."

God had given the people cause for great joy. . . . The joy of the people of Jerusalem could be heard far away. NEHEMIAH 12:43

Think about the last time you celebrated something. It might have been a birthday, an anniversary, a promotion, a birth. Did you put your heart and soul into it, or did it warrant only a partial smile? halfhearted interest? How sad if that's the extent of your excitement. True celebration is quite a party worth attending.

We celebrate what brings us joy—the more joy, the bigger the celebration. Since God is the true source of joy, those who know him have reason to celebrate huge all the time. If you were to list the joys in your life, before long you may notice a similarity among them. Everything on that list points to one main blessing: God's goodness. His goodness is reason enough to hold a celebration in your heart every moment. If your heart belongs to him, here are a few thoughts to jump-start your celebratory spirit:

Your eternity is secure, and you will spend it with him.
You are never alone on earth.
You are loved thoroughly.
You have a purpose greater than yourself.
You have an opportunity to share his joy.
You will be healed and whole one day.
You have spiritual family on earth, and you will take them with you into eternity.

Are you catching the spirit yet? The dedication of the new wall of Jerusalem sent the spirit of celebration throughout a nation that had suffered and grown and rebuilt together, all under the protective shelter of the Lord's goodness. When the work was finished and they looked toward a renewed life of worship, it was time to say thanks to God for his faithfulness and his future promises.

Whether you celebrate out loud or gently within your heart, let your spirit of thankful celebration be heard all the way to the heavens.

TALK TO HIM

"God, sometimes when life stresses me out, I lose sight of you and your goodness to me. Now I would just like to say thank you. You are my reason to celebrate!"

Celebrate each breath that carries you into the next one
that eventually lasts a lifetime. Each one is a gift from God.
ANONYMOUS

May 18 ESTHER 1:1-8

"My goodness should be a greater reason for celebration than your own success."

The celebration lasted 180 days—a tremendous display of the opulent wealth of his empire and the pomp and splendor of his majesty. ESTHER 1:4

How sad for King Xerxes that he was his own biggest celebration! Six months of reveling in everything about himself. That is half a year of precious life spent glorying in his own identity. Even when Xerxes threw a banquet for everyone at the end of that time, nothing indicates that God was invited to the festivities, much less as the Guest of Honor. Xerxes had a lot of power over what appeared to be a very large world; but in reality, his world was very small if he was its center.

How unfulfilling that lifestyle would become! We aren't created to be satisfied with a world that revolves around ourselves. God wants much more for us; he wants us to find our greatest cause for rejoicing in him. When he is our center, he opens up for us the world as he sees it. When we see from his expansive view, we notice the world others live in, we grow in understanding of others' needs, and we feel grateful that he is the Almighty instead of pretending we ever could be. In short, we become more authentic instead of existing in a dream world where we rule.

King Xerxes could have benefited from some authenticity. Fortunately, as we see later in the book of Esther, God broadened Xerxes' world to the needs of others. When Xerxes took part in saving the Israelites, he surely witnessed their celebrations of God's goodness. And if his heart had grown at all, he rejoiced with them at the opportunity to be used for good in other people's lives.

If we're wise, we will find reasons for authentic celebration within the expansiveness of God's goodness. Don't limit yourself to small reasons for joy when you can have the Source of joy within you, filling your world with his goodness.

TALK TO HIM

"Lord, thank you for showing me reasons to celebrate that go far beyond me and my little world. Thank you for your goodness. I will love to celebrate you for eternity."

Joy is the most infallible sign of the presence of God.

TEILHARD DE CHARDIN

"Prejudice tells more about those who judge than about whom they judge."

He had learned of Mordecai's nationality, so he decided it was not enough to lay hands on Mordecai alone. Instead, he looked for a way to destroy all the Jews. ESTHER 3:6

Depending on world and national events when you read this, different people groups could come to mind when you think of prejudice. Humanity never seems to be free of hatred toward its own. Hate has been a powerful catalyst but a lousy excuse for history's most heinous crimes.

However, prejudice shows itself often in more "innocent," everyday injustices that most of us are guilty of occasionally. We gasp at Haman's evil plot to destroy the Israelites, and well we should. But are we really as free of prejudice as we think?

Before answering yes, consider the question carefully. Prejudice includes any ill will that lurks inside us toward someone because of race, religion, sexual preference, gender, age, social status, or for any other reason. Prejudice sees a classification instead of a human being, a reason to judge instead of a human heart that needs God's love. Prejudice has its own standards of right and wrong for others and condemns a soul God loves, but misses its own sins of hatred and judgment. Prejudice reveals more about those who are guilty of this sin than about those they judge.

Haman obviously viewed the Israelites as disposable, worthless, and subhuman. Yet, his attitude and actions illuminate the darkness in his heart so clearly that we don't even look at the people he's pointing his finger at. All we can focus on is his appalling wickedness.

Loving others as we love ourselves is one of God's greatest commands for us, second only to loving him (see Matthew 22:37-39). Notice where we ourselves rank in these commands—no higher than anyone else. This leaves no room for prejudice.

Guard your heart against Haman's poisonous example; the end results for him were not pretty.

TALK TO HIM

"Heavenly Father, please show me if I am holding on to traces of prejudice. Give me your heart for others, and help me to be a healing resource in this world where hatred twists your truth."

It is well that there is no one without a fault,
for he would not have a friend in the world.
WILLIAM HAZLITT

May 20 ESTHER 4:1-17

"When you're committed to me, I always ensure you're at the right place and time."

"Who knows if perhaps you were made queen for just such a time as this?" ESTHER 4:14

Are you comfortable in your life in general? We all have our comfort zones where we feel sheltered and safe. Even if we venture out occasionally, we like to choose our adventures so we don't get lost outside our area of familiarity.

If you have ever been booted from your comfort zone by no choice of your own, you know how it feels to be out of your element. Wherever "out of your element" is, it's an alienating place where you wonder how to fit into a situation that doesn't suit you.

Queen Esther was out of her element in King Xerxes' harem. A Jewish girl suddenly separated from everything familiar and comfortable, she was thrust into the role of Persia's queen, forced to adapt to her new station and to the king's bed.

However, God had a plan for Esther that required her to move beyond what she had always known and all that made her feel safe. Without consulting her, God changed her life in ways that shook her to the core of her faith. The key truth that prompted her to move forward in that strange new world, despite her misgivings, came as a question from her uncle Mordecai (verse 14). Once she considered that God was behind the odd events of her life, she found the courage to accept the challenges in faith.

If your heart is tuned in to God, he will make sure you're at the right place and time to accept his next move for you. He might not consult you about it; in fact, he most likely won't. But he definitely will meet you there and see you through it.

If your ultimate comfort zone is in his presence, then you can feel at home and fulfilled anywhere he leads. Go with him, and grow with him.

TALK TO HIM

"Father, my circumstances don't feel good, and I feel out of my element. But I trust that you will guide me and work your will through me. In fact, thank you for not consulting me; you know best."

So often we try to alter circumstances to suit ourselves, instead of letting them alter us, which is what they are meant to do.

MOTHER MARIBEL

"Fighting for your pride creates a very small world; fighting for my honor expands your horizons."

"Whom would the king wish to honor more than me?" ESTHER 6:6

In the reading several days ago, we saw how King Xerxes' celebrations of himself trapped him in a small world. Well, in today's selection, we see someone again create a tiny environment with himself at the center. This time the culprit is Haman, and his own pride is in his way.

You have to love Esther 6:10 when King Xerxes—unaware of Haman's wicked ego—orders Haman to honor Mordecai with the prizes Haman drooled over for himself. If we were more childish, we might blow raspberries to Haman or croon a "nonny nonny boo boo." Fortunately we aren't that immature. We just keep our flaunting to ourselves and pretend we're above such responses.

Truth is, don't we all love to be the big cheese at times? Head honcho? All that and more? Even though we wouldn't go to Haman's evil lengths to exalt ourselves, we carry a thread of his pride.

Problem is, when we try to enlarge our world where we're the center, we end up creating a smaller world for ourselves. Our pride has us believing we deserve grandiose attention, but it actually works against us, alienating us from the real world.

We enlarge our scope by looking beyond ourselves at God. In pursuing his honor, we see increasingly broader horizons of life than is possible from a prideful vantage point.

Pride in ourselves is limiting, so we're wise to guard against being fooled by it. Esther and Mordecai showed a better way by fighting for God's name instead of their own. Consequently, God used them to bless an entire nation and its descendants. As it turns out, their names are remembered with honor as well. Funny how a godly focus works best all around.

TALK TO HIM

"Lord, I want my life to be about you, but my pride challenges my best intentions. I wonder if I will ever have completely pure motivations to make you look good instead of hoarding the honor for myself. Please work your excellent character in me more each day."

O God, our Shield, let wickedness
And pride be put to shame,
Till all shall know that Thou dost rule
And all shall fear Thy Name.

AUTHOR UNKNOWN, "PROTECT AND SAVE ME, O MY GOD"

May 22 JOB 1:1–2:6

"Satan's power is always limited by mine."

"All right, do with him as you please," the L*ORD said to Satan. "But spare his life."* JOB 2:6

Is there no limit to evil in the world? Senseless crimes, hatred and prejudice, death and destruction . . . evil is everywhere. Even the womb isn't safe for countless souls whom God loved enough to send his Son to the cross.

Has Satan gotten the best of him? Surely almighty God could prevent at least some of the pain humans endure. What was the point of sending Jesus if Satan still has free reign over the earth?

Back up to that last sentence, specifically the word *free*. In that word we find the truth. Satan is not free to do as he pleases. Although God temporarily gives him a long leash, God still limits his every action and deception. God never will give up control to the devil. He put boundaries on Satan's power over Job, and he holds Satan back from destroying us. If we could see into the spiritual realm, we would have far greater faith in God's power over evil. This minute he could be saving your life or the soul of someone you love.

We may not understand God's temporary allowing of evil. It's true that he is giving more people time to turn to him before he destroys wickedness forever. But even knowing that, we can have difficulty accepting God's ways when we experience evil's effects.

Coming to terms with the reality of evil comes down to trusting God to be God, ruler of all, including the devil and his forces. We are stretched to our limits to hang on to God when hurts tear us up. But those with tenacious trust will one day see God put the final limitations of utter destruction on Satan. Then finally we will rest in God's limitless peace.

TALK TO HIM

"Lord, I am so tired of hearing stories of suffering—not because I'm not compassionate, but because I am. I can't stand the thought of horrific pain. Lord, please be God again today. Protect as you know best, and please don't delay your final destruction of evil."

Let wickedness that raged in power
Now rage in impotence;
But I will glory in Thy strength,
My Refuge and Defense.

AUTHOR UNKNOWN, "PROTECT AND SAVE ME, O MY GOD"

"Don't speak on my behalf unless you're willing to show my love."

"Do you think your words are convincing when you disregard my cry of desperation?"

JOB 6:26

Someone somewhere once said she would love God if it weren't for Christians. Where would she get an idea so strongly set against God's followers? She would probably point toward people who claim the religion of Christianity but fail to claim the love part of it—the crucial part.

Christianity at its heart is all about love because God is love. Anyone who comes up with a religious system that fails to show Christ's love fails to really know God. God's truth cannot be filed in a separate category from his love. We would be better off not speaking as God's mouthpiece unless the truths that come out of our mouths are cushioned in love.

Job's friends knew all kinds of facts and accusations based on how they saw right and wrong. The problem with their approach, though, was that they forgot that Job needed compassion, not a slap on the wrist.

Our words, even our promises to pray for others, are worthless unless we are willing to back them up with actions based on love. True caring expresses itself in ways that matter to others—not necessarily in ways that come easily to us—until the people we are caring for benefit from our genuine concern.

The easy way to live a form of the Christian life is to abide by the rules in the Bible. Yet if our story is only about rules and neglects God's love, we've missed his whole point, as Job's friends did. They ended up causing him more harm than good.

If you're going to speak for God, make sure the message you're passing on includes the love he undeniably would show.

TALK TO HIM

"Lord, your love is better than life. Please help me to make it my primary goal to show your love. Thank you that your truth and love are inseparable."

It is this intangible thing, love in many forms, which enters into every therapeutic relationship. . . . And it is an element which binds and heals, which comforts and restores.

KARL MENNINGER

May 24 JOB 12:1-25

"Be careful not to assume you know someone else's heart; that skill is mine alone."

"You people really know everything, don't you? And when you die, wisdom will die with you!"

JOB 12:2

If there's one theme to take from Job chapter 12, it is that God is supreme. He's the One in charge, the authority over everything—calming truth for those who love him, and a little disconcerting for anyone who doesn't respect him.

It should be a bit unnerving as well for anyone who assumes the ability to read other people's hearts. God doesn't share that skill with anyone. Verse 13 says counsel and understanding are his, and that includes the ability to see all that goes on in someone else.

Aren't there times when you aren't sure even what's inside your own heart? We battle mixed motives, halfhearted desires for goodness, and a bevy of character flaws that fall short of God's standards. Who would want anyone else to see inside us? It's not a pretty picture, even for someone who appears pure and holy.

Job's sarcastic answer to his friends about wisdom dying with them was an effort to help them realize their nerve in thinking they knew his inmost thoughts. It seems they wanted to be right more than they wanted to help him.

We're better off not trying to play God for others. We weren't created to be anyone's holy spirit or conscience. Thank the Lord! What a burden we would bear if we were required to point out everything we think is wrong about others; not only would we face the pressure of having to be right, but we would also need to make sure our own lives were faultless before we cast judgment on others.

God gave us a gift by not granting us the ability to read other people's hearts. Be grateful that in this case ignorance really is bliss.

TALK TO HIM

"Lord, thank you for keeping me ignorant of the deep places of other people's hearts. Please help me to value your Spirit working in them as well as in me to mold each of us as you see fit, and please help me not to intrude where I don't belong."

If we had no faults of our own, we would not take so much pleasure in noticing those of others.

FRANÇOIS, DUC DE LA ROCHEFOUCAULD

"Many times the best way you can show my love is by being quietly available to others."

"If only you could be silent! That's the wisest thing you could do." JOB 13:5

As a generality, we humans talk too much. We love to hear our own opinions, as if spreading them validates us as wise people.

Yet true wisdom often shows itself through silence, particularly when dealing with someone else's difficulties. Our hearts may be in the right place; we want to help them cope however we can. But why must we revert to talking? Surely someone going through a confusing time already is plagued by introspection, questioning their circumstances, praying that things will change, asking God to soothe their aches.

Just as we can't see the hidden parts of someone's heart, as yesterday's text showed us, we can't know exactly what words to use to comfort someone. A wounded heart needs extra tenderness and sensitivity; a bevy of words can end up trampling it. Old standbys like "It'll be okay" or "I know how you feel" only twist a grieving person's hurt deeper because only God can utter those sentiments with any real reassurance.

However, quiet availability brings comfort every time. Not hovering, mind you, but a simple offer to be there with open ears, a warm hug or hand squeeze, or even a suggestion to help out in practical, everyday ways like bringing a meal or running an errand.

Quiet availability is a sure-win way to touch someone whose spirit might feel as if it's on life support. Your unobtrusive presence, whether right there or a phone call away, might be the healing balm the situation needs.

Save your plethora of words regarding the circumstances for God, but limit your tongue as you open your heart in quiet availability to a hurting person.

TALK TO HIM

"Lord, please grant me sensitivity to keep my words to myself more often than not when I want to solve someone's troubles. I've messed up in this area before, but I want to grow as you use me to bring healing to someone today."

The habit of common and continuous speech is a symptom of mental deficiency. It proceeds from not knowing what is going on in other people's minds.

WALTER BAGEHOT

May 26 JOB 19:1-29

"If you suffer, don't assume I'm punishing you."

"How dare you go on persecuting me, saying, 'It's his own fault'? You should fear punishment yourselves, for your attitude deserves punishment." JOB 19:28-29

Perhaps one of the greatest secondary burdens of suffering is our often unanswered question, Why? We want to make sense of things that happen to us, so if we must endure something hard, at least tell us the reason for it. At least give us that much, God.

Right?

Suffering often plunges us into introspection, where we rehash how we may have earned such awful consequences. Surely God wouldn't let us hurt so badly unless we deserved it as punishment.

Right?

Not so fast. It's anyone's guess where we got the idea that suffering must be a consequence of sin. Sometimes God does allow suffering as discipline, but that is only sometimes. Pain is an unavoidable part of life. It's here to stay until we're with God for eternity.

Look at Job's life. God was extremely proud of Job for the way Job lived, yet he allowed Satan to test Job's faithfulness. Not a shred of Job's pain came as a result of sin. Job wasn't merely a halfway good man; he was "blameless—a man of complete integrity. He feared God and stayed away from evil" (Job 1:1). If anyone did not deserve to suffer, Job was that man.

God's purpose in allowing Job to bear huge pain was the opposite of punishment. He held up Job before Satan's sneering face as a pillar of integrity (see Job 2:3), a man who brought glory to God, a man whose life put Satan in his place.

If you're having a difficult time, consider how your life can be a testimony of faithfulness to God rather than a tale of sin's woes. You might be amazed what God will do through the situations that hurt you.

TALK TO HIM

"Lord, I don't like that pain is part of life, but I'm eternally thankful that you're so gracious to spare me from the suffering my sins deserve. Please help me to honor you even when my questions remain unanswered."

Here is a mystery: one man's experience drives him to curse God, while another man's identical experience drives him to bless God. Your response to what happens is more important than what happens.

CHIP BROGDEN

"Trust my reasons for allowing evil in the world; and trust that it is temporary."

"Why doesn't the Almighty bring the wicked to judgment? Why must the godly wait for him in vain?" JOB 24:1

Job's *why* questions strike at our hearts with their poignancy. His outpouring of anguish transcends time and distance and calls to us with raw urgency. We don't know how he felt. But then again, we do—to a degree. Pain is pain, and even if we haven't experienced exactly what someone else is going through, we can relate to hurting in general. This chapter sends our emotions plummeting over the endless forms of cruelty in the world. We don't have to endure any one of those specifics to understand the hopeless feelings involved.

Back on May 22, we looked at the limits God puts on Satan and touched on the reasons God allows evil to continue. Today it is time to focus more on the joy we can have knowing evil is temporary. The second half of chapter 24 is like refreshing rain to those who have thirsted for justice. In what may have been a rallying cry to bolster his own faith, Job listed examples of how the wicked will come to a terrible end.

God is watching even now. If he seems to take a passive stance on evil, rest assured he is on the move. Our idea of fixing things differs from his in both method and time frame. However, we can trust that his plans for justice will be entirely worth the wait.

Our job in the meantime is to hold on to our faith in him and refuse to let anything budge it. Job did it, and God blessed him richly.

You can hold on too.

TALK TO HIM

"Lord, sometimes I feel like I can't hold on any longer. I'm desperate for you to fix my circumstances. Please change the situation or change me to handle it. I know you will be faithful. Please help me believe more."

The evil and suffering in this world are greater than any of us can comprehend. But evil and suffering are not ultimate. God is. Satan, the great lover of evil and suffering, is not sovereign. God is.

JOHN PIPER

May 28 JOB 29:1–30:1

"When you are hurting, know that I am still your greatest Friend—and I am still here."

"When I was in my prime, God's friendship was felt in my home." JOB 29:4

One of the most troublesome truths to come to terms with is that God allows suffering for those he considers friends. Our instinct is to protect those we care about. We wouldn't let a loved one continue hurting if we could make it better. Why would God do things differently?

How do we go through life with a firm grasp of pain's existence—and the potential for it to hit us personally—without becoming pessimistic, cynical, or incapable of celebrating the good times for fear of coming disaster? That is a question for the ages.

As usual, the answer points us to God's heart. When we plant ourselves firmly in his presence, his love glows from his heart over our lives. It warms, comforts, and covers us when clouds darken our world.

Instead of continuing to ask why God allows heartache, we need to train ourselves to wear blinders of a sort that fix our gaze on him to protect us from being sideswiped by suffering. Without that fixed gaze, we lose sight of him for all the cares crowding our peripheral vision, and we assume he is the one who lost track of us.

Keep him in your sights. Just because he lets you hurt more than you ever thought he would, or should to your way of thinking, doesn't diminish his position as Best Friend for eternity.

Hang on. He is still with you.

TALK TO HIM

"Lord, I don't understand your reasons, and I don't always like them. But you have the right to be God, and I will take you at your word that you are my Friend above all friends. I know you will be faithful to me, even when life hurts."

Friend Who never fails nor grieves us, faithful, tender, constant, kind;
Friend Who at all times receives us, Friend Who came the lost to find.
Sorrow soothing, joys enhancing, loving until life shall end;
Then conferring bliss entrancing, still, in heaven, the sinners' Friend.

C. NEWMAN HALL, "FRIEND OF SINNERS, LORD OF GLORY"

"I see your innocence; wait for my justice."

"Let the Almighty answer me. Let my accuser write out the charges against me. I would face the accusation proudly. I would wear it like a crown." JOB 31:35-36

Every now and then a story shows up on the news about someone who served time for a crime he or she didn't commit. After years behind bars, the person was finally released when new evidence found someone else guilty.

Free at last, the acquitted person faced an uphill battle to restore his or her life. Time lost with loved ones, devastated reputation, destruction of others' trust, stilted career advancement, financial instability, insecure future, missed vacations . . . those are only a few of the enormous consequences the wrongly accused paid unnecessarily.

Can anything be done to make it right? Is it even possible to recover lost time? And where was justice when it was originally needed?

Justice by human scales is faulty, to say the least. We're rarely able to see every hidden truth necessary to dole out justice accurately—obvious when an innocent person's life is derailed by a wrong verdict.

Being wrongly accused is humiliating and embarrassing. It cuts to our core, although we have no reason to feel guilty. The idea that others look at us as guilty twists us up inside because we're better than that accusation. We want to be seen for the honest people we strive to be.

In addition to his other losses, Job bore the pain of a loss of reputation. Every time he opened his eyes, he looked into someone else's that questioned his character. How heart-wrenching it must have been to see doubt muddle compassion from others. The only thing that kept him going was his trust in the Almighty as his final defense. God saw everything and knew Job's innocence.

When there is no earthly reason to rest, rest in the knowledge that God sees you. He knows your innocence. His justice on your behalf will be supreme.

TALK TO HIM

"Father, I am grateful that the scales of your justice are faultless. I am counting on them to be so. Please help me to trust you with my innocence."

God's mill grinds slow, but sure.

GEORGE HERBERT

May 30 JOB 38:1–40:2

"In your questions for me, do not lose sight of who I AM."

"Do you still want to argue with the Almighty? You are God's critic, but do you have the answers?" JOB 40:2

When we're going through something difficult, it's easy to start excusing our doubts, confusion, and even bitterness toward God because we're at the end of our strength. When we think we can't take anything more, our questions often take on a cynical tone, as if we're attempting to hold the reins on our full venting—as if we could cover the true depths of our negativity from almighty God.

Job reached that point. He wanted to give up. He wished God would let him give up. And he spoke his mind fully about his disappointment in the God he had obeyed faithfully—the same God who continued to let Job hurt so much. None of it made sense to Job, and his doubts about his circumstances veered too closely into becoming doubts about God's goodness. He didn't turn his back on God, but he did lose clarity of God's character because God did not act within the patterns Job had previously experienced of him. Job's life was great before everything fell apart. He had lived above troubles until he nearly drowned from a sudden deluge of them. The waves crashing around him blurred his vision of the God he had known his whole life.

Although God undoubtedly grieved over Job's hardships, and he certainly blessed Job after the terrible season was over, he spared no words clearing up his identity for Job—and Job's rightful place of humility before him.

God will always be true to his character. He will always be good and loving. Always, always.

Don't let your pain blur your vision of him.

TALK TO HIM

"Lord, please don't just clear my vision—please help me plant myself before you, so closely that I can't see problems to the right or left. Thank you for remaining true to yourself—and to me."

Be Thou my Vision, O Lord of my heart;
Naught be all else to me, save that Thou art.
Thou my best Thought, by day or by night,
Waking or sleeping, Thy presence my light.

TRANSLATED BY MARY E. BYRNE, "BE THOU MY VISION"

✿

"I may test your loyalty to me; never underestimate the importance of every thought, word, and action to make sure they pass the test."

"I was talking about things I knew nothing about, things far too wonderful for me." JOB 42:3

"I had only heard about you before, but now I have seen you with my own eyes." What profound thoughts Job wrapped up in those words from verse 5! Although he had lived obediently to God long before God allowed his faith to be tested, Job really got to see God through his trials. With his better vision, he came to understand the importance of his loyalty to his Lord, and he realized that he hadn't voiced his complaints from an attitude of resting faith.

God knows we hurt sometimes, and he shares all our sorrows with us. Yet in our grieving, he also wants us to carefully watch our attitudes, words, and actions so our trust in him speaks more loudly than our complaints. Keeping a lid on our negativity doesn't diminish the validity of our pain; however, it will please God, and it may even protect our outlook since negativity usually compounds itself. Once we give in to it, it's hard to stop it.

Instead of spending our energy reserves (that are already limited by difficult circumstances) venting our frustrations, we're much better off giving our best efforts to God by trusting him to bring us to a healing place. As we do that, we will notice there isn't room in our lives for time wasted on unhelpful attitudes when we need the benefits of a positive outlook more than ever.

Job realized these truths after God pointed them out. We can think of Job 42 as advance warning to make sure we pass life's tests with heaven's highest marks.

TALK TO HIM

"Heavenly Father, when I'm too tired to speak or even think positively, please quiet me with your presence. Help me to wait well while I trust you to move me through this difficulty."

The usual fortune of complaint is to excite contempt more than pity.

SAMUEL JOHNSON

June 1 PSALM 5:1-12

"When you come to me, expect me to respond."

Listen to my voice in the morning, LORD. Each morning I bring my requests to you and wait expectantly. PSALM 5:3

After many days of studying the heaviness of Job's story, it's time for the refreshment of the Psalms. One theme that carries over from Job is that of expecting God to hear and respond. Like Job, King David poured out his heart to God with the expectation that he would be heard and cared for.

When people complain about their prayer life or think God doesn't answer their prayers, perhaps some of the fault is their own because they pray without faith instead of praying expectantly. God loves it when we take him at his word, believing that we have a captive audience in him. He loves to hear from us, and he loves even more when we believe that he longs to listen and respond to us.

David packed huge emotion into his writings, holding nothing back from the Lord he loved and served. From his psalms, it's easy to imagine that God filled David's first waking thoughts each day. Even when agony consumed his words, he turned his thoughts in a more positive direction by the end of the psalm. He believed God. That much is obvious.

We can believe God every bit as much as David did because God assures his presence with us just as he did for David. When you pray, expect him to be waiting on the receiving end. Your prayer life is one area in which it is good to assume. It's good to take for granted that he hears you because he promises the comforting guarantee of his attention to those who belong to him.

You have all his attention all the time. He is your God, and he's waiting now to hear from you.

TALK TO HIM

"Father God, I'm humbled that you wait for me to approach you and blessed that you want me to expect you to respond. Thank you for your attentive love. Please help my life speak to others of the closeness they can have with you too."

They never sought in vain that sought the Lord aright!

ROBERT BURNS

"Do you know the lengths I go to save you?"

He led me to a place of safety; he rescued me because he delights in me. PSALM 18:19

Why does God save us? Not only did he choose to be our eternal Savior, but he rescues us daily from dangers only he knows about. Someday in eternity, if we have a chance to watch events of our lives, we'll be shocked to see how often he came to our aid when we had no idea we needed help.

But again, why does he do it? Having existed for an eternity before he created us, God had it made. No chaos, no evil, no sinful humans messing up his world—pure and simple peace. Yet he exchanged all those perks for an eternity with unholy creations who would bring him heartache until he'd have to fix everything.

A human being wouldn't bother. How fortunate we are that God is not human!

God loves to love. He loves to shine his glory on us, despite the turmoil we bring him every day. Even when we think our hearts are his, we still are one breath away from making a mistake because we're faulty—there's no way around it. Yet he loves us enough to storm the skies to rescue us. Psalm 18 provides incredible behind-the-scenes imagery into his passionate love that defeats dangers threatening his own. Nothing can stop him from saving you.

If you haven't discovered that you are his delight, it's time to study Psalm 18. Who would fight this much for anyone he didn't cherish? The God of the universe adores you. Take that knowledge into your day, and rest in his rescuing embrace.

TALK TO HIM

"Father God, I'm so thankful to be safe with you. Please remind me that my enemies are not safe with you, and that I can rest assured."

The chariot! the chariot! its wheels roll in fire,
As the Lord cometh down in the pomp of His ire!
Lo! self moving it drives on its pathway of cloud,
And the heavens with the burden of Godhead are bowed.
The glory! the glory! around Him are poured
Mighty hosts of the angels that wait on the Lord;
And the glorified saints and the martyrs are there,
And there all who the palm wreaths of victory wear.

AUTHOR UNKNOWN, "THE CHARIOT"

June 3 PSALM 24:1-10

"Do you know what it means for you that nothing can defeat me?"

Who is the King of glory? The LORD, *strong and mighty; the* LORD, *invincible in battle.*

PSALM 24:8

When King David worshiped, he really worshiped. Without holding back, he laid himself out before the Lord's supremacy.

But who is this God you worship? He is invincible. Invincible. And his invincibility means a great deal for you. It means, first of all, that you chose the right God—make that the only God—worthy of your soul-deep worship. But beyond that primary truth, his invincibility also guarantees your invincibility. There's a mind-blowing thought. Yes, you win some and lose some in this life. But your ultimate, eternal victory is sure when you stand on God's side.

David knew about battles, in actual warfare as well as struggles personally and as king. He knew the thrill of entering his city gates as the victor, welcomed by streams of devoted people, hailed with cries of support and praise.

For anyone who needs a victory cheer, this psalm is it. Reading Psalm 24 with greater understanding of David's perspective adds to the passion of his words. He is with the King of glory today—how surreal. He put his heart into worshiping God while he lived on earth; imagine the joy he pours into worship now that he can do it in person.

Because David followed God, he found out firsthand what it means that nothing can defeat him. What victory do you need today? Lay your heart out before the King of glory, and let him lead you straight into his arms with his overcoming power.

TALK TO HIM

"I'm so glad, God, that you are the ultimate winner. Thank you for sharing your invincibility over death with me. Please help me walk through this life in your victory."

David with a shepherd's sling and five stones,
Met the giant on the field all alone,
Trusting in the Lord, he knew what God had said,
By faith he saw the victory ahead.
Victory ahead, victory ahead,
Through the blood of Jesus, victory ahead.
Trusting in the Lord, I hear the conqueror's tread,
By faith I see the victory ahead.

WILLIAM GRUM, "VICTORY AHEAD"

"Learn the hidden joys of waiting on me."

Yet I am confident I will see the LORD*'s goodness while I am here in the land of the living.*

PSALM 27:13

Anticipation. When it revolves around something positive, we love it. When it focuses fearfully on something dreaded, we can't shake it off quickly enough.

Psalm 27 is loaded with David's anticipations. From preparing himself for coming uncertainties, to seeking God's protection during trouble, to letting his excitement grow at the thought of God's goodness yet to come, David's words carry great anticipation for the future.

Anticipation involves waiting. For many of us, this in-between phase is a difficult road to travel when we either can't wait for the future or we shake our heads at the thought of it. We want to get to the point already, and we don't appreciate a horizon that seems to hang forever unreachable in front us.

We don't like to wait for God's timing, but as verse 11 alludes to, waiting is prime training ground for learning how to live. It's by walking his path that we reach his full blessings for us at the horizon.

Waiting well requires courage and patience, as David noted in verse 14. And, as verse 4 states, it also takes deliberate resolve about our main priority—that is, to make God number one in our lives.

God offers us unique joy during the waiting periods. We focus on him more determinedly, and we don't bother with trivial side roads because we just want to stay close to him to discover where he will lead us.

We're all waiting for something all the time. Whether you're anticipating a major event or are looking forward to the smallest perk, learn the joys of waiting on God.

TALK TO HIM

"God, I'm going to be honest. I hate to wait. There, I said it. It's out. But, Lord, you have things to teach me in the between times, so please help me learn to wait well—and even to enjoy anticipating all you'll do."

There are not three stages in spiritual life—worship, waiting, and work. Some of us go in jumps like spiritual frogs, we jump from worship to waiting, and from waiting to work. God's idea is that the three should go together.

OSWALD CHAMBERS

June 5 PSALM 34:1-22

"Discover how my presence in you can radiate through you."

Those who look to him for help will be radiant with joy. PSALM 34:5

Although it isn't officially summer yet, depending on where you live, you very well could be feeling summer heat already. As spring days brighten and lengthen, the sun radiates with increasing warmth over the land, beckoning us outdoors, where new life explodes everywhere. Our faces color beneath the rays, and energy pulses freshly through our veins. There is something healing about summer, as creation is refreshed and heavy layers of clothing are shed for lighter garments that allow us to breathe easier.

God's joy is to our souls what the sun's rays are to a winter-weary world. Radiant heat like the sun's works best the closer we move to the source, which explains why the climate stays warmer near the equator. Similarly, God's joy emanates through us best when we remain close to him.

David discovered God's joy through the circumstances that tested his faith and drove him close to his Protector. When he was desperate, he prayed and experienced God's help and goodness. He turned to God for protection and found that living within the Almighty's presence brought him everything he needed. He stayed near to his heavenly Father during his many troubles, coming to understand personally how it feels to be rescued from a crushed spirit.

Throughout it all, he planted himself near God, and God radiated joy through David in increasing measure.

Whether or not you're in a winter season of life, draw close to God's warmth, shed the heavy layers of burden, and let him radiate joy through you.

TALK TO HIM

"Lord, I'm ready for lightness. Whether or not you change my circumstances, I will stay close to you where your joy will radiate through me."

Stay with me, God. The night is dark,
The night is cold: my little spark
Of courage dies. The night is long;
Be with me, God, and make me strong.

A SOLDIER—HIS PRAYER

"I created your heart and its desires; discover what it means to make me your delight."

Commit everything you do to the LORD. Trust him, and he will help you. PSALM 37:5

Psalm 37:4 is a favorite verse of many. It isn't difficult to see why since it's all about getting what we want. Be happy about your relationship with the Lord, and he will give you your desires. Pretty cut-and-dried.

Or is it?

Taken out of context, it appears to be a simple formula that says, "Go to God for happiness, and he will give you what you want." However, its message is not about our desires being the be-all-end-all purpose for making God our top priority. We do not exist for ourselves; in fact, God doesn't exist for us either. He loves to pour blessings onto his children, but his primary goal (and his right as God) is to glorify himself.

Verse 5 illuminates verse 4's true meaning. When we commit our whole selves to God to do with us as he pleases, he will help us with our desires. In other words, he will plant the desires in our hearts that he wants us to have. His desires will become ours, and he will find joy in granting us what he wants for us. When we are tightly linked to his heart, we will want those same things instead of the selfish desires we used to chase.

And in a clever twist, once we make God our main purpose, we're not so concerned with our own pleasures because he fills us deep down with himself. All earthly pleasures—even the genuinely great ones—pale in comparison.

Your Creator knows what's best for you. He loves to see you smile from an overflowing heart of joy. He has your desires in mind, so you can take your own mind off of them and focus on him. That shift in focus is the way to discover what it means to be delighted in God.

Leave your desires with him, and find out what else he has for you.

TALK TO HIM

"Father, my heart is filled with wants, many of them oriented around myself. Please help me find my true delight in you and leave all those other desires to you to handle."

Praise God, from whom all blessings flow!
DOXOLOGY

June 7 PSALM 46:1-11

"Find out what it means to know that I am God."

"Be still, and know that I am God!" PSALM 46:10

Psalm 46 opens with a world in turmoil—earthquakes coming, mountains trembling and crumbling, oceans roaring and surging. It's an earth on the verge of destruction.

But then the psalmists switch their focus. The scenes of devastation fade into the quietness of a gentle river tripping along through God's beloved city. Its waves carry joy into God's dwelling place, and his presence protects the city from threats of annihilation.

The focus changes again, this time to explain that, yes, the world is bent on ruin. However, almighty God is bent on destroying anything that opposes him and his people. So enemies, watch out. His victory is sure, and he ferociously defends the ones he loves.

If you belong to God, you are that city where God dwells. He calls your heart home and takes seriously his role as your defender. Your heart welcoming him makes him glad, and he will move heaven and earth to protect his investment in you.

God's presence is utterly real in your life, whether you feel it or not. Sometimes you might sense him close by when a trickle of peace meanders through your thoughts. Other times you hope to hear his thundering voice command his armies in your defense.

Just as you would give all to keep your home safe, God already gave everything to ensure his home in you is secure. Once his Spirit lives within you, invading enemies cannot set up camp. They may attack. In fact, they will attack. But they cannot take over what God has claimed. Your future is stable when you invite God to rule and protect your life.

Allow yourself the luxury of being quiet with him now. Enjoy being sheltered by your King and Defender, the Love of your life.

And know that he is God once more today.

TALK TO HIM

"Lord, I'm so glad you decided to live within me. Thank you for the ever-present peace and protection you offer. Please help me rest in the understanding of what it means that you are my God."

When you close your doors, and make darkness within, remember never to say that you are alone, for you are not alone; nay, God is within.

EPICTETUS, DISCOURSES, BK. I, CH. 14

"Let me love you despite your mistakes."

Purify me from my sins, and I will be clean; wash me, and I will be whiter than snow.

PSALM 51:7

It's gardening time. If you have a green thumb, you have probably worked it into the soil by now, nurturing flowers, fruits, vegetables, grass seed . . . a cornucopia of budding growth. You also have the mud-stained clothes to prove it. Anyone who has won against a ground-in stain would vouch for the cleaner that made their whites whiter and rejuvenated filthy fabric.

Those who have fought stains may also gain a glimpse into God's heart when it comes to cleansing the stain of sin from our souls. King David wrote Psalm 51 at a point of remorse for his adultery with Bathsheba. Without God's cleansing, he would have been forever stained by his actions. Fortunately, he knew God's purification was worth humbling himself for; he needed to be clean, but he also needed to come to terms with God's desire to make him clean.

Facing our mistakes is humbling; letting ourselves receive love despite them is doubly so. We want the ability to clean up our act so we don't have to owe anything more to anyone. When we're already feeling lousy because we've made a mess, it's even tougher to let someone carry the burden of making things right. It's as if we've lost the chance to make ourselves feel better through penance.

Yet God invites us to let him be our Cleanser. It's useless for us to try to fix ourselves, anyway, because we're so steeped in sin. Someone who is up to their elbows in mud can't expect to clean up someone else without adding their own filth to the process. We can't do it for others, and we can't do it for ourselves.

But God can, and he longs for the opportunity. He sees more than your mistakes. Let him wipe the mud from your eyes so you can see what he sees.

TALK TO HIM

"Lord, I'm a mess. I try to cover it up, but I know the truth. I am tired of hurting you, so please clean me up because I can't do it myself."

Oh! precious is the flow
That makes me white as snow;
No other fount I know,
Nothing but the blood of Jesus.

ROBERT LOWRY, "NOTHING BUT THE BLOOD"

June 9 PSALM 61:1–62:12

"Let me be for you a rock of refuge and rest, a safe tower where no enemy dares to tread."

Lead me to the towering rock of safety, for you are my safe refuge, a fortress where my enemies cannot reach me. PSALM 61:2-3

When someone has a chronic case of complaints, we joke that the world is out to get them. Some people stay so wrapped up in whatever is wrong with their lives (whether it's real or perceived) that they develop a skewed view of reality.

It's unlikely the entire world is against anyone. However, it's entirely likely that most of us feel at times like no one defends us, a reality that isn't much better than imagining a world of enemies.

We don't know when David discovered God as his refuge, his place of safety and peace. But it's certain that he did. From what we can tell from the Bible, he started getting to know God at a fairly young age. That means he walked with God through a variety of vulnerabilities, from those of youth to greater ones as he led God's nation. As a shepherd boy, he faced dangers from wild animals and Goliath. As a king-in-waiting, he faced dangers from King Saul and his own limited wisdom to lead his men. Then as king, he dealt with enemy nations and again his own limited wisdom to lead the Israelites.

He needed a place of refuge and security to cope with everyday pressures. As God led David deeper in life to prepare him for increasing challenges and more responsibilities, life led David deeper with God.

When you feel like you don't have a friend in your corner, God is your safety. Even if you feel like the world is yours to command, God still is your only place of true security.

Life is uncertain, and those uncertainties are unnerving. Seek God as your rock and your rest, and rise with him above it all.

TALK TO HIM

"Lord, thank you for holding and protecting me."

Let nothing disturb thee,
Let nothing affright thee,
All passeth away,
God alone will stay,
Patience obtaineth all things.
Who God possesseth, is lacking in nothing
God alone sufficeth.

TERESA OF AVILA

"Look for the awesome miracles I do in your life; I fit them uniquely to you."

Come and listen, all you who fear God, and I will tell you what he did for me. PSALM 66:16

If you could ask God for anything, what would it be? Think along the lines of impossibilities, otherwise known as miracles. What would you love to see him do, perfectly suited to your need? Do your thoughts flicker to a health issue? a financial need? a wayward family member? Whatever burden crosses your mind, you may feel as though it's an impossibility to bother hoping for a miracle because God seems to send those few and far between, and generally not to you.

Don't sell him short.

It's obvious by the mention of the Red Sea parting that this psalmist had heard ancient stories of God's miracles on the Israelites' behalf. After generations of slavery in Egypt, surely the Israelites weren't sure how God would save them. Many of them probably doubted he would. Behind them, the Egyptians raced to catch up; in front of them, the deep waters flowed menacingly. No doubt they prayed for God's rescue; possibly some of them wondered if their prayers were in vain. Probably not too many, if any, expected God to split the sea so they could walk through on dry land.

God must have smiled.

God knows your need is every bit as enormous to you as the Israelites' need for a solution at the Red Sea. We tend to think of only his big answers as miracles, but he works miraculously anytime he does something we couldn't do ourselves.

He gave the Israelites the answer he knew they needed. He will answer you in a way precisely suited to your need. However, he will answer in his way and time. He didn't part the sea until the people stood on its brink, yet he allowed plenty of time for their complete rescue and their enemies' destruction.

He will get to your need on time too.

TALK TO HIM

"Father God, I trust you with my needs. Please use those needs to teach me to look for your miraculous touch in my life."

There are only two ways to live your life. One is as though nothing is a miracle. The other is as though everything is a miracle.

RICHARD CRASHAW

June 11 PSALM 80:1-19

"Feel my face shining down on you."

Turn us again to yourself, O God. Make your face shine down upon us. Only then will we be saved. PSALM 80:3

Imagine all the mistakes you've made in your lifetime—not pleasant memories, but consider them purposefully for a few minutes. Now imagine the number of your mistakes quadrupled, and suppose that's how many you could have made if God hadn't altered your course through discipline.

What a relief that God corrects us!

Wherever did we get the idea that discipline is a bad thing? Just because it feels uncomfortable at the time, we lose sight of the good it does us and the trouble it spares us. In reality, God shines his smile on us when he loves us enough to turn us back to himself. Discipline shows its glow because it wears the purity of God's character. It proves that we are loved and cherished by the King of kings, who doesn't let his own go without fighting for them.

It is only through his guiding hand that we are saved . . . for eternity, yes, but on a daily basis as well here on earth. Sometimes mercy and love must use the hook end of the shepherd's staff to pull us back to a safe path. Better a little discomfort for the short term than to suffer untold pain forever.

Get to know God's face of discipline as he shines on you. The glow of his smile will light your way back to him and lead the way to heaven with him someday. His is a face you'll know forever. Accept his discipline by looking to him and returning his smile.

TALK TO HIM
"Thank you for your sweet smile, Lord. Even when I don't deserve it, you shine your light on my way and draw me back to you. Thank you for proving your love by disciplining me."

May God's eyes lighting my way keep me from tripping over my own foolishness.
AUTHOR UNKNOWN

"I can turn your low times into seasons of deep refreshment."

When they walk through the Valley of Weeping, it will become a place of refreshing springs.

PSALM 84:6

You've heard the saying, "The higher you rise, the farther you fall." It's sort of a depressing thought. Flipping it around, we get a more encouraging picture: The lower you fall, the deeper God goes to rescue you.

Suppose your circumstances look like a pit in the ground. The farther you sink, the harder it is to climb out on your own. Descend far enough into that depression, and others can't reach you either. Sometimes it's easy to feel lost and wonder whether anyone even knows how low you are. However, those deep places are prime situations for God to prove the lengths of his arms to reach down and save you.

We can find God's deepest refreshment oftentimes at our lowest points. It might seem backward, but there is a bright spot in the darkest depths because we meet God alone there and learn to know him in new ways.

We love the good times. But they don't usually drive us to go deep with the Lord. We tend to coast without putting our all into pursuing him. Yet when he's our only light and our only hope, our desperation sends us cruising to him. In our search for a way out, we discover we crave his presence even more than a quick rescue.

As good as life is, it still tosses us into the pits now and then. When you're down, open your eyes to God's light. He is there with you, and his presence can calm you enough to wait with him until he settles you on solid ground. Until then, get to know your heavenly companion. If you haven't seen his light in the low places, ask him to reveal himself. He loves to show you greater depths of himself. When he does, the low places look vastly brighter with his light refreshing your world.

TALK TO HIM

"I have been in the pits for a while, Lord, and I'm ready to see more of you. I know I am not lost when your light reveals yourself to me. Please open my eyes to see you better."

God stooping shows sufficient of His light
For us i' the dark to rise by. And I rise.

ROBERT BROWNING

June 13 PSALM 94:1-23

"I am your God who avenges you."

Joyful are those you discipline, LORD, those you teach with your instructions. You give them relief from troubled times until a pit is dug to capture the wicked. PSALM 94:12-13

Have you noticed that life's lessons build on each other? The reading two days ago focused on how God shines on us to discipline us to turn back to him. Yesterday's selection illuminated truths about God's light as refreshment when we are in the pits. Psalm 94:12-13 wraps those themes together and then moves forward with a focus on how God deals with those who make themselves enemies of his loved ones.

Our low times might come at the hands of others, and when they do, God shines his justice. Their audacity at thinking God won't avenge his people eventually will return to haunt them. Verse 23 says, "God will turn the sins of evil people back on them. He will destroy them." God's vengeance casts them into the pit, but it's a pit where God's light does not shine.

Although God's discipline results in joy for those who turn back to him, his vengeance against his enemies serves up nothing but doom. He does not shine his light as comfort and warmth for them. His presence is nowhere to be found for their refreshment.

We can be comforted knowing our place is secure with him, and comforted further still knowing a day is coming when God will end all wickedness so it can never hurt us again.

God takes care of his own. There is no denying that suffering can reach extremes we think we can't survive. But rest your remaining energy on his faithfulness. His hope reigns in any suffering if we turn toward his light and trust him to provide us another moment of faith to keep looking for him.

Look for him once more.

TALK TO HIM

"Lord, thank you for avenging me. Please help me to wait on you for that, trusting that the harm others have done won't go unpunished by you."

Wait on the Lord and keep His way;
He will exalt thee, nor delay
To give the land to thee;
And when the wicked are cut off,
The wicked who against thee scoff,
Their judgment thou shalt see.

AUTHOR UNKNOWN, "THE GOOD MAN'S STEPS ARE LED ARIGHT"

"Spare yourself trouble by learning from others' mistakes."

"Your ancestors tested and tried my patience." PSALM 95:9

There really aren't any new ways people find to reject God. As depressing as it is, human nature has been twisted for so long, plenty of time has passed for sin to perfect itself. You would think that we would have learned not to insist on making the same mistakes people have made since Adam and Eve's day, but apparently we're not as smart as we would like to think. Either that, or intelligence doesn't automatically assume good habits.

When we sin by opting for anything that doesn't please God, we choose a road of heartache. We complain about our troubles because we don't enjoy feeling pain, yet we deliberately bring them on ourselves when we try God's patience through disobedience. Disobedience never brings blessing, just as obedience always brings it. The effects may be delayed for a time, but our behavior—good and bad—always impacts us and usually affects others as well.

Instead of trying out sin to discover its consequences, the wise option is to study what others through the ages have endured because of it. Not only do we have the benefit of testimonies from other believers today, but we have a storehouse of lessons at our fingertips in the Bible.

Today's generations have more reason than ever to do what's right because we have more collected wisdom of the past to build our lives upon. This very day holds countless opportunities to choose well.

TALK TO HIM

"Lord, thank you for the benefit of the lessons in your Word. Please help me pay attention to what others have experienced because of sin so I can avoid the trouble it brings."

The time is always right to do what is right.

MARTIN LUTHER KING JR.

June 15 PSALM 103:1-22

"When you experience my forgiveness and healing, you will never be the same."

May I never forget the good things he does for me. He forgives all my sins and heals all my diseases. PSALM 103:2-3

One of God's greatest gifts to us is the gift of recollection. With it we can bring to mind pleasant thoughts of things we've done and remind ourselves how far we have come.

Even the memories steeped in sorrow serve a purpose because when we experience God's healing, past hurts take on a precious ache instead of an outright pain. They are evidence of God's gentle, personal touch that tells us he knows what we've been through and the thoughts that are forever imprinted within us.

Our memories also serve to keep us grounded on the basic foundations of our faith, namely that God forgave us and saved us from our sins. How quickly our minds overflow with here-and-now urgencies! Yet the here and now someday will fade to distant memories. On the other hand, our eternity with God will be completely free of a time frame. When we are finally with him, all we will know is his presence and his glory forever. We are wise to remember him often during this lifetime because everything we do on earth affects our heavenly rewards.

We were not created for the here and now. We were created for eternity. Be conscious about filing your experiences on earth into your memory bank. Make your memories—all of them, positive and negative—purposeful by letting his forgiveness and healing remind you of his Spirit working in you. Remember where he brought you from and his transforming power in your life. Take joy in knowing that your memories with him let you know you are continually changing to reflect his likeness.

TALK TO HIM

"Father God, someday I will look back on my life and remember the times I've pleased you and failed you. Please help me invest in memories yet to be made by investing myself in a deep, ever-growing closeness with you. Thank you for your beautiful salvation and healing touch."

While memory holds a seat
In this distracted globe. Remember thee!
WILLIAM SHAKESPEARE

"Enjoy my creation."

O LORD, what a variety of things you have made! In wisdom you have made them all.

PSALM 104:24

When God created the world, he could have done it with a snap of his fingers. He could have waved a careless hand and made things fall into place. He could have tossed a massive glob into space and let everything fall where it may.

He could have done any of those things. But he did not.

Far from taking the haphazard approach, God formed every detail with care, and Psalm 104 revels in the wonder of his methods. We are the beneficiaries of his intelligent design. His thoughtful wisdom infuses the starry curtain of the heavens, the winds that are his messengers, and the streams that gush down from the mountains to provide water for the animals.

What an awesome thought that we are formed by him. We received his personal touch to bring us to life, and if our hearts are sensitized to him working in the world, we can see his imprint whenever we look outside.

Forming anything requires care and time. It requires skill and patience, and a sense of ownership and pride. God invested all of those resources into his creation, and he still invests himself in our world.

You were formed by God Almighty, King of the universe, Creator and Lord over all. His touch, the very touch that brought you life, sustains you today. It comforts you when you hurt and offers peace during uncertain times.

Enjoy being his creation. He took great pride in forming you before you were born, and he still thrills to see you respond to his refining touch.

TALK TO HIM

"Lord, please never let me lose sight of you as the One who formed me and who knows me inside and out. Thank you for your ever-present touch on me and in your world. I love seeing your imprint everywhere!"

The planets in their stations list'ning stood,
While the bright pomp ascended jubilant.
Open, ye everlasting gates, they sung,
Open, ye heavens, your living doors; let in
The great Creator from his work return'd
Magnificent, his six days' work, a world.

JOHN MILTON, PARADISE LOST

June 17 PSALM 107:1-22

"What can you praise me for today?"

Has the LORD *redeemed you? Then speak out!* PSALM 107:2

Everyone has a story to tell, and everyone who has met God has something extra special to share.

Where does God appear in the pages of your story? Perhaps you became aware of him near the beginning, the table of contents of your life, when you learned early to anticipate his next appearance. Or maybe you first remember him around chapter three, well into the plot of your life but with plenty of action left. Others meet him after much of their story has unfolded, as twists and turns head toward a wonderful ending.

The Bible contains countless stories of God showing up in individual lives, sometimes quietly, other times with thunder, but always with life-changing effect and always with his glory and our redemption in mind.

God is all about praise and salvation—his praise and our salvation. Your story includes reasons to praise him that are universal, such as for his salvation, holiness, goodness, love, patience, and power. You also have reasons specific to your story, ways he has shown his love uniquely to you. His love fits each person, and the story he's writing with your life fits you and only you.

No one else can tell your story from your perspective. Someone God places in your life needs the encouragement of hearing how God moves in you. Someone will observe why you praise the Lord. And God himself deserves to hear from you, so let him have your praise, and let others hear it as well. Your story might not seem worthy of inspiring awe, but a life in God's hands is always miraculous. Don't hold back what God might want you to share about him.

TALK TO HIM

"Heavenly Father, only you can complete the story of my life to make it usable for someone else's benefit. Please help me know what to share and when, and please take all the credit for anything worthwhile about it."

I love to tell the story; more wonderful it seems
Than all the golden fancies of all our golden dreams.
I love to tell the story, it did so much for me;
And that is just the reason I tell it now to thee.

A. KATHERINE HANKEY, "I LOVE TO TELL THE STORY"

"Enjoy the stillness after the storm."

What a blessing was that stillness as he brought them safely into harbor! PSALM 107:30

Lightning shocks the darkened sky, and thunder trembles the sea air. Torrents of water cut through the atmosphere. Wave rolls upon wave, tossing boats over the crests, as the depths surge with unease and a storm takes over the earth. Then finally the rain stops. The clouds pull back their fury, and the waves cease the binge and purge of everything in their path. Quiet permeates with audible stillness.

Such are the storms in our lives. Troubles scramble our circumstances and batter our emotions, then eventually retreat when God calls them down from their rampage. After he preserves us through a tumultuous season, he plants our feet on restful ground to give us time to process what we endured. Our minds settle, and our hearts resume a normal, tolerable rhythm. Freed from the constant din of stress, our ears welcome the sound of peace.

Peace is always a feel-good emotion, but peace after a storm is especially sweet. We appreciate peace and quiet more when we've experienced their lack. It's amazing how something can be so powerful in its nonexistence, but when peace is absent we feel it.

The Israelites knew what the absence of peace felt like while they were exiled to Babylon. Their world had been capsized during storms of war. Some dealt with their losses well; others turned from the safe harbor of the Lord's presence. Finally God calmed the downpour of suffering and returned them to their homeland, where they rejoiced in the stillness and safety of his harbor.

Whatever he has brought you through—or is seeing you through—take time to enjoy the safety of his harbor. Soak up the rays of his peace, and thank him for holding you in the storm and bringing back the calm.

TALK TO HIM

"Father, I love your peace, but so often it feels fleeting. Please help me soak up you during the stormy times as well as the calm ones. Then I will enjoy your peace regardless of the weather in my life."

God moves in a mysterious way
His wonders to perform;
He plants his footsteps in the sea
And rides upon the storm.

WILLIAM COWPER, "GOD MOVES IN A MYSTERIOUS WAY"

June 19 PSALM 112:1-10

"I love to see you follow in the footsteps of my generosity."

Light shines in the darkness for the godly. They are generous, compassionate, and righteous. . . . They confidently trust the LORD *to care for them.* PSALM 112:4, 7

Generosity in a Christian is oftentimes one sign of a secure faith. Generous people don't need to hoard their resources for fear of running empty because they are confident that God will provide all they need.

When we measure our wealth first of all by the depth of our relationship with the Lord, we always come out rich indeed if we have given our whole lives to him. God withholds nothing of worth from those who belong to him. Our experiences of his generosity prompt us to follow his lead as givers. Because he is God, he needs nothing. And because he takes care of his children, we need nothing more than what he provides.

What does his wealth look like? Well, it's true that he provides financially for us. But those gifts only hint at his other ones. Many of his blessings hold value to his followers but are lost to a world that chases material wealth as its highest goal. Peace and joy, discernment and wisdom, hope and strength—these are benefits that increase in worth as our faith grows richer.

We receive those blessings through his Holy Spirit within us, and we can have as much of him as we seek. His Spirit's wealth is directly linked to how passionately we want to experience him. He is ready to fill us and show us how to bless others by sharing the wealth he shares with us.

God's wealth is meant to be passed on, not stockpiled for our use alone. There is plenty of it to go around, more than we could ever think of using up.

Don't miss true wealth during your lifetime. Getting ahead in material gains could leave you behind for eternity if you pursue it to the expense of a vital relationship with God as your Savior. Investing in your relationship with him and with others will bring you more riches than you ever could spend.

TALK TO HIM

"Thank you, Lord, for being so lavish with your goodness. Please help me share willingly of your love and the blessings you have given me."

Not he who has much is rich, but he who gives much.

ERICH FROMM

"My love for you will grow your love for me."

What can I offer the L*ORD* *for all he has done for me?* PSALM 116:12

Do you know why you love the Lord? Before running through a list of common reasons given, consider what specifically you have grown to love about him. No one's list will look exactly like yours because no one has your history with him.

So now, why do you love him? Although true love isn't based on what others do for us, our hearts often are won by the outpouring of someone else's unselfishness. God woos us with his abundant love and by revealing himself to us in the circumstances of life.

The writer of Psalm 116 learned to love God for his listening Spirit and his kindness, goodness, and mercy. In finding protection, rest, healing, salvation, and freedom in a relationship with God, the psalmist's heart was won over as God changed his life forever. In the privacy of his innermost heart, he came to know the depths of God's love and couldn't help but return it.

Unless we are closed to God's love, it pulls our hearts toward him. As we learn to love him in return, our natural desire deepens to give our best back to him as an offering. While it's true that we never can love him to the extent that he loves us, he only wants all we have—nothing more, nothing less.

Spend some time thinking through specific ways God has worked to win you to himself. He knows all about you, and he loves his history with you. You are not common to him; he cares uniquely for you as if you were the only one to shower with his love. It is nothing short of amazing. Act on your heart's response to him. Don't hold back the love that yearns to grow closer to him every day.

TALK TO HIM

"Father God, I don't always understand love, but I am so grateful you do. Please pull me closer to you so I can feel your heart more fully and know your love more deeply."

Love is an image of God, and not a lifeless image, but the living essence of the divine nature which beams full of all goodness.

MARTIN LUTHER

June 21 PSALM 119:1-72

"I wrote my Word for you so you can hear from me daily."

Give me life through your word. PSALM 119:37

Somehow through the years the Bible has developed a reputation for being a book of dos and don'ts, mostly don'ts in many people's opinion. Psalm 119 straightens out the true nature of God's Word.

God gave us his Word for the purpose of life and freedom, not to bind us to an existence of rules and regulations. Just look at a few of the benefits we receive in the Bible:

We find knowledge and reasons to praise him (verse 12).
We find joy in remembering his words (verse 16).
We learn to long for his regulations (verse 20).
We soak up good advice (verse 24).
We're refreshed by studying what he wrote to us (verse 25).
We receive his encouragement and comfort for our sorrows (verse 28).
We learn to look at ourselves honestly (verse 29).
We're privileged to know his instructions (verse 29).
We're freed from shame (verse 31).

Who knew the Bible contained so much practical help that reaches into the confusion of life and blesses us in the midst of good times and bad? God is thoroughly spiritual, but he is also utterly practical when it comes to knowing what we need. He sees beyond what is immediately evident, straight into the crevices that shelter our true needs. He is about so much more than squeezing us into an unexciting, generic mold to suit himself.

Ultimately, he gives us life through his Word. Soak up the life-giving nature of this psalm, and take delight in the letter of life and love he wrote to you.

TALK TO HIM

"Father, I love to read your Word and imagine you writing it to me. Thank you for your life that flows out of it."

The Bible, read in the right spirit and with the guidance
of good teachers, will bring us to Him.
C. S. LEWIS

"What if I were not on your side?"

The LORD keeps watch over you as you come and go, both now and forever. PSALM 121:8

If we could see what God sees, we would either be scared out of our wits or we would never stop thanking him for watching out for us.

Psalm 121 begins today's reading by getting our minds to consider God's 24-7 attentiveness to us. Then Psalm 124 comes in with a wallop by going deeper into our imaginations and prompting us to wonder just what his care spares us from.

What if the Lord were not on your side today? Would you even be here reading this if he hadn't been on your side yesterday? And how about tomorrow?

That near miss on the expressway . . .

The last-minute inspiration as a work deadline ran out . . .

The surge of energy to help you through a tough workout . . .

The boost of willpower to help you remain patient . . .

If we could see the resources we have because of God's power, we would approach each moment with purpose and deliberateness. We would bask in the security of knowing he truly does have us covered. And we would never cease to show him our amazement and gratitude for saving us time and again.

We can't see everything he sees, but we can trust that he rescues us constantly. And we can praise him for all the ways he works for our good that remain unknown to us during this life.

Sometimes what we don't see is heavenly when it helps us learn to trust him more.

TALK TO HIM

"Lord, trusting in you should be the easiest thing in the world to do, yet it seems to be a lifelong learning process. Thank you for being so trustworthy in ways I can't even see."

Some things have to be believed to be seen.

RALPH HODGSON

June 23 PSALM 130:1–131:3

“When was the last time you let me quiet your soul?”

I don’t concern myself with matters too great or too awesome for me to grasp. Instead, I have calmed and quieted myself. PSALM 131:1-2

Anxiety is a real energy drain. It twists up our insides, and regardless of how calm we might appear to others, we know the truth. When we’re a bundle of nerves, it’s tough to maintain clear thinking and common sense. Molehills become the proverbial mountains, growing larger until they loom over us and block our view of reality.

But anxiety doesn’t stop there. No, it starts shaking those mountains until the world around us seems to tremble with uncertainty and instability. Nothing feels secure, and we yearn for that far-distant last moment when we felt any sort of peace.

When we become deluged by an avalanche of anxiety, our thought life can’t manage to escape for a moment to be free of our troubles. Our concern compounds itself until there seems to be no way out from beneath the burden.

But those who know their God know the path through the mountain to the other side where calming freedom waits. Where is the entrance to that path? It is always at the place where we stop our racing thoughts and cease our attempts to solve issues that God never meant for us to solve. Some things are simply too complex, as ironic as it sounds.

When anxiety threatens to bury you, remember that God has already covered the issues that you can’t resolve on your own. So take the quiet route out of anxiety. Purposefully hand over your cares to God, and let him teach you to rest in the cover of quiet that he draws over your spirit.

TALK TO HIM

“Faithful Lord, I love your calming touch when I am full of nervous energy and lacking restful calm. Please speak into my anxieties and remind me to live simply in your care.”

Quiet, Lord, my froward heart,
Make me teachable and mild,
Upright, simple, free from art,
Make me as a weanèd child. . . .
What Thou shalt today provide,
Let me as a child receive;
What tomorrow may betide,
Calmly to Thy wisdom leave.

JOHN NEWTON, “QUIET, LORD, MY FROWARD HEART”

"What if I were all-powerful but not good?"

Praise the Lord, *for the* Lord *is good. . . . The* Lord *does whatever pleases him throughout all heaven and earth.* PSALM 135:3, 6

When you think of God, do you dwell more on his power or his love? Talk with people long enough about God, and it isn't too difficult to figure out whether they view him more as a harshly powerful dictator or a tender, loving Father. The responses depend to a great degree on people's backgrounds and their early experiences of religion.

For better or worse, we bring into adulthood many ideals that we observed or were taught during childhood. Also for better or worse, we tend to project our general view of authority onto God. If we have had bad experiences with rule makers or powerful people, we find it tough to believe that someone with control could use it for our benefit instead of merely as a restraint. Give a human the means and the right to rule unquestioned, and any one of us eventually would bring disaster on those under our control.

How fortunate we are that God is perfectly superior to us! He is the only One who truly has the right to do whatever he pleases, which in fact he does. Just think what that would mean if it pleased him to hurt us as much as possible. Just think what it would be like if Satan were more powerful than God.

Instead of favoring either his power or his love, revel in knowing the two work together as inseparable characteristics of the almighty lover of your soul. If you belong to him, rest assured that you are not only safe, but also cared for more than you can imagine.

TALK TO HIM

"Almighty Father God, my first love. You teach me every day what it feels like to be loved by the greatest Being in the world. That is a very humbling truth, and I am so grateful that your goodness and might work together. Thank you for being completely strong and utterly good."

God is not merely good, but goodness; goodness is not merely divine, but God.

C. S. LEWIS

June 25 PSALM 136:1-26

"Imagine being loved by me forever."

Give thanks to the L*ORD, for he is good! His faithful love endures forever.* PSALM 136:1

If you were to illustrate forever, what would it look like? Forever could resemble a sky full of clouds, where you keep jumping from one to the next without ever reaching the end. Or perhaps forever is like a bucket that never runs out of water to refresh your thirst or nurture a garden. Or better yet, forever could be an endless feast of your favorite foods that always fill you up but never make you too stuffed to stop eating.

It's challenging to imagine forever, even more so to imagine endless love. When God offers his love for eternity, we receive a double blessing. First of all, his love is blessing enough; but to think that he promises it to us forever is doubly good, beyond what we can get our minds around. He will never take a break from us—no hiatuses or furloughs or sabbaticals.

No matter how much we love someone, it's nice to have our own space now and then. We grow weary of giving and being on call for others. Most of us probably wouldn't mind a break from ourselves once in a while!

But God chooses to be with his children every minute, and he even wants to share forever with us, giving and loving and shining his glory over us. We can't understand why he offers us so much because we have limited capacities for showing patient love in our human strength. But we can find peace and hope in trusting that he is mighty enough to stay true to his plans by sticking around.

God's love for you endures through the joys and sorrows. It remains when life gets ugly and you are not your most attractive self. It holds on determinedly through everything his children throw at him.

Breathe deeply knowing his love will be there for you today, tomorrow, and until you no longer bother counting tomorrows because they will all be spent in his presence.

TALK TO HIM

"Lord, thank you for your enduring love. I count on you more than I realize, and I am so grateful that you are reliable with your forever love."

God's love here on earth is a taste of the wealth of eternity.

ANONYMOUS

"My hand always holds you, my custom creation."

I can never escape from your Spirit! I can never get away from your presence! PSALM 139:7

If you have ever studied astronomy, then you've probably felt awestruck by the universe. Even though our galaxy is on the medium to small side, it is still beyond what we can comprehend, and it's expanding all the time—just like the countless other galaxies out there.

Now take the image of our galaxy and place yourself in the middle of it. It's almost laughable how insignificant one human being appears compared to the scope of Creation—laughable until you realize you're that one human being, and sometimes you feel so insignificant that it panics your heart. The world can be a lonely place. Even with billions of other people filling the earth, it's possible to feel alone every day. Quite frankly, most of those billions probably do feel alone more often than the rest of us know. And the rest of us likely feel alone the remainder of the time.

Let's face it. We're small.

Well, God had the idea first that good things come in small packages because he made us insignificant humans to be his masterpieces, each one a reflection of his image. We might feel lost within the vastness of the universe, but the thing is, the universe fits in God's hand. We never leave his reach, and we are never without his touch.

We may be physically small, but when we invite him to be at home inside us, our hearts can grow large like his. They expand to share more of his Spirit with others; then, in welcoming God and others close to us, we lose that feeling of aloneness.

Next time loneliness hits, imagine yourself resting in the shelter of his palm, and realize being alone is an impossibility since his hand never lets you go.

TALK TO HIM

"Thank you, Lord, for banishing 'alone.' I love being held by you; please help me find ways to invite others into your sheltering touch."

The hand that was nailed to the cross of woe,
In love reaches out to the world below;
'Tis beckoning now to the souls that roam,
And pointing the way to the heav'nly home.

HARRIET H. PIERSON, "THE HAND THAT WAS NAILED TO THE CROSS"

June 27 PSALM 142:1–143:12

"People will let you down, and life will let you down. But I won't fail you."

Then I pray to you, O LORD. I say, "You are my place of refuge. You are all I really want in life."

PSALM 142:5

Do you have a drink handy? Water, tea, soda . . . anything to satisfy your thirst? The mention of it probably sent you reaching for a beverage.

Thirst carries an urgency not even hunger touches. It comes on unexpectedly sometimes, and when it does, it's almost impossible to ignore. Nothing else satisfies, and really nothing can take our minds off it. It's impatient and desperate.

David understood thirst of a different nature. He compared his desire for God to the thirst of a parched land. Nothing else could satisfy his need for God, and nothing made him so desperately aware of God's vital Spirit in his life. All around him, David felt the carnage of his failed faith in other people. Enemies hunted him, others ignored his needs—everyone let him down except God. Only God satisfied his soul's thirst because only God offers unfailing love and unrelenting presence. As a result, David discovered that God was all he really wanted. When God quenched the thirst of his soul, ultimately all was well. Without God, David was sure to die of a parched spirit.

Your thirsty soul must be satisfied as well, and like David, you won't find it in other people. As fulfilling as a healthy human relationship is, no mere person has God's ability to refresh and rehydrate your soul. Enough relational letdowns will leave you thirsting for him so much that the mention of his name sends you searching his Word and longing to connect with him in prayer.

When the thirst for him hits, drink up. His love for you will never run dry.

TALK TO HIM

"Father God, I understand soul-thirst, but I often need reminding that only you can quench it. Please help me turn to you sooner next time I need your hydration."

Jesus the water of life will give,
Freely to those who love Him.
Come to that fountain, oh drink, and live!
Freely, freely, freely;
Come to that fountain, oh, drink and live!
Flowing for those that love Him.

FANNY CROSBY, "THE WATER OF LIFE"

"Will you put your greatest energy into a relationship with me?"

Let all that I am praise the LORD. PSALM 146:1

We all have compartments in our lives: home, family, work, recreation, friends, church, spiritual life. Sometimes those areas overlap; sometimes one takes over for a time while the others suffer a bit. We only have so much energy and a limited number of hours each day, and more often than not we struggle to give as much attention as needed to all our compartments.

We would love to spend more time with family, but work deadlines loom. Ideally we want to break out of our everyday responsibilities; but our "free" moments get clogged like the sink, the water heater leaks, and the cat didn't make it to the litter box again. Pretty soon our storehouse of energy is empty.

Where is God in all this? Because he doesn't often take the role of the squeaky wheel, it is easy for us to grease the other areas, so to speak, just so they'll quiet their cacophony of chaos.

But we have it backward when we let our communication with God fall by the wayside. In addition to the plain fact that he deserves the best portion of our energy, he has a way of extending our resources for the other compartments when we give him first place. When we spend time praising him, we end up with greater peace, longer patience, and joy that transcends higher levels of stress. Not only that, but our efforts in the other areas become avenues to praise him more because we discover that we can worship him as we spend time with family, while we take time for recreation, or even as we work hard to meet job deadlines.

God is number one, and when we prioritize him in our lifestyle, we give him his due honor and set ourselves up for handling life more capably.

TALK TO HIM

"Lord, thank you for reminding me that you deserve top priority. Please help me give you my all, trusting that you will help the rest of life fall into proper place."

Put first things first and we get second things thrown in:
put second things first and we lose both first and second things.

C. S. LEWIS

June 29 PSALM 147:1-20

"I don't want you to prove you are powerful; I want you to show that you are mine."

He takes no pleasure in . . . human might. No, the LORD's delight is in those who fear him.
PSALM 147:10-11

If you could make sure the world knows one thing about you, what would that one thing be? Maybe it is most important that they remember you for your kindness—or maybe for reaching the top of the corporate ladder. How about for raising a solid family?

All are noteworthy achievements; some more than others, depending on who you ask. It is healthy to find satisfaction in doing a job well. We are created for purpose, and at the end of the day it feels good to know that the air we used was spent on worthwhile accomplishments. No one enjoys feeling useless. Yet if we get too caught up in our agendas, or in making names for ourselves, we lose focus of what God desires from us. More than anything, he wants us to be his.

He isn't impressed by the initials after your name pronouncing degrees earned. He cares far more about your soul than about the title on your business card. And although he desires that you value your relationships, particularly those at home, he wants more for you than even your loved ones offer.

For all your successes that earn you earthly recognition, God cares more that you belong to him. He wants your lifestyle to leave a trail of his Spirit's aroma of grace and peace and salvation. He also wants all your successes to point others to him, not to yourself.

Back to the original question about the one thing you want others to know about you. More than anything else, will they remember that you belong to God?

TALK TO HIM
"Father God, I am floored knowing I belong to you. It's the most amazing reality, but also easy to neglect. Please help me to be yours above all self-centered goals."

Am I willing to reduce myself simply to "me," determinedly to strip myself of all my friends think of me, of all I think of myself, and to hand that simple naked self over to God? Immediately I am, He will sanctify me wholly, and my life will be free from earnestness in connection with everything but God.

OSWALD CHAMBERS

"When it's all said and done, praise me."

Let everything that breathes sing praises to the LORD! Praise the LORD! PSALM 150:6

Since you're reading this, you obviously haven't said good-bye to the day yet. Therefore, you have a choice about how your day will end. By the time you're ready to put your head to the pillow tonight, you will likely have dealt with bunches of stresses, countless responsibilities, and only God knows how many issues that await your fix-it skills tomorrow. By the time you close your eyes tonight, you may not feel like praising.

But just for a moment, imagine ending each day with praiseworthy thoughts of God. Imagine looking to him before closing your eyes and offering him the final word on the previous hours. Imagine asking for his redemptive touch on the problems and concerns that barked at you all day long.

No matter how rotten a day can be, you have the opportunity every twenty-four hours to let the Lord have the last word. How sweet that is! The stressors and anxieties cannot reign over your awake time, and they need not rule your dreams, when you make a point to turn your last waking thoughts toward praising your Lord.

Psalm 150 provides a few suggestions for putting the day to bed. Read it tonight, and quiet yourself as you spend time with your Creator. Do it to refuse giving your struggles the power to get you down. Do it to remind yourself who really owns your time. Do it because God deserves it.

But by all means do it. Praise him with your last thoughts tonight.

TALK TO HIM

"Father, by the end of the day I'm so tired. But I know there is refreshment in praising you, and I know you deserve it. Please accept my offering of worship as I close my eyes tonight."

Angels, help us to adore Him;
Ye behold Him face to face;
Sun and moon, bow down before Him,
Dwellers all in time and space.
Alleluia! Alleluia!
Praise with us the God of grace.

HENRY F. LYTE, "PRAISE, MY SOUL, THE KING OF HEAVEN"

July 1 PROVERBS 1:1-19; 2:1-11; 3:1-12

"Don't become so stuck in your opinions that you lose your willingness to learn from me."

My child, listen to what I say, and treasure my commands. PROVERBS 2:1

One of the profound lessons of growing older is finding out that the more we know, the more we realize how much we have to learn.

As we age, we risk losing flexibility with our ideas of how the world should work, as well as our willingness to be wrong and to keep learning. When we become convinced of our own level of understanding, we lose sight of where we might be misinformed; and as soon as we become sure of our opinions, we're sure to be proven wrong. It's tough to see an accurate view of our shortcomings from such a narrow, close-up vantage point—it's so much easier to spot the faults of others! Thinking we know all that and more is a dangerous mind-set we are wise to avoid.

It seems a sign of true maturity is acknowledging that our opinions need to leave room for error. God never put a cap on our learning potential; in fact, he filled this world with endless treasures to pique our curiosity, and he intended that we keep growing right up to our last breath.

There is wisdom in remaining childlike when it comes to regarding the world with wide-eyed wonder and allowing ourselves to be wrong and to keep learning. When we refuse to think we've mastered all we will ever know, we keep our guard up against making childish mistakes.

King Solomon wrote the book of Proverbs to share insights he had learned over the course of his life. Throughout the book, he encourages people to continue seeking God's wisdom and guidance. Human knowledge is limited, and we need the Lord's discipline to succeed in this journey called life.

Take advantage of his experience, and challenge yourself to keep growing in spiritual wisdom every day.

TALK TO HIM

"Lord, thank you for sharing the wisdom of your Word with me. Please keep me from thinking I know all I need or understand as much as I can. I never want to stop growing with you."

Never mistake knowledge for wisdom. One helps you make a living; the other helps you make a life.

SANDRA CAREY

"Sticking to my ways requires a deliberate, ongoing choice of your will."

Mark out a straight path for your feet. . . . Don't get sidetracked. PROVERBS 4:26-27

If you've ever watched a bird build a nest or ants or bees go about their daily business, then you've seen determination that's tough to match. It takes force to get them off their course. God instilled them with his purposes for them, just as he did for us humans. The only thing is, we are much more distractible than most of his other creations. Perhaps that's because we have a will that is unmatched by any other creature.

Birds and ants and bees don't have a choice whether to serve their purpose or not; they simply operate as instinct tells them, no questions, no second-guessing, no rabbit trails. In contrast, our will allows us more freedom, yet it also leaves us plenty of room to veer off God's safe course for us.

It is said that our greatest strength is also our greatest weakness, and we can see that truth whenever we exercise our will for good or bad. The same determination that steers us wrong also gives us the push to stay on track, and the same will that curses us when we go the wrong way also blesses us whenever we go God's way.

We have endless options every day to move ahead with God or take side roads that inevitably lead us into pain. Heartache may not be straight ahead or even just around the next bend, but it lurks along those sidetracks all the same, ready to cause us to stumble, as verse 19 says.

How many times will your will lead you toward God or away from him today? The more you practice using it, the stronger it will guide you in the direction you have made its habit. Ask God to help you toughen your will to follow him; it's always his will that you do.

TALK TO HIM

"Father, thank you for giving me a will. But please, Lord, help me use it wisely. I need your constant help to stay on track; thank you for being there to see that I do."

If passion drives you, let reason hold the reins.
BENJAMIN FRANKLIN

July 3 PROVERBS 8:1-36

"If I gave you what you ask of me today, would you regret your request later?"

Wisdom is far more valuable than rubies. Nothing you desire can compare with it.

PROVERBS 8:11

King Solomon lived to have some regrets, but his request for wisdom as a new king was not one of them.

When God promised to grant anything Solomon asked for, Solomon wisely opted for wisdom to lead God's people. Although Solomon made his share of mistakes, his words in Proverbs 8 show us that he never regretted choosing wisdom over riches. He would know, too, because God was so pleased by Solomon's smart choice that he gave the king unmatched riches to boot.

Solomon knew the value of rubies and the pleasures that gold and silver afforded him, yet he advised his readers of Proverbs to choose wisdom above those treasures. He may have wanted material wealth, but he knew he needed wisdom to be successful in God's plans for him. In choosing to ask for the greatest asset he could offer his nation, instead of merely what looked appealing at first glance, he brought blessings to himself as well.

What do you want? Is it what God knows you need? Fast-forward your imagination years down the road and envision whether your request would yield eternal rewards or unwittingly buy you worldly troubles.

Solomon was known as the wisest man of his time, so his advice is worth heeding. Seeking the treasures God desires for you is the way to ensure that you will look back with no regrets. Give yourself that gift today by taking wise care with your requests.

TALK TO HIM

"Father, my heart can be greedy at times for things I'm not sure you want me to have. Please help me to yield to your wisdom. Show me what to ask, and give me the will to stick with those requests."

I don't think much of a man who is not wiser today than he was yesterday.

ABRAHAM LINCOLN

"Hard work pleases me and brings you freedom."

Work hard and become a leader; be lazy and become a slave. PROVERBS 12:24

Even though King Solomon had many perks handed to him, it seems he still understood the meaning of hard work. As King David's son, he watched his father pour into their nation, not shirking his responsibilities to lead by example. David learned a solid work ethic as a shepherd boy and didn't forget his humble heritage when it came to passing it on to his son.

David's and Solomon's efforts paid off because their hard work helped them achieve great successes as kings. It was through their work that they learned leadership, and it was also through their work that they earned freedom for their people. David led many battles as the head of the Israelite army, and Solomon's wisdom and wealth brought peace and prosperity—and most importantly a Temple to worship God.

Hard work has always paid off in one form or another. Changing times will never change that truth. Nor will it change the leadership skills we gain through our efforts. True leadership is servant leadership, and the nature of servanthood necessitates work.

Whatever God gives you for work these days, put your all into it, knowing that with each hour you are learning how to be a servant leader who pleases the Lord. Your work may not feel fun all the time; it may not feel fun most of the time. However, when you work with the attitude of a learner and the goal of pleasing God, your hours will reward you, your peers will respect you, and you will know the feeling of inner freedom coming from a job well done.

TALK TO HIM

"Father God, you set the example of hard work. From the days of Creation until today, you have not stopped working on my behalf. That's very humbling, Lord, but it also inspires me to follow your lead. Thank you for the ability and the privilege to honor you with my work."

The average person puts only 25 percent of his energy and ability into his work. The world takes off its hat to those who put in more than 50 percent of their capacity, and stands on its head for those few and far between souls who devote 100 percent.

ANDREW CARNEGIE

July 5 PROVERBS 16:1-33

"Check your deep-down motivations; I see them even before you do."

People may be pure in their own eyes, but the LORD examines their motives. PROVERBS 16:2

A pastor posed the question to his congregation: "If God were to show the past five minutes of your thoughts on-screen for all of us to see, would you mind?"

Yikes! Who of us might be horrified? Few people, if anyone, would escape a moment of panic, at the very least. Found out . . . a thought life laid bare. Again, yikes!

Even if we were caught at one of our more innocent five-minute time frames, just think about the mess that still lurks within our minds—the hidden reasonings, the mixed motivations. In our purest moments, who of us doesn't harbor threads of selfishness in our relationships? Not a bit of jealousy behind that compliment you paid yesterday? How about a sliver of pride that you never would have made your coworker's blunder last week?

Okay, maybe that moment of panic is setting in now.

Before you resettle yourself in the comfort that the pastor's question is only hypothetical, remember that your thoughts are posted for God all the time. If he were less gracious, he could replay them for all of heaven—or he could ensure that each fault you attempt to cover up gets found out here on earth.

How fortunate we are that our God isn't petty or manipulative! How fortunate that he isn't us!

Consider what God thinks of your thought life of recent days. Would he be pleased? Really pleased?

Thank him for not hiding his deepest motivations from you, and ask him to show you what he sees lurking inside your mind. He will help you to be wholly pure like him if you will only ask.

TALK TO HIM

"Lord, I would be horrified if the world knew what you know about me. Thank you for being the only One who sees it all, and thank you as well for helping me clean up the hidden motives that don't belong in your child."

Searcher of hearts, from mine erase
All thoughts that should not be,
And in its deep recesses trace
My gratitude to Thee.

GEORGE P. MORRIS, "SEARCHER OF HEARTS, FROM MINE ERASE"

"Choose wisely who you become close to; they will influence your character."

Don't befriend angry people or associate with hot-tempered people, or you will learn to be like them and endanger your soul. PROVERBS 22:24-25

Sometimes we love them. Sometimes we rue the day we discovered them. But most often, our feelings fall between those two extremes when it comes to (drum roll here) . . . *relationships.*

You've heard the saying "Can't live with 'em, can't live without 'em." Let's be honest. Have you ever cared for someone from whom you *didn't* need a bit of space every now and then? We get wrapped up in other people, and our baggage mixes with their issues until a point comes when we can't remember which person started out with which qualities. Didn't he have the bad temper? Wasn't she the one with the whinier voice? Surely it wasn't me!

When we spend enough time with someone else, we take on each other's attributes—the good, the bad, and the not-so-attractive ones. And we do this without realizing how our personalities had slowly been melding.

Solomon offers bucketfuls of advice, and a good portion of it centers on how we deal with others. Given his position as king, he saw a great deal in his kingly duties. From servants to advisers to common folk to enemies and finally to his abundant family—Solomon's experiences with people left little room for wondering how we influence each other. Who knows what memories prompted his advice in verses 24 and 25?

People haven't changed much over time—not deep down in our heart of hearts. We still need to guard ourselves against negative influencers every bit as much as people did in Solomon's day.

Are your relationships influencing you for the good?

TALK TO HIM

"Thank you, God, for putting people in my life who inspire me to become more like you. But please help me guard against adopting qualities from others who don't seek you. Instead, Lord, please help your Spirit in me to influence them for good."

Associate yourself with men of good quality if you esteem your own reputation, for 'tis better to be alone than in bad company.
GEORGE WASHINGTON

July 7 PROVERBS 23:1-35

"Truth, wisdom, discipline, good judgment: Discover from me why these are so important for you."

Get the truth and never sell it; also get wisdom, discipline, and good judgment.

PROVERBS 23:23

One of the great understated lessons in life involves learning when to quit. Quitting flies in the face of what society hollers at us. We're taught never to do it. Don't give up. Keep going.

That's well and good in many areas, but there are times when it's best to stop, times when moderation can be a beautiful thing indeed. Proverbs 23 might be called the moderation chapter because line after line encourages us to keep our obsessive tendencies in check. From overeating to overworking to overspending to overtalking . . . we exhaust ourselves with our overdoing.

Solomon knew a lot of things, as we're finding out. One more thing he knew about was overdoing. For much of his kingly life, he was not familiar with moderation. Or, if he had heard of the concept, he certainly didn't practice it in all areas of life. Fortunately, he realized before his life was over what the costs of overindulging can be.

In this chapter, he offers encouragement through wise words about truth, wisdom, discipline, and good judgment. What do all those qualities have in common? They help us to know when to stop. Truth reveals right from wrong actions—a good starting place. Moving on to wisdom and good judgment, we gain a gut feeling about whether we should get involved in something. And finally, discipline develops the willpower to act on what God is showing us about a situation.

When truth, wisdom, good judgment, and discipline work together, we have what it takes to live with moderation instead of continuing on destructive paths of overdoing that leave us overwrought and underenergized.

TALK TO HIM

"I've overdone it again, Lord. Please help me to study your Word for greater truth, wisdom, discipline, and good judgment regarding when to say no. Please help me to practice moderation."

Quit while you're ahead.

NEW YORK TIMES, 16 APRIL 1954

"Learn self-control in your speech and actions."

A person without self-control is like a city with broken-down walls. PROVERBS 25:28

A controlling personality isn't regarded as virtuous unless it applies to self-control. No one enjoys being dominated like a puppet by someone else, but who of us wouldn't welcome a greater dose of self-control, especially if we don't have to work hard to get it?

Well, the bad news is that there doesn't appear to be any better path to finding it than old-fashioned discipline and conscientious effort. The very word *self-control* suggests hard work; so if you want it, you have to apply yourself. The good news is that we're all capable of increasing our share.

God doesn't tell us to do things in his Word without giving us the ability to obey him. So when he issues commands through Solomon's proverbs, he sees us as fully capable of following through on them.

If Proverbs 23 was the moderation chapter, then Proverbs 25 is the self-control one. It's all about carrying ourselves well with other people and having the backbone to live authentically. Solomon says a lot about dealing productively with troublemakers and other enemies and about exhibiting high character in the big and little circumstances of life. We always have a choice to show self-control in any situation, and when we view self-control as the blessing it is, we will work doubly hard to build up ours.

Self-control blesses us. It works as a hedge of protection around us in the same way that walls protected cities in Solomon's day. Without it, we're vulnerable to bad judgment calls, to temptations, and to misguided priorities. With it, we are more fit to talk and behave in God-pleasing ways.

Add some control to your life by practicing self-control today.

TALK TO HIM

"Lord, thank you for giving me a will. Please strengthen my 'will's power' so that I practice better self-control. Thank you for self-control so I can choose how to behave in every situation."

What it lies in our power to do, it lies in our power not to do.

ARISTOTLE

July 9 PROVERBS 28:1-28

"Pray for the leaders in your home, church, and government."

But wise and knowledgeable leaders bring stability. PROVERBS 28:2

Yesterday's topic used the analogy of a town's crumbling walls to symbolize a person without self-control. Carrying the image of instability further, Solomon moves on to the subject of leadership.

A close look at the wording of verse 2 raises our curiosity with one of our favorite little introductory words, *but*, in the second clause. With that word, Solomon sets up a contrast, in this case between wise and knowledgeable leaders and the moral rot of an unstable government.

You don't have to look far to see the carnage of bad leadership. It is far more prevalent than the good variety. That's because anyone can assume the role of a leader, but few can truly lead. That goes for large governments as well as smaller units, such as families, businesses, churches, and others.

Healthy things grow; that is a fact of nature. Well, healthy leadership grows a group as surely as bad leadership crumbles it. As our Creator, God designed us to grow. Therefore, we need to talk with him about our leaders at home, across town, and around the world. We can actually take the lead by reinforcing our leaders in prayer. More than any other asset, they need to experience God for themselves before they can become godly leaders and examples to those they guide.

Pray that God would move personally in and reveal himself to each leader in your life. Pray that they will pattern their character and integrity after God, as well as their heart for unselfish giving.

Your prayers for your leaders will bolster the fortifications of the group and guard against forces that threaten to crumble it.

TALK TO HIM

"Father God, you are my ultimate leader. Even though I get frustrated by many of the leaders I see, I know that you put them on my heart so I can pray for them. Thank you for showing me how I can take the lead in this way."

I do not pray for success, I ask for faithfulness.

MOTHER TERESA

"I have planted eternity in your heart; how are you using your time to grow it?"

God has made everything beautiful for its own time. He has planted eternity in the human heart. ECCLESIASTES 3:11

Eternity and beauty are echoed in the same verse. Make no mistake; that is no coincidence. The two concepts belong together because God, the Eternal One, is also Lord, the Beautiful One.

Everything he does lasts forever, and everything he does is beautiful. He plants his Spirit of eternity in the hearts of his people, creating in us a spirit of beauty that will reflect his own forever. A while back we imagined what forever looks like. Here we see that forever is intricately associated with beauty, and both are gifts from God.

God offers us many gifts of eternal beauty—salvation, love, hope, joy, and peace, among others. What we do with his gifts is up to us. We can grow them by planting our hearts at his feet and worshiping him daily. We can nurture them by letting his love soak into us and then returning it as an offering. And we can multiply them by spreading his love to others. Whatever we do, we are wise to remember that all we do with his gifts today impacts eternity.

Today might seem like an insignificant blip in your life, less important still in the limitless scope of forever. But don't be fooled; this very second holds precious opportunity to turn your heart toward him and soak up a beautiful dose of eternity. And keep in mind that this second always leads to the next one, which may be the very one that holds an opportunity to share his love with someone else.

Are you making growing space for the beauty of eternity in your heart, or are you so wrapped up in today's agenda that these twenty-four hours seem more valuable than the rest of forever?

God wants to shed beauty on your day. Look for signs of it, and prepare for forever by cherishing his beauty today.

TALK TO HIM

"Lord, you are my beautiful King and my eternal Savior. I love to learn more of your love! Please help me to care for the eternities of others by sharing your love with them today."

Beautiful tho't to me,
We shall forever be
Thine in eternity.

BARNEY E. WARREN, "BEAUTIFUL"

July 11 ECCLESIASTES 5:1-17

"Beware of drivenness that distracts you from the true life I offer."

Throughout their lives, they live under a cloud—frustrated, discouraged, and angry.
ECCLESIASTES 5:17

A story has circulated for years about a wealthy businessman who traveled to a remote island to teach the natives how to grow rich and enjoy a better life. Sitting on the beach one day with one of the islanders, the businessman explained that with lots of hard work and the willingness to sacrifice sleep, rest, and time with family, the native eventually could retire in style, sleep in every day, spend his days napping in a hammock and his nights relaxing under the stars with his wife.

The native listened patiently, his brow furrowing deeper the longer the businessman talked. Finally he had a chance to reply.

"Why should I follow your plan and wait for such a life when every day I already sleep in, work a bit, take a nap in the afternoon, and spend my nights relaxing under the stars with my wife?"

We think we're so wise with our "advanced" ideas and our high-tech lifestyles. But what does our drivenness earn us that truly enriches us and lasts beyond our stressed-out lives on earth? Does it teach us how to live, or does it fool us into thinking that decades of overdosing on busyness are worth a few years to unwind in retirement?

We're driven to distraction by drivenness! We don't even realize how tightly wound we are because we don't know any different.

God calls us to hard work, but he doesn't call us to obsess about getting ahead to the detriment of a calm mind, healthy human relationships, and most importantly, a rich relationship with him.

Lose the frustrated edge on your spirit by releasing your misguided need to push ever more intensely. Get to know God's idea of balancing work and play, and let him teach you the art of rest.

TALK TO HIM

"Lord, I don't know who I would be if I let go of my driven tendencies. Please show me why I keep pushing, and then please show me true rest in releasing my drivenness to you."

If we could learn how to balance rest against effort, calmness against strain, quiet against turmoil, we would assure ourselves of joy in living and psychological health for life.

JOSEPHINE RATHBONE

"Do you have the patience to finish?"

Finishing is better than starting. ECCLESIASTES 7:8

Do you ever wonder why Solomon paired certain concepts together? For instance, why would the thoughts of verse 8 go together? Do finishing and starting and patience and pride have anything in common?

We don't know what Solomon's reasoning was for combining those ideas, but we can make some logical guesses. First of all, think about a young person starting out, new in the work force, full of ambition to change the world—and oftentimes with a tad too much pride.

Now consider the average sixty-year-old—doing the career thing a long time, a portfolio of personal accomplishments to show for it, nothing more to prove. All that's left is to find patience for the final stretch until retirement—possibly the greatest career challenge yet.

Solomon may have linked his ideas of verse 8 together because he discovered that the patience necessary to finish a job well reveals more character and class than the prideful gusto required to get started.

We refer to our modern world as a microwave society because we want everything fast, faster, and fastest. We don't have time for time to move slowly; there are simply too many important things we important people have to do. We're easily distracted, too, and we are hard pressed to stay the course when we get bored, continuously longing for something new.

Perhaps we are not so different from people in Solomon's world. From verse 8, it appears that those folks struggled with patience and character to finish as well.

What have you begun that requires high character to complete? Patience is a virtue that will push you further than the showier quality of pride. Practice it well, and it will lead you to the finish line in a way that earns God's deeper, well-earned pride in you more than merely starting out with a bang.

TALK TO HIM

"Lord, the finish line looks far away. Please help me exercise the patience to keep moving toward it, trusting that you will help me get there with character and class, caring more about your pride in me than my own."

Get a good idea and stay with it. Do it, and work at it until it's done, and done right.

WALT DISNEY

July 13 ECCLESIASTES 10:1-20

"Develop class-act quietness."

A quiet spirit can overcome even great mistakes. ECCLESIASTES 10:4

Although Solomon's nuggets of wisdom seem to be grouped rather randomly at times, as we noted in yesterday's reading, thoughtful study often uncovers an overarching theme within sections of verses.

Case in point: Chapter 10 may have you wondering why Solomon spent his precious kingly time on simplistic statements about falling into wells and endangering yourself while chopping wood. But take care not to write it off too quickly. Taken as a whole, this chapter holds wonderful wisdom about foolish living, and what better way to enlighten us about such a topic than by putting the truth in simple terms?

Tucked in toward the chapter's beginning lies a statement, unobtrusive in its simplicity, that shines the glow on the other verses as if to say, "This is it: the point!" The glow is cast by the classy little second half of verse 4, which reveals a character trait in stark contrast to foolishness.

When foolishness seems to shout its shortcomings, a quiet spirit gently reveals its class. All of us act unwisely at times; that's to be expected from human beings. However, we can make up for many of our foibles simply by holding ourselves back to quiet our impulses and give ourselves time to consider a next move that shows more class.

Isn't it more shocking when someone who once appeared foolish begins to show maturity than for someone who was always known for classiness to continue acting wisely? Ironic as it is, a quiet spirit shocks us with its rare gentleness and by offering a divergence from the cheap blather of fools, who are a dime a dozen.

Go for the shock value. Exhibit the depth of a quiet spirit when you're on the right track and even after you've temporarily driven off course. Give yourself time to pull your integrity together, and step forward like the class act God created you to be.

TALK TO HIM

"Father, when I mess up, I panic to save face. But God, please remind me that my actions following a foolish mistake are critical for reestablishing class-act maturity that should define your children."

Many individuals have, like uncut diamonds, shining qualities beneath a rough exterior.

JUVENAL

"When I create love between two people, my timing is perfect; don't rush it."

Promise me . . . not to awaken love until the time is right. SONG OF SONGS 3:5

Timing is everything. We wish it would slow down to linger over the sweet moments, and we strain to push it forward through a rough season. Far too often, we wish God's timing would match ours.

Well, we can thank God that it usually doesn't.

When it comes to love, we can't get enough moments with those we care about, and we tug on the reins when true love seems to remain in the distant future. What can we say? We love love and can't wait for more of it.

Yet, God's timing for our love life shows his perfect wisdom in holding back what we're not ready to handle with the care it deserves. Either we need more character refining to appreciate the treasure of true love, or he wants to illustrate through us a picture of waiting well for his time frame.

By churning impatiently while the clock ticks at his pace, we cheat ourselves of some precious moments with him, our first love. And suppose he were to send us that special someone of our dreams before he finished preparing us for each other? We would receive a half-done gift that wouldn't give us its full potential of satisfaction, and God would be cheated of the joy of providing for our dreams in his perfect method and time.

God knows the whole span of your life, and he has built into it enough minutes and days and years to hold every bit of the love he has in mind for you. When you rest in his timing, you receive his best.

TALK TO HIM

"Oh Lord, love is hard to wait for—both for its start and for its perfection as you mature it. Please help me to live joyfully within your timing; I know it is truly the best."

The richest love is that which submits to the arbitration of time.

LAWRENCE DURRELL

July 15 SONG OF SONGS 6:4–7:13

"A love that I create for you has unlimited potential for blessings."

Turn your eyes away, for they overpower me. SONG OF SONGS 6:5

When God sends us blessings, sometimes they are nearly overwhelming in their perfection, as the lover's eyes were to her guy. They were almost more beautiful than his heart could take.

In his uncompromising way, God desires only the best for us. With that desire always in mind, he goes to joyful lengths to make his blessings an ideal fit for each of us, particularly when it comes to love, which he takes very seriously (being love himself, after all).

Since he created marriage as a picture of his relationship with his church, it goes without saying that he puts the utmost care into creating our love relationships. He desires that our marriages exhibit such deep love that partners are awestruck by his blessings. Through our marriages he also wants to show an example of his love to a world that doesn't understand its unconditional quality, a world that starves for more than its own unsatisfying imitation of the real thing.

Whether God already has given you a spouse, is in the process of bringing you together, has yet to reveal your true love, or simply wants you to know him as your truest love, he wants to shower you with his unlimited love. When you experience it, you won't be able to comprehend its richness. It will have you praising him endlessly, as the two lovers in Song of Songs couldn't seem to find enough ways to express their feelings for each other.

Learn of his love, lean on it, and let yourself trust it to guide you further into its unlimited blessings.

TALK TO HIM

"Heavenly Lord, your love is beyond my understanding, and I thank you for it. Please broaden my experience of it more each day so my ability to love grows more complete, and so others will be blessed by your loving character in me."

Loved with everlasting love, led by grace that love to know;
Gracious Spirit from above, Thou hast taught me it is so!
O this full and perfect peace! O this transport all divine!
In a love which cannot cease, I am His, and He is mine.
GEORGE W. ROBINSON, "I AM HIS, AND HE IS MINE"

✿

"It's settled for me, so let it be settled for you: I want to forgive you."

"Come now, let's settle this," says the L*ORD. "Though your sins are like scarlet, I will make them as white as snow."* ISAIAH 1:18

A good lawyer is known for debating with such authority that anyone listening can't say anything to refute the argument. Well, God isn't called our Defender, Advocate, and Counselor for nothing. Once he takes a case, it is as good as settled because he argues with ultimate authority, and he always wins.

Who, though, would have imagined he would argue against us for us?

We're guilty. We know it, and he knows it. However, sometimes we struggle to accept his forgiveness. For one reason or another—whether a guilt complex or a backward sense of pride, thinking we don't deserve to be off the hook—we remain in bondage to our guilt.

This might sound humble and holy, but in reality both of those attitudes disrespects the price God paid to free us from guilt. We are sinners; that nature isn't up for debate. But God not only sees all the evidence of our sin; he also takes it upon himself to clear our names and restore our record to a cleaner state than it originally was. That's some deal he works on our behalf! To go back and try to pay the penalty ourselves is like telling God his way wasn't enough.

You can argue with God all you want about your sin, but the facts won't change. He still sent his Son to die for you, and accepting his sacrifice is all you need for forgiveness. Actually, it's the only way to forgiveness.

Your case was settled in God's courtroom long ago. Accept his verdict and his forgiveness, leave your chains behind, and move on into the life of freedom he bought for you.

TALK TO HIM

"Thank you, Father, for being my heavenly Advocate and for releasing me from the guilt of my sin. Please remind me not to cheapen the price you paid by trying to pay it again myself."

A forgiveness ought to be like a canceled note, torn in two and burned up, so that it can never be shown against the man.

HENRY WARD BEECHER

July 17 ISAIAH 6:1-13

"When I send you, will you say yes?"

"Here I am. Send me." ISAIAH 6:8

They say talk is cheap. Whoever "they" are, they have become somewhat jaded by the overuse of passionate phrases that lack the promised follow-through. Consider these meaningful expressions that are often tossed around like common lingo:

I love you.
I hate you.
Everything will be okay.
I know how you feel.
You're the best.
You always do that.
You never do that.

The list goes on. If God were to make a list of phrases we glibly say to him, one that might appear toward the top is "Here I am. Send me." When we've known God for any length of time, it's likely that we've felt pressured (by others or by an inner need to feel like a better Christian) to say this to God while secretly hoping he won't send us outside our comfort zone.

God asked the prophet Isaiah to take his messages to the Israelite people. Any study of the prophets reveals that their jobs were never easy. In fact, no one in his or her right mind would accept the challenges without truly knowing that path was God's choice.

In another day when talk was cheap (again, humans don't change much over the millennia), Isaiah meant his yes. He showed that his talk held integrity and commitment to be God's on a much deeper level than mere lip service.

Commit to enrich, not cheapen, your spiritual life through the words God gave you the ability to speak.

TALK TO HIM

"Lord, I want my words to matter. Please help them to glorify you with their trustworthiness and enrich the lives of others with their dedication to your truth."

An acre of performance is worth whole world of promise.
WILLIAM DEAN HOWELLS

"Your thoughts should reflect mine, not those of the world around you."

"Make the Lord *of Heaven's Armies holy in your life. He is the one you should fear. He is the one who should make you tremble."* ISAIAH 8:13

Most people, when given an instruction, want to know *why. . . . Why shouldn't I have that second piece of cake? Why do I have to fill out a time card to justify my work? Why can't I go five over the speed limit?* We're typically okay with yielding to authority, as long as we can see the value in its direction.

Sometimes we question God's commands because we think they don't apply to us, or they feel limiting. Isaiah 8:13 might fall into one of those categories. The *why* of that verse can be understood in the context of verses 20-21. Why should we fear the Lord and make him holy in our lives? Because, according to those later verses, "People who contradict his word are completely in the dark. . . . They will rage and curse their king and their God."

The connection? Fearing God and seeking his holiness guard us with his truth in a world that opposes his word, a world that lives in dark confusion and anger because of its stance against him. When we pursue holiness, God's Spirit patterns our thoughts after his, protecting us against half-truths and misconceptions of him and of our purpose. Our holy fear of him keeps us on track and helps us avoid useless, empty living.

God gave us our curiosity, and if we look to him for guidance, he will steer us toward the right questions to ask, such as, Why would I follow any path that doesn't lead to him? Now, there's something worth asking.

TALK TO HIM

"Father God, your guidance is my lifeline, your authority my truth. Please help me turn to you with my questions and submit to your answers so my thinking reflects yours. Thank you for protecting my mind."

I have the responsibility of keeping my spirit in agreement with His Spirit, and by degrees Jesus lifts me up to where He lived—in perfect consecration to His Father's will, paying no attention to any other thing. Am I perfecting this type of holiness in the fear of God?

OSWALD CHAMBERS

July 19 ISAIAH 9:1-7

"I planned to provide you a Savior, and I offered hope generations before I sent him."

For those who live in a land of deep darkness, a light will shine. ISAIAH 9:2

After yesterday's thoughts about seeking God's holiness in a world that lives in darkness, today's musings shed light on how God brightens our days with his hope.

In his gracious love, God saw a world of people who were lost and hurting, longing for a reason to hope beyond their circumstances. Instead of merely letting them wait until his timing was right, God sent many messages through the prophets about their coming Savior. Isaiah was one of those prophets, and chapter 9 is one of those messages.

Known as the Light of the World, Jesus is our reason for hope. As our Savior, he shines through the confusion that muddies the world's thinking. Sent by his heavenly Father to be our salvation, Jesus' mission on earth was the result of God's thoughtful planning from before he created us.

In the same way that God offered people hope generations before actually sending Jesus, God planned for your life before you were born. He knew every bright spot and dark day you would face; not one comes as a surprise to him. You may feel thrown by unexpected health issues, expenses, hurts from other people, or career failures, but God remains your steady beam of light to guide you through all of it.

Jesus came to give you hope for always, that's true. But he also came to give you reason to hope for just this day. He has the broad view of your life in mind, as well as the smallest details of this hour.

Look toward the light he sends your way. He was the hope of the world before he came to earth, and he remains your hope now and into eternity.

TALK TO HIM

"Thank you, God, for offering hope in a hopeless world. Thank you for knowing the challenges I will face and for never being caught off guard by them. Please help me to put my hope in your faithful planning."

We must accept finite disappointment, but never lose infinite hope.

MARTIN LUTHER KING JR.

"Get to know the stability of my perfect peace."

You will keep in perfect peace all who trust in you, all whose thoughts are fixed on you!

ISAIAH 26:3

How does God keep in perfect peace all who trust in him? He surrounds them with the walls of his salvation.

Salvation isn't only a grand pinnacle we reach at the end of time. Salvation guards us every minute of every day in this life. Safe within its realm, we find God's perfect peace.

Peace is inextricably linked to salvation by the word "keep." It's quite nice to experience fleeting moments of peace, like breaths of fresh air that offer brief respites from stress. But to be kept in peace, and not just peace but perfect peace, is a whole other experience.

Did you ever realize that you can dwell in peace all the time? Consider what that would mean for your mind-set, your relationships, your ability to concentrate at work, and your ability to truly relax.

Just as a wall is fixed, immovable, so are you when you fix your thoughts on the God who saves you. The walls of salvation mentioned in verse 1 illustrate the stability God's perfect peace provides. Working as a team, salvation guards us with peace, which stabilizes us against ferocious onslaughts of trouble. Even during those rare seasons when circumstances cooperate with us, we still need the peace and security available within God's salvation.

Wherever your day takes you, keep your mind fixed within the walls of God's salvation, and enjoy extended times of perfect peace.

TALK TO HIM

"Lord God, you are my mighty Savior, and I'm so thankful for your walls of protection, salvation, and peace. Please help me to fix my thoughts on you so I can dwell within—not just visit—your stable place for me."

Peace is the mark of the sons of God. . . . Peace is the rest of blessed souls. . . . Peace is the dwelling place of eternity.

LEO THE GREAT

July 21 ISAIAH 30:15-26

"I am constantly available, waiting to show you compassion. But you must move toward me."

The LORD must wait for you to come to him so he can show you his love and compassion.

ISAIAH 30:18

The saying "God helps those who help themselves" isn't from the Bible, but the concept is worth considering in light of the Bible's teaching.

First, though, a bit of clarification lest we present God in a wrong light. God doesn't expect the helpless to buck up and help themselves. He loves to shower compassion on the needy, and he cherishes the weak.

However, for the millions of healthy, able-bodied folks who make up the rest of the population, God doesn't hand us everything on a silver platter. He expects us to use the abilities he gave us. As his children, we should reflect his good sense, willingness to work, and love in action. We also should show that we realize we need him by making an effort to stay close to him.

During times of weakness—which even the strongest people face—we should go to him, admit our reliance on him, and trust that he is ready to help us, all the while guarding against our knack for using him for his blessings. We're spoiled by all he gives us, and sometimes we get bent out of shape if he expects what feels like too much effort from us. But how reasonable are we to expect his perks without committing to follow him?

God is our provider, and he already has gone to extremes to give us heaven's treasures. But he deserves to be wanted for himself more than for his blessings. We must want him enough to give to the relationship as well. When we show that we understand our reliance on him, he will spare nothing to meet us at our need with all the compassion he is known for.

TALK TO HIM

"Lord, I praise you for being loving and kind. Thank you, also, for not giving me everything I need without building character in me that's willing to apply myself to our relationship. Please use my needs to help me move toward you."

The Holy Spirit . . . wants to flow through us and realize all these wonderful possibilities in the world—if we only open ourselves and allow it to happen.

BROTHER DAVID STEINDL-RAST

"In this world full of changes and no guarantees, I am unchanging and sure."

"The grass withers and the flowers fade, but the word of our God stands forever." ISAIAH 40:8

If it hasn't already, summer is nearing its peak. Everywhere you look, the vibrant colors of spring soon will begin to fade under the sun's burning heat. Flowers wither, desperate for water. Grass crisps and browns. Trees begin to drop a few early leaves to preserve precious moisture. For all its fun, summer flies past us and leaves behind a world closing up for cooler fall temperatures.

Every season begins with fresh life and ends with the promise of something new to come. The seasons remind us that the world is full of change, and just as no one can predict the exact weather from day to day, no one can be sure what life will unfold as time passes. Sure, we can guess that summer will be warmer than winter, the same as we can assume certain basics about our daily lives like what we'll eat and when we'll get tired. However, surprises come up now and then, both in our climate and in our personal world. Sometimes uncertainties cause us to crave a guarantee.

Isaiah 40 serves as a memory jogger about all that God is, namely that he is the guarantee we all need. With God, there are no shocks, no changes, nothing but sureness. He is incomparable, unwearying, everlasting, and in charge.

The One who keeps the universe in order from season to season guarantees your life. The hand that holds the oceans also holds your soul, and the mind that knows the weight of the earth also knows the weight on your heart.

He will be your ever-present help and saving power today just as he always has been and will be forever.

TALK TO HIM

"Lord, my heart breathes a sigh of relief knowing you will never change. Thank you for being the solidness I crave."

Unchanging God, hear from eternal Heav'n:
We plead Thy gifts of grace, forever given. . . .
From hope's sweet vision of the thing to be,
From love to those who still are loved by Thee.

SAMUEL J. STONE, "UNCHANGING GOD, HEAR FROM ETERNAL HEAVEN"

July 23 ISAIAH 43:1-13

"Have you considered what it means to me that you are mine?"

"I have called you by name; you are mine. . . . No one can snatch anyone out of my hand."
ISAIAH 43:1, 13

God loves to love you. He isn't reluctant about it in the least. To prove his love, here is a recap of some basics that he has done and continues to do for you:

He created you in his image.
He planned for your salvation before you were born.
He sent his innocent Son to die in your place.
He fills you with his Holy Spirit.
He calls you his child.
He gives you the rights of heavenly royalty.
He watches over you every second.
He listens to you.
He responds to you.
He works on your behalf.
He guards you from being snatched from him.

You have quite the package deal with him. No one would offer all that unless it meant something to the giver. So what does it mean to God to make you his own?

Well, since he created you in his image, he must think you are beautiful indeed. And since he planned for your salvation long before you even needed it—and since he gave his perfect Son to buy you back from your sins—he must treasure you. By filling you with his Holy Spirit, he shows his vested interest in your connection to him. By watching over, listening, and responding to you, he is keenly aware of what it takes to work on your behalf. And then there's the ongoing protection he offers to ensure your soul is secure with him.

Do you need more proof of his love? Talk to him today, keep looking into his Word, and he will continue to show you the depths of what it means to him to love you.

TALK TO HIM

"Heavenly Lord, your love for me amazes me. But to think of what it obviously means to you to give me so much—it's overwhelming. 'Thank you' seems so inadequate, but I give you my thanks, along with all my heart."

One way or another he will make his love real to our heart.
JILL BRISCOE

"I am the God of newness; never think I am finished with you."

"I am about to do something new. See, I have already begun! Do you not see it?"

ISAIAH 43:19

Summertime brings with it the thrill of dipping your toes in a pool of water, cool to the touch and refreshing to your very core. Ahh! Can't you almost feel it just thinking about it? There is nothing quite like being rejuvenated after feeling dried out and shriveled, whether we're talking about physically, spiritually, mentally, emotionally, or even financially. Fresh is good; we love a new start because we love imagining how things could be better.

God finds great joy in providing the refreshment of a new start. He loves rebuilding, reforming, and re-creating, and he loves to see us get excited about the hope of new beginnings. With infinite power to do whatever he pleases, he is pleased to find endless ways to amaze us with his ability to change our circumstances and grow us.

He knows what you're going through, but more importantly he knows where he wants to take you and who he wants you to become. The God who made a path through the seas is at this moment creating a way for you through your present troubles; but he also is forming your character, refreshing it with his own.

Count on refreshment on the other side, but don't miss the signs of God at work between here and there. They are evidence of his delight in refreshing and re-creating you. He is a visionary who offers glimpses of his coming attractions if you will keep your eyes poised on him, looking always for what he is about to do.

Only a God so gracious would give you constant reason for hope in the future while blessing you with the refreshment of his presence along the way. He is not finished with you. Stay close and see what he does next.

TALK TO HIM

"Lord God, it's easy for me to get stuck in the here and now, stagnant in my thinking that you are done working in me. Please forgive me for being so shortsighted about you, my mighty Savior. Please do in me whatever comes next."

God loves us the way we are but He loves us too much to leave us that way.

LEIGHTON FORD

July 25 ISAIAH 49:8-26

"I will be your perfect parent."

"See, I have written your name on the palms of my hands." ISAIAH 49:16

As surely as an attentive father stays alert to his child, God stays clued in to the depths of you. In fact, he understands you far better than you understand yourself.

There is no love quite like a parent's, but even the best human parents fail their children at times. Not so with God. He is our lifeline of sustenance much as a nursing mother is to her child. We live off of him. The idea of a mother forgetting her nursing baby is nearly impossible to fathom; well, the idea of God forgetting us is impossible.

The concept of God as a parent might seem foreign to you. If you didn't have the benefit of a happy, secure childhood within your parents' home, then a part of you might resist looking to God for parental direction even while another part of you still yearns for that type of nurturing as an adult.

Be encouraged. It is never too late to learn how to be God's child. While none of us can go back and redo the past, we can turn to God for healing for the future. God sees each ache and pain you carry, and in fact, each one went through him before it touched you. If you doubt that's true, take another look at verse 16. Your name is branded on his palms. Branding is painful, but he bore your pain so you could be healed.

Branding also is permanent, which means you cannot be erased from his heart. He saved you forever; there will be no going back on his part. God knows what's going on with you, and you are always on his mind. Let him be your perfect parent and love you with the completeness you've always needed.

TALK TO HIM

"Father God . . . I want to pause to let your name sink in. You are my Father. What a complex but wonderful truth! Please help me learn to simply be your child and welcome your loving guidance. Thank you for imprinting me permanently on your hands that hold me."

God's hands that bore your pain and your shame
also hold your salvation and hope.
ANONYMOUS

"I took on your emptiness so you can be whole."

When he sees all that is accomplished by his anguish, he will be satisfied. ISAIAH 53:11

Was Jesus' death worth it to save you? The first few verses of Isaiah 53 may have you turning toward the heavens and asking, "Why? Why did you do it?" The question reverberates through our souls—not from a lack of gratitude, but from a sense of awe that anyone, much less our perfect God, would endure so much for us. The harassment, torture, agony, ridicule, rejection, beatings, whippings, humiliation, grief, separation from God the Father . . .

It's almost more than we can hear about. And let's not even waste time wondering if we would be willing to suffer what he did on our behalf, the very ones who doled out all that anguish. We wouldn't.

Isaiah 53 reads like a tragedy until the final three verses reveal what will make it all worth it. God's plan to crush his Son, Jesus, in our place will accomplish immeasurable victory, both in the spiritual realm and in our lives. The spikes that pierced his wrists left holes that he filled with our souls. Those holes are not empty since he carries in them those who accept his salvation. In a beautiful twist of irony, those holes made it possible for him to fill up our emptiness with his wholeness.

Is your existence worth his death? Long ago, he thought so. He died to give you life and hope for this very day, July 26. And now that today is here, he still thinks it all was worth it to see you lift your heart to him and accept his gift of forever.

TALK TO HIM

"My Savior God, there is no way I can thank you enough. There is no way I can even understand all you went through for me. And to think you did it all, knowing my simple humanness never could comprehend your full suffering. Thank you, God. Thank you again today."

The Cross did not happen to Jesus: He came on purpose for it. . . . The Cross is the point where God and sinful man merge with a crash and the way to life is opened—but the crash is on the heart of God.

OSWALD CHAMBERS

July 27 ISAIAH 55:1-7

"Please accept my invitation of all invitations."

"Come to me with your ears wide open. Listen, and you will find life." ISAIAH 55:3

As kids, we were thrilled, and always a little relieved, when we "made the list" and received a party invitation. Of course, we were excited about the celebration itself, but we also felt a sense of belonging that someone remembered to include us.

God sent you an invitation long ago, and there is no topping the hoopla of this event. It's the Celebration of Life, and God would love for you to show up and stay awhile—say, for all eternity.

As you might expect, there's a dress code for this all-important gala. On the other hand, it may surprise you to know how casual that code is. You are to come as you are—whatever burdens and faults you're wearing these days, whatever ones you've worn to shreds because you haven't traded them in for God's clothing of forgiveness.

Oh, there is one other prerequisite for the guests of this party. Anyone who accepts this invitation of all invitations needs to come with open ears in order to find the Celebration of Life. Don't be discouraged; the directions really aren't difficult. But many times guests complicate them by not listening and trying other routes besides the one God included in his invitation. Just follow Jesus' path, and he will lead you home to his Father's house, where the party will last forever.

It will be the gala event of all time when Jesus returns home with you at his side, and together you will join with God and the other guests in celebrating eternal life.

If you haven't given him your RSVP, don't delay. Time is running out, and you don't want to miss this event. Not if your life depended on it (which, incidentally, it does).

TALK TO HIM

"Lord, no doubt you throw a celebration like no one has ever dreamed. I hardly can wait to find out all you have planned. Please show me how to live in preparation for eternity."

Thou hast long been waiting
For some better time,
But today He's calling,
Come and claim Him thine. . . .
He will lead thee gently,
All along the way,
In the path that shineth,
Unto perfect day.

LIZZIE AKERS, "COME, OH, COME TO ME"

"My thoughts and ways are far above yours—but they are on your side."

"My thoughts are nothing like your thoughts," says the L*ORD*. *"And my ways are far beyond anything you could imagine."* ISAIAH 55:8

If only we could know what God is thinking right now. . . . Wow, that thought jump-starts worlds of ideas.

First of all, *how would knowing God's thoughts change our lives?* Perhaps our reaction would depend on whether we think we can please him. Knowing God's mind would either instill anxiety or security. It would bring us to our knees or lift our heads high. And it could lead us to gratitude or guilt, remorse or rebellion, mercy or justice.

Secondly, *how would knowing God's thoughts change how we feel about ourselves?* Would we feel proud or humbled? encouraged or disciplined? settled or confused?

Our perceptions of God's thoughts have everything to do with how we view the world and, specifically, ourselves in relation to it. God lays it out for us in verses 8 and 9—his mind works so far beyond ours that we can't even imagine his thought processes.

Our attitude about those verses reveals our openness to him. Someone who assumes that God holds his infinite intelligence over our heads like a dictator will rebel against his authority, shrink from it in terror, or obsessively work to earn a place in his good standing. However, anyone who reads these verses with God's loving character in mind will welcome the stability of knowing that Someone bigger and higher and greater is in control.

Even though God's supremacy gives him every right and ability to misuse his power, he shows us incredible respect. In fact, he applies his higher, greater thoughts for our good.

There is no need to take sides with him, as if he has competition. His thoughts show that he is on your side. Are you on his?

TALK TO HIM

"Thank you, Lord, for being so far above me. It gives me immeasurable comfort to know that you never are confused or misled, and you always are thinking of ways to draw me closer to you. Please help me let go of my resistance and enjoy you as you reveal your thoughts to me."

In Christ we are promised both the "know-how" and the "know-when" that we cannot possibly know without him!

JILL BRISCOE

July 29 ISAIAH 57:1-2, 14-21

"For those who know me, the end of life on this earth is the doorway to true life."

No one seems to understand that God is protecting them from the evil to come.

ISAIAH 57:1

This life isn't everything you've been waiting for.

Are you breathing a sigh of relief? Thank heaven this life isn't as good as it gets! Hardly. God created a beautiful world for us, but this life is merely a staging area for the real deal to come. While we're alive on earth, we wait at the door of eternity. We don't understand everything about life and death as we witness it here. Our viewpoints take in only an eighty- or ninety-year perspective of what it means to go through life and run out of years.

Because of those limitations, we mourn what we cannot see. We grieve the losses of loved ones even when we know they knew Christ as Savior and thus are in a better place. We grieve for ourselves, but we also grieve for those who have passed on, particularly if it seems death claimed them too early. We feel they have been hurt by what they will miss on earth.

Oh, if we could grasp the truth, we would be so comforted. According to Isaiah 57:1, God in his grace sometimes brings people home to be with him sooner than we would like, but for the very purpose of saving them from future harm. We think death hurt them, but if they had stayed alive, life on earth would have hurt them more. The death of their mortal bodies blessed them by releasing them from chains of humanness into freedom at Jesus' side.

For those who know Jesus as Savior, this existence isn't all there is. Remember, God's ways are far above ours, and his perspective is that this life on earth is something to be saved *from*, not *for*.

TALK TO HIM

"Father God, my Savior, I am thankful that your perspective holds so much more than my own. Although it's difficult to come to terms with loss, I am grateful that you save people from the limitations of this life. Amen, Lord. You are good."

Death is simply a shedding of the physical body, like the butterfly coming out of a cocoon. . . . It's like putting away your winter coat when spring comes.

ELISABETH KÜBLER-ROSS

"I want your real worship, not just your actions."

"They act so pious! . . . They ask me to take action on their behalf, pretending they want to be near me." ISAIAH 58:2

Only Jesus' death and resurrection gives us God's salvation. But what does it take to please God? Does pleasing him include its own set of have-tos?

Many of us accept his gift of salvation as a gift we can't earn—hence the term *gift*—only to strive from that point to earn his approval. A backward approach! Since he accepted us when he saw us as sinful and unforgiven, we don't have to earn his acceptance after we have Jesus' sacrifice cleansing us.

God knows we will sin even after we accept his salvation. The point where people confuse whether they have his ongoing acceptance centers on their wholeheartedness in making him Lord. Did they commit their lives to him for real? God sees through phony attempts to appear righteous. He knows the state of every soul, whether it truly wants him or not. Any spiritual act that doesn't come from a heart devoted to him disgusts him because it mocks his limitless knowledge and his right to our unhindered worship.

He is most pleased when he sees honest desire to please him. Everyone makes a mess of things now and then, but God is pleased regardless when he looks into a person's soul and sees his Son's mark of salvation and a heart that seeks to become more like himself.

If you are his child, he rejoices over you, and he is even more pleased when your heart continues moving toward him honestly, not trying to cover up for devotion that should be there but isn't.

Make it real, and don't doubt his pleasure over you, his accepted child.

TALK TO HIM

"Father God, please help me to be honest with you. Thank you for seeing me as more than the sum of my actions. I am so grateful that you look for genuine devotion and refuse to accept halfhearted, self-centered attempts to take all I can get from you."

> *[God] can't be used as a road. If you're approaching Him not as the goal but as a road, not as the end but as a means, you're not really approaching Him at all.*
>
> C. S. LEWIS

July 31 ISAIAH 64:1-12

"You aren't fooling me about your sins, so don't waste time trying to fool yourself."

When we display our righteous deeds, they are nothing but filthy rags. . . . Yet no one calls on your name or pleads with you for mercy. ISAIAH 64:6-7

Those Israelites struggled with phony faith, and Isaiah continued to hit them hard with God's truth. Yesterday he called them on their false efforts to earn God's acceptance without offering their wholeheartedness. Today he goes after another load in their laundry pile of sins with a rebuke about their lack of authenticity with themselves.

In Isaiah 64, we see the Israelites finally admit that their best "righteous" efforts were like filthy, stinking rags. God's anger wouldn't relent until they came clean about their degenerated hearts and asked for his mercy.

What better way to get messed up than to fool ourselves into believing our sins aren't so bad? We don't like false flattery from others; why do we accept it from ourselves? For all our modern, "evolved" attitudes about living with authenticity, we all have room for more. If you don't agree with that . . . point made.

God already is aware of everything we do wrong. Confession isn't for bringing him up to speed with our sins. We aren't showing extra character by going to him with a "God, you deserve to know this." Instead, we confess for the humbling goals of agreeing with God about where we've erred and coming to terms with our sinfulness. Only when we acknowledge our need for his forgiveness can we receive his help to change our ways.

Like filthy rags, our sins mold and stink when we let them build up without receiving God's cleansing. The sooner we admit the state of our hearts, the less likely we will need his pressure-washer method of cleaning us up!

TALK TO HIM

"Lord, I want to be as honest with myself as you are with me. You see it all, Father, all my dirty laundry that stinks to the high heavens. Please reveal areas that need your cleansing so that I'm pure and clean as your children should be."

Yea, only as this heart is clean
May larger vision yet be mine,
For mirrored in its depths are seen
The things divine, the things divine.

WALTER C. SMITH, "A CLEAN HEART"

"Consider the costs of fear; I created you to rise above it."

"Get up . . . prepare. . . . Go out . . . tell them. . . . Do not be afraid of them, or I will make you look foolish in front of them." JEREMIAH 1:17

God isn't known to mince words when it comes to giving us wake-up calls about unhealthy patterns. His words are full of compassion and love, but they also get the job done when we need a swift boot to jolt us from a bad habit.

Fear is a bad habit. It isn't usually thought of in those terms, but habits are created through repetition, and fears are encouraged or destroyed through repeated use or consistent quelling.

Bad habits always cost us something. In the case of fear, we lose a sense of empowerment. We also may lose face in front of others, as was the situation God brought to the Israelites' attention in this first chapter of Jeremiah. If they gave in to fear, God wouldn't protect their image in front of their enemies. They would have to face the shame of looking foolish if they didn't take courage from the strength he offered them. Tough love, but again, God doesn't waste time getting to the point when he knows action is necessary.

God hates fear when we allow it to diminish our willingness to move forward with him. We can't overcome fears by sitting around waiting for them to get the best of us. Therefore, God told his people to get up, prepare, and go out. Sometimes action involves nothing other than choosing to rest in faith; when that's what he wants from us, that's all we need to do.

Don't let fear cost you victory, honor, integrity, or deeper faith. Take action against the issues that make you afraid by heeding God's commands and moving confidently with him.

TALK TO HIM

"Lord, I understand why you hate fear because I hate it too. Please help me only fear missing out on a deeper relationship with you that would result from giving in to other fears. Thank you for being my courage."

There is a time to take counsel of your fears, and
there is a time to never listen to any fear.
GENERAL GEORGE S. PATTON

August 2 JEREMIAH 2:1-37

"Will you be desperate to keep loving me or desperate to hold on to your other gods?"

"They worshiped worthless idols, only to become worthless themselves." JEREMIAH 2:5

Desperation is a quality that serves us well when we're pursuing wholesome desires, such as saving a life or committing fully to God. But it isn't so attractive when it means trading our integrity for shameful behavior.

Case in point: Jeremiah 2. Throughout this chapter, Jeremiah used images that convey the idea of desperation, such as eagerness to please God and following him through barren wilderness (verse 2); searching desperately (verse 23); and running and panting, unable to stop (verse 25). The Israelites were desperate for something. Unfortunately, they turned their passionate efforts away from God.

We read this chapter and think how ridiculous it was that the Israelites "exchanged their glorious God for worthless idols," as verse 11 states. How could they commit such a sin as idolatry? But seconds later we gulp over verse 23: "'You say, "That's not true! I haven't worshiped the images of Baal!" But how can you say that? Go and look in any valley in the land!'"

As we're gulping, we can't help but wonder what God would find if he looked in the nooks and crannies where we hide our less-than-holy habits. We swallow hard again realizing he sees it all 24-7. We can't hide anything. We don't like to think we have idols in our lives, but when we withhold parts of ourselves from God, we hold them above God. Anything that we place above God is an idol.

We don't wipe out idolatry once and for all without ever having to purge it again from our lives. Other interests constantly try to take over where only he belongs, so we constantly have to remain on guard.

Stay desperate for more of God so you don't end up desperately chasing worthless attractions.

TALK TO HIM

"Lord, I want to stay passionate about you, but my humanness gets in the way. Even the desire to be close to you has to originate from you. Please do what's necessary in me to keep me desperate for you."

'Tis mad idolatry
To make the service greater than the god.
WILLIAM SHAKESPEARE

"When you put anything before me, you hurt yourself."

"I will be merciful only if . . . you stop harming yourselves by worshiping idols."

JEREMIAH 7:5-6

God commands us to serve only him for a couple of reasons. First and foremost, he deserves exclusive worship. That reason on its own is enough.

Yet there's another reason he wants to retain his number-one place in our lives. He wants us to be safe. The only way that can happen is if we guard against harmful influences. No matter what happens in and around our lives, we're perfectly safe when we live within his will. Circumstances might get messy. Fear might knock loudly on our door. But our souls are not in danger.

Unless . . .

We cast off his protection by failing to recognize his lordship. If we are callous to him and toss aside his love out of preference for unholy desires, we remove ourselves from his safety net. A soul he saves is still safe eternally, but we place our lives on earth in jeopardy. We can't expect to receive the blessing of mercy from him while we run on a path that leads away from him.

You'd think we would process all this logically and conclude that it's best to stick only with him as our God. We might be smart enough to agree with that statement. But good logic does not automatically equate with good behavior, and we do not always do what's best for ourselves.

We think it's best for us to receive more of God's mercy, and we're right about that. But we must stay in proximity to him in order to accept that mercy. There are no good outcomes from putting anything before God. None. Moving outside of God's will by disobeying him will always, always lead to pain.

Life with God offers enough adventure without adding guaranteed hurt to the journey. Desire his best way, and then follow up by living his best way.

TALK TO HIM

"Lord in heaven, you are gracious and merciful, and I thank you for keeping my soul safe. Please help me to help myself by living in obedience to you."

The strength of a man consists in finding out the way in
which God is going, and going in that way too.

HENRY WARD BEECHER

August 4 JEREMIAH 9:12-24

"Your confidence is only as good as the One you place it in."

"Those who wish to boast should boast in this alone: that they truly know me and understand that I am the LORD." JEREMIAH 9:24

When people reject God or turn away temporarily, an attitude of overdone confidence lies at the heart of their actions. They are confident that they don't need him, or that they can be excused from potential repercussions, making a sin worthwhile to their thinking.

Confidence is good, and God desires that we enjoy the security he offers. However, the strength of our confidence depends entirely on what, or whom, we place it in. We can be wholly confident that a chair will support us, but if that chair is made of toothpicks, our confidence likely will prove futile. Athletes might rejoice in their strength, but their power cannot save them from a deadly disease. Atheists who boldly proclaim there is no God one day will discover their confidence was in vain. And scholars who live as though they've learned it all are sure to discover somewhere in eternity that God withholds a few surprises from us until he deems the time is right.

God's point in verse 24 is that confidence placed anywhere besides in him is guaranteed to eventually come up short. The only confidence that will never fail is the one that relies on God.

Our humanness is nothing to brag about. Our faith is nothing to brag about either. The only thing worth boasting about is the Lord's lordship over the world. We can boast about his qualities and never fear that he will be unable to live up to our confidence.

Point your confidence at God, and don't settle for placing your trust in securities that hold no guarantees.

TALK TO HIM

"Lord, I trust that my confidence in you is secure. Thank you for the reminder that nothing else is secure in this life or for eternity."

Great confidence in unstable things will yield small results. Small confidence in a big God can yield results yet unmatched in their significance, and how much more a big confidence in that same big God.

ANONYMOUS

"Be discerning about spiritual leaders; many do not stick to my truth."

"As for the people to whom they prophesy—their bodies will be thrown out into the streets. . . . For I will pour out their own wickedness on them." JEREMIAH 14:16

God did not create us to be victims. True, evil and wickedness do victimize, but when we have the ability to guard against forces that seek to destroy us, God expects us to use the resources he provides. One of those resources is a sound mind to discern when someone doesn't speak God's truth.

The world has never lacked for liars and other dishonest people who show hatred for the Lord's truth. And the world has never lacked for gullible folks who allow themselves to be taken in by smooth words.

God's response to people who buy into the messages of false teachers might seem harsh—how could he penalize those "victims" simply because they believed leaders who work against him? Well, consider his viewpoint in light of the intelligence and discernment he offers his children. Those supposed victims may not have used their God-given resources to learn for themselves whether a message lined up with God's truth.

Through his Spirit in us, God gives us spiritual fortitude to stand up to incorrect doctrine. He did not create us to be spiritual wimps, but to grow into spiritual giants. However, many times we lack the discipline to study his Word for truth and clarity that help us recognize when someone is off base.

He wants us to use the good minds he gave us, along with the discernment of his Holy Spirit, to defend ourselves against the onslaught of mistruths.

Arm yourself with his unmatchable wisdom and his guard over your mind by studying his truth as he laid it out in the Bible. He created you to stand up for his Kingdom ways, but you will need Kingdom help in order to be successful.

TALK TO HIM

"Father God, you are the creator and imparter of intelligence and discernment, but you don't offer handouts when we're fully capable of applying your resources. Please help me use what you've provided me to guard the truths you've entrusted to me."

It requires wisdom to understand wisdom.

WALTER LIPPMANN

August 6 JEREMIAH 17:5-18

"My hope translates to strength during difficult times."

"Blessed are those who trust in the LORD *and have made the* LORD *their hope and confidence."*

JEREMIAH 17:7

Healthy things grow. Like "trees planted along a riverbank, with roots that reach deep into the water" (verse 8) are those who put their hope in God. Hope sounds good, but what is it really? What does it look like, practically speaking, in someone's life?

Moving through verse 8, we see that the trees planted along a riverbank aren't bothered by heat or worried by long drought. In human terms, the verse seems to indicate that hope provides the soul nourishment we need to withstand intense pressure and stress, as well as trials and disappointments—anything that feels like heat weighing on us.

To deepen our understanding of the helper that is hope, think about what excessive heat does. It's midsummer now; the sun's rays burn with ferocity, and the green world is gradually fading to brown. Without the refreshment of rain, lakes and rivers shrink from their banks as their waves evaporate under heat waves. Heat makes us gasp for life-giving air; breathing requires more effort, and inhaling feels like weight lifting. We might worry whether we'll make it through the dry times. Thriving seems out of the question; we are weary from the effort to survive.

Jeremiah 17 begs to differ. Not only can we survive through each ordeal, but we can revel in the hope God offers us, feeling strengthened to grow even when circumstances threaten to evaporate our vitality.

Hope looks beyond the bleak browns of here and now and dares to draw nourishment from God's supply. Hope sees refreshment and life in the midst of drought seasons. Hope is strength that doesn't wither beneath a furnace of worry.

Hope withstands—and even hydrates your spirit—despite what you're dealing with today.

TALK TO HIM

"Father God, you are my sustainer. Please help me to live on hope in you, trusting you for health and wholeness deep in my soul during this dry time."

Sometimes our fate resembles a fruit tree in winter. Who would think that those branches would turn green again and blossom, but we hope it, we know it.

JOHANN WOLFGANG VON GOETHE

"I understand your hurts, but maintain your faithfulness to me because I am still with you."

The LORD stands beside me like a great warrior. JEREMIAH 20:11

Jeremiah knew about the lowest of the lows. He had been there, done that, didn't like it. He had been arrested, whipped, humiliated, and forsaken to the point that he wished he had never been born.

Life doesn't always feel worth living. When we face the worst, we think there has to be something more than this, something better. When something better doesn't appear, we might begin to wonder what God is doing. When time continues to pass, but the "better days ahead" don't come, doubts we tried valiantly to quell begin to bite more fiercely.

Jeremiah knew all about this pattern, and he was honest with God regarding his feelings. He even spoke frankly with God about how he felt God had misled him—bold words to speak to the Almighty.

However, as we've seen with other biblical heroes such as David and Job, Jeremiah turned his frustrations around and refocused himself on what he knew to be true of the Lord. Even though Jeremiah couldn't see God, he knew the Lord still stood beside him "like a great warrior" (verse 11).

Just as negative thoughts snowball, a person's determination to remain faithful compounds itself. As soon as he reminded himself that God hadn't abandoned him, Jeremiah felt compelled to praise. It was as though a lightbulb went on in his mind, a thoughtful "Oh yeah, I almost forgot I'm not alone."

Your determination to stay faithful to what you know about God will stretch you to meet the next challenge and enable you to endure the long road of uncertainty and disillusionment.

As we studied about hope yesterday, faithfulness to God will be your strength when all else fails.

TALK TO HIM

"Lord God in heaven, thank you for staying near me on earth. Please help me to choose faithfulness when everything looks bleak. I know you will never leave me, and because of that I can hope."

Assisted by the Holy Author . . . , I do, with all conscience of truth, required therein by Him, who is the Truth itself, report the wonderful displays of His infinite power, wisdom, goodness, and faithfulness.

COTTON MATHER

August 8 JEREMIAH 25:1-14

"Whether or not I grant you worldly success, strive to live successfully for me."

"For the past twenty-three years . . . the L*ORD has been giving me his messages. I have faithfully passed them on to you, but you have not listened."* JEREMIAH 25:3

Success is a big deal to us. Too often we tend to base our worth on our accomplishments, buying into society's influence that places the highest value on people with the most possessions to show for their efforts. Forget that we're cherished by God simply because we're his creations; the trendsetters on earth say we must give an account of what we do with the space we consume on the planet: Not measuring up? Move over, because there is someone coming behind you with a bigger name and flashier credentials.

For most of his career, Jeremiah was a failure by those standards. He toiled with no success for twenty-three years—not an iota of accomplishment to show for his efforts to turn the people back to God. We breeze over those verses and think that was okay with him because he was on God's mission, and it was so long ago. Surely he knew he would go down in history as a spiritual giant who stayed the course despite a track record of zero success.

But twenty-three years! He would have been virtually unemployable today because his résumé looked so grim. Jeremiah was as human as we are. Surely he grew discouraged over day in and day out failure. Questions likely plagued him with relentless mockery: Where am I going wrong? What must everyone think? Am I doing right by my family? Is this worth it? How much longer do I have to keep at this? Is this all there is to life? Can't I have just one success, Lord?

Jeremiah's only hope throughout such a dry career came from knowing that God had called him to the work. The only success worth measuring was how faithfully he stuck to his task. In God's eyes, Jeremiah was a great success.

What does God see in your work?

TALK TO HIM

"Heavenly Father, thank you for establishing my purpose. Please burn on my heart that you determine my success, and my faithfulness to you is my priority. Please close my ears to the world's opinion of my efforts."

Don't confuse fame with success.

ERMA BOMBECK

"You will see me when you look with your whole heart."

"If you look for me wholeheartedly, you will find me." JEREMIAH 29:13

God loves when we give our hearts to him—our whole hearts, that is. Since he isn't a half-way God, he doesn't cherish the gift of a partial heart. To him, that kind of mediocre offering is the same as giving him nothing.

If he gave us himself half the time, we would lose more than half of our ability to trust him. We would lose all of it. How would we know if our prayers would reach heaven during his on-duty time? Half-trustworthy translates into untrustworthy, because trustworthy requires guaranteed availability.

Our whole heart is required to discover a whole relationship with God. He can work with whatever we give him, but he shows us more of himself the more we open our hearts to his Spirit within us. It's almost like peering inside a half-open hand. You can see part of what's hidden inside, but part remains in the dark. The only way to discover the entire treasure is to open your hand wide.

Two half people cannot make one whole relationship because healthy relationships are not fifty-fifty commitments. Imagine how quickly a marriage or friendship would disintegrate if the two parts gave only a portion of their energy, affection, love, or time. Each person must give 100 percent.

God will reveal himself to you in proportion to how fully you release yourself to his care. Sure, he will continue putting all of himself into your relationship, but you will miss experiencing everything he wants for you if you don't seek him with all you have.

He has amazing plans for you, "to give you a future and a hope" (Jeremiah 29:11) But you must want him wholeheartedly if you hope to discover the full treasure that he is.

TALK TO HIM

"Father God, you are my treasure. Please help me to open wide my heart, and give me greater desire to seek you. Keep me from being satisfied with a halfway effort at our relationship."

Whole-hearted thanksgiving to Thee I will bring
In praise of Thy marvelous deeds I will sing;
In Thee I will joy and exultingly cry,
Thy Name I will praise, O Jehovah, Most High.

AUTHOR UNKNOWN, "WHOLE-HEARTED THANKSGIVING TO THEE I WILL BRING"

August 10 JEREMIAH 31:1-40

"Imagine being completely restored by me."

"I will rebuild you. . . . You will again be happy." JEREMIAH 31:4

You have probably heard of the burgeoning career known as flipping houses. The goal is to buy a fixer-upper, do a whirlwind renovation, then sell it quickly for a profit. Flippers turn the structure inside out to give it a new lease on life.

God has been in the renovation business for generations; in fact, it's his family business, and people are his fixer-uppers. He has been known to breathe freshness into the most decrepit soul, clearing out dust that clogs our spiritual filters, tearing down faulty supports we've erected as coping mechanisms to keep us functioning. He cleanses the mold and mildew of unhealthy patterns, and he removes debris that clutters and compromises our foundation.

The Israelites understood surviving on unsteady support beams and breathing toxic fumes from their surroundings. Living in captivity left them longing for home sweet home. Jeremiah 31 describes the Lord's commitment to rebuild them. In the Lord's own words, he acknowledged their desolation. But instead of doing a complete demolition on them, he emptied them to a shell in order to make something whole and new. His compassion, forgiveness, and faithfulness resound in his words. All along, he kept his dream for them alive, and one day he would welcome them back to himself, restored and beautified through his renovating work.

Just as run-down houses look shabby and depressed, over time we show signs of the world's wear and tear. We all need a dose of God's renovating power every now and then. Expertly skilled with the tools of the trade, he chisels and forms and repairs our damaged places until we stand tall and strong, with hearts ready to make a healthy home for him.

TALK TO HIM

"Father God, sometimes your construction hurts, but you do beautiful renovation work. I am tired of the worn-out places inside myself. Thank you for loving me too much to let my soul deteriorate."

Surely in temples made with hands,
God, the Most High, is not dwelling;
High above earth His temple stands,
All earthly temples excelling;
Yet He whom heavens cannot contain
Chose to abide on earth with men,
Built in our bodies His temple.

NIKOLAI F. S. GRUNDTVIG, "BUILT ON THE ROCK"

“Will you trust me when justice seems unlikely?”

“What have I done against you, your attendants, or the people that I should be imprisoned like this?” JEREMIAH 37:18

Jeremiah hit bottom again in these chapters, this time literally at the bottom of a dry cistern. Caught in King Zedekiah’s turbulent reign, Jeremiah faced more attacks on his reputation. Accused of defecting to the enemy Babylonians, he again was whipped, imprisoned, and left to fear for his life. Jeremiah had every reason to revolt at the mistreatment by the king’s officials.

Not much triggers our desperation like being at the wrong end of injustice. We typically can handle punishment when we have done wrong, but our sense of justice kicks in if we feel we are getting the raw end of the deal. Our hackles rise in self-defense. We want things made right. Perhaps because innocence is so rare, we like ours to be known. We want our true hearts to be revealed with no misunderstandings about our loyalties.

Some issues, however, will be made right only when God has his final say: childhood abuse when the abuser is nowhere to be found, the driver who hit us and lied about fault, divorce proceedings that turn ugly. Every day we face circumstances that smart of unfairness but hold little hope for justice anytime soon. Life is not fair.

Truthfully, we have many reasons to thank God for not being fair to us, namely for withholding what we truly deserve in lieu of mercy. God’s justice favors us—favor that we don’t deserve because we aren’t innocent in our heart of hearts. Our souls are naturally corrupt, and it is only by his grace that we don’t have to spend eternity behind spiritual bars, so to speak.

Our desire for justice can be complicated, and we lack wisdom on our own to dole it out properly. Trust God with justice, and know that he has you covered despite circumstances that beg to differ.

TALK TO HIM

“Lord, I can’t stand feeling trapped by injustice. Sitting still and waiting on you goes against my instincts that want to solve things my way right now. Please help me to be patient, trusting that you will make everything right in the end.”

Injustice is relatively easy to bear; what stings is justice.

H. L. MENCKEN

August 12 JEREMIAH 50:21–51:14

"I don't doubt my victory on your behalf, so why should you?"

"Who is like me, and who can challenge me? What ruler can oppose my will?"

JEREMIAH 50:44

Confidence is contagious, and God has lots of it. Think about his pride when he says his own name: "His name is the LORD of Heaven's Armies" (50:34). Can you hear his voice thunder those words? Does the image make you want to sign on to his team? He has an undefeated track record . . . make that undefeatable.

We like to be on the winning team, and we like to associate ourselves with confident people because they instill positive feelings in us. We want what they have. They don't trouble themselves with useless self-doubts that drain their energy. They wear security like a hero's cape, and if they are generous as well as confident, they might let us in on their secrets of success.

God's confidence is unique because he alone has reason to be downright arrogant about his strength; yet he is not. Contrast his self-possession with the audacity he accuses the Babylonians of in verses 31 and 32, and you will see that he uses his abilities for the good of others, as verses 33 and 34 indicate. His confidence is all the more appealing because of his other characteristics such as kindness, thoughtfulness, selflessness, gentleness, holiness, and graciousness.

God is supremely confident in his ability to handle your troubles. The grief that suffocates, the pain that intensifies, the heartache that twists, the question that plagues—all are opportunities to trust his confident victory on your behalf.

Nothing challenges him, not even your doubts. So put them to rest, and rest instead in his coming victory.

TALK TO HIM

"God Almighty, you are supreme, and I am grateful for your sure victory. Please help me trust you even now, when I cannot see how you will get me through this situation. You are the Lord of Heaven's Armies, and right now I cherish even more that you're my Lord."

While leaning on His arm alone
I cannot know defeat;
The glory shall be all His own
When victory is complete.

JAMES M. GRAY, "VICTORY IN MY SOUL"

"Be refreshed with a new dose of my mercy every day."

His mercies begin afresh each morning. LAMENTATIONS 3:23

God is supremely generous, but two things he will not lend us are yesterday's or tomorrow's mercies. Is he suddenly stingy? Heavens no! He simply wants us to receive the freshest of fresh mercies from him, because they are new every morning. That means yesterday's aren't sufficient for today, and we haven't received tomorrow's dose yet.

Consider the implications of not having tomorrow's mercies right now. We need mercy to withstand Satan's attacks and to see us through our failures. Wouldn't it be wonderful to get it ahead of time, to build it up for future use in case we need extra one day? Apparently not, or God would work out a different schedule for mercy giving. In supplying us with mercy to fill only the present day's needs, he does a number of things in us.

First of all, he grows our trust as we wonder, *Will he be enough for me again today?* Next, he strengthens us against worry since we have to learn not to borrow trouble from the future. And finally, he reasserts his sovereignty by showing very practically that he is Lord, and he decides how things will be done. As a result, we exercise our muscles of surrender to him by either bucking the system and getting angry at him or releasing our desire for control in exchange for his greater wisdom.

God's mercy brings refreshment, and because he provides the day's supply one day at a time, our daily dose is sublimely fresh and perfectly fitted for the challenges of that twenty-four hours.

He knows what things you need mercy for today. Your needs are not the same as they will be tomorrow or next week, but you can count on receiving an ideally handcrafted supply for those days . . . but not until then.

TALK TO HIM

"You are a wise, wise God, my heavenly Father. Thank you for your gift of mercy that teaches me so much about waiting and relying on you."

Among the attributes of God, although they are all equal,
mercy shines with even more brilliancy than justice.
MIGUEL DE CERVANTES

August 14 EZEKIEL 2:1-10

"Does your obedience to me extend to situations that seem hopeless?"

"You must give them my messages whether they listen or not. But they won't listen, for they are completely rebellious!" EZEKIEL 2:7

"Okay, Ezekiel, this is your Father speaking. It's time for you to wake up and be Mr. Sunshine for the nation. Here's a scroll to eat. Feast on its words of gloom and doom; then spread the word to the people."

Who wouldn't be tempted to raise an eyebrow to God and dash off in the opposite direction? To be assigned the job of declaring sorrow day after day—what fun! Ezekiel's work was shaping up to resemble Jeremiah's. Such was the life of an Old Testament prophet.

Actually, God doesn't promise blue skies and roses to his followers today either. His call still doesn't include get-out clauses if things become difficult to the point of appearing hopeless. Gray days are still part of our earthly journey, and they don't warrant time-outs or hiatuses from living for him.

Even though God is extremely compassionate, sometimes he shows his unwavering side that challenges us to remain strong when we want to cave under pressure. For all his tenderness, he is tough. But he needs to be tough when dealing with stubborn humans, and his toughness works only for our good.

He doesn't shy away from telling us to deal with situations and people that seem hopeless because his message needs to be shared regardless of who will listen. As we continue to put one foot in front of the other in our walk with him, he strengthens our spiritual muscles and fits us for greater tasks. All the while in our training, he becomes our hope amid the hopelessness around us.

Choose obedience no matter what pressures you face. Obedience to God is the ultimate path out of hopelessness.

TALK TO HIM

"Lord, you're greater than the problems around me. I'm easily discouraged when I focus on the world's hopelessness. Please keep me walking in obedience to you no matter how much stress weighs on me."

Turn away for one second out of obedience, and darkness and death are at work at once. All God's revelations are sealed until they are opened to us by obedience. You will never get them open by philosophy or thinking. Immediately you obey, a flash of light comes.

OSWALD CHAMBERS

"Digest my Word; it is for your nourishment."

"Fill your stomach with this," he said. And when I ate it, it tasted as sweet as honey in my mouth. EZEKIEL 3:3

When you read God's Word, do you think of it as nourishment? It's the greatest food you could give yourself—even above the whole grains, fruits, and veggies the wisest nutritionist would prescribe.

God's Word is soul food, and when your soul is fed and healthy, your whole being functions better. The more you ingest his Word, the better your body learns to digest it and make the most use of its vitality. As a baby gradually learns to handle grown-up food, we learn to take in God's truths better the more we turn to him for sustenance. We get out of it what we put into it.

If our spiritual diet consists of a few Scripture verses fed to us on the weekends at church, we can't expect to thrive and think God will fill out the empty corners of our spirit. However, when we discipline ourselves to eat of his Word daily, letting ourselves chew on what it says, then surely he will fill us up. We will be satisfied and overflowing with desire to share this good feast with others.

Not only is God's Word filling, but it also tastes sweet to those with an appetite for it. "We are what we eat," and we develop a taste for whatever we consistently put into our bodies. The more we taste God's Word, the more we will crave it, and the less satisfied we will be with less nourishing input.

Take a bite of his Word today, and see if he doesn't whet your appetite for more of his soul satisfaction.

TALK TO HIM

"Father, it's odd to think of your Word as nourishment, but the more I digest what you have written to me, the more I understand how much I need the Bible's truths to thrive. Thank you for providing such unique sustenance."

Feasting, I am feasting,
Feasting with my Lord;
I'm feasting, I am feasting,
On the living Word.

JOHN S. BROWN, "FEASTING WITH MY LORD"

August 16 EZEKIEL 6:1-14

"Do you understand the depth of my emotions?"

"They will recognize how hurt I am." EZEKIEL 6:9

We might know a lot of things about God, but do we understand him? Do we really understand his emotions? Because God is invincible, infallible, infinite, omnipotent, omnipresent, and omniscient—not to mention all-seeing, all-consuming, all-perfect, and altogether awesome—we forget that he is also a God of extraordinary feeling. He can do all and see all, but he can also feel all we feel. He is strong and unyielding to run the universe, but gentle and kindhearted to understand our fragile selves.

A God who created us with our emotional range, and who created us in his image, knows the highs and lows we experience because he feels them as well. Most often, we're the catalysts for his emotional responses, as Ezekiel 6 describes.

God had had it with the Israelites when he told Ezekiel to warn them what they were in for. He shared his anger toward the people, but he also exposed his tender heart when he expressed his pain over their sin.

Do we ever consider God's big heart as being filled with pain? Furthermore, do we take ownership for his heartache? God's pain bears our names, each of our sins like a whiplash that cut Jesus' back before he went to the cross. He aches over our waywardness and longs to help us see his light and turn back to him. The God who collects our tears hurts over each one before he dries them from our eyes.

When other people hurt, we offer comfort. But how does one comfort God? Can we presume to offer solace to the Almighty? It seems a mite audacious, as if he needs anything from us.

Instead of afterthought pats on his back, God simply wants our obedience. A cessation of the behaviors that hurt and anger him would be nice. In fact, a worshipful life is what he has wanted from us all along.

May you understand God's heart more today than yesterday.

TALK TO HIM

"Father God, thank you for not being heartless in your perfection. Although you don't need my comfort, please help me care for your beautiful heart by refusing to grieve it."

The heart that broke over your sin breaks also over your hurts. As only the heart of God can do, its brokenness brings you to wholeness.

ANONYMOUS

"Is my glory welcome in you, my temple?"

The glory of the L*ORD moved out from the door of the Temple.* EZEKIEL 10:18

Burning coals, spinning wheels, and four cherubim with sixteen faces? Priceless.

As was the norm for Ezekiel's messages from the Lord, this news foretelling future events wasn't pleasant. God went to great lengths to convey one thing: He was removing his glory from the Temple. His people were about to lose something precious, but most of them wouldn't recognize its pricelessness until it was gone. Once his glory left the Temple, the people would realize the treasure they had given up in favor of a lifestyle that didn't welcome God's purity.

What is God's glory? Glory is a difficult concept to define. We know it has a wow factor. We also can assume his glory invites, even commands, our reverence. But can we see it? Why would God use such complex imagery to convey his glory?

There is no telling for sure, but perhaps he wanted to express its otherworldliness. He is wholly beyond anything we can touch on our own, yet he makes himself accessible to us. His indescribable qualities attract, awe, and humble us. Such a vision as he gave Ezekiel stuns us with its creativity.

God's glory cannot share space with impurity, but it doesn't force its way where it isn't welcome—at least not until the final battle between good and evil. Then God's glory will have the last say. In the meantime, if you belong to God by accepting his salvation, then you are his temple, the home of his glory. Do you guard a welcoming environment for him to shine through you?

You have a priceless treasure within you. You are wise to treat it as such.

TALK TO HIM

"Lord God Almighty, you reign in the universe, and you reign in me. Let my life be a shining point for your glory."

The glory of God makes possible the . . . realization that we are not sufficient unto ourselves, that we have received our life and being from another. In a decision that reaches the roots of our most intimate self and demands the renunciation of belonging to that self, we . . . acknowledge the illusion of control and open ourselves to the reality of God.

BRENNAN MANNING

August 18 EZEKIEL 16:1-34

"A broken relationship with me is as painful as infidelity."

"I wrapped my cloak around you . . . and declared my marriage vows." EZEKIEL 16:8

The intimacy of marriage between true soul mates cannot be equaled on earth. Souls laid bare, nothing hidden from each other, two spirits refining one another through life's joys and sorrows—that unity must be experienced directly. It can't be manufactured or felt secondhand. It's a gift from above, and it deserves the utmost care and protection.

But God offers us something even better. Long ago he made a covenant with us that humbles the best of human marriages. With him, we can experience heights of fulfillment and growth that nothing else can touch. We also come to know the true meaning of forever as we look forward to eternity with him, our heavenly Bridegroom.

Yet there is a vulnerable side to any marriage, earthly or heavenly. Along with sublime unity comes high vulnerability to imperfections and unfaithfulness. We are unfaithful people by nature. Even our best intentions fail at times, and infidelity can devastate the strongest connection. When unfaithfulness tears into a marriage, it shreds trust and love. The effect is like separating two papers that had been cemented together. It can't be done without both sides leaving parts of themselves attached to the other. They can be patched, but the damage goes deep.

Our connection to God needs protection from unfaithfulness, too—ours, that is, since he is unwaveringly true to us. Protect your heavenly Spouse by guarding your unity with him. Let nothing intrude on your relationship—not sin or other attractions or a too busy schedule. Life will always lay its demands on you and threaten to undo your connection with your Lord. Don't let it. What God has joined together, let nothing separate!

TALK TO HIM

"Lord Jesus, I want to be faithful to you always. Please help me to stay true in good times and bad, for richer or poorer, in sickness and health, till death brings us together forever! Thank you for being the Soul Mate beyond my dreams."

Jesus, lover of my soul,
Let me to Thy bosom fly. . . .
Hide me, O my Savior, hide,
Till the storm of life is past;
Safe into the haven glide,
O receive my soul at last.

CHARLES WESLEY, "JESUS, LOVER OF MY SOUL"

"It's easy to blame me for the world's troubles, but look again and see who's at fault."

"Yet you say, 'The Lord isn't doing what's right!' Listen to me, O people of Israel. Am I the one not doing what's right, or is it you?" EZEKIEL 18:25

God blessed humans with many skills, including our ability to think and process information. However, we're good at using that gift in less-than-admirable ways.

When we go into rationalization mode, there's no stopping where our thoughts can take us—more specifically, how they attempt to excuse our wrongs. We can twist anything to lay the blame for our problems anywhere besides our own laps. *I wasn't raised right. In time I probably would have thought of that coworker's great idea. My spouse had that sarcastic comment coming.*

Yet God says we answer for our behavior. No one makes us sin. He doesn't lay secondhand blame, nor does he give secondhand credit. You may have heard that God doesn't have grandchildren. Grandma Harriet's ministry on Skid Row can't speak in our favor, but neither will Dad's abuse earn check marks against us.

Even more seriously, we can't blame God for the trouble we bring on ourselves with our sin, claiming we didn't know better. As the archenemy of holiness, sin is huge to God; it sent his Son to the cross and continues to break his heart. And we humans are full of it. We can't expect him to spare us the consequences of living apart from his standards.

He isn't mistreating us when he corrects us, even painfully, for walking away from him. He will never give in to our faulty rationalizations for bad behavior because he wants more for us. He even longs for the wicked to turn back to him so he can save them—not the attitude of a God who enjoys punishing unnecessarily.

Kick the urge to rationalize, and develop the character that accepts blame when blame is due.

TALK TO HIM

"Lord, I don't like messing up, but please help me show the integrity to admit it and accept the consequences. Thank you for not letting me get away with rationalizing my sins; they're serious to me because they're serious to you."

Whoever wants to be a judge of human nature should study people's excuses.

FRIEDRICH HEBBEL

August 20 EZEKIEL 24:1-27

"I notice the losses you take for my sake."

"With one blow I will take away your dearest treasure." EZEKIEL 24:16

Would your heart break more over the loss of a loved one or the loss of your connection with God?

Your answer is as telling of your humanity as it is of your spiritual desire. We want heroic faith that doesn't swallow hard before answering. We want to love God, and we do love him—with the deepest of loves, actually. We say he is first in our hearts, and we mean it.

Yet if we were forced to choose between God and the person most precious to us, we'd be dishonest to say the decision wouldn't bring us to our knees. Even when there's no real decision because we absolutely would choose God, we would still be left to deal with mind-numbing sorrow from losing someone irreplaceable.

A strong faith does not negate our emotions over extreme loss. Anyone who criticizes Christians for feeling depression and heartache would grow from studying this chapter or several psalms about approaching God honestly.

God knows exactly how brokenness feels because he feels every bit of it with us. We don't carry our pain alone, no matter how our feelings plead otherwise. God knows, and God feels. We can only handle so much at once, so at least let the question of aloneness rest when waves of heartache threaten to drown you. If you are God's child, you are not alone.

Being a hero of faith does not make the tough questions easier to hear, but it does keep the answers clarified and your intimacy with God worth it all.

TALK TO HIM

"Father, you know how I feel, but when the pain won't subside, I find little comfort even in that truth. Somewhere deep down it helps to know that you are here, even when I can't feel your presence. Please give me grace to keep choosing you. I can't do it without your help."

Transcendence means that God cannot be confined to the world. . . .
Immanence, on the other hand, means that God is wholly involved with us,
. . . that he is here in his mysterious nearness. . . . Disregard of God's
immanence deprives us of any sense of intimate belonging, while
inattention to his transcendence robs God of his godliness.

BRENNAN MANNING

"I care for you myself; I do not hire another to get the work done."

"I myself will tend my sheep and give them a place to lie down in peace, says the Sovereign Lord." EZEKIEL 34:15

One way people manage busy lives is by subbing out a few tasks here and there. Weeding and trimming in the summer, window cleaning in the spring and fall, house cleaning whenever. . . . We appreciate those folks who build careers from the overflow of our schedules! Usually the jobs are B-level, leaving us more time to give our best attention to higher priorities.

Imagine if God subbed us out. . . .

How would we feel being B-level people in his heart? What would that do to our trust in him, much less our desire to emulate his character? We are fond of being loved, and we have quite a deal being heirs of divine royalty.

All tongue-in-cheek banter aside, though, we have a genuine and deep need to know that God cares for us himself. We know angels serve him as messengers and warriors. But when it comes to cherishing our hearts, drying our tears, strengthening us with his Spirit, filling us with joy, and nudging us back on track when we stray, God does not send anyone to deal with us as B-level concerns.

He does his own work in us, and the peace we have in him comes directly from his heart. He is our rescuer, our guide, and our nurturer. When we are lost, he does not rely on angels or any other beings to search for us. We have the real, one-and-only Lord of the heavens and earth nearby at all times.

He loves being our Savior and sustainer—our God, the great I Am, who carried his people long ago, is faithful to us today, and promises himself to us for eternity.

You are always A-level to him.

TALK TO HIM

"Lord God, thank you for doing your own work—yet more reasons to praise you for who you are. You are good and faithful, and I love being a top priority to you! Awesome and humbling all at once."

The Shepherd of Love knows His sheep by name,
And tenderly leads the way;
O weary one, come to the Shepherd's fold,
He's calling, calling today.

ALBERT S. REITZ, "THE SHEPHERD OF LOVE"

August 22 EZEKIEL 37:1-14

"Death is powerless over me."

"'Breathe into these dead bodies so they may live again.'" EZEKIEL 37:9

There is a type of death that exists among the living, far more tragic than physical death. It is spiritual death, and it claims people without anyone knowing it, including those who have succumbed.

You may be able to spot it, although there is no way to see for sure the state of someone else's soul. It may appear as apathy, bitterness, fear, hopelessness, or obsessiveness. It could take the form of an -ism: workaholism, alcoholism, rageaholism. You might see it in a shopaholic or a drug addict, the soccer mom across the street or the pastor across town. It doesn't cater to rich or poor, young or old, churched or unchurched. It is pervasive, ruthless, and tricky to identify because it poses as characteristics like depression and fatigue that even those with healthy spiritual lives experience from time to time.

Lying to its victims, this death tells them their exhaustion is part of life; sometimes it attempts to fake true life with coping mechanisms of busyness and material wealth, all the while cheating people of joy and peace. When it has them by the throat, it deals a final blow by robbing them of God's truth that holds the power to save.

God spoke to Ezekiel about spiritual death and illustrated with extraordinary creativity how he would restore his people. Anyone who hadn't experienced his ability to conquer death might find the whole vision unbelievable, but God's resurrecting power is that miraculous.

All our good efforts cannot make up for the dead state of sin we inherited as humans. A lifestyle of sin isn't the only identifying factor of spiritual death, which is why someone in ministry is just as susceptible to it as a death-row inmate.

Only a saving relationship with God can conquer spiritual death. God's breath that gave us life at Creation also restores us to eternal life. Our role is simply to breathe him in and accept the salvation he offers.

TALK TO HIM

"Lord, I appear healthy and whole, but I still need your life-enriching breath every day to overcome these burdens. Thank you for your never-ceasing ability to refresh."

Power again, power again,
Our hearts have been tuned to the sweet refrain,
The breath of the Spirit brings power again.
CIVILLA D. MARTIN, "THE BREATH OF THE SPIRIT"

"Let my glory overwhelm you."

Suddenly, the glory of the God of Israel appeared. . . . And the whole landscape shone.

EZEKIEL 43:2

Several days ago we wondered what God's glory looks like. How do we recognize it? What is its effect?

Today we find out more. With a roar of rushing refreshment, God's glory returned to the Temple. It came with suddenness, power, and light. Ezekiel recognized it since he had experienced it previously, but it still floored him with its impact and filled the Temple with its consuming nature.

God's glory does not arrive halfway. It alters the environment it saturates, slipping in to shed light on everything it touches. It is the sign of God's authority and majesty, his sovereignty and fidelity, his purity and sanctity. All is well when God's glory is present.

Living in the light of God's glory humbles us, as it did Ezekiel, who dropped to the ground at its awesome arrival. We are put in our place by its awesomeness, yet privileged to witness it and blessed to dwell in its proximity.

Life looks different when viewed in light of his glory, which softens the edges of pain, tenderizes hardened hearts, and increases our awareness of the world as he sees it. We can't remain the same after tasting his glory. Its sweetness leaves us craving more, even while its sustenance fully satisfies us.

Most of all, his glory points us to himself, and we understand more completely that our existence is not about us but about praising him for being *God.*

TALK TO HIM

"Lord, I don't understand how to define your glory, but I want to witness it today. I invite you to shine into my surroundings. Thank you for being the God of all glory who shares yourself with me."

The obscure yet real, penetrating, and transforming experience of his incomparable glory . . . awakens a dormant trust. Something is afoot in the universe; Someone filled with transcendent brightness, wisdom, ingenuity, and power and goodness is about. In the face of overwhelming evidence to the contrary, somewhere deep down a Voice whispers, "All is well, and all will be well."

BRENNAN MANNING

August 24 EZEKIEL 47:1-12

"Life flourishes wherever I am."

"Life will flourish wherever this water flows." EZEKIEL 47:9

Healthy things grow. Sound familiar? We have seen that truth evidenced in previous days' readings, and here it echoes again. Anytime God repeats an image or phrase in the Bible, he does so to emphasize a point. Over and over, using a variety of symbolic illustrations, he shows himself as a life giver. In this chapter, he again displays himself as the source of never-ending refreshment.

Like a flowing river, so runs his constancy. The farther we travel with him, the deeper we can experience his nourishment. And the more his presence surrounds us, as deep waters rose around Ezekiel, the better fitted we are to stand tall in the midst of other turbulence because we have learned to balance ourselves in him.

Life that flourishes does not mean life without trouble. In fact, the deeper we go with him, eventually we must learn to tread in faith when the ground moves out from under us. We can't see beneath the waters that rise around us, nor are we hidden from storms that rage through our world. Yet in him we can draw continual strength and ongoing comfort as water refuels and hydrates a worn-out body. Sometimes we feel drowned, but we are not, because his water is safe.

You can flourish in any circumstance when you turn to the Lord as an oasis. Dry times will come, no doubt about it. They will feel powerful and suffocating, and they will threaten to cut off your air supply and rob you of growth. When you feel as though you're gasping for your last breath, surrender to the Deep that is God's life-giving arms enveloping you. Far from suffocating you, his Spirit will help you learn a new way to breathe and thrive.

TALK TO HIM

"Thank you, Lord, for being my spiritual thirst quencher. As I grow deeper with you, please teach me more about flourishing in waves of uncertainty instead of drowning."

God does not see deserts as you see them, as unreachable horizons with no refreshment. He knows he is your Oasis just up ahead where life and growth come if you'll keep moving toward him.

ANONYMOUS

"Wisdom takes the time to seek my direction."

Daniel handled the situation with wisdom and discretion. DANIEL 2:14

Daniel is one of the Bible's greats. Nowhere in his book can we find an instance when he failed to act honorably on God's behalf. His biggest secret of success was the fact that it was no secret to him that he would fail on his own. He knew he needed God.

Cast into the unfortunate situation of an exile to Babylon, Daniel landed in King Nebuchadnezzar's palace service, where his faithfulness to God was tested time and again. The tests that proved his loyalty weren't the run-of-the-mill challenges we know in our daily lives. He repeatedly encountered situations that meant life or death and required superhuman intuition. In each one he sought God and found what he needed.

When he was called on not only to interpret Nebuchadnezzar's dream but also to know the details of that dream, he wisely took a time-out to ask for God's help. Instead of panicking or reacting rashly, he responded with self-control and spiritual maturity that established him as a trustworthy adviser and showed the king and officials that Daniel's God was worthy of worship.

Being God's followers doesn't give us any greater abilities in our own power. Instead, our connection with the Lord shows us how much more connected to him we need to be. The more we know of him, the more we know we need him. Daniel was keenly aware of this truth; in fact, he put his life on the line in deference to this truth.

Only God knows how many circumstances will cross your path today that will require his extra wisdom, and only he knows what specific wisdom you'll need for each one. When you have no idea what to do, and the urge to panic strikes, invest the time to ask for God's help. He knows you need him, and your first step of wisdom is to acknowledge that need as well. Instead of losing time or wasting it with human logic, you will find the moments spared for him will pay off with life-changing results.

TALK TO HIM

"Thank you, Lord, for not being limited by anything. Please help me not to limit myself with my own wisdom, but instead to invest time seeking yours."

Every second spent with God protects every future second.

ANONYMOUS

August 26 DANIEL 6:1-28

"Take care of my business, and I will take care of you."

So Daniel prospered during the reign of Darius and the reign of Cyrus the Persian.

DANIEL 6:28

As children, many of us had big dreams of playing the hero and overcoming astounding obstacles. We knew we were unbeatable—couldn't stop us, couldn't even hope to contain us!

But then we reached adulthood and practicality set in. We still like the idea of adventure—from the safety of our armchair. We still have dreams, but they typically fall more in line with real life and keeping ourselves and our loved ones secure and happy. When those dreams are threatened, we would rather not have to be heroes. We would just like the status quo back, thank you very much.

Daniel had many dreams stolen, and his life's business was not his own to direct. Even though he rose to some influence in the palace of Babylon and admirably served three kings, his status as an exile limited his freedom. Add to that the occasional deadly test of faith, and Daniel was forced to get used to stepping up and acting heroically.

Many times he walked unknowingly into everyday situations that called for heroic faith—a lesson for us to note. His normal habits, such as praying, suddenly placed him on the most-wanted list of criminals, and he found himself facing execution. But instead of wallowing in fear, he continued to make his life about God's business and trusted God to handle everything else.

We may be more in tune with God when our lives are turned upside down, as Daniel's was, which is a bright-and-shining silver lining in the clouds of trouble. Sometimes the greatest heroism happens in the ordinary events of our days.

Always the greatest heroism happens when we live for God and let him handle our business. May you be his kind of hero today.

TALK TO HIM

"Lord, I don't like being shaken out of my comfort zone. Although I want to be a hero of faith and make you proud, I am still very drawn to a secure existence. Please remind me that the safest place is found in living for you."

Our prayers are answered not when we are given what we ask but when we are challenged to be what we can be.

MORRIS ADLER

"My love extends beyond your sin."

"I will win her back once again. I will lead her into the desert and speak tenderly to her there." HOSEA 2:14

The English language contains many words with meanings we take for granted. Consider the word *beyond,* for instance. No one gives this preposition much thought, but when it comes to God's love and our sin—wow, it packs eternal import.

We know God loves us in the midst of and in spite of our sin. Amazing. But he also loves us beyond our sin. Beyond implies that he takes us past our errors, stretching us farther than sin can reach. *Beyond* paints a picture of God leading us outside sin's realm. He doesn't leave us in the muck of our sins, powerless to change. He has more in store for our good, including a safe place of salvation and rest beyond lifestyle sins we can't overcome on our own.

How does he love us beyond our sin? Look closer at verse 14, which foretells a day when God will return his people to relationship with him. Let the imagery form in your mind. God winning back his beloved . . . leading her into the desert with tender words. . . .

Into the desert? Sometimes he removes us from sin's clutches by taking us into a desert place where he finally has our undivided attention. Sin can't reach its talons as far as God's goodness woos us.

We view dry seasons of life as times to get through, times of barrenness and little growth. But those desert phases take on refreshing meaning in light of God's love that guides us straight into them, beyond our sin, in order to woo us to himself.

He loves you deeply in the desert. His tender voice calls your name, inviting you to freedom with him so he can water your soul and bring you back to a thriving condition.

Let him take you beyond, right into the desert, to meet him more intimately than ever.

TALK TO HIM

"Lord, please take me beyond myself so I can know you more fully. Thank you for the desert places of growth."

In the deserts of the heart
Let the healing fountain start,
In the prison of his days
Teach the free man how to praise.

W. H. AUDEN

August 28 HOSEA 14:1-9

"My ways make a safe path for those with hearts for me, but they will be stumbling blocks for those who reject me."

The paths of the L*ORD are true and right, and righteous people live by walking in them. But in those paths sinners stumble and fall.* HOSEA 14:9

Considering the world's dangers, and that God doesn't guarantee us a problem-free journey, just what is God's definition of safe? Surely the ancient Israelites wondered, as we wonder today.

Life clearly is not safe, even when we follow God. Evil doesn't discriminate between religious or pagan, rich or poor, male or female, young or old. Diseases and disasters don't pick and choose, either. So is God really a protection for people who live for him? How can he claim to keep us secure when countless dangers lurk along that "safe" path?

The answers come by viewing things as God does. He sees this earthly time frame as a mere introduction to eternity. The eternal condition of our souls is far more important than the security of these temporary bodies. That's not to say he doesn't care about our mortal bodies, but he allows us to face the same terrors and trials as those who run from him because we are still part of this earth.

Being saved for eternity doesn't exempt us from trouble during these finite decades of human life. We're steeped in the wear and tear of sin on earth; yet when we place our souls in God's keeping and let him guide us into eternity, he doesn't let anything threaten our forever with him.

On the other hand, those who refuse him now might not answer for it until eternity, when it will be too late. They will have spent years stumbling over the truth that could have saved them. In essence, they will have tripped over their own perspective—the stumbling block that kept them from God.

God is a God who leads us to safety. But he also is a God people trip over when they run the opposite direction.

TALK TO HIM

"Lord, help me to choose your way, remembering you provide ultimate safety despite temporary hazards."

We are traveling on through a world of sin,
Walking in the good old way;
Though our foes are strong we have peace within,
Walking in the good old way.

FANNY CROSBY, "WALKING IN THE GOOD OLD WAY"

"I am eager to forgive; but you must turn to me first."

Return to the LORD your God, for he is . . . eager to relent and not punish. JOEL 2:13

A fearsome army marches with vengeance, a battalion so vast it shadows the wide horizon, "like dawn spreading across the mountains" (verse 2). The precision of the soldiers' approach shows their impeccable training. They are an intimidating sight, and we hope they aren't coming after us.

Then with sudden clarity, we recognize the Lord at the head of the column. Our fear dissipates and we exhale, remembering that the Lord won't come after those who love him; he will come for them. Both warrior and Savior, God stands ready to forgive instead of to destroy, but he requires one thing of us: repentance. Our repentance before God makes him our greatest source of relief instead of our most provoking catalyst for fear (verse 6).

As our final shivers of fear settle, we come to verse 13 and discover that God looks forward to forgiving us. In fact, he passionately pursues us in his desire to save us. Do you imagine God eager to forgive? More pointedly, do you imagine him eager to forgive you?

Your answers to those questions hold the key to your understanding of God's feelings for you, as well as your impression of him. If in your mind he is the ferocious warrior out to get you, then it's time to check your heart. Do you have trouble repenting, turning aside from sin, or do you need a greater understanding of God's desire to forgive you?

He pursues you out of love, not out of vengeance. Let that truth transform your thinking today, and set your sights on the beautiful horizon where the Lord longs to come for you.

TALK TO HIM

"Lord God, you are the warrior who saves me. Please help me keep my heart clean and pursue you as you pursue me."

No word of anger spoke He
To them that shed His blood,
But prayer and tenderest pity
Large as the love of God.
For me was that compassion,
For me that tender care;
I need His wide forgiveness
As much as any there.

CECIL F. ALEXANDER, "FORGIVE THEM, O MY FATHER"

August 30 AMOS 1:1-15

"In whatever work you do, you can be a spiritual warrior."

This message was given to Amos, a shepherd from the town of Tekoa in Judah. AMOS 1:1

God loves the unassuming because their egos don't get in the way of his work. Amos fit that bill. Even the book of the Bible named after him is only nine chapters long, but its words tell the story of how God used one unpretentious shepherd for a very important work.

The Bible doesn't record Amos's reaction at being called by God, but we can assume he responded willingly because there is no indication that God had to talk him into it. In fact, the sparseness of detail about Amos's calling could lead us to think he received God's visions and immediately acted in obedience, as if obeying the Lord was Amos's everyday, default response. Amos's life surely changed drastically from that point on, but we have no reason to think he chafed at the interruption to his life in progress. His simple existence as a shepherd hadn't earned him acclaim, but the previous absence of fame might have disciplined him for greater work without tempting him with a desire for fanfare. It seems he lived for more than himself.

God views this type of self-disinterest as heroic. In many ways, living consistently for God day in and day out is more difficult than making it through a short-term crisis. We can dig deep and come up with strength that peaks then wanes, but staying the course without seeking pats on the back can prove more challenging for our spiritual maturity.

Whatever your everyday ventures, keep in mind your calling to go about God's work in the drudgery of anonymity, for his name instead of your own. Spiritual heroes often are discovered in those very circumstances.

TALK TO HIM

"Father, please help me to value the heroism of a life lived simply for you. Thank you for calling me to step outside my desire for self-promotion to a lifestyle that breathes your name."

Drudgery is one of the finest touchstones of character there is. Drudgery is work that is very far removed from anything to do with the ideal—the utterly mean grubby things; and when we come in contact with them we know instantly whether or not we are spiritually real.

OSWALD CHAMBERS

"I rule the universe, but more than that, I want to rule your heart."

The LORD's home reaches up to the heavens, while its foundation is on the earth. AMOS 9:6

One of the most brilliant delights of life on earth is gazing away from earth at the expansive universe. Even though our scope of it seems limitless, the space we see is hardly a pinprick in relation to its entirety. The universe is so large, our most powerful telescopes haven't even touched its grandeur. It is beyond awesome to think that God made it all.

Something so immeasurably vast defies our comprehension, yet God knows every inch of it. And something so spectacular must be God's masterpiece, yet he holds us dearer to his heart. Instead of endowing the vastness of the universe—galaxies, solar systems, planets, stars—with his image, he chose to give us immortal souls and gift us with the honor of being created to reflect his character.

He glorifies himself throughout the universe, but he reveals himself to us. He unquestionably rules the skies and seas, the earth and heavens, but he is a gentleman when it comes to ruling us. He knows he will have the final say over all aspects of his creation, but he gives us time to exercise our free will to obey him.

It is his universe, and we are his creations. He never had to allow us to live and move and exist (see Acts 17:28), but he invites us to the grand celebration of life that he hosts. He is the ultimate Host with the Most.

We don't care to be ruled, but he deserves that role, and we desperately need him to maintain it. His rule results in our good.

When you look into the blackness of night, rest securely in the hand that holds its depths yet nurtures you as his treasure.

TALK TO HIM

"Lord, you have many names, but one of my favorites today is 'Master.' I am so grateful that you are mine. I love belonging to you."

Ruler of the hosts of light,
Death hath yielded to Thy might;
And Thy blood hath marked a road
Which will lead us back to God.

AUTHOR UNKNOWN, "RULER OF THE HOSTS OF LIGHT"

September 1 OBADIAH 1:1-21

"Watch out for your pride; it is a great deceiver."

"You have been deceived by your own pride." OBADIAH 1:3

We know pride is bad. It puffs us up and deflates others. But pride is harmful in another way. It is a chronic liar, and the primary victims are also the culprits: ourselves.

When we let unhealthy pride and its accomplices, defensiveness and rationalization, chatter away in our minds, we usually end up liking what they have to say. . . . *You are so much more mature than she is. . . . You would never lose your temper like he did. . . . At least you don't spend your money as carelessly as they do.* Why wouldn't we like to hear that stuff? We come across golden!

But pride is a big excuser. It sets us up higher in our thinking than we deserve—higher than we can handle. It tells us we're okay, even great, when in reality we have issues to face and sins to deal with, not the least of which is pride itself. Pride lies to us by casting others in a shadow of negativity and ourselves in angelic beams of light. However, that light eventually exposes the grunge lurking beneath our pristine facades.

Pride is ironic in its gullibility to believe its own lies yet grow defensive toward believing the truth. When proud people are confronted with an error, their response smacks of arrogance when they cop an appalled attitude that anyone would dare accuse them.

Obadiah confronted the nation of Edom with God's message of judgment. One of their most destructive sins was pride. They basically wagered their security on their manmade fortress and fell prey to pride's lie that they were indestructible. God knew the truth, though, and he clarified it for them through Obadiah: The Edomites were going down, and their downfall would be that much more diabolical because their pride had lifted them up to heights that would prove too much for them.

Knock out pride before it catches you with its deceptions. Refuse its excuses, and opt for a holy dose of God's honesty.

TALK TO HIM

"Lord, please enlighten me to my pride. I want to live honestly and accept your truth."

The intelligent man who is proud of his intelligence is like the condemned man who is proud of his large cell.

SIMONE WEIL

"Keep in mind that disobedience to me affects others, as does obedience."

"Why has this awful storm come down on us?" they demanded. "Who are you?" JONAH 1:8

What was the sailors' tone in their accusations toward Jonah? Were they fearful? angry? offended? They were probably all that and then some. Whatever words we find to describe their reaction to Jonah, it's certain they did not take kindly to the trouble his disobedience brought on them. Even being rugged sailors did not secure their safety in the midst of a raging sea; they knew the powerlessness of being caught in the middle of someone else's sin.

Obedience always brings blessing. We've heard it before. It is as sure as its polar-opposite truth that says disobedience always brings heartache. However, those guarantees don't apply only to the one doing the obeying or disobeying because our actions have ripple effects like a stone dropped in a pool of water. The rings shake up everyone as far as their reach extends. The sailors felt those ripples on a grand scale when Jonah's attempted escape from God landed them all in rough water.

No matter how we try to protect others from our mistakes, we do not sin in a vacuum. God created us to bless and refine each other as we share this planet earth. But along with the benefits of togetherness come unavoidable problems that stem from our sin nature. Even though our sins impact others, we still don't like being on the receiving end of theirs.

God calls us to love people, and one way we can accomplish that is by obeying him, not only for the sake of doing what's right by him, but also doing right for those we care about—and quite possibly for those we don't even know.

TALK TO HIM

"Thank you, God, for reminding me that my actions affect people you love. Please help me to put my heart into obeying you by remembering that so many other hearts are affected by my obedience."

When we walk with the Lord in the light of His Word,
What a glory He sheds on our way!
While we do His good will, He abides with us still,
And with all who will trust and obey.

JOHN H. SAMMIS, "TRUST AND OBEY"

September 3 JONAH 3:1–4:11

"Your attitude toward those still blinded by sin says more about you than about them."

"Didn't I say before I left home that you would do this, LORD?" JONAH 4:2

The gall! The nerve! The self-righteousness! Oh, how we love to judge Jonah for those character flaws that soured his spirit. How full of himself he was to scold God for showing compassion to the Ninevites, those dreadful sinners!

And how full of ourselves we are to point long fingers at his guilt when we carry our own loads of junk that are every bit as ugly and every bit as blinding!

We are creatures of irony, and one of the most prevalent ironies of Christendom is our habit of penalizing unforgiven sinners for being blinded to their sins when we ourselves are blinded by our judgment of them.

Which is worse, really, the lost person acting lost or a saved person stomping that lost person into the ground, so to speak, for being lost? We are messed-up souls, indeed.

God calls his people to be tools of healing, a role that is impossible to accomplish when we carry a spiritual bat in one hand and a spiritual club in the other to wallop anyone who doesn't fit God's moral code. Yes, obedience to his standards is important; but more important still is loving others simply because we've been loved and forgiven so much that we can't help passing it on.

Our attitudes toward other people shed more light on what's going on in our hearts than in theirs.

Are your eyes open to the true state of your heart? Do you want the best for those who don't yet know God?

TALK TO HIM

"Father God, please do what is necessary to keep my eyes open to see clearly my deep-down attitudes. Please clean me up where I need it, and grow me to love simply because I can't help it."

A long habit of not thinking a thing wrong gives it
a superficial appearance of being right.
THOMAS PAINE

"Be courageous enough to hear my tougher messages."

"Don't say such things," the people respond. "Don't prophesy like that. Such disasters will never come our way!" MICAH 2:6

What would you rather hear: a truthful negative statement or a dishonest flattering one? Let's try this question on for comfort. What's your first reaction—your gut-level, instinctive response—to these comments someone hypothetically makes about you?

Yellow really isn't your color.
You're quite self-absorbed.
Yellow looks so good on you.
I appreciate how you value honesty.
You're the funniest person I have ever met.

Any number of words could describe the emotions those comments triggered inside you: shock, pride, humility, indignation, defensiveness, outrage, contrition, self-effacement, disbelief, gratitude. How about appreciation? Sure, bring on the praise! Okay, but how about appreciation for the negative ones?

Putting aside those insulting comments intended to hurt, if we truly value honesty, then a stinging yet truthful remark from someone who has our best at heart should prompt some introspection—or at least our open heart and listening ear, for starters.

Tying into yesterday's reading, we keep ourselves blinded to reality when we put a wall up against hearing difficult things about ourselves. The only way we can live in the freedom God offers us is by having the courage to face the truth, no matter how icky and uncomfortable it feels. And when it's a truth from God himself, we show not only courage, but wisdom and maturity by listening up quickly.

Dishonesty hurts in more insidious, hidden ways than kindhearted honesty because it blinds us to how we're really doing in life. Like life, the truth can be messy. But living in it is the only way to keep a clean heart before God and others.

TALK TO HIM

"Lord, the truth hurts, and sometimes I want to push it away. But I know there is a unique kind of security in knowing all the facts instead of being fooled by something that just sounds good. Please show me your light inside even the most difficult realities."

Maturity is reached the day we don't need to be lied to about anything.

FRANK YERBY

September 5 MICAH 6:1-16

"It all comes down to this. . . ."

The Lord has told you what is good, and this is what he requires of you: to do what is right, to love mercy, and to walk humbly with your God. MICAH 6:8

Life is as simple as this verse's three steps: Do right, love mercy, walk humbly with God. Got it. Now that we know everything, we can all go home. Right?

Not so fast.

The complexity of our sin natures muddles the simplicity of that verse and makes right living, mercy loving, and humbly walking impossible without lots of help from above.

The first seven verses in chapter 6 lead up to this one that stamps God's clarity on the whole message. In those first few lines, God expressed his exasperation with his thick-headed people.

Their response? They wanted to complicate their way back to God by showering him with extensive offerings, bowing in grand genuflection, and even making wicked offerings—hey, God, how about our firstborn? Would that do the trick? Is that the right formula to earn your approval?

We imagine God answering back with a shake of his head. "People, people," he said, guiding them to sit beside him and listen closely. "It all comes down to this. . . ." Then he shared with them his heart's desires.

All God wants from us is that we live a simple life of obedience, share the mercy he shows us, and accept his acceptance of us with humility that doesn't involve self-recrimination or inflated egos.

Those three requirements address our relationships with him, others, and ourselves; they cover every aspect of life. We live by his standards to maintain our connection with him; we show his mercy toward others, which we can do only by understanding his mercy toward us first; and we practice a healthy attitude about ourselves that understands we have worth because of his love for us.

It's as simple as three phrases and as difficult as turning to him for help to practice them.

TALK TO HIM

"Heavenly Father, I love that you bring everything in life back to one point: yourself. You are what life is all about. Please help me dwell on that refreshing simplicity."

God gives us always strength enough, and sense enough,
for everything He wants us to do.
JOHN RUSKIN

"The world's evil will pale in comparison to the horror of being my enemy."

"I am your enemy!" says the L*ORD* *of Heaven's Armies.* NAHUM 2:13

What do abundant arrogance, a heart full of hate, and a flock of foolishness have in common? All are characteristics of God's enemies. It takes either a boatload of pride, hate, or stupidity to risk opposing the Lord. In order to dare side against God, a person either is blinded to whom they are dealing with, or they have deliberately chosen a self-destructive path that heads away from God and directly toward evil.

Let's look at the difference between willful and passive rejection of the Lord. Unless a person has willfully chosen evil over holiness, thus sealing his or her future apart from God, a true understanding of the Lord of Heaven's Armies draws reverence, awe, and humble gratitude instead of arrogance, hate, and foolishness. But in addition to spreading terror across the globe, evil acts as a blindfold on hearts that are closed to God's holiness. It stalls people from seeing God's authority over the universe, as well as how seriously he views his right to receive worship, and his abhorrence of wickedness. Does God fight to win back those who are blinded? Yes! He is divinely gracious. God knows people's hearts, and he will remove blinders. He won't allow evil to snatch someone with a heart for him.

God takes the gentlemanly stance for now when it comes to dealing with his enemies, but one day he will deliver the deathblow to every creation of his that doesn't honor him. As we see from his words to ancient Nineveh, he will defend his own. He will receive his rightful worship eventually, even from his opposers, but it will be at great penalty to them.

We can take comfort in this evil-deadened world that God's vengeance will silence wickedness because his patient mercy will run out for those who haven't turned to him. Evil's effects will pale in comparison to the punishment God's enemies receive when his majesty radiates over the universe for eternity.

TALK TO HIM

"I am grateful, Lord, that you plan to destroy evil. My mind understands why you delay, but sometimes I wish you would hurry. Please help me to trust your perfect timing."

Among the things God is serious about, these three top the list:
His glory, our salvation, and evil's doom.
ANONYMOUS

September 7 HABAKKUK 1:1–2:3

"Let me turn your doubts into deeper faith."

I will wait to see what the LORD *says and how he will answer my complaint.* HABAKKUK 2:1

Thank the Lord for questions! By gifting us with the ability to question, God gave us the route to receive his answers.

Imagine living day after day surrounded by problems, yet not having the mental capacity to wonder where they came from, why you are forced to deal with them, or how God could help you solve them. What a trapped existence you would struggle through! You would have not only no way out, but no way to understand life or God better.

Questioning God often gets a bad rap in some Christian circles, as if asking him why and when and how is unholy or disrespectful. And in truth, sometimes we are guilty of attacking God with questions laced with anger and bitterness.

However, when we pour out our confusion to him from an attitude of humbly wanting his direction and comfort, wanting to grow closer to him, or needing his clarity on a situation, he loves listening to us and revealing himself through his answers—even when his answer must be silence for a reason only he knows.

It is often through our doubts and questions that we hand God a bigger part of ourselves so he can grow it. As we share our doubts and wonderings with him, he utilizes our greater attention on him to deepen our faith and help us trust him more.

Be thankful for your questions instead of being wracked with guilt for not having all the answers. God never expected you to be completely self-sufficient. If you were, you wouldn't need him, and that is an impossible state because God wired us to need him.

Lift your questions to God with a yearning to be closer to him, and watch him grow your faith in ways it couldn't have if you had never asked.

TALK TO HIM

"Can you hear my sigh of relief, God? Thank you for the freedom to pour out my questions to you. Please grow my faith through your answers."

Ask what thou wilt, believing heart,
The answering time will come;
Pray and believe—that is thy part,
The answering time will come.

MARY B. WINGATE, "THE ANSWERING TIME WILL COME"

"It's one thing to hear about me, but true change comes by experiencing me."

His coming is as brilliant as the sunrise. HABAKKUK 3:4

Slow down a moment, settle the thoughts interrupting your time with God, and review this wonderful chapter that sings of his presence.

Picture the vast universe—dark, mysterious, and awesome. Now zoom in through the clouds for a bird's-eye view of earth. Skim your gaze over the land, taking in snowcapped mountains, glistening lakes, foaming oceans, windswept prairies. Across the miles, buildings dot the landscape. You might even notice traffic on the interstates and a lonely truck stop along a desert highway.

Suddenly in the midst of the quiet, the earth starts to tremble, perking your attention more acutely. In the distance, a mountaintop explodes; seconds later the entire range crumbles. A light more brilliant than you've ever seen flashes across the sky. Lightning cracks, trumpets sound.

God has arrived.

Sometimes God comes silently, and sometimes he comes thunderously, such as when he unleashes his anger or defends those he loves. But no matter how he makes his presence felt, he changes everything in his wake. He comes as a destroyer to those who face his wrath. But for those who seek his heart, he arrives to rebuild and restore, to freshen and provide new landscapes of beauty. Life looks and feels different after an encounter with him.

No one and no thing can remain the same in his presence. We can read and study about his glory and his power, but our understanding becomes wholly more real after experiencing him firsthand. If we really want true change in ourselves, we need to spend time with him one-on-one. We can't know him by merely knowing about him.

Plant yourself in his presence and hold on for the adventure of experiencing the Almighty. His changes will rock your world.

TALK TO HIM

"Thank you, Lord, for loving me too much to leave me unchanged. Please keep refining me with your presence."

We may ignore, but we can nowhere evade, the presence of God. . . .
He walks everywhere incognito. And the incognito is not always
hard to penetrate. The real labour is to remember, to attend.
In fact, to come awake. Still more, to remain awake.

C. S. LEWIS

September 9 ZEPHANIAH 3:9-20

"Can you see me smile at you?"

"The Lord *your God . . . will take delight in you with gladness. . . . He will rejoice over you with joyful songs."* ZEPHANIAH 3:17

We hear a lot about rejoicing in the Lord, finding our joy in him, and being glad in his presence. And indeed, his presence gives us a lot to delight in. But how odd it sounds that he delights in us! Hearing that carries our joy to a whole new level. Our God and Lord, Maker of heaven and earth, the One worthy of more praise than we ever could give, that sovereign ruler smiles and sings over us. We can't understand it all, and we couldn't have it any better.

We busy ourselves with responsibilities and immediate cares that surround us, interrupted now and then by the realization of God's love as it steals over us at unexpected moments—a brush of peace, a sigh of contentment, a whispered sentiment that our inner heart recognizes as the Holy Spirit. Those moments bring relief to our scattered selves because we know God is reminding us of his ever-present love.

But in addition to sharing his love, he also is letting us know that he smiles on us. A smile not only shows love, but it also shows that someone likes us. God by nature is love; but we often adopt a mixed-up view of him that paints him in a haze of frowns and angry-browed expressions.

How unfair we are to assume he prefers to be grumpy instead of joyful toward his children! What loving parent wears a chronic frown for a precious child who messes up now and then but who earnestly wants to please? God loves to smile on us as he helps us to grow. Our behavior may not always earn a smile from him, but our identity as his children always does.

As he calms your soul, let your mind adopt a new picture of him—as your heavenly Lord who smiles on you, his delight.

TALK TO HIM

"Lord, the thought of your smile makes me want to live more fully for you. I want to bring that smile to your face often. Thank you for delighting in me."

God's smile sets the flowers in bloom, the sun to shine, and his child at peace.

ANONYMOUS

"When your priorities are mine, your life will be full of my richness."

"You have planted much but harvest little." HAGGAI 1:6

We love success! We're addicted to accomplishments—bigger and better and most of all, more! We may have moments when we long for rest from the race for more, but old habits die hard, especially when they make us feel purposeful and successful.

The beginning of verse 6 feels like criticism for not seeing success from our efforts. We try and try, but when we don't produce much for the time and energy we've applied to our goals, we end up unsatisfied. Broken and discouraged, we wonder where our lives spun off track.

But when we read verse 6 in light of the surrounding verses, we see a broader scope of how God views our drive for success. Through his prophet Haggai, God set the Israelites straight about a classic mistake. They were guilty of building their own kingdoms at the expense of God's. For all their striving and searching for satisfaction, they needed to learn the difference between chasing their own agendas versus pursuing the priorities of God's heart.

God gives us a gift when he halts our wheels from spinning toward self-centered success. We can thank him for failure if that's what it takes to straighten out our focus. We need him as our center if we are to handle life's bumps well. When we revolve around anything but him as our hub, we inevitably cycle through seasons of dizzy confusion, wearing down our spiritual treads until he realigns us.

Although failure stings like skin against pavement, we can thank God that he isn't near-sighted like us. He sees the long-range beauty of his eternal Kingdom, and he wants to fit us for the journey.

By making his priorities our own, we set ourselves on track for a life filled with his richness.

TALK TO HIM

"Lord, I'm tired of the cycle of striving for my own success. Please hinder my accomplishments, if that's what it takes, to focus me on your Kingdom."

> *The being cured, with all the pain, has pleasure too: one creeps home, tired and bruised, into a state of mind that is really restful, when all one's ambitions have been given up. Then one can really for the first time say "Thy Kingdom come."*
>
> C. S. LEWIS

September 11 ZECHARIAH 3:1-10

"Wear my salvation well, like fine new clothes."

"I, the LORD, reject your accusations, Satan. Yes, the LORD, who has chosen Jerusalem, rebukes you. This man is like a burning stick that has been snatched from the fire."

ZECHARIAH 3:2

Oh, how sweet it will be to hear those words from Jesus—to watch him crush the accusations Satan makes against us, to see Satan's rage toward us crumble under the authority of Jesus, our Savior and Defender.

All of us have a date with the Lord, the lover of our souls, when we will face the accusations of Satan, the hater of our souls. Naturally, we will want to dress for the occasion—an outfit designed for success, a spiritual power suit, so to speak. We can spend this lifetime searching for it, trying to design it with our own skills. Or we can read Zechariah 3 and discover that Jesus holds out to us the most beautiful clothing sewn of his purity. It truly is the only outfit that will wear well and resist the stain of threats Satan throws at us.

No matter how we dress up our lives with good behavior and kind acts, we are clothed in filthy rags until we receive the beautiful new clothing of salvation from Jesus himself. He died and shed his blood, pouring it over our souls, washing us in rich crimson to make us as white as his own purity. We can stand strong and beautiful as members of God's royal family if we are wearing Jesus' clothing—the clothing fit for our King.

Satan has a date to face the Lord too; however, his will end badly. Before God, the heavenly hosts, and God's sons and daughters, Satan will be stripped of the evil power that he wears as the prince of wickedness. He will be humiliated and defeated before God throws him into the very fire that our Savior, Jesus, snatched us from.

As you face today, reach for your spiritual garb of Jesus' purity. Remember, if you know him as Savior, you will be dressed for success as his beautiful, pure child.

TALK TO HIM

"Jesus, thank you for your clothing of purity. Please help me to wear your salvation well, as a joyful child of spiritual royalty."

God's purity enfolds us in his beautiful love and
drapes us with his glorious presence.
ANONYMOUS

"Learn what it means to walk by my Spirit."

"It is not by force nor by strength, but by my Spirit, says the LORD *of Heaven's Armies."*

ZECHARIAH 4:6

"Walking in the Spirit." Sounds fancy, doesn't it? But if we don't understand their spiritual significance, those words just spell consternation.

Although the idea of walking in the Spirit might seem confusing, it is a lifestyle encouraged by God in his Word. As we mature in our faith, we learn to depend on the Lord's direction through his Spirit's power in us. In fact, the deeper we go with God, the better we understand how much we need to rely on him. The more we live our days in the Spirit's power, the greater clarity he brings to our lives, and the more we crave him.

Walking in the Spirit means inviting him into our day. It means observing his majesty in creation, talking with him about large and small issues, praising him for who he is, and sending a smile from our hearts to his for the simple reason that we want to communicate our gratitude. Walking in the Spirit also involves handing over our burdens and asking him to stabilize and strengthen us beyond our capabilities. We can stifle the Spirit's power in us through sin we haven't come clean about, but we can also invite the Spirit to increase his work in us by heeding his nudges.

One of the most empowering spiritual lessons we're wise to learn requires disciplining ourselves to listen for the Spirit. Learning his language takes time and practice, but we experience greater joy and peace as we know him better. As we walk with him, we realize the inadequacy of our strength in light of his, and our ever-growing appreciation for him makes us want to remain in his power and worship him all the more.

When we realize he is our lifeblood, we know we can't walk well through life without him.

TALK TO HIM

"Lord, please quicken my spirit to pay attention to yours. Thank you for the gift of walking with you. Please grow my sensitivity toward your Spirit's voice."

Never pump up joy and confidence, but stay upon God.

OSWALD CHAMBERS

September 13 ZECHARIAH 8:1-23

"Extend honesty to your deepest parts."

"Stop your love of telling lies that you swear are the truth. . . . Love truth and peace."
ZECHARIAH 8:17, 19

It sure would be nice if lessons we learn would stick for the rest of our lives. But life often seems like a cycle of rehashing the same old stuff, repackaged in new circumstances every few years.

Take honesty, for instance. We love honesty, don't we? We love hearing the truth, speaking the truth, and being truthful with ourselves.

Okay, if we were truly honest, most of us would have to admit that only a part of us actually loves honesty. The other part isn't so fond of the discomfort that often accompanies a word of truth. We like honesty when it doesn't reveal our failures, and we like it when it clears up someone else's wrong and sets us in better light. But truth often brings guilt along with it, forcing us into either dishonest denial or difficult discipline.

God knows honesty is vital to our growth, which is why he expected it of his ancient Israelites and why that expectation still stands for us today. He was ready to bless his people after they had been disciplined through a time of exile. However, he warned them of the one thing they needed to incorporate into their lives. They needed to be people of truth—no excuses or halfway agreements allowed.

Anything less than wholehearted honesty with ourselves—which in turn can't settle for dishonesty toward others—puts distance between us and God because we don't go to him with genuine hearts.

Lay out your heart before God today, and let him show you potential areas that could use complete truth. Once you do, you will be able to enjoy the deeper intimacy and freedom with him that he longs for you to experience.

TALK TO HIM

"Lord, I want to be honest (big sigh). I'm a little afraid of what the truth might reveal, but I don't want to settle for less than whole and healthy relationships with you and others. Please help me, Father."

Many people today don't want honest answers insofar as honest means unpleasant or disturbing. They want a soft answer that turneth away anxiety.
LOUIS KRONENBERGER

"You will shine like silver and gold through my purifying fire."

"I will bring that group through the fire and make them pure. . . . I will say, 'These are my people,' and they will say, 'The LORD is our God.'" ZECHARIAH 13:9

God's greatest act of love was sending his Son to die for us. In essence, he handed us holiness.

However, he shows his love in another way, one that seems harsh apart from his perspective. He loves us by putting us through his refining process.

Many are thrown off by his willingness—even his proactive efforts—to let us suffer for our good. Indeed, it makes little sense to us why he would offer a gracious (i.e., easy on us) salvation, but then submit us to troubles with the intention of growing us to be more like him. Is he making us pay for our sin after all?

That is a question we each need to settle solidly, because our interpretation of it impacts our view of God and where we stand with him. Simply put, the answer is a resounding no. God's refining fire is not a way to eke out a payment plan for our wrongs. We aren't earning his love through his refining.

God doesn't love us because he refines us. He refines us because he loves us.

If he didn't give us the attention of beautifying us with his own character, he would be a negligent parent who allows his children to continue in destructive, dangerous habits. What caring parent lets his precious offspring endanger themselves and others with immature (not matured) behavior? He wouldn't be true to his identity as our heavenly Father if he didn't act in our best interests.

We must reject the idea that pain is bad when it is from God's hand for our benefit. Through the pain, we learn to return to him, to cling to him, and to be like him. In essence, we learn to wear the holiness of the salvation that he gave us at such great pain to himself.

TALK TO HIM

"Heavenly Father, I don't like the pain of your refining fire, but I appreciate it. Thank you for loving me into becoming like you. Please keep going."

Father, make us loving, gentle, thoughtful, kind;
Fill us with Thy Spirit, make us of Thy mind.
FLORA KIRKLAND, "FATHER, MAKE US LOVING"

September 15 MALACHI 3:1-18

"Do you treat your finances as mine?"

"Bring all the tithes into the storehouse so there will be enough food in my Temple. If you do," says the Lord *of Heaven's Armies, "I will open the windows of heaven for you."*

MALACHI 3:10

We love gifts—receiving them, definitely. But we also love to see the joy in others' eyes over a gift we've given. Their response makes the effort and expense worthwhile, and we wish we had offered it to them sooner.

God is a lavish gift giver. But he also loves to be on the receiving end, particularly because everything we give back to him shows our gratitude to him for giving us everything. By offering part of that "everything" to him, we acknowledge that we owe him all we typically view as ours, when in truth, all we have belongs to him. One gift we can give to God every day is the wise use of our finances, or rather, his finances that he entrusts to us.

You have heard statements like these: We came into this world with nothing, and that's how we'll leave it. All we have comes from God. They roll off the tongue as we nod piously. Yet, we show whether we truly buy into them through our attitudes about giving to the Lord's work. Heartfelt generosity that motivates our gifts to God shows that his priorities are ours as well.

Money issues create one of life's greatest stressors. How much less anxious we would be, and blessed with peace and joy, if we would take Malachi 3 to heart and release our hold on "our" financial situation. God challenges us to lay before him the money he gives us and to expect him to open his storehouses of blessing through our offerings, given of course from a genuine spirit of generosity and gratitude.

As you reach into your wallet today, remind yourself that the funds to pay off that credit card, the balance in your bank account, and the health of your 401(k) belong to the Lord. How will you treat his finances?

TALK TO HIM

"Lord, thank you for your finances that you have entrusted to my use. Please give me your wisdom and generous spirit to handle them well."

The miracle is this—the more we share, the more we have.

LEONARD NIMOY

"My Son's name, 'Immanuel,' is an eternal reminder that I am with you."

"They will call him Immanuel, which means 'God is with us.'" MATTHEW 1:23

Choosing a name is among the special joys of having a baby. What will this child be known as throughout his or her life? Will the moniker evoke a sense of honor, beauty, whimsy, elegance, or strength? We put a lot into our names; they're like our brand—our "brand name," so to speak.

Names were especially important to the Israelites. We see often throughout the Bible that babies were named to symbolize events surrounding the birth or for prophetic reasons impacting a circle of influence wider than one family, even as great as the entire nation.

It's interesting that Matthew began his Gospel with a long list of names leading up to Jesus' birth. We rattle through the genealogy, wanting to get past the long, unpronounceable names, in order to get to the real story. However, that genealogy should not be scanned casually because it serves as a drumroll building toward the thrilling announcement of our Savior's birth and naming.

The genealogy reveals a slice of history—many generations who waited for their Messiah to come. Finally, one unassuming night in Bethlehem, he was born. As we might guess, knowing a bit about the stock the nation put into their names, God chose an exceptional one for his precious Son: Immanuel.

With the simple naming of his Son, God sent a message to his people that he would be with them forever. Immanuel was a promise, a hope, a fulfillment of prophecy, and the beginning of a legacy—the turning point of eternity.

You are living in Immanuel's legacy. Today, many generations after Jesus received his name, God still is with you. What's in a name? When it comes to Jesus' name . . . everything.

TALK TO HIM

"Thank you, Lord, for being my hope with every utterance of your name. May my life point others to its meaning for them."

Immanuel, we sing Thy praise;
Thou Prince of Life, Thou Fount of Grace,
With all Thy saints, Thee, Lord, we sing;
Praise, honor, thanks, to Thee we bring.

PAUL GERHARDT, "IMMANUEL, WE SING THY PRAISE"

September 17 MATTHEW 2:1-23

"Watch for me, and learn to recognize my voice—your life depends on it."

God had warned them in a dream not to return to Herod. . . . An angel of the Lord appeared to Joseph in a dream. MATTHEW 2:12-13

We owe a thank you to those wise men. If they hadn't tuned in to God's voice, our Savior's story would read very differently. Their sensitivity in following God's guiding star translated into wisdom when they heeded God's hand of protection and avoided revealing Jesus' location to King Herod.

Within two verses that cover a brief time, God shows his behind-the-scenes protection of Jesus and his family. That same God works just as protectively in our lives. Those verses teach us about God's reliability and communication to us; he gets the job done, and he leads continuously. They also set an example about paying attention to his voice. The wise men had to actively look for the star in order to find the baby Savior. Their watchful eyes kept them going along the path God laid out. And their willingness to alter their course—to be interrupted from their plans—saved Jesus from Herod's murderous scheme.

We can extend our thanks to Joseph as well. He let God lead the way when he took his young family into the safety of Egypt. Only God knows how tragic Jesus' early days may have been if it weren't for the sheltering care of Joseph's spiritual sensitivity. We know God would have saved Jesus' life in order to give us salvation, but who's to say Mary or Joseph wouldn't have been at risk, thus altering Jesus' preparation for his purpose on earth?

We have no idea the grief our spiritual eyes and ears spare us. Maybe someday God will show us a play-by-play of his interventions on our behalf. Whether he does or not, we can be certain that he will use our attentiveness to him for our good and for the good of others.

TALK TO HIM

"Father, thank you for guiding me. Please help me to listen up and look closely for you."

Lead us, O Father, in the paths of right:
Blindly we stumble when we walk alone,
Involved in shadows of a darksome night;
Only with Thee we journey safely on.

WILLIAM H. BURLEIGH, "LEAD US, O FATHER"

"You can understand your other needs only in context of your primary need of staying connected to me."

"The Scriptures say, 'People do not live by bread alone, but by every word that comes from the mouth of God.'" MATTHEW 4:4

As God, Jesus had it all: purity, perfection, power. As man, he had all our experiences of need. He knew what it felt like to be hungry and humbled, submissive and spent, weakened and weary, tempted and troubled. One of Jesus' first recorded experiences as an adult was when the Holy Spirit led him into the wilderness so Satan could tempt him at a time when Jesus likely felt all those human limitations. Through three different enticements, Satan appealed to Jesus' physical hunger, the steadiness of his faith in God, and his desire for significance.

In Jesus' emptied state after forty days of fasting alone, his sense of need surely peaked to new heights. His weakened condition made him especially vulnerable to losing sight of his greatest need, the one that puts all others in perspective. Above all, he needed to stay connected to his heavenly Father to see through the lies Satan fed him about what would bring true fulfillment.

Our wilderness times render us particularly needy as well. Any need—physical, spiritual, financial, or emotional—can threaten our resolve that knows God must retain his rightful position as our greatest desire, above everything we think we lack. Removed from the context of God as God, our humanity takes over, and we are more likely to give in to temptation than resist it.

Only by keeping him in view at all times can we see clearly the reality of our lesser needs. When we keep ourselves rooted in him, he reminds us that he will provide for every hunger, he will always be faithful, and he will always be the only One worthy of worship.

Don't be fooled by the clamor of your desires. Go to God, let him fill you, and then look again at your other dreams in his light.

TALK TO HIM

"Lord, it's difficult to differentiate between needs and desires. Please help me to stay grounded in you, and be my strength and vision about what's important."

A true need, when fulfilled, leaves you satisfied. A desire stubborn enough to wear the disguise of need often continues to demand more.

ANONYMOUS

September 19 MATTHEW 6:1-34

"Deepening your understanding of me sheds light on the worthlessness of worry."

"Can all your worries add a single moment to your life?" MATTHEW 6:27

What triggers the worry valve inside you, letting loose a chorus of doubts and insecurities, fears and anxieties?

We worry for a host of reasons, but at the root of them lies our self-preservation. We also worry about the well-being of people we love; but those worries also play into our self-preservation, because if they hurt, we hurt.

We want to be safe and happy, and we want uncertainties to right themselves and become certain. We don't like unknowns because they could lead to disappointment. We don't care for troubles because they're already disappointing. We don't like worry itself because it reminds us that we can't control everything, and oftentimes the forces we have least control over, like cancer or natural disasters, are the most threatening of all. If we would calm ourselves long enough to look at the negative effects of worry, we would worry about the harm we are causing ourselves by giving in to worry!

Worry is exhausting. It is debilitating and humiliating. It robs us of respect, both from ourselves and from others. It steals the sparkle from our eyes, the smile from our lips, the joy from our hearts, and the faith from our souls.

There is nothing positive about worry. Nothing.

God speaks strongly about the futility of worry. Our worries are like slaps in his face because we are really communicating to him that we're unsure of the quality of his care for us and unconvinced that he can help us weather the difficulties of life.

He knows all the reasons we have to worry, but he also knows that our reasons for trusting him far outweigh our worries. Extend the life in your days by deepening your faith in the God who loves you. Risking worry's effects is far more stressful than the "risk" of faith.

TALK TO HIM

"Today, Lord, I give you my worries, and I refuse to take them back. I choose your gift of trust and will rest in your care, whatever shape that takes."

Worry affects circulation, the heart and the glands, the whole nervous system and profoundly affects the heart. I have never known a man who died from overwork, but many who died from doubt.

CHARLES H. MAYO

"Guard against cares that crowd me from your day."

"All too quickly the message is crowded out by the worries of this life." MATTHEW 13:22

Gardens represent life and sanctuary. We escape to them for recreation, relaxation, peace, and beauty. We breathe easier among the plants, which in God's exquisite design give us the oxygen we need to thrive.

Gardens play important roles in the Bible. A garden served as the first humans' home. Jesus spoke of vineyards, planting, growing, and harvesting. He also spoke about weeds, a garden's great enemy.

Just as weeds suffocate a garden's healthy plants, the weeds in our lives choke out God's sustenance. If a garden represents our heart, then we are wise to guard against invaders. To do so, we must learn to recognize the weeds that masquerade as flowers, because even weeds can appear beautiful as they carry out their hostile takeover.

We could spend all day listing issues that crowd God from our hearts: work obligations, friend and family responsibilities, financial stresses, ministry commitments, health concerns, social issues, national tragedies, global unrest. Most of those hold validity for pressing on our time and our nerves; after all, we can't neglect our responsibilities or live in a bubble.

However, we can guard our hearts from becoming crippled beneath our burdens by asking God to strengthen our spiritual muscles to pump more vitality into our hearts. By deepening our roots in God, we become more efficient at weathering the effects of weeds that crop up. We can continue to grow in godliness that helps us to care for others, gives us wisdom for decision making and prioritizing, and provides perspective in confusing circumstances.

God is our spiritual oxygen to keep our heart's garden flourishing despite weeds that threaten to crowd his life in us. Every moment you spend with him acts as weed killer to your cares. Linger with him, and as you know him better, watch him beautify the garden of your heart.

TALK TO HIM

"Lord, as Gardener of my heart, you know what helps me grow and what threatens my spiritual vitality. Please help me thrive as I deepen my roots in your Word."

There's a sacred and hallowed retreat,
Where my soul finds a fellowship sweet,
Where the Lord of my life I may meet,
In the garden of my heart.

HALDOR LILLENAS, "THE GARDEN OF MY HEART"

September 21 MATTHEW 23:1-36

"Beware of nitpicking others into accepting a version of spirituality; instead, point others to me."

"You cross land and sea to make one convert, and then you turn that person into twice the child of hell you yourselves are!" MATTHEW 23:15

Nitpickers beware! Jesus had choice words for them in this chapter, and as it happened, he discovered a bevy of them among Israel's religious leadership.

They were quite an impressive bunch, in their own eyes most of all. They held the people to impossible standards but left no room for grace. Perfection was their priority—for others, anyway. They could do as they pleased. In their self-observed grandeur, they assumed the role of holy spirits—make that "holier-than-thou spirits"—who pounded guilt onto those less worthy in their estimation. People who submitted to their pressure became doubly hypocritical and nitpicky; those who didn't faced their wrath. Their idea of spirituality looked pristine on the outside, but it covered their hypocritical hearts and nitpicking natures that hindered the passing on of true spirituality rooted in a loving relationship with Jesus.

Although they ignored Jesus' condemning response since their hearts were so twisted, we would be wise to look closely at the spirituality we pass on to others. First and foremost in our self-examination, we ought to ask ourselves if we're emphasizing a list of rules or introducing others to Jesus. If we're unclear about the difference, most likely we're pushing the rules to the detriment of someone's soul.

The world is fully capable of creating and enforcing rules. We have governments; we have laws. However, there is no fabricating a personal relationship with the Lord. Laws do not equal relationship. When Christians push laws instead of showering others with Jesus' love, those nitpicky rules might yield the desired behavior, but behavior alone doesn't mean a saving relationship exists.

When you speak of spiritual things, do others hear a language of rules or the language of Jesus' love?

TALK TO HIM

"Lord, I know rules are important. But please help me break the ones that put greater importance on following them than on knowing you."

I know no method to secure the repeal of bad or obnoxious laws so effective as their stringent execution.

ULYSSES S. GRANT

September 22

"Live today as if it's your final one before I return; one of these days will be."

"You also must be ready all the time, for the Son of Man will come when least expected."

MATTHEW 24:44

One of the most curious questions raised in Christian circles, from scholars to those new to the faith, revolves around Jesus' return. When is he coming back? We would love to know the answer to such a crucial concern. It's frustrating to wonder why God left it a mystery, even from Jesus. He didn't even tell us why he didn't tell us. Doesn't he know how our lives depend on the answer? We are just sitting around here, biding our time until true life can begin. How about now, God? Now is good for us.

Okay, say God did reveal his time frame for sending his Son back for his followers. Let's imagine we have seven years left on earth. Or seventy, or even seven hundred. What would we do differently if we knew for sure?

You might say you would live each moment with a greater sense of urgency. You might resist a familiar temptation one more time because you can see the finish line in sight and want to end strong. Or maybe you would show more patience toward your loved ones since you would soon be face-to-face with Jesus, the lover of your soul. And of course you would look for opportunities to share the news of Jesus' imminent return so others could prepare as well. You wouldn't want anyone to miss eternity with the Lord.

But (sigh) too bad we don't know when he is coming back. We would live so differently if we only knew.

TALK TO HIM

"Father God, I am starting to think you didn't reveal your time frame so that we would preoccupy ourselves with living each day to the fullest instead of wasting precious hours wondering when to start getting ready. Please help me live today as if you're coming today, since you just might."

Precisely because we cannot predict the moment, we must be ready at all moments.

C. S. LEWIS

September 23 MATTHEW 27:11-31

"Get rid of envy; envy killed my Son."

He knew very well that the religious leaders had arrested Jesus out of envy. MATTHEW 27:18

You know the feeling. That wriggling in your gut when you see something you want—in someone else's possession. That squirming is the worm of envy, otherwise known as jealousy. When we give it life, it begins its tumultuous rampage throughout our body, mind, heart, and soul. As it consumes us, it leeches into other parts of our lives—namely our relationships.

The longer we let envy grow, the more it eats us up, devouring our strength and vitality, our energy and creativity, even our inner and outer beauty. The worm of envy cannot be satisfied because as soon as it consumes what it wants, it turns its green eye onto something new to satiate its hunger.

Envy is a destroyer; it murdered our Savior, so we certainly are not immune to it in our own strength. Envy drove the Israelite leaders to arrest and kill Jesus because he drew a following away from them. He embodied forgiveness and hope, qualities their souls were too diseased to appreciate.

Both a root issue and a symptom of deeper sickness of the spirit, envy is the cause of other problems as well as the effect of looking for fulfillment anywhere but in Jesus. Because envy had blinded those religious leaders to Jesus' true identity, and thus their need for him, they rejected him instead of embracing him as the Messiah they had waited and still longed for—the Savior who was ready and willing to cure them if they would only own up to their sickness.

Don't be fooled. The worm of envy may begin small, but it will destroy you unless you destroy it first. We hate its presence, and we hate even more to admit it affects us. But we must admit it if we want God's Spirit to cure us. He will cleanse the effects of envy and fill up the empty places it has eaten away until someday we will be immune to anything that empties us. You can be cured, but you must go to God for his antidote.

TALK TO HIM

"Lord, I'm sick of allowing envy to sicken my spirit. Please heal me and fill me with your satisfying Spirit."

Let age, not envy, draw wrinkles on thy cheeks.

SIR THOMAS BROWNE

"What is your response time to me?"

They left their nets at once and followed him. MARK 1:18

Imagine sitting at your desk one day, preoccupied with everyday issues that demand your attention, when suddenly a stranger walks up and invites you to follow him. You know he's not talking about accompanying him to lunch; he means follow him for life, requiring a total 180-degree reverse of your priorities and time commitments. Your friends and family would feel the effects; your finances could take a nosedive; your previous dreams would be cast aside permanently as far as you would know. Life would never be the same. Change like that would require a bigger-than-life catalyst; it would require a God-size nudge. Basically, it would take an emergency.

We usually think of an emergency as something life threatening enough to make us drop everything and alter our course. Fire. Terminal illness. Danger. Those are emergencies.

Meeting Jesus created emergency situations for all who met him because their response times were very short—immediate, to be exact. He instigated immediate responses from people who followed him, demons who feared him, and illnesses that fled when he showed up. From the disciples who dropped their nets, to the crowds who persisted after him, to the demons and sicknesses that scattered in his presence, one thing is sure: The time to act was immediately if not yesterday.

Responding to Jesus is an emergency every bit as urgent as fire, terminal illness, and danger: We need his salvation from the fires of hell; we are terminally (and eternally) ill without him; and we are in danger of Satan's evil unless we place ourselves in Jesus' eternal protection.

When you let him change your entire course, he steps with gracious authority into your days; he invades with gentle power and loving presence, inviting and urging you to a future of salvation that rescues you from a path of decay.

But you must respond.

Keep your response time short when it comes to answering Jesus' invitation. Time eventually will run out on this emergency.

TALK TO HIM

"Jesus, thank you for saving me from the emergency of eternity without you. Please help me respond to you without delay."

A true emergency shocks us into the necessity of action;
from then on, the greatest danger is inaction.
ANONYMOUS

September 25 MARK 2:1-28

"Discover simple, radical trust in me."

Jesus knew immediately what they were thinking, so he asked them, "Why do you question this in your hearts?" MARK 2:8

Jesus was a lawbreaker. We gasp at that statement, but it's true . . . and it isn't heretical or sacrilegious or a bit shocking to God. God raised his Son for the purpose of bucking the system of twisted rules the religious leaders had attempted to pass off as righteous.

Jesus didn't fast like the Pharisees thought he ought to. He let his disciples harvest on the Sabbath. For that matter, he himself healed on the Sabbath—horrors, all of them. And he surely must have been a dangerous criminal because those were the folks he chose to hang with—very suspicious.

Radical actions often appear most suspicious to those harboring something in themselves that isn't quite right. The Pharisees kept their hearts' corruption hidden as much as possible, but as verse 8 shows, they couldn't hide from Jesus. They wanted perfect actions from people; Jesus cared for people's hearts, knowing that pure actions were an overflow of a heart purely loved. As a result of his radical behavior, he became a threat to the Pharisees, who grew obsessed about catching him breaking any law they could find or fabricate.

Jesus wasn't really a lawbreaker in God's perspective. In fact, he was perfectly obedient to God. As a Jew and God's own Son, he respected and honored the Old Testament law of Moses. However, he knew his purpose was to bring us a way of life and freedom beyond that law. He embodied grace that gives us inner freedom, spiritual freedom we can't have by merely conforming to rules and regulations.

Jesus invites us to live by radical trust in him. For all the radical living people today praise themselves for doing, Jesus' way still tops them all.

TALK TO HIM

"Heavenly Father, I want to know the freedom of radically trusting you. Please help me cast off the chains of unnecessary dos and don'ts and opt instead for a wholehearted pursuit of knowing you."

> *[A Christian] puts all his trust in Christ: trusts that Christ will somehow share with him the perfect human obedience which He carried out from His birth to His crucifixion: that Christ will make the man more like Himself.*
>
> C. S. LEWIS

"Though it may sound simplistic, you can 'just have faith.'"

But Jesus overheard them and said to Jairus, "Don't be afraid. Just have faith." MARK 5:36

"Just have faith. Just believe. Just let go and let God."

Agggghhhhhhhhhhhh!!! Do you ever want to react that way to people's trite comments about faith? Usually spoken with simplistic flippancy that proves the speaker has no clue what we're going through, those "just have faith" remarks prompt us to want to "just let 'em have it."

We might be surprised, then, to learn that Jesus himself uttered the phrase, and to a father whose daughter was dying. Was he being trite and simplistic? Surely Jesus, who knows everything, would have understood and sympathized with the man's devastation.

Of course Jesus understood, which is what makes us dig deeper so we can understand why our Savior offered what we typically view as little comfort requiring little effort. Jesus' understanding becomes clear with the word *but* that begins verse 36. Verse 35 just revealed the messengers' tragic news that the girl had died. All hope was lost; the voices of doubt had won.

Until we come to *but*: "But Jesus overheard them." In the face of impossibility, Jesus encouraged Jairus that faith had not lost. Faith is most important when all looks lost. In fact, our blindness to the outcome is what makes faith faith. Faith can win no matter what circumstances look like because it doesn't look at circumstances; it looks to all-powerful Jesus.

Jesus' "just have faith" counters the voices of doubt. He didn't spare Jairus from hearing them. Instead, he allowed Jairus to rise above doubts and choose faith more decisively. Jesus doesn't always spare us from circumstances that tempt us to wonder if he will be trustworthy again. That would cheat us from strengthening our trust in him.

You will hear the voices of doubt—no doubt about that. But you can trust that Jesus hears them, too, and he still wants you to just have faith.

TALK TO HIM

"Lord, please help me listen for your voice that tells me to trust you. Your voice is quiet, but you can help me hear it over the shouts of doubt."

Faith is to believe what we do not see; and the reward of this faith is to see what we believe.

SAINT AUGUSTINE

September 27 MARK 6:30-44; 8:1-10

"I can turn your nothing into abundance."

They ate as much as they wanted. Afterward, the disciples picked up seven large baskets of leftover food. MARK 8:8

Nothing. Nada. Zip. Zero. Zilch. We don't like the idea of nothing. Nothing means being gypped, left out, overlooked, forsaken, emptied.

As you might guess, Jesus' ideas about emptiness are very different from ours, and for that we can be eternally grateful. Think of the miracles in the Bible. Jesus showed up when things looked bleakest, when people had no more options. Those miracles were miracles precisely because people had run out of formulas and methods for fixing things themselves. Each time, Jesus turned their nothing into everything they never knew they had always needed. Their negatives were his opportunities to shine in their lives and to introduce them to his abundance.

Emptiness holds blessings in disguise. Someone whose life is going fairly well, minus a few average-sized troubles, can draw on their own coping mechanisms and become accustomed to living with less than God's abundance. Those people become programmed to accept halfway living as all they should expect. After all, life is messy and tough, right?

Well, yes. Jesus' abundance doesn't negate the difficulties we deal with. The thousands he fed with loaves and fishes had already gotten hungry. He didn't stop that reality. Instead, he revealed his glory to them by filling up their emptiness.

When we truly are running on nothing, we can't escape our need. We can't pass it off as all there is to life. We need help, and we need it now if we're going to make it.

Reserve room in your emptiness for a bit of excitement to sneak in, because it is prime time to experience Jesus' abundance. He may fill you with so much of himself that what you thought you needed wasn't what he knows you need. But he will provide abundantly for you if you trust him with your emptiness.

TALK TO HIM

"Father, thank you for giving me hope for my lowest times. Please help me to hang on for you to fill up my emptiness. I gladly trade my nothing times for your abundance, however you see fit to fill me."

Fill me now, fill me now,
Jesus, come and fill me now;
Fill me with Thy hallowed presence,
Come, O come, and fill me now.
ELWOOD H. STOKES, "FILL ME NOW"

"Do you recognize me?"

"'Surely they will respect my son.'" MARK 12:6

God went to great lengths to prepare people for Jesus' coming. He wanted to help us recognize Jesus as the promised King, the One generations had built their hopes around.

God sent prophets to tell of the saving King whom God would send someday. He even spoke of Jesus as far back as Genesis 3, when he told Satan the serpent that Adam and Eve's offspring (Jesus) would strike a fatal blow to Satan's head.

And then Jesus came and spoke in his own words about his purpose. He taught and healed and loved as no one had done before or could do again. He fulfilled prophecies that should have led the people to understand his identity, that he was more than the good man they saw him as or the corrupt criminal their leaders thought he was.

They should have recognized him. Even the least educated Israelites were versed in their history because their religion was a way of life, not just a side order of practices. They knew the prophecies. They watched him teach. They saw his miracles. They joined the hysteria welcoming him into Jerusalem.

Days later they shouted to crucify him. They did not recognize him as the King whom God had promised. For all the history and hype, they missed the moment they had been anticipating.

Although Jesus no longer walks the earth, he still speaks to us through his Spirit. He still teaches, heals, and loves. He still is the saving King our hearts yearn to know. God filled his Word with prophecies of Jesus' return. Now we are the generations awaiting an unknown day.

Jesus turned the world upside down the last time he arrived; next time he will make an even bigger impression. Until then, his Spirit calls, urging you to know him so you will be prepared to meet him.

Will you recognize him as King when he appears in your life?

TALK TO HIM

"Jesus, you are my King. I worship you now and when we meet face-to-face. Please help me recognize you in the details of today as I wait for you to return."

With shouting and singing, and jubilant ringing,
Their arms of rebellion cast down;
At last every nation the Lord of salvation
Their King and Redeemer shall crown!

MARY B. SLADE, "THE KINGDOM IS COMING"

September 29 MARK 12:28-44

"Is your love recognizable?"

"'Love the LORD *your God with all your heart, all your soul, all your mind, and all your strength. . . . Love your neighbor as yourself.'"* MARK 12:30-31

How do we recognize love? We can learn about it in books; we can hear about it on TV; we can experience the agony of living without it. But what qualities make love apparent?

Love cannot be perfected through secondhand means like reading or hearing about it, a point made obvious by Jesus' description of the religious leaders in verses 38-40. As we observed yesterday, the leaders knew about the Messiah, but they didn't know Jesus. Today we see that they knew about love, but they didn't know love.

If they had known love, they would have been givers instead of takers—one of the primary "giveaways" about love, no pun intended. The Pharisees fed their pride by preferring the receiving role. They loved to attract impressive looks and respectful greetings while they graced the synagogues with their presence and took the best seats. They loved to love themselves. But love others? Not so much.

Contrast them with the poor widow who had virtually nothing but gave it all anyway. In doing so, she revealed her heart's greater richness that put the religious leaders to shame.

True love cannot be contained. It simply shows. Love must express itself by giving its best. When we love with all our hearts, souls, minds, and strength, we offer everything we have to the object of our affection. That is the love God gives and the love he asks for himself.

God alone deserves this kind of love, yet he lavishes it on us even as we hog it for ourselves. We can't enrich his existence by loving him. He already has the world at his fingertips and his own goodness at his disposal. But he longs to have our love because he is glorified when we reflect his loving character.

Is your love for God and others surprising for its believability or its rarity?

TALK TO HIM

"Lord, I want others to see in my love a reflection of your perfect love. Please show me how to love more as you do."

There is no surprise more magical than the surprise of being loved. It is God's finger on man's shoulder.

CHARLES MORGAN

"I would rather have your loyalty that goes the distance than dramatic promises of great love."

He said to Peter, "Simon, are you asleep? Couldn't you watch with me even one hour?"

MARK 14:37

Peter the passionate. That's what we could call him. Either that or drama king. Peter was one to act fast and maybe get around to thinking later.

While we can't fault him for wanting to do right, his follow-through often didn't measure up to his rash promises. His story serves as a wake-up call regarding our loyalty to God. Are we really as devoted as we claim, as committed as we would like to believe?

Jesus wasn't impressed by Peter's determination to stay true, but there's hope for all of us because Jesus never gave up on Peter. We shake our heads at Peter's weak will that promised so much but couldn't keep him awake to pray when Jesus was hurting so badly. Yet how often do our thoughts wander and our eyelids droop when we talk to God?

We imagine facing a crucial hour of do-or-die loyalty to Christ, and we probably imagine we would come through fine.

But would we?

Being called on our failures to stand up for Jesus is humbling and painful; however, if we are devoted to learning greater devotion, as Peter showed later on, then Jesus' reprimands will urge us to loyalty in action rather than simply in word.

We can be grateful for the humility of coming to terms with our own lack because often we have to see the worst in ourselves before we're motivated to make genuine changes.

God wants the real thing from us, just as he wanted from Peter. And just as he helped Peter grow into rock-solid devotion, he can help us develop actions that prove our promises.

Your loyalty will prove itself by going the distance through consistency from one minute to the next.

TALK TO HIM

"Lord God, I want to show my loyal love for you. Please help me to learn greater devotion that will go the distance."

O hear, ye brave, the sound that moves the earth around,
'Tis loyalty, loyalty, loyalty to Christ;
Arise to dare and do, ring out the watchword true,
Of loyalty, loyalty, yes, loyalty to Christ.

E. TAYLOR CASSEL, "LOYALTY TO CHRIST"

October 1 LUKE 1:26-56

"Accept my difficult blessings because you believe in me."

"You are blessed because you believed that the Lord would do what he said." LUKE 1:45

We can only imagine the jumble of thoughts and emotions Jesus' mother, Mary, felt upon learning she was carrying God's Son.

On second thought, no, we really can't imagine that. Never before nor since that awesome day has anyone received such shocking news. In all likelihood, Mary was a young teen at that point. Who of us would have the presence of mind, much less the spiritual maturity, to handle that responsibility with a portion of the grace Mary showed? God knew his girl's belief in him, and he was about to bless her big-time for it.

However, Mary welcomed God's news about the Messiah growing within her not because she craved blessings, but because she craved God, the giver of those blessings. She accepted his unbelievable news because she believed her Lord.

Only a God so wonderful that we need his assistance to understand his ways could be capable of producing a Son through a virgin. It's a miracle unbelievable to human hearts that haven't been prepared by God to accept it, a miracle many would not want to be blessed with because it brought a great deal of heartache along with it.

Mary had to love her Lord in order to see the gift of being the Messiah's mother as a blessing. To remain faithful and grateful despite the scandal of being an unwed, pregnant teenager and the threat of losing her fiancé's trust . . . those challenges required a heart that truly desired God at its deepest places. A lesser faith would not want such blessing.

Mary was blessed because she chose God no matter what extra difficulties his blessings for her included. She was blessed because she knew and returned God's love. She was blessed because she believed God had blessed her.

Some blessings may be yours only through difficulty, but take God at his word that he is blessing you just the same.

TALK TO HIM

"Lord, please help me not to run from your difficult blessings, but to believe you for the 'impossible' job of seeing me through."

The Christian life is gloriously difficult, but the difficulty of it does not make us faint and cave in, it rouses us up to overcome.

OSWALD CHAMBERS

"I will meet you at your crisis of belief."

"Master," Simon replied, "we worked hard all last night and didn't catch a thing. But if you say so, I'll let the nets down again." LUKE 5:5

You have a crisis of faith. We all do.

Our crisis of faith comes from struggling to believe that Jesus' miracles could mean something for us today; modern society views him as old and outdated, not having anything of value to offer our advanced age. Funny how that mind-set reflects the opposite crisis of belief of two thousand years ago. Those people who watched Jesus in person wondered what to think of the stranger who stepped into their midst with all manner of new theories and amazing feats.

No matter when we live or what our background is, on some level we all struggle to believe. Even the most churched person doesn't escape human nature's desire to see all the facts before risking our all-important intelligence. And no one can run from the decision point of believing or not when we face a very personal faith crisis.

We wonder if belief makes sense when we've never seen something done before, like Simon Peter, who wondered why they should bother taking Jesus' advice about fishing after they'd just proven there were no fish around to catch. Or how about the man with leprosy, who risked being shunned by yet another person, Jesus, the man whom he viewed as his final hope? And then there was the paralyzed man who relentlessly pursued Jesus with his need to walk.

In every crisis of belief, Jesus met the people at their specific needs. He didn't mix things up by curing the paralyzed man of leprosy or handing the leper a net full of fish or sprouting extra legs on the fishermen in case theirs went lame.

He gave them what they needed.

Our needs represent a crisis point of believing in Jesus' specific power to help us. As it was back then, his timing will be perfect and his methods precise.

He will meet you at your crisis point with exactly what you need.

TALK TO HIM

"Jesus, my Lord, you are a miracle. Please help me look for you in my crisis of belief."

Faith is like radar that sees through the fog—the reality of things at a distance that the human eye cannot see.

CORRIE TEN BOOM

October 3 LUKE 9:21-27, 51-62

"Let me show you how letting go and hanging on work together."

"If you try to hang on to your life, you will lose it. But if you give up your life for my sake, you will save it." LUKE 9:24

Let go and rest. Hang on to faith. Loosen up on the things of this world. Hold tight to Jesus. Let go, hang on, loosen up, hold tight—which is it?

Spiritually speaking, it's all of those things. And as it might seem, it takes a lifetime to learn how to balance holding on and letting go. Fortunately, God gives each of us a unique lifetime and a training manual (aka the Bible) to help us do just that.

Jesus showed what letting go and holding on look like because he spent thirty-three years putting human dreams to the side for the sake of guarding his God-given purpose on earth. We might not think Jesus had human dreams, but the Bible says he was tempted in every way, yet didn't sin. Surely he had to choose between finite dreams that would've distracted him from God's plans for him or faithfulness to his heavenly Father's will. Anything we want to put above God works as a temptation. No doubt Jesus as fully man had to decide repeatedly to put his godly calling above immediate human desires. Since Jesus succeeded at "taking up his cross" (verse 23) and "putting his hand to the plow" (verse 62), he can help us succeed at those disciplines as well.

There is no denying the struggles we face when it comes to trading our humanness for God's better way. But when we release our hold on a lesser perk to free our hands to grip immeasurable treasure, our hope can soar into eternity as God intends it to.

As you let go of this life, hang on to Jesus for the one to come.

TALK TO HIM

"Heavenly Father, thank you for sending Jesus to set the example of letting go and holding on. Please help me learn to balance those disciplines from day to day."

Hold Thou my hand, and closer, closer draw me
To Thy dear self—my hope, my joy, my all;
Hold Thou my hand, lest haply I should wander,
And, missing Thee, my trembling feet should fall.
FANNY CROSBY, "HOLD THOU MY HAND"

"I am a relentless pursuer of those I love, and I love you."

"When he has found it, he will joyfully carry it home." LUKE 15:5

They say repetition is the mother of learning. Well, Jesus must have wanted to impress something huge on his listeners, because he told the same story in three different ways.

The theme he was passionate to share? God's pursuit of us.

By comparing tales of lost sheep, coins, and sons, Jesus increasingly opened our ears to the extent of God's love for us. By the time we reach the end of chapter 15, we're rejoicing right along with God over the lost son whose father welcomed him home with open arms. Like an orchestra building to a crescendo, God sweeps us off our feet with the grand lengths he goes to for us.

How amazing God is as the eternal pursuer of our souls! We don't have to chase him down or convince him to forgive us and take us back. He is the One seeking to win us. He doesn't offer us salvation grudgingly or with reservations or strings attached. He longs to lavish us with his goodness while we spend eternity worshiping him.

If your soul hasn't yet been captured by God's relentless pursuit, know that he longs to bring you into his fold as your heavenly Shepherd. He owns the wealth of the universe, yet he seeks you like one small lost coin he would rather die for than live without. And no matter how ugly the trail of your sins or the worthlessness of your past actions, he waits for you to return to him and accept his glad welcome.

This God—this Shepherd, Seeker, Father—loves you. He broke his own heart in pursuit of yours. Do you want him to repeat himself again? Listen, and you will hear his "I love you" today.

Listen and let him catch you.

TALK TO HIM

"Father, sometimes I can be deaf to your gentle song of love. Sometimes I tune you out because I can't fathom why you keep pursuing me. Please remove everything that plugs my heart's ears to you. I want to be caught by you."

Ye sinners, come, 'tis Mercy's voice;
The gracious call obey;
Mercy invites to heav'nly joys,
And can you yet delay?

ANNE STEELE, "THE SAVIOR CALLS"

October 5 LUKE 18:1-14

"Learn the power of humble, persistent prayer."

"Don't you think God will surely give justice to his chosen people who cry out to him day and night?" LUKE 18:7

Even an unjust judge did it. When we doubt that God hears and responds to our prayers, we are basically viewing him as less loving than an uncaring, ungodly judge.

How's that for a wake-up call about our perspective on prayer?

Human beings seem to have a default setting on disappointment: When things don't go the way we think they should, we automatically toss the blame on God as being unfair. But as today's reading shows, God isn't out of touch with us when he delays answering prayer. Often he wants us to persist through unbelieving attitudes that hinder our prayers.

The widow relentlessly pursued the judge for help because she knew he was her only resort. God welcomes our humble acknowledgment of our need for him because only when we see the end of ourselves do we truly realize how dependent we are on him. When we look at our troubles from God's viewpoint, we see that our most desperate circumstances are really our least desperate because he is about to move on our behalf—another wake-up call on how we view troublesome times. The Pharisee who felt such "gratitude" that he didn't need as much grace as the humble tax collector had no idea how much he was missing from learning to depend on God.

But we must keep asking. We must show stubborn trust and humility of spirit that God adores responding to. He chose to create us and save us. Surely he chooses to sustain us as well.

Don't shortchange your prayers by imagining the Lord you call out to sits on his throne with his hands covering his ears. When you're exhausted from crying out to him, let him know. Pour out your need and trust tenaciously that his ears perk to your every word.

TALK TO HIM

"Father God, I am not going to stop praying until I receive your answer. Please give me patience while that answer is 'wait' and faith that trusts in your loving timing."

What we usually pray to God is not that His will be done, but that He approve ours.

HELGA BERGOLD GROSS

"Does your heart delight to connect with mine?"

They said to each other, "Didn't our hearts burn within us as he talked with us on the road and explained the Scriptures to us?" LUKE 24:32

Jesus has a sense of humor. Anyone who doubts that just needs to read Luke 24. The scene is almost comical in a wondrous, miraculous way. In fact, the humor we can see in it adds to the story's sheer refreshment.

It didn't begin too well from the two followers' viewpoint. At the lowest of lows, swallowed up by grief over Jesus' death, they were confused about the previous days' events at the Crucifixion, clueless about Jesus' identity as the Messiah, and oblivious when he joined them on the road. So Jesus set them straight, and finally the lightbulb lit in their minds: Of course! How could we have missed it—all the signs were there! Even our hearts burned in his presence! Jesus, our Messiah!

And then the fun began. Picture Jesus next appearing to a group of disciples. He showed up out of nowhere, so naturally they were shocked and a tad scared. Even after seeing the scars in his hands and feet, they just stood there, rooted to the floor in surprise. So Jesus continued with the next order of business—food! Profound.

Can you imagine a smirk toying at Jesus' mouth at their dumbfounded expressions? Someone—speechless as far as we know—managed to come up with a broiled fish for him. Grinning up at them around the food in his mouth, he enjoyed his first good meal that we read about since his resurrection.

Jesus seemed to take great delight in his time with those disciples. After their adjustment period of realizing he was back, perhaps they chuckled with him over their initial reaction. We don't know; but we do know through this passage that Jesus affected people.

From burning hearts to surprised disbelief to utter shock, people reacted to him. Jesus doesn't leave people unchanged by his presence today either.

Do you find surprise and delight when you meet with him?

TALK TO HIM

"Lord, I'm ready for a new adventure in your presence. Please surprise me with fresh awareness of you."

Jesus is full of surprises for those who stick around for the adventure.

ANONYMOUS

October 7 JOHN 2:1-12

"Remember that my miracles show my personal care for you."

This miraculous sign at Cana in Galilee was the first time Jesus revealed his glory. And his disciples believed in him. JOHN 2:11

Jesus always had personal purpose for his miracles: personally for him, to reveal his power; personally for us, to meet a need.

The Cana wedding was when Jesus first showed his power, which resulted in the disciples' belief in him. Through the miracle of turning water to wine—the finest of wines at that—Jesus touched a group of guests. But he also personally touched several people's hearts.

First of all was the bridegroom. Running out of wine in that culture was humiliating. It simply wasn't done in respectable society. If not for Jesus, the groom would have faced shame in front of his guests and his new bride.

Then there were the disciples, who witnessed their leader do something extraordinary. Whatever their motivation had been for following him, no doubt it multiplied exponentially when they tasted that heavenly wine.

And finally there was Jesus' mother. We don't know the countless ways her son had wowed her as he grew up. But surely she looked upon him with more than a mother's pride when she saw that miracle at Cana. That was her boy. He had been changing her life for the previous thirty years, and he was about to change the world.

Every time the Lord acts on his people's behalf, he performs miracles. From what appears to us as mundane events of everyday life, from the rising of the sun to the flowing of the tides, God showers his power over creation. He shows his glory to all of us; yet he also reveals his glory to each of us.

God fills every moment of your day with signs of himself. He works on your behalf to get your attention and to reveal his faithfulness. Will his miracles move your belief in him?

TALK TO HIM

"Lord, every day is a miracle when I consider your hand on the details. Please help me to look for your personal care for me in the things you do today."

Where there is great love, there are always miracles.

WILLA CATHER

"Do you want my healing?"

When Jesus saw him and knew he had been ill for a long time, he asked him, "Would you like to get well?" JOHN 5:6

Every now and then we come across a line in the Bible that jumps out in its simplicity. Jesus' question in verse 6 is one of those instances. Why would Jesus bother asking the man if he would like to be healed?

Think about our tendency to get stuck in status quo, to grow complacent—not content, but complacent—with our lives. People give up on themselves, and worse still on God, all the time. Living in a messy world, we become used to thinking our current situation is the end of the road.

Jesus came to earth to blast that shortsighted thinking off the planet. In order to change, though, we must first anticipate a different situation. In order to get ready, we must face some questions: Do we really want change enough to keep hoping? Do we want to rely on Jesus to move us on?

The lame man had forgotten what it was to imagine himself healed. Not only was his body decaying, so were his soul and his spirit. He needed a jump start to consider a new picture for himself.

Jesus' question got the man's hope flowing again. Follow his thought processes: *Do I want to be well? . . . Huh, there's a thought. Me . . . healed. Whole. Is that possible? What would I be like? What would I do tomorrow?*

A lifetime of built-up, buried dreams probably flashed through the man's brain in those milliseconds after Jesus questioned him. He had to want to be healed in order to rise to the changes Jesus had in store. He also had to look closely at the man who posed the question, the Savior who would restore his dreams and add eternal ones as well.

Jesus is ready to restore the hopes you've given up craving. Risk one more time that Jesus' healing power can change you.

TALK TO HIM

"Lord, please remind me that you have more in store. Please help me to risk hoping in you."

Lay hold on the hope set before you,
A hope that is steadfast and sure;
O haste to the blessèd Redeemer,
The loving, the perfect and pure.

FANNY CROSBY, "THE HOPE SET BEFORE YOU"

October 9 JOHN 8:1-20

"I see where you've come from, and I see where I want to take you."

"If you follow me, you won't have to walk in darkness, because you will have the light that leads to life. . . . For I know where I came from and where I am going." JOHN 8:12, 14

Getting comfortable in our own shoes takes most of us into early adulthood to accomplish. None of us survived childhood without scars because even loving parents are imperfect. When school days arrived, imperfect teachers didn't always fill our heads with positive feedback, while the playground crawled with peers who often didn't treat us as worthwhile. It didn't take much negativity to imprint our psyches with our perceived failures.

As we grew, we developed coping mechanisms that still either fight for our self-worth or bury our hurts. Either way, we learned to deal with life in healthy and not-so-healthy ways. We might enjoy brief bouts of confidence, but just when we think we've overcome our issues it's time to revisit the same old, repackaged junk.

Crises of identity are some of the oldest troubles known to humankind. From Adam and Eve's first sin we have faced an uphill battle against the human nature that cripples us and separates us from God.

But Jesus came to earth to reestablish our identity with his heavenly Father. Jesus never wasted energy wondering who he was or whether he was worthwhile, and he doesn't wonder that about us. He was entirely comfortable in his own sandals because he knew his Father so well, and he knew the greatness of his Father's heart.

When we follow Jesus, he leads us to deeper understanding of God's love for us. He lights the path through our confusion about ourselves, and he invites us into the wholeness he enjoys with Father God.

God loves you and sent his Son to tell you so. No matter where you've come from, God offers you a secure future with him.

You are cherished by your Creator. Enjoy being his treasure.

TALK TO HIM

"Father, it's tough to fight the negative thoughts that shout inside me. Please replace them with your words of love, and help me to move forward with you."

Lead me gently, Lord, through my mess of self-doubt.
Lead me to the safety of your heart.
ANONYMOUS

October 10

"Learn from me how to have twenty-twenty spiritual eyesight."

"You remain guilty because you claim you can see." JOHN 9:41

To see or not to see? That is the question of the day. Actually, it's a question for life. As Jesus is so skilled at doing, he wove together daily events into a beautiful tapestry of life lessons about what it means to really see.

The story began years before Jesus met the blind man, back all the way to when the man was born. Being blind from birth, the man had no idea what it was to see. Trees? He had no concept of a brown trunk or green leaves. To him, trees were things to lean against, scratchy to the back, but good relief from the hot sun and pleasant to hear as a breeze brushed their leaves.

Although the man had no idea what Jesus looked like, he recognized something about Jesus that the Pharisees missed. He had twenty-twenty spiritual eyesight that enabled him to "see" without his physical eyes.

Maybe his blindness had humbled him. It at least had acclimated him to his own weaknesses—a quality that's a blessing in disguise but foreign to the proud Pharisees who weren't aware of their spiritual pride that blinded them. If the man's blindness served to open his heart in a way that the arrogant Pharisees couldn't relate to, then hallelujah for his physical eyes that didn't see.

If God gave the man insufficient eyes at birth because he knew that was the only way to grow the man's spiritual vision, then blindness was the man's greatest reason for gratitude to God—quite a shift in perspective from how the world views shortcomings.

As the Bible has shown us already this year, our weaknesses teach us our need for the Lord, and in that way, they are assets. Is your spiritual vision twenty-twenty, allowing you to view your shortcomings through God's eyes?

TALK TO HIM

"Heavenly Lord, you are a sight for sore spiritual eyes. Please give me greater vision to see my weaknesses through your eyes."

Be Thou my Vision, O Lord of my heart;
Naught be all else to me, save that Thou art.
Thou my best Thought, by day or by night,
Waking or sleeping, Thy presence my light.
DALLAN FORGAILL, "BE THOU MY VISION"

October 11 JOHN 11:1-44

"You can see me clearly through your tears."

"But even now I know that God will give you whatever you ask." JOHN 11:22

Martha earned a name for herself through her busyness. She was the sister who slaved in the kitchen and complained about Mary lounging idly near Jesus instead of helping her (see Luke 10:38-42). But before casting worker-bee Martha in with the Bible's problem children, let's take another look at her motivations.

She was a striver. She wanted to make things perfect, possibly because she was a perfectionist, but probably because she truly wanted to show her love for Jesus. Her genuine faith in him shows up in today's reading when she risks looking foolish for the sake of believing Jesus had more in store.

Her brother had died. No one was denying that fact, no one including Jesus. Most people would have caved in to their despair and taken it as a given that Jesus had passed them over.

Not Martha. Her tenacious personality carried into her spiritual life, and she could not give in to the temptation that teased her, saying that Jesus must not have cared—or worse, that he wasn't all she believed him to be.

Martha's faith had matured enough to know that Jesus had a greater explanation for why he hadn't shown up in time to save Lazarus. She trusted that "even now"—even after Lazarus had died—God would come through for them according to whatever Jesus asked.

Martha, the worker, put her trust to work and should be remembered for seeing Jesus clearly through her tears.

What does Jesus look like through your tears?

TALK TO HIM

"Lord God, I know you don't stop every tear from flowing, but I believe you catch them all. Please keep my eyes on you, seeing your love clearly despite my tears—clearer still because of them."

Be grateful for tears; their flow flushes out debris that
keeps our eyes of faith from seeing God.
ANONYMOUS

"You can know my peace, the only kind that lifts you above trouble."

"The peace I give is a gift the world cannot give." JOHN 14:27

We live in a peaceless world. (Surprise, surprise.) For all the bumper stickers and peace symbols and New Age promises, this world has no clue what real peace feels like because a world that rejects God also rejects any potential for lasting peace.

Peace is a gift that comes from Jesus alone. Period. People can fabricate it, fake it, and fantasize about it, but no one can conjure up the real deal because we lost peace way back in the Garden of Eden when Adam and Eve first sinned. We cannot get it back without accepting it as a gift from Jesus, who made it possible through his death and resurrection.

Peace is the security that comes from an unhindered connection with God, which explains why we lost it when Adam and Eve's sin broke our intimacy with our Creator. It also explains why we can experience it again through Jesus, since he is our bridge back to God.

Just as God lifted Jesus to heaven after the resurrection, his peace lifts us above our earthly troubles. We're still on this earth for our human lifetime, and we still endure all the messes and heartaches that go along with that. But God's Holy Spirit in us has the power to hold us above the stresses we encounter here. It is truly miraculous that we can be in this world but enjoy the safety of having our souls sealed with God, and our spirits kept healthy and whole by his. Peace is a sure by-product of intimacy with Father God. If we're not experiencing it, then the glitch is on our part.

Let those times when peace feels lacking draw you back to your heavenly Father's heart. Use those empty phases as catalysts for your spiritual growth and for seeing God glorify himself by refilling you with the peace he promised long ago.

TALK TO HIM

"I've heard so much about peace, Lord, but haven't witnessed much of it. Please show me the real thing for your glory, my good, and the good of others whom I can point to you."

There's either peace with God or no peace at all.
ANONYMOUS

October 13 JOHN 15:1-27

"The only way you will thrive in a world that refuses me is to stay connected to me."

"I have told you these things so that you will be filled with my joy. Yes, your joy will overflow!" JOHN 15:11

All God's promises are vital, but one that affects our daily life perhaps the most is the one about staying connected to him as branches on a vine. We need that connection to thrive with joy, mentioned like a breath of freshness in this chapter.

Like the peace that we studied yesterday, God's joy is the only real variety. No making it up, no mimicking it, no measuring it to ensure we don't run out. When we have it for real, we have it without limit. But the only way to experience that joy is by sticking close to God, or in Jesus' words, by remaining in his love.

In the same breath that he spoke verse 11, Jesus emphasized his love again, so it's common sense to connect his love with his joy. The two miracles go hand in hand, and they're true miracles because the real versions come only from the Lord.

We're wise to connect his love with his overflow of joy. But there is more we need to know because this life is full of threats to both love and joy. The second part of the chapter continues with advice about hardships Jesus' followers can expect. It is smart to connect his words about love and joy with his prophetic ones about difficulties.

How do they work together? The joy we experience as a by-product of his love serves as protection and strength in seasons of heartbreak. Joy doesn't differentiate between good times and bad because it isn't at the mercy of circumstances, as mere happiness is.

Thrive in joy today by connecting with your loving Savior who promises to sustain you.

TALK TO HIM

"Lord, I am so thankful that you love to lavish joy on your own. Please help me stay connected to you through today's ups and downs."

Joy seems to me a step beyond happiness—happiness is a sort of atmosphere you can live in sometimes when you're lucky. Joy is a light that fills you with hope and faith and love.
ADELA ROGERS ST. JOHNS

"Anticipate the joy to come when I return for you!"

They were filled with joy when they saw the Lord! JOHN 20:20

We learn to trust people in part by observing their lifestyle—how they carry themselves and interact with us and others. Even though we haven't met Jesus face-to-face, the fact that he lived so relationally with people of his day speaks volumes about how he relates to us through his Holy Spirit. We can anticipate what to expect from him based on his interactions on earth two thousand years ago.

So when he spoke Mary's name and instantly became recognizable to her, we begin to understand that he calls us by name too. And when he didn't let a few locked doors bar him from appearing among the disciples, we hope that he will defy our limited experience to show himself in new ways to us. And when the disciples were filled with joy at the sight of him, we start to anticipate the joy we will feel when he returns someday for us.

Jesus proved repeatedly in big ways and small that he is ever present and ever engaged in our lives. He isn't a ghost bent on spooking us or an arrogant wonder-worker set on amazing us with heroic feats only to abandon us when we need to know he is with us.

We learn something of his character from what we read about him. And based on our own experiences of him, we can let ourselves get excited about meeting him in person someday. Our hopes for someday should increase our joy today.

So go ahead and dream about what's to come with him, and let those dreams lift your spirit today since you know he doesn't wait to call out to you. Your name is on his lips even now.

TALK TO HIM

"Jesus, my Savior, Lord, and King, I'm listening for your voice. Thank you for calling me by name and helping me to recognize you in my life. And thank you for all I can anticipate with you."

Jesus calls us! By Thy mercies,
Savior may we hear Thy call,
Give our hearts to Thine obedience,
Serve and love Thee best of all.
CECIL F. ALEXANDER, "JESUS CALLS US"

October 15 ACTS 1:1-11

"My purpose in your life might be different from your original expectations."

When the apostles were with Jesus, they kept asking him, "Lord, has the time come for you to free Israel and restore our kingdom?" ACTS 1:6

We don't get it till we get it. It took the disciples a long time to understand Jesus' purpose for coming to earth. Their confusion, in turn, affected their grasp of God's plans for their lives. Considering that they lived closely with him for three years, listening to his teachings, watching him interact, observing his miracles, is it any wonder that we can be a little dense, too, about his plans for us?

If you were to ask a hundred people today why Jesus came to earth, what might be some responses you would hear? Maybe he came to

. . . teach peace and love.
. . . bring hope to us.
. . . take over the kingdom of Israel.
. . . who really knows?

Well, we can know why he came, and we need to know if we're to understand his dreams for us. Jesus came to restore us to God. When we realize that purpose, we also begin to learn that his life in us inspires us to point others to God's holiness and love. Everything God allows in our lives is part of his grand plans to glorify himself and share his love with us.

The disciples expected Jesus to free the earthly kingdom of Israel from the Roman Empire. It wasn't until after Jesus returned to heaven that they realized he came to bring freedom to their souls.

Those who think God is all about making their purposes come true are selling their dreams short and missing out on the greater—the greatest—adventure of knowing him. Allow room in your plans for God to show you something bigger and better. You might be surprised to discover what you didn't know you were missing.

TALK TO HIM

"Lord, please loosen my grip on my plans and help me welcome your changes to what I think I need. I want your dreams above all."

Release yourself to God's purposes to discover a life
you can't envision apart from him.
ANONYMOUS

"My Spirit in you is limitless when you welcome me."

"How can this be? . . . What can this mean?" ACTS 2:7,12

When God sent Jesus to us, he delivered a bundle of newborn innocence to an unassuming couple. After Jesus returned to heaven, God sent his Holy Spirit, this time with a bit more drama.

Sounds of a windstorm roared through the new believers' meeting place, and flames settled on everyone. As the Spirit filled them, they spoke in different languages, all understandable to each other. The attention-grabbing scene was exactly what the situation called for. Jesus' victory had rendered the old system of justification with God unnecessary; the era of grace had come, and God was on the move with a new way of approaching him.

Change is exhilarating and unsettling, and the Spirit delivers both. When he moves, we know it. Like God the Father, who sent his Son and Spirit, and like Jesus, who came to us, the Holy Spirit is an initiator. He comes ready to fill us, but we need to stay attuned to him. When we welcome his changes, there is no limit to what he will do.

Through him, people related to God and each other in new ways. God knew the believers would be hard pressed to communicate his salvation around the globe, so his Spirit simply removed those language limitations. God also knew how much they would need each other for the difficulties ahead, so he sent his Spirit to a group instead of to only one couple, creating instant camaraderie through shared life changes. Their growing community began sharing meals, homes, possessions—their daily lives. The Holy Spirit altered their entire way of living.

The Holy Spirit knows no limits in us except for barriers we put up to keep him from doing all he wants. We must encourage his changes if we are to experience his unhindered majesty, but when we do, we can expect to be constantly awed.

TALK TO HIM

"Father, although your Spirit undoes my comfort level, I am so thankful for him. Please keep me from hindering your power in me."

Whenever the Holy Ghost sees a chance of glorifying Jesus, He will take your heart, your nerves, your whole personality, and simply make you blaze and glow with devotion to Jesus Christ.

OSWALD CHAMBERS

October 17 ACTS 7:51-60

"Look up in the midst of trouble, and feel my glory shine on you."

But Stephen, full of the Holy Spirit, gazed steadily into heaven and saw the glory of God.

ACTS 7:55

We've come across another crucial but: "But Stephen, full of the Holy Spirit. . . ." Stephen experienced God's comforting presence and glory despite hindrances. His filling was in spite of rage leveled on him from the Jesus-hating Jewish leaders.

Beware of passing off Stephen's sacrifice as heroism reserved for only a few. His nerves exploded in agony with every rock that battered his body. To think that his faith put a barrier between him and the pain would be to cheapen the price he paid to be faithful to Jesus. Life can take us to the end of ourselves. Stephen wouldn't argue with that. He knew what torture felt like, and he was no stranger to feeling like an outcast when he saw hatred in the faces glaring back at him.

But Stephen stopped looking around and looked up to discover the infinitely kind eyes of his Savior. God graciously gave him a glimpse of what awaited him if he would hold on through the pain.

This "but" transforms our approach to hardships. We will face them, absolutely. We've heard it before, but a part of us still resists hearing it again: God doesn't shield us from every hurt, and not even the hope of a painless eternity removes us from the realities of this earthly life. We don't like it, but it is what it is.

Given all that, how precious to us is the unobtrusive word *but* in verse 55. We can have the power of God's Spirit to strengthen and comfort us through torrents of pain. We might even see God's glory more profoundly smack-dab in the throes of our lowest times.

Hold on to the exception God grants you through a little word like *but*, and know that his glory outshines any trouble you will endure.

TALK TO HIM

"Lord, when I reach the end of my strength, frankly I have trouble wanting to hold on to hope. But no matter what, I can't ignore your right to receive glory through it all. So glorify yourself in me today."

I don't think of all the misery but the beauty that still remains.

ANNE FRANK

"I excel at opening eyes and healing lives."

He fell to the ground. . . . "Who are you, lord?" Saul asked. ACTS 9:4-5

Recently we've studied about physical and spiritual eyesight. The blind man saw with his spiritual eyes what the proud Pharisees missed with their physical ones (see John 9:1-41). The man's humbled state of being born blind had prepared his heart to recognize his need for Jesus, thus making his physical inability an eternal blessing.

The apostle Paul, originally known as Saul, experienced an opposite miracle, but one that worked in much the same way. God blessed him as an adult with the gift of blindness in order to open his spiritual heart to see. It's more than a little ironic that he had enjoyed an illustrious, if brutal, career as a Pharisee. Call it poetic justice from God's hand?

Sometimes God doles out grace gently, as he did for the blind man. Other times his grace hits like thunder, or lightning, in Saul's case. He needed a walloping dose of God to get his attention. He had no idea of his need until God brought him to his knees and removed all pretensions and inaccurate assumptions of his own merits. God literally floored him.

Saul's story and the blind man's experience illustrate a key truth about how God works. Because he is a very personal Lord and Savior, God knows exactly how to get our attention. The blind man needed only Jesus' gentle touch. Saul required God's version of a Mack truck. Both methods resulted in opened eyes and healed lives.

God is perfectly good at what he does. There is no greater expert at being God because there simply isn't any possibility of improving on him. He knows exactly how to help you through your struggles, including the ones you carry in your spirit.

Ask him, and he will remove all barriers keeping you from seeing him and being restored by him.

TALK TO HIM

"Lord God, truly, utterly, in every sense, you are the best, and I'm so thankful to be at your mercy. Thank you for your grace fit just for me. Please get my attention whatever it takes."

God's grace is light as a feather, more powerful
than a tsunami, and a perfect fit for you.
ANONYMOUS

October 19 ACTS 10:34-48

"Prejudice does not exist in my love."

"God shows no favoritism. In every nation he accepts those who fear him and do what is right." ACTS 10:34-35

Surely you've asked and been asked, What's your favorite . . . ? Book, song, verse, color, etc. It's actually kind of a draining question when it puts you on the spot, or when you can't honestly answer one thing over another.

It also can be convicting when it reveals an unfair or hurtful preference. Imagine the pain a child feels from a parent who favors a sibling. Or think about the atrocities people have suffered worldwide because of favoritism, otherwise known as prejudice. Playing favorites can be innocent enough when it comes to a preferred ice cream flavor, but there is no way to undo the damage to someone's heart because of prejudice.

Thankfully for all of us, the only favoritism in God's heart is the kind that says we're all his favorites. Originally he picked the Israelites as his chosen people, but when Jesus came and died, he died for all of us, regardless of race, gender, age, sin history, education level, or any other reason. No favoritism means no favoritism. God loves equally every person who has ever lived, and his love will continue to be available in measures just as great to everyone yet to be born.

We can't do anything to lose his love, but we also can't do anything to earn more of it. Consider the refreshment of that truth. God's unprejudiced love not only frees us from eternal death, but it also frees us from striving to earn his acceptance in this life and for the one to come.

We've got his heart! How exciting that is!

Now the question remains . . . does he have yours?

TALK TO HIM

"Father God, thank you for making me your favorite! Please help me to be grateful for that status with you, while treating others as your favorites as well."

God's heart is infinitely big enough to hold all his favorites at once.
ANONYMOUS

"Do you think nothing can shock you? How about my freedom?"

Peter finally came to his senses. "It's really true!" he said. "The Lord has sent his angel and saved me!" ACTS 12:11

We love freedom. We crave it, fight for it, and feel abused when we lack it. From physical to emotional to spiritual and so on, we experience freedom or bondage in every area of life. Sometimes we're aware of chains that keep us down, as Peter clearly understood in Herod's prison. Other times the chains aren't so obvious.

Take emotional bondage, for instance. We have carried some emotional burdens for so long that we don't notice them anymore, or we have lost hope of breathing easily without a weight pressing on our lungs. We would be shocked to wake up refreshed without the ache of stress. Freedom is shocking, and that is partly why it's so wonderful. Freedom surprises us with refreshment.

Spiritual freedom is the most fantastic of all because it not only affects our earthly lives, but it also determines our eternity. Yet many people don't know what it means for them, so they muddle through life assuming it merely involves the space to worship whomever and however they please.

True spiritual freedom comes only from the Lord, and it impacts all other freedoms. To understand more, look closely at verse 11. Even though Peter was in prison, he was spiritually free because he knew that Jesus had died to save him from sin. Herod and his guards were the ones truly in bondage because they didn't know Jesus as Lord. Peter's spiritual freedom brought him temporary physical bondage, but his soul was infinitely better off than Herod's and the guards', whose physical freedom did nothing for their souls' enslavement.

When God freed Peter physically, he illustrated how shocking freedom is, and how victorious we are when we're spiritually free. He stopped at nothing to save our souls from death; surely he will do all he can to keep us free.

Ask for more of his freedom in the areas he knows you need it, and prepare for the shock of an eternal lifetime.

TALK TO HIM

"Lord, thank you for being the authority on freedom. When I feel bound by weakness and sin, whether mine or someone else's, please free me in your way and time."

Freedom is the oxygen of the soul.

MOSHE DAYAN

October 21 ACTS 14:8-20

"My creative acts should lead you to worship me, not my miracles."

"In the past [God] permitted all the nations to go their own ways, but he never left them without evidence of himself and his goodness." ACTS 14:16-17

You finally did it! After months of dreaming and preparation and effort, you finally finished the gift you believe to be the lifelong dream for someone you love. What a joy it was to create! Sure it took lots of effort. Sure it required your heart-and-soul passion. But your efforts reveal your deep love, and you hope your loved one will see your heart in the gift.

Never once do you consider how you would feel if the receiver took your gift and walked away, ignoring you while showering kisses all over the object of your efforts.

Unfortunately, that's the response God gets from most of humankind. What must he think when he sees people loving his miracles more than him? To add insult to injury, he knew even before he created the world that we as a creation would be more inclined to worship his gifts than him, yet he lavishes us with signs of his love anyway.

Why do we do this to him? The reasons are endless and shameful. We are arrogant and proud, ungrateful and lazy, and we love to take, take, take when we know Someone is willing to give, give, give. How much better when that Someone is God himself, who has more riches than we can fathom and loves to shower them on us. What a deal for us!

However.

God knows a key truth that is a secret to those whose hearts are still blinded in "take mode": We miss out on his very best gift (a close relationship with him) when we have our eyes plied to the next greatest miracle cure for our every want.

The people in Lystra missed seeing God because they were so awed by his miracle. The true miracle is God's love for us; his actions on our behalf only serve to point us to him. Don't favor the evidence of his love over the Lover himself.

TALK TO HIM

"Lord God, I'm awed by your love because it reveals your greatness. I worship you only, and I thank you for gifts that show who you are."

To love a gift, love the giver.

ANONYMOUS

October 22

"My Son died to give you freedom, not more rules."

"Why are you now challenging God by burdening the Gentile believers with a yoke that neither we nor our ancestors were able to bear?" ACTS 15:10

When you think of traditions, you might think of special holiday or birthday events, or unique ways to commemorate meaningful times. Traditions anchor our memories and establish group identity. When they're deeply rooted, we can't imagine ignoring them.

When Jesus died and did away with the old system of law, the rules and regulations regarding sacrifices and being justified before God weren't necessary anymore. However, the people had been practicing them for so long that many had a hard time letting go of the way of life generations had followed. The old rules felt like traditions they couldn't imagine discarding.

However, Jesus' purpose on earth showed that some traditions were meant to be released in favor of a better way. The old system served its purpose for a time, but it became a distraction from the wonderful new system of grace.

Jesus came to free us from the burden of rules that remind us of our sin but no longer do anything to earn favor with God. Instead, Jesus offers us new traditions, joyous ones that remind us of his gift of eternal life. In him, believers can enjoy traditions of helping grow his church, praying and worshiping together, celebrating his birthday and resurrection day, and anticipating as a group the wonder that awaits us with him forever.

The law of Moses that Old Testament Israelites followed made them acceptable to God. But it wasn't meant to be permanent. If you belong to God through Jesus' sacrifice, enjoy the freedom that's your gift as his child. Sticking with the old traditions to earn your way into God's heart is like tossing in his face everything Jesus died to offer you.

You are free! Start a new tradition of living like it.

TALK TO HIM

"God, thank you for a better system of traditions to celebrate your victory. Please keep me from burdening myself and others with rules you don't require."

Now we are free, there's no condemnation,
Jesus provides a perfect salvation.
"Come unto Me," O hear His sweet call,
Come, and He saves us once for all.

PHILIP P. BLISS, "FREE FROM THE LAW"

October 23 ACTS 16:16-40

"Praising me through suffering reveals my presence in unexpected ways."

Paul and Silas were praying and singing hymns to God, and the other prisoners were listening. ACTS 16:25

How did they have energy to praise God? Perhaps that thought crossed your mind. Here's a quick review of the details:

> Paul and Silas weren't just in a fistfight for their faith; they were beaten without freedom to defend themselves.
> And they weren't just beaten; they were beaten with wooden rods.
> And they weren't just beaten with wooden rods; they were severely beaten with wooden rods.
> And after they were severely beaten with wooden rods, they were thrown in jail.

Few of us will face the violence Paul and Silas endured for faith, but their experiences in Philippi make us shudder. Experiencing any difficult hurt helps us understand the mind-numbing heights excruciating pain can reach. It takes quite a faith to suffer as they did and praise God through it all. Their wounds hadn't healed yet. Their faces crackled with dried blood and dirt whenever they spoke. As with Stephen's story, to assume that praise came easily for them might actually cheapen their sacrifice of praise.

But in the midst of their physical agony, God's Spirit shone through them and filled their jail cells with glory. Despite all they had been through, the weary faces of Paul and Silas were lit with a peace we cannot comprehend apart from the Holy Spirit. We don't know whether God allowed them to go through such torture to grow them, but verse 25 definitely shows that he used their praise in the lives of the other prisoners who listened and the jailer whose life was spared on earth and for eternity.

God was very present with Paul and Silas during their torment. He doesn't leave his people to suffer alone, no matter how lonely it might feel. Make that sacrifice of one more word of praise, and ask him to turn it into something that glorifies him beyond what you could imagine in the midst of your hurts.

TALK TO HIM

"Lord, although I can barely stand up under this pain, I praise you. By your grace, I praise you and give you the glory."

For this I bless you as the ruin falls. The pains You
give me are more precious than all other gains.
C. S. LEWIS

"Your unique story of meeting me has power to touch others."

"'The God of our ancestors has chosen you to know his will and to see the Righteous One and hear him speak.'" ACTS 22:14

Although it might seem strange, it's fairly common to take a grass-is-greener approach to our spiritual journey. There will always be someone with a more magnanimous story and a testimony that defies all odds. And someone who has endured great suffering holds a unique attraction to us because they received the difficult mercy of going deeper with God through hardships. On the other hand, a person with a picture-perfect Christian family heritage might inspire envy because they've had it so easy.

Taking the grass-is-greener approach is never a good idea.

First of all, every person who has given his or her heart to God has a testimony that defies all odds. Even the most seemingly innocent person was on the fast track to eternal separation from God if not for his grace through Jesus' death. And the worst of all saved sinners can minister in ways people with less complicated backgrounds cannot.

Be assured, God wants to touch someone through your story as no one else's can. Not only that, but he will ensure that your paths cross in his way and time. Remember this: Your life matters for someone else. If it didn't, you would be unnecessary, and God does not create unnecessary people.

You are unique and useful in the Lord's Kingdom. Whether your history involves great sin like the apostle Paul's or a fairly clean slate, your salvation required God-size grace that cost Jesus' life. To assume you require more or less grace than the next person is to distort God's view of sin and devalue Jesus' sacrifice.

Put that way, your story is quite miraculous, isn't it?

TALK TO HIM

"Father, sometimes it's hard to look back and appreciate where I've been, but I will always appreciate where you've brought me and where you're leading me. Please, Lord, help me learn to respect the beginnings you granted me because they speak uniquely of what you can do with a life."

When you feel insignificant, consider your spiritual significance to the soul you'll meet in heaven whom God touched with your story.

ANONYMOUS

October 25 ACTS 27:27–28:16

"I have unexpected blessings for you even on unwanted detours."

It was three months after the shipwreck that we set sail. ACTS 28:11

Oh, how we hate interruptions! We pack our schedules, and heaven forbid anything or anyone intrudes! Yet Paul's shipwreck adventure teaches us a great deal about the value of a God-orchestrated detour.

A few things about detours . . .

First of all, they never show up at good times to our way of thinking.

Second, they always mess with our plans.

Third, although they cause stress, they often take us to places (geographically, emotionally, spiritually) that hold unexpected blessings.

Think what Paul's shipwreck meant to Publius's father. Consider what the disaster at sea did for the commanding officer's respect for Paul, and as a result, the officer's potential openness to God. And then take into account the unity built between prisoners and sailors through shared hardship. Finally, don't forget what Paul's shipwreck did for his own spiritual life.

As a former Pharisee, Paul was programmed to get his way without interference or delay. He had come a long way since those days, but an occasional reminder of what's been learned along the way serves as reinforcement to anyone's faith. Paul received many opportunities to see God work in and through him, to point people to God's power instead of his own, and to worship God as he welcomed God's will above his own plans.

Detours don't just happen for God's people. Each one is either allowed or ordered by God himself, and since all God's actions hold purpose, so does every detour.

Don't miss this detour's importance for your life and others' lives because of a hard-and-fast hold on your vision of how things should move along. You could cost many people, yourself included, lessons and blessings of a lifetime.

TALK TO HIM

"Lord, it comes as a surprise to hear myself say this, but thank you for this circumstance that seems to be in my way. Every hindrance orchestrated by you is a chance to grow my faith in you; therefore, there really are no true hindrances with you. Thank you for that truth."

Leaving room for interruptions is leaving room to be awestruck.

ANONYMOUS

"Do you know the potential for your own sin?"

Claiming to be wise, they instead became utter fools. ROMANS 1:22

No one appreciates a know-it-all. To set the rest of us at ease (for certainly none of us fit the category), here are a few truths about those folks:

Number one: Know-it-alls contradict themselves. Number two: Know-it-alls harbor a fool inside. And number three: Know-it-alls are on a path to self-destruction.

Actually, if we are set at ease about those facts, then we have more to learn about mercy, but that's a topic for another day. For now, let's get back to why people who consider themselves utterly wise aren't doing themselves any favors.

How do know-it-alls contradict themselves? Any imperfect human being who acts like he or she has the corner on wisdom lacks the humility necessary to see the need for God, the source of wisdom. Being misguided about one's own level of wisdom qualifies as a mistake, which a true know-it-all would know in advance and thus would not make.

The pursuit of knowledge can be very healthy and productive when we are seeking to know God better and when God keeps us humble enough to recognize his exclusive corner on knowing everything. But a human being apart from the Lord is a frighteningly foolish force whose first victim is himself or herself. According to the Bible, when left to our own intelligence, we are bent on a path of dark confusion, like a snowball careening downhill that gathers uncontrolled speed and gobbles up everything in its way.

On the other hand, a person growing in God's wisdom recognizes his vulnerability to drown in his or her own sin and takes care to make consistently wise choices to yield in obedience to God. No one is perfect, and we all sin, but when we live God's way we won't become trapped by ongoing patterns of sin.

The first step in growing godly wisdom is to acknowledge the capabilities of your spiritual destructiveness. Take that step, let God be your Know-It-All, and find yourself traveling with him on the road to true wisdom.

TALK TO HIM

"Lord, thank you for being my wisdom. Please keep me humble about my need for you as my Know-It-All."

One of the functions of intelligence is to take account of the dangers that come from trusting solely to the intelligence.

LEWIS MUMFORD

October 27 ROMANS 3:9-28

"I offer only one way to myself, but it is the only way you need."

We are made right with God by placing our faith in Jesus Christ. ROMANS 3:22

Is God narrow minded or openhearted? There's a question for the ages. Actually, arguments could be made for both. He doesn't accept our efforts to earn his forgiveness; but then again, why does he seem easy on evil? Lest you think God is an unbending ruler or a passive defender, let's figure out how he is both restrictive and welcoming.

Some might argue that God is narrow minded because he doesn't let us work our way into his good graces. Given only that argument, sure he seems harsh. On the other hand, others complain that God isn't harsh enough on those who do wrong.

But let's consider a broader scope to both cases. If we open up the truth that God doesn't allow us to earn forgiveness by taking into account that he sent Jesus to pay for our sin, doesn't that make God supremely gracious and welcoming? It isn't that he doesn't allow us to earn our way to him; it's that we can't. So he made an utterly loving way that costs us nothing. If that's restrictive, then so be it.

Now think more about the "freedom" God grants evil. Because we can't earn our way to him, and because we're eternally lost until we accept his salvation, God is in a holding mode for destroying the evil of sin. Just as "God was being fair when he held back and did not punish those who sinned in times past" (verse 25), he is being fair now by waiting to punish the world's sin. He is holding off to give people time to turn to him—again, supreme grace, not weak passivity.

We can be grateful he's narrow minded because he provided one way back to him; and we can be thankful he's openhearted to give people time to turn to him.

He is the best of both.

TALK TO HIM

"Thank you, God, for being just and merciful. Please help me understand how you blend the two so perfectly."

If God were only just, we'd wish for his mercy. If he were only merciful, we'd yearn for justice. Thank God he is both.

ANONYMOUS

"As my child, you have my power to choose not to sin."

Letting your sinful nature control your mind leads to death. But letting the Spirit control your mind leads to life and peace. ROMANS 8:6

How many words can you spell taking some of the letters in *freedom*? Try these: Contentment. Health. Space. Choice. Goodness. Joy. Hope.

The mere sound of "freedom" lifts our spirits and fills us with a positive outlook. It draws a contented sigh because freedom implies something better—the ability to manage ourselves, and room to move unencumbered. Obviously freedom is worth fighting for because people have battled to the death to secure it for themselves and those they love.

God is a freedom fighter, too, only his main objective is spiritual freedom, a fight many people don't appreciate. Although we associate positive things with freedom, we have a hard time understanding the relationship between God's freedom and his standards. But if we would grasp two key truths, how free indeed we would be! First of all, freedom doesn't mean the absence of limits. And second, freedom doesn't exist apart from God.

When Jesus died for our spiritual freedom, he felt the confines of death and hell and Satan's wrath. He endured the greatest imprisonment so we could experience the heights of freedom. However, when we (freely) choose to accept his sacrifice on our behalf, we don't truly experience his freedom until we (freely) choose to accept the Holy Spirit's power to break old sin patterns.

We detest being confined and balk at threats to our choices, but we can't be free until we understand that we will head directly back into sin's trap unless we (freely) choose to live out our freedom within God's standards of safety.

We are free to "free-fall" off a bridge, but that choice would result in long-range limitations to our freedom. Similarly, sin plunges us into destruction. Like its master, Satan, sin is a liar that promises bigger, greater, better perks. But in the end it buries us.

God's freedom awaits, but only within his safety net.

TALK TO HIM

"Lord, thank you for true freedom. Please help me to feel the warning of sin so powerfully that I run directly to your safety net."

Freedom is the right to choose the habits that bind you.

RENATE RUBINSTEIN

October 29 ROMANS 8:18-39

"As my child, you live with the ultimate hope."

With eager hope, the creation looks forward to the day when it will join God's children in glorious freedom. ROMANS 8:20-21

One of the wonderful by-products of yesterday's topic about freedom is hope. To understand the relationship between the two, let's ask ourselves a few questions:

What are we hoping for? Freedom.

Freedom from what? Death.

How do we receive freedom from death? Christ's sacrifice purchased for us hope that extends beyond death.

So hope extends beyond death. That's great news for after we die. But what about while we're alive and struggling on earth? Now there is a question to keep us busy for a while. We know hope for the afterlife is crucial; we have no argument there. But how grand it would be to also enjoy the blessing of feeling hopeful about our daily life on earth! After all, we are shortsighted humans who need a pick-me-up in the here and now if we are to make it through the next several decades in one healthy piece. We need the real deal of hope now.

Fortunately, God's brand of hope is up to the task. His hope isn't a halfway deal. Partial hope, a smidgen of hope, or even mostly hope doesn't cut it. Either we have his hope or we lack it. Period.

All that might make experiencing hope seem hopeless, but according to Romans 8, we have every reason to hope eagerly. The eager part shows present action. Hope involves enthusiasm that transforms how we live today while we wait for all that we're hoping will happen in the future.

God offers us hope for tomorrow in order that it will brighten today as well. If you're his child, then enjoy his ultimate hope right now.

TALK TO HIM

"Lord, I love the feel-good gift of hope. I couldn't make it through life without it. Your understanding of that is one more reason to praise you for your kindness."

There is one thing which gives radiance to everything.
It is the idea of something around the corner.
G. K. CHESTERTON

"I delight to see you delighting in 'you first' habits."

Take delight in honoring each other. ROMANS 12:10

Honor isn't something we think about every day, but when a person's integrity is characterized by honor it's unmistakable in his or her lifestyle. Honor is about taking the high road, choosing the best actions because good behavior reveals good character. Honor does what is right simply because it is right, not out of coercion or obligation. The beauty of genuine honor lies in its freedom from an unnecessary need to prove itself; it just exists quietly, graciously, contentedly.

When we honor others, we reveal a "you first" approach to life, respecting their uniqueness, pointing out their successes, and acting in their best interests. God is pleased when we treat others well, but even more so when we do it enthusiastically, without being standoffish or grudging with our acknowledgments.

There is no room for jealousy in honoring others or for harboring hopes that we will shine brighter than them. In fact, we're more pleased for someone else's success than for our own. Honoring others sounds wonderful in theory, but in reality it doesn't come easily because we're more selfish than giving by nature.

In order to honor others, we must be secure in our own place in life, which only happens when we rest in God's acceptance of us. Honor begins at the foot of Jesus' cross, where he humbled himself and died in our place. Enduring such a death certainly did not come easily for him; it was no less traumatic for him than it would have been for us. But he cared for our well-being above his own. So without fanfare or a need to boost his ego through heroism, he quietly laid down his life for our good.

The security of knowing we are loved that much by our Savior frees us from self-centeredness and sets the example for honoring others.

Delight in putting the well-being of others above your own, and you will honor God as well as them.

TALK TO HIM

"Thank you, Jesus, for showing me about honor. Please remind me of your love so I can trade my desire to prove myself for the desire to live for others' good."

No person was ever honored for what he received.
Honor has been the reward for what he gave.
CALVIN COOLIDGE

October 31 ROMANS 14:12–15:7

"Love allows room for weakness."

Accept each other just as Christ has accepted you so that God will be given glory.

ROMANS 15:7

Weakness is a pain in the neck. Okay, that's pretty rude, but that's how we typically view it. We fear the vulnerability of our own weaknesses and get angered by the inconvenience of others'. Confidence attracts us far more—that and the appearance of having it together. We don't enjoy feeling dragged down by too many needs. We don't have time for them among our important responsibilities. Forbid that we might ever become too needy!

Have humans always been short-tempered with frailty? Who knows? Maybe modern life does exacerbate the problem. We hear all the time nowadays about our want-it-yesterday society that requires not only speed but the power to support that efficiency. If someone can't keep up, that person loses value in the eyes of many. How tragic!

We would be wise to slow down and discover what God says about the subject. As we might expect, our natural tendency steers us down a path away from his best. According to him, love involves accepting weakness in ourselves and others and showing patience when strength is at a minimum.

Weakness can be a surprising gift because it eliminates the charade of "having it together." It exposes what is really underneath the image we work hard to project and protect. Weakness causes us to get real and is actually a powerful force for driving us to go deeper, to care for someone's heart beyond what we see on the surface. Weakness teaches us that love cares about the whole person.

Instead of viewing weakness as a pain in the neck, take the opportunity to lift someone's face to see God's love better through the acceptance in your eyes.

TALK TO HIM

"Thank you, Lord, for a reminder about the strength of weakness. You never cease to surprise me by taking a higher approach than I do—a weakness in me? Definitely. But please grow me through it."

Resolve to be tender with the young, compassionate with the aged, sympathetic with the striving, and tolerant with the weak and the wrong. Sometime in life you will have been all of these.

ROBERT H. GODDARD

"Less is more with me."

This foolish plan of God is wiser than the wisest of human plans, and God's weakness is stronger than the greatest of human strength. 1 CORINTHIANS 1:25

God is not ashamed of our weaknesses. Nor is he surprised by them. Instead, he is moved to reveal himself in the thick of them. And for that, we can be grateful once again for our human limitations.

As God's children, we're actually stronger when we reach the end of our pride, our intelligence, and our strength. Why? Because God is already at the end of ourselves, waiting for us to get there—or rather, to admit that we have arrived.

Although our limitations don't catch God off guard, sometimes they take us by surprise, wounding our pride with the reality that we're more fallible than we had guessed. Once we recover from that shock and accept ourselves as God does, hang-ups and all, we finally give God room to be more.

God reserves a special place in his heart for the needy, the weak, the poor, and the useless. He loves our humility because it primes us to recognize the less in ourselves that needs more of him. God adores less when it comes to our swelled, if somewhat misguided, egos, but he resists those who don't sense their need for him.

When we're familiar with our need for God, we're more attuned to the storehouse of wisdom he would love to reveal to us. He is a God of mystery and secrets, but he longs to share himself with hearts tenderized to him.

God's secrets are incredible in their simplicity but mind-boggling in their wisdom. Therefore, we need his Spirit to help us understand him. Since it's through our weakness that his Spirit shows his power in us, we have every reason to get comfortable in our shortcomings because they're the pathway to discovering more of him.

Whoever imagined our weaknesses would prove to be such treasures? That is exactly what they are when we let them lead us closer to the Lord.

TALK TO HIM

"Lord, I'm not sure I will ever welcome feeling weak among people who don't understand your strength. But Father, I want to filter the world through your wisdom. Therefore, please remind me how much I need you."

Admitting weakness is the first step toward strength.

ANONYMOUS

November 2 1 CORINTHIANS 5:1-13

"Don't be surprised when those who don't know me don't follow my ways."

I wasn't talking about unbelievers who indulge in sexual sin, or are greedy, or cheat people, or worship idols. You would have to leave this world to avoid people like that.

1 CORINTHIANS 5:10

Christians often earn a reputation for being judgmental toward people who don't share our faith. And while a life lived apart from God usually isn't lived according to his standards, Christians make a mistake by acting surprised by a world that acts like it doesn't love him. Instead of forcing our opinions on people who aren't interested, let's spend our energy rethinking our approach.

As his children, we should grow in his wisdom and love. The wisdom of 1 Corinthians 5 reveals us as his loving followers when we heed it. Our job as reflections of him on earth is not to turn off those who don't know him. But that's what we do when we make our faith about expecting a lost world to conform to standards he calls his children to obey.

Not living by his truth is wrong for Christians and unbelievers alike. But our role is to love others, not to condemn them. We can and should show love to people who don't know the Lord regardless of whether their lifestyle lines up with the Bible. We can know someone's behavior is wrong but still draw that person closer to Christ through the quality of our love for them.

The world sorely lacks love, and many people's sin patterns result as coping mechanisms for past hurts. We have no business stomping someone's heart with condemnation, particularly when that heart has grown accustomed to mistreatment. God calls us to a higher love that cares first about the person.

When God's own, who are dearly loved by him, thumb our noses at those who desperately need to know what real love feels like, we do his reputation more harm than good. Instead of being surprised by the world's sin, surprise the world with real love.

TALK TO HIM

"Lord, please help me to be a messenger of your love, and don't let me forget that a person living in sin is a person living in pain."

Where did we get the idea that responding to wrong behavior with hateful behavior could improve someone?

ANONYMOUS

"I want to be your first love; let me handle your other loves."

I want you to be free from the concerns of this life. 1 CORINTHIANS 7:32

"I want you to do whatever will help you serve the Lord best, with as few distractions as possible" (verse 35).

Ah, here is the crux of our faith journey. Whatever habits keep us focused on God, they are the center of the lifestyle we should pursue. Actually, there is more to it than staying focused to serve him; serving the Lord best involves loving him most. When he is our priority, we are free to let him handle the other issues of our hearts, namely our other loves.

Since God is love, he has a lot to say about the subject. His expectation that we keep him number one doesn't negate our earthly loves—quite the opposite. We love others better when we love him first because intimacy with him teaches us genuine love.

But since we're easily sidetracked, God tells us not to chase after other ways to meet our hearts' needs because we will inevitably focus our passions on them more than on him. Instead, he asks us to release our human loves—their existence, their timing, and their issues—into his safekeeping. He isn't withholding anything from us—again, quite the opposite. He wants what's best for us, and therefore he must remain our highest desire—because he deserves it, but also for our good.

Life can feel lonely, even when we know God loves us. But chasing after human love is not the cure-all. We need other people. Even more, we need God to provide those loves as he sees best.

Whatever the current status of your love life, hand your heart's distractions back to God. Commit to keep him first, trusting wholeheartedly that he will do right by you.

TALK TO HIM

"Lord, I know you love me, but I also crave arms that hold me and eyes that smile at me. When I feel distracted by those desires, please help me to enjoy the freedom of letting you care for my heart."

God knows quite well how hard we find it to love Him more than
anyone or anything else, and He won't be angry with us
as long as we are trying. And He will help us.

C. S. LEWIS

November 4 1 CORINTHIANS 8:1-13; 10:23-33

"Your love is more valuable than all the knowledge you could pursue."

While knowledge makes us feel important, it is love that strengthens the church.

1 CORINTHIANS 8:1

The world is a smorgasbord of information. Like an expanding universe, our knowledge base never stops increasing. Schoolchildren today have their work cut out for them tackling a curriculum that makes what we learned look elementary in comparison. The value we place on knowledge reveals itself in the emphasis we give to test scores, diplomas, and degrees. The drive for knowledge has even infiltrated our entertainment in TV game shows and trivia board games. We love to know a whole lot of stuff, whether it's useful or not.

But what value does God place on knowledge? According to today's reading, knowledge is most helpful in the Christian faith when it causes us to love more genuinely. The more we know about what defines love, the smarter we can love. But knowledge on its own does not equal love, create love, or measure up to love. Knowledge may be somewhat valuable to God, but love is utterly precious to him.

Why is that? Knowledge is good, right? Of course it is. Knowledge serves many wonderful purposes, and we have every reason to be grateful for our ability to retain facts. So what then makes it second-rate compared to love?

Well, consider one of our primary motivations for collecting knowledge. Knowledge makes us feel good, but love makes others feel good. It's the trade-off from self-focus to others-focus that God prizes. Very often our craving for knowledge is to better ourselves, but truly loving someone is all about making things better for that person.

Those who drive themselves for more knowledge may receive great recognition on earth, but the person who loves is the one God recognizes. Now, based on all we know about God's view of knowledge, which ambition—love or knowledge—is the smarter goal?

TALK TO HIM

"Lord, I love all that you want to teach me. Please help me learn to love first of all."

The greatest bit of knowledge is knowing how to love.

ANONYMOUS

"I see your behind-the-scenes work, and I am proud of you for it."

Some parts of the body that seem weakest and least important are actually the most necessary. 1 CORINTHIANS 12:22

You know the saying "I feel like I'm missing my right arm"? It doesn't take a medical expert to understand how drastic the loss of a right arm would be. But what if you heard someone moan about missing their left big toe? How about a kneecap? an eyelid? Oh, the under-appreciated lives of big toes, kneecaps, and eyelids!

We laugh, but consider what the losses of unsung heroes would mean for God's Kingdom, those behind-the-scenes saints who run the sound at church or shovel the walk or clean the bathrooms. As unglorious as it seems, at least half the work happens behind the scenes where most people don't notice and where the givers often go unrecognized.

Does recognition or the lack of it reduce the importance of what goes on when no one's around to applaud? Not by a long shot. But every now and then we all enjoy hearing that our efforts make a difference. When other people are slow to offer thanks, we can always know that God smiles on our work. And in his smile lies a promise of rewards to come when we faithfully continue our roles in his spiritual family, regardless of pats on the back or the thumbs-up we receive on earth.

So all you behind-the-scenes givers, hear this: God sees you, and you make him smile with pride. He looks at you and says to his Son next to him, "That's my child! What a gift, and what a giver!"

Wouldn't you rather have his praise than a whole congregation's worth of applause?

TALK TO HIM

"Father God, thank you for seeing my efforts. It isn't about earning praise, but oh how good it feels anyway to know that you're happy with what I do. Please help me notice and take the time to thank other behind-the-scenes workers."

Just as there are no little people or unimportant lives,
there is no insignificant work.
ELENA BONNER

November 6 1 CORINTHIANS 13:1-13

"Release selfishness to me."

[Love] does not demand its own way. 1 CORINTHIANS 13:5

Another great day to study love. Can you feel the warm fuzzies? Hear the big, contented sigh? Love is wonderful, and it's wonderful to experience God's unshakable kind. But for we humans still perfecting it, our love is vulnerable to our imperfections, many of which are listed in 1 Corinthians 13:4-7.

The truth these verses instill in us is that love considers not only its actions but also its motivations and attitudes. Sure, we can shore ourselves up to show good behavior even when we're secretly boiling over with unhealthy, unhelpful emotions. We might fool others and even ourselves for a while. But God sees what goes on inside, and that's the part that matters most to him.

Perhaps the quality of love that embodies all the others is selflessness, or not demanding our own way. We can't fake selflessness for long because eventually our human nature kicks in and tires of putting others first. True love is difficult to keep up because it requires constant checks on the deep-down condition of our spirit. Most people are too . . . well, selfish, to put that much effort into it.

We can be fooled into thinking mere affection or giving a compliment or thinking good thoughts equals love. However, love gives up its comforts to meet someone else's needs, and not just once or twice, but over and over again with relentless faithfulness. Love extends itself to others instead of hoarding its goodness, and sacrifices itself in favor of someone else. Unselfish love is redundant, really, since true love cannot be selfish.

Developing a lifestyle of love takes time to learn because we prefer to receive love rather than give it, that is, until love is perfected in us. If you want to appreciate giving more than receiving, take heart in the unselfish direction that one desire already is leading you, and ask God for opportunities to develop selflessness.

TALK TO HIM

"Thank you, Lord, for your perfect love. Mine is so faulty by comparison, but I'm thankful for your loving guidance to help grow me. Please help me learn to be a giver."

Love is not measured by how many times you touch each other but by how many times you reach each other.

CATHY MORANCY

"My comfort is not stagnant; I give it to you to pass on to others."

When we ourselves are comforted, we will certainly comfort you. 2 CORINTHIANS 1:6

There's an extra depth of comfort we receive from someone who has been there before us.

Pain is universal, that is true, which is why we're able to share a measure of grief with anyone. But when we're hurting, we often seek out others who have gone through similar levels of heartache because there is comfort in knowing they really know. Someone who lost a spouse is able to understand the searing pain of death more than someone whose greatest loss was a stolen bike, no matter how compassionate the person. We understand the breathtaking weight of grief only as far as we've carried it ourselves.

No matter how much pain you've felt, Jesus can understand it. He grew up on earth and experienced the highs and lows we do. So he understands our hearts more than by simple observation. In fact, he endured pain so crushing that we will never truly understand all he went through. Selfish as it sounds, in a way we can take comfort that his compassion was born in the fires of agony. There isn't a shred of triteness in his tenderly whispered "I've been there."

God provided us with a comfort system that travels. When pain threatens physical, spiritual, emotional, mental, relational, or financial life, others can offer support that breathes life back into the dying. In that way, comfort takes on a life of its own, moving throughout our world, refreshing stagnant spirits.

All of us will suffer, and each of us has unique opportunities to provide refreshment for someone else. Instead of enduring pain only to let it go to waste, make it worthwhile by showing someone that Jesus' comfort eventually will transcend all pain.

We can't do away with pain on earth, but we certainly can do something through it.

TALK TO HIM

"Father, thank you for the gift of comfort. Please help me treat it as a gift that keeps giving by passing it on to someone else in need."

[You have] suffered many a day,
Now [your] griefs have passed away,
God will change [your] pining sadness
Into ever springing gladness.

JOHANNES G. OLEARIUS, "COMFORT, COMFORT YE MY PEOPLE"

November 8 2 CORINTHIANS 3:1–5:10

"I want you to care for others' eternity more than for your lifestyle."

We live in the face of death, but this has resulted in eternal life for you.

2 CORINTHIANS 4:12

"We live in the face of death." These are heroic words from Paul, a great hero of faith who gave up his life of comfort for the sake of other people's souls. He lived in dangerous times when spreading the Good News of Jesus' salvation meant putting his security on the line.

Our lives are pretty comfy today, religiously speaking. Typically we don't risk our necks in the name of faith. Most of us won't have to endure beatings; most of us won't die as martyrs. Has faith gotten easier, or are we merely opting for an easy way around the hard stuff? Let's go one further: Is our faith missing something because we don't know what it's like to choose Christ over death?

We could feel guilty because we've been given an easier road in some ways, but we would do better to spend that time gratefully looking for other ways to put God first. After all, souls are as much at stake in our privileged society as they are in nations that don't have the same luxuries. As long as there are people who need God's truth, we will have opportunities to stand up for Jesus and prioritize other people's eternal well-being over our everyday perks.

When we give our comforts lower priority, we may face death of a different sort, such as a loss of reputation, career advancement, or relationships with people who reject us because of faith. Anytime we place God above everything else, someone will resist. But we need to tone our spiritual muscles if we are to survive in the less cozy circumstances that are coming. Wise preparation means toughening our faith by focusing on eternity.

Enjoy your blessings, but not at the expense of someone else's opportunity to see Jesus in your lifestyle. Make the effort to spread God's dream of eternal life for all who seek him. Then when you meet Jesus face-to-face, you can enjoy knowing you cared for other souls more than for your own passing comforts.

TALK TO HIM

"Heavenly Lord, I'm grateful for so many blessings on earth. But Father, please don't let me desire comfort over someone else's salvation."

God first. Others second. Yourself a distant third.

ANONYMOUS

November 9

"Your generosity gives others a reason to be grateful."

When we take your gifts to those who need them, they will thank God.

2 CORINTHIANS 9:11

Do you realize that every act of generosity provides triple blessing? The first—a blessing for a need met. Second—giving someone an opportunity to feel grateful. And third—building unity. The first blessing of meeting needs is obvious, so let's look more closely at the other two, less apparent ones.

Feeling gratitude is a gift in itself because it soothes weary emotions. Remember the last time you felt it? Like curling up in a blanket in front of a fire while a snowstorm blew outside, gratitude is sweet.

As for building unity, generosity and gratitude work together on that one. As we receive someone's generosity, our gratitude pulls us beyond our needs and inspires us to pass along the treasure of generosity however we're able. In this way, generosity and gratitude pair beautifully as a power team that overcomes many wants and increases the joy of both giver and receiver.

Second Corinthians 8:2 says, "They are being tested by many troubles, and they are very poor. But they are also filled with abundant joy, which has overflowed in rich generosity." When we're in a position of want, or when we're the one giving, we learn the give-and-take relationship that God intended as a means of meeting needs and serving each other.

We will all have opportunities to give and receive, and we're smart to learn to do both with respect. As Paul wrote in 8:14, "Right now you have plenty and can help those who are in need. Later, they will have plenty and can share with you when you need it. In this way, things will be equal." As we experience the roles of giver and receiver, we come to understand each other's struggles better. In this way, unity is nurtured. And where there's unity, you might have guessed it . . . there's more generosity.

And the gift keeps giving.

TALK TO HIM

"Lord, what better words to say to you today than 'thank you!' You are the original Gift that keeps giving, and I'm grateful to learn from the best."

Never hesitate to hold out your hand; never hesitate
to accept the outstretched hand of another.

POPE JOHN XXIII

November 10 2 CORINTHIANS 13:1-14

"You were created to grow."

Grow to maturity. 2 CORINTHIANS 13:11

Children, vegetation, spiritual lives. All are beautiful creations of God; all need nurturing; and all are meant to grow. We know that a mature child looks like an adult, and a mature sapling looks like a tree. But what does a mature Christian look like?

A mature Christian bears several characteristics—first and foremost the power of God. A growing faith is one that acknowledges its weakness and chooses to live by God's strength. Paul readily admitted he was not strong (verse 4), but he grew to such confidence of Jesus' Spirit in him that he promised his readers proof that Christ would speak through him (verse 3). He had matured enough to understand living by the Spirit's power.

Next, a mature Christian embodies the courage and honesty of self-examination. A weak faith wouldn't face difficult realizations about itself; it's more concerned about image than genuineness. It's reassuring in a way that a mature faith doesn't mean a perfect faith; otherwise we would have no cause to examine ourselves. Rather, a tested faith is willing—even eager—to discover areas it needs to grow so nothing holds it back or hinders the Spirit's power.

Even though it isn't perfect, a mature faith doesn't allow ongoing sin to create division between itself and God or his people. Someone growing in spiritual maturity should exhibit godly behavior that flows from a heart in love with the Savior. And while a mature Christian faith respects authority, it doesn't typically require micromanaging because it behaves in God-honoring ways.

When we're growing as healthy spiritual children of God, our lives show evidence of our others-oriented hearts. We make a point to encourage each other and to promote peace in God's family.

You were created to grow in Christ's love and maturity, and in turn help to grow his Kingdom. So feed on his Word and watch the Spirit's life spring up in yours.

TALK TO HIM

"Lord, thank you for a spiritual life that wasn't created for stagnancy. Please keep me growing, Father."

To grow is to find more life beyond what you've known.
ANONYMOUS

November 11

"I am serious about your freedom."

I died to the law—I stopped trying to meet all its requirements—so that I might live for God.

GALATIANS 2:19

"Stop!"

What immediately comes to mind when you hear that word? Getting caught? Being warned? Feeling hindered? Although it often carries a negative connotation, the word *stop* is beautifully freeing when God says it to halt us from trying too hard to earn his approval.

He says, "Stop!" to our pious airs about our perceived goodness, to our fears that we haven't done enough for him, and to our overdone efforts that teach our children that we must work our way into eternal life.

God had many rules for his Old Testament followers. To them, "Stop!" would have fit right in with all the dos and don'ts of his law. But Jesus' defeat of death introduced a system of love, forgiveness, and salvation. We only have to accept those gifts with the humble understanding that we need him and can't live without him. Then we're freed from obligation to the old law. Now a "Stop!" from God can mean, "Give up trying to earn my love; it is already yours."

If we'll take our spiritual freedom as seriously as God does, we'll understand what his freedom means for us. Far from restricting us with suffocating boundaries, God's "Stop!" tells us to give up the exhausting pursuit of a goal we can't achieve. Not only will we never earn salvation in our humanness, but we'll waste time and energy that's much better spent in gratitude and worship of Jesus. It's actually by ceasing to fit a certain mold that we're free to accept his grace and live for God.

We can't live for God until we give up the idea that we can punish ourselves into heaven, because living for God involves joy, peace, hope, love, worship, and gratitude—all of which work together to create the wondrous freedom his Son died to give us.

He was serious enough about our freedom to trade Jesus' life for it. Let's be serious about enjoying it.

TALK TO HIM

"Father, your freedom is amazing! Please help me to treasure what it cost you."

The cause of freedom is the cause of God.

SAMUEL BOWLES

November 12 GALATIANS 5:1-26

"Take care with your subtle treatment of others."

"Love your neighbor as yourself." . . . Beware of destroying one another. GALATIANS 5:14-15

Let's travel today. No worries; it's a free trip, and you don't even have to pack for it because you can stay right where you are. It's a trip through your imagination, and your destination is the Grand Canyon.

You instantly had an image in your mind, didn't you? Even if you've never been there, you've seen enough pictures to imagine soaring over high canyon walls beneath a clear blue sky. Below you the Colorado River cuts its way through the hardened earth as it has for generations too numerous to count. Amazing, isn't it, that a bit of meandering water could carve such a geographic masterpiece? The river hasn't stopped its work and will continue to wear through the rock for many more generations.

Like the river, our actions affect others. We might not realize the subtlety of our day-to-day words and behaviors, but little by little we create beauty or destruction in our relationships. A roll of the eyes, an exasperated sigh, a hint of sarcasm all work remarkably well to wither someone's sense of security in our presence. Yet a gentle smile, an attentive look, or a patient demeanor encourage someone by sending the message that they're safe and accepted with us. We express ourselves at least as much through nonverbal communication as we do with our words. We're constantly either subtly enhancing others' lives or tearing them down.

It's your choice how you want to affect the precious people God sends your way. Will you be a beautiful blessing God sends their way?

TALK TO HIM

"Lord God, you are the creator of beautiful relationships and the refiner of my heart. Please help me be an encouragement to the treasured souls you give me the privilege to know."

A friend is someone who makes me feel totally acceptable.

ENE RIISNA

"Perfect and blameless are not the same to me."

God . . . chose us in Christ to be holy and without fault in his eyes. EPHESIANS 1:4

It sure would be nice to be perfect—flawless and faultless, with no fear of mistakes coming back to haunt us. No troubles due to our jealous temper. No wasted energy covering up our hang-ups. No insecurities about our worth . . . what a dream!

Actually, it's a dream that can come true for anyone. Well, not perfection; that quality is reserved for God. But perfection and faultlessness aren't the same. Perfection implies pristine condition, free of errors and flaws. Being faultless—or blameless—allows for faults but is free from condemnation. God's children are blameless in his sight. And since he desires that everyone accept his salvation, the dream is open to anyone.

We humans are bogged down with imperfections. For all our kind intentions and best efforts, we're still sinful. Thankfully, God knows this. He knew it before he created us, which is why he sent his Son to correct our situation. Jesus was perfect, quite the opposite of us; yet he took the blame for us. And what a lot of blame we loaded on him! Our faults were so great that God had to turn away from Jesus on the cross because all he could see was our ugly sinfulness suffocating and burying his precious Son.

Now if you're his child, God sees only Jesus' perfection in you. You're still a sinner capable of doing wrong and causing hurt. But you're completely blameless in the sense that Jesus' blood cleansed your soul, and no one can condemn you to eternal separation from God—not Satan, not you, not any other person.

In Jesus Christ, you are God's forgiven, holy masterpiece. Making you his blameless child "gave him great pleasure" (1:5), so "praise God for the glorious grace he has poured out on [you] who belong to his dear Son" (1:6)!

TALK TO HIM

"Lord, that you see my Savior's perfection in me is a miracle. Thank you, God. Thank you."

We learn, on the one hand, that we cannot trust ourselves even in our best moments, and, on the other hand, that we need not despair even in our worst, for our failures are forgiven.

C. S. LEWIS

November 14 EPHESIANS 2:11–4:5

"You're part of something exciting, something beyond yourself."

You have been called to one glorious hope for the future. EPHESIANS 4:4

Extra! Extra! Hear all about it! It's time to get excited about news that trumps any headline. Our excitement begins with God's love. In case you haven't heard—he loves you! But there's more to his love for you than you.

Once we get a taste of his love, we begin to see our place in his plans, and we realize that our individual faith is a mere glimpse of his story. As our understanding of his love grows, we realize the privilege we have to share our faith.

When we're loved by God, our faith grows more vibrant as we draw life from him. Vibrant faith, like love, can't help sharing itself. If our faith doesn't thrill us to overflowing so others can see it, then it's missing something vital.

But let's be honest; being open about our faith makes many of us cringe. From lack of confidence to wanting to avoid being a pushy Christian, we often opt to keep our news to ourselves. However, getting excited about God's love doesn't mean we confront others awkwardly and demand that they think as we do. Nor does sharing our faith mean we adopt an us-versus-them attitude, letting such a distinction interfere with relating naturally with "them." A healthy faith is inviting, courteous, and sensitive, and it shows consideration by not stomping on hearts that aren't ready. An exciting faith loves gently instead of pushing obnoxiously.

Our inhibitions about spreading God's love aren't good reasons to keep us from doing it. As Paul wrote (3:7), we're privileged to talk about God's truth and the hope that he offers, especially considering that so many people don't even know they need it.

If you know Jesus as Savior, you're part of something huge and extraordinary. You have a gift of wonderful news to share. Offer it generously and thoughtfully, but by all means, get excited about giving it!

TALK TO HIM

"Thank you, Lord, for being my reason to get up every morning. As I begin another day, please awaken my excitement to share your Good News."

Why bother with a faith that isn't the thrill of a lifetime?

ANONYMOUS

"I don't do anything halfway; I will finish your story."

God, who began the good work within you, will continue his work until it is finally finished.

PHILIPPIANS 1:6

You may have seen a commercial in recent years about a dad who was known as "the finisher." He was famous for telling his kids to finish their homework, finish their supper, finish up and get to bed. We relate to his desire because we, too, appreciate completion and the joy of putting finishing touches on something we've poured our heart and soul into.

God goes by many names, but perhaps a new one could be the Great Finisher. He leaves nothing halfway completed, namely his children. From his initial plans of Creation through the rest of eternity, he pours his heart into us and finds God-size joy in finishing what he starts.

What does a finished life look like anyway? A life completed by God exhibits several characteristics, all of which reflect God's gracious character. According to today's reading, when we're finally complete, our love will consistently overflow, and our knowledge and understanding will be full grown. We will maintain unwavering right priorities about what really matters without getting sidetracked by the less important perks of this world. To top it off, we'll have hearts that are completely filled with Jesus' righteous character, and we'll love to point the glory to God.

In the process of being made complete, we will probably recognize those wonderful "finished" qualities in increasing measure. But if we're honest, we will admit we still have a ways to go before they're perfected in us.

We can take heart during this growing phase knowing that God is always working on us. His promise not to leave us undone—that we will one day be finished, whole, exquisite reflections of his glory—must mean that every day he is helping us to move closer to his "finish" line.

Enjoy today's leg of the Journey with your Great Finisher.

TALK TO HIM

"I'm so glad, Lord, that you will finish your work in me. Please help me to get rid of any habits or sins that delay reaching your finish line."

To begin well is admirable; to finish well, extraordinary.

ANONYMOUS

November 16 PHILIPPIANS 2:1-30

"Learn my secrets of living in unity."

You must have the same attitude that Christ Jesus had. PHILIPPIANS 2:5

There's an old saying about relationships that if two people always agree, one person isn't necessary. Either one person is highly controlling and the other is excessively passive, or the saying is wrong and they've mastered Philippians 2:2 to an exceptional degree.

Since most of us don't have much trouble speaking our minds when push comes to shove, how do two people work together with "one mind and purpose"? Does the Bible set us up for failure with that command?

Hardly. Since we usually have more trouble keeping our opinions to ourselves than preserving peace, instead of setting us up to fail, the command opens our eyes to our tendency to miss the mark. It encourages us toward a higher way of dealing with each other.

Notice the three words directly following verse 2: "Don't be selfish." Unity begins with casting off our selfish tendencies, humbling ourselves, and "thinking of others as better than [ourselves]."

Ultimately, we "must have the same attitude that Christ Jesus had" (verse 5). The secret to achieving and maintaining the unity commanded in the first part of the chapter lies in the verses that follow it. Hmm. Sounds logical! But unless we're paying attention to God's directions, we easily miss the connection that seems obvious after closer inspection.

In the same way that we gain more from God's Word when we take time to look more closely, we learn more about Jesus' attitudes the more we study his actions and words in the Bible. As we know him better, we'll be more successful at sensing his Spirit moving in us, urging us to put aside selfishness for the sake of unity.

Like studying God's Word and knowing Jesus better, relating well to other people requires us to pay attention to issues that may not be readily noticeable but impact our unity, nonetheless. As we grow more like Jesus, we'll be better equipped to sense the more subtle nuances of unity with others as well.

TALK TO HIM

"Thank you, Father, for creating us to need one another. Please help me prioritize unity above my own desires."

We must all hang together, or assuredly we shall all hang separately.

BENJAMIN FRANKLIN

"Rest in my peace."

I have learned the secret of living in every situation. PHILIPPIANS 4:12

The year's official hurricane season is winding down. Anyone who keeps up with the news inevitably has been schooled in tropical storms and hurricanes. They can cause horrendous damage as they blast onto shore, destroying buildings, reforming landscape, and devastating lives and livelihoods. Their effects are anything but peaceful.

How ironic that at the center of a churning system of high-powered winds and precipitation lies the eye, a place of peace and calm! Despite a hurricane's fearsome force, it holds beautiful symbolism for resting in God's peace when life rages. Peace in any situation sounds incredibly appealing. But how do we catch peace, much less hold on to it, when out-of-control circumstances jettison us every which way?

The key lies in God, whose peace blows troubles out of the water. If we focus on the storms around us, their spinning force will make us sick with dizziness. But if we look up to God, he becomes our Eye, our center of peace.

Although we don't understand how he does it, God grants peace that is divinely gentle yet powerful to conquer any threat. It sounds too good to be true, but we know God doesn't bother with the word *impossible*. We know the apostle Paul discovered how to live within God's peace. It was his "secret of living in every situation."

We'll take peace anytime, rain or shine, but it's much more meaningful to experience rest and quiet in our soul when all forecasts say we should be swept away by stress and pain.

Can you hear peace whisper its secret from within life's storm? Transfer the effort you would normally spend worrying into open, honest, gratitude-filled prayer. Then God's peace will guard your heart and mind as you focus on him, your beautiful Eye in the storm.

TALK TO HIM

"Father, I'm having trouble seeing you through the rough weather in my life. Please sharpen my focus on you, my loving source of peace."

Peace, peace to my soul
Flows like a beautiful river;
Peace, hallowed and pure,
Constant abiding forever.
O loving Redeemer . . .
In tempests or sunshine,
I'll follow Thee still.

FANNY CROSBY, "PEACE TO MY SOUL"

November 18 COLOSSIANS 1:1-29

"No one twisted my arm to save you—I love you."

God in all his fullness was pleased to live in Christ, and through him God reconciled everything to himself. COLOSSIANS 1:19-20

When someone asks a favor of us, don't we occasionally, if not often, smile and agree while biting back an excuse about being too busy? On one hand we truly do enjoy helping others; but we also love to have our time to ourselves without interruptions.

Have you ever wondered whether you're an interruption to God? No one has more going on than he does, and certainly no one has more people hitting him up for favors. God's kindness is part of what draws us to him. We're ashamed to admit it, but a random check on our motivations would reveal a time or three when we've used him. Yet he's God, right? If we can't go to him with our needs, then where does that leave us?

Although God doesn't appreciate being used, he certainly doesn't need his arm twisted to coerce him into being our God. No one had to pose the idea to him about saving us. Just as he initiated creating us, he saw our inevitable downfall and came up with a plan to reconcile us to himself. Nowhere in the Bible do we see him lay a guilt trip on us for costing him so much.

But we do read over and over again how much he loves us. Sure, he's bluntly honest about our sins and our need for him. However, all those references are in the bigger context of his loving salvation. Everything he's ever done and said has always been for his glory; and part of what brings him glory is the loving character he reveals through his care for us.

God favors you with his constant presence and help because he loves you with God-size love. He'll never have to stifle an exasperated sigh because you need him so much. He loves being "interrupted" by you.

TALK TO HIM

"Lord, thank you for your constant availability with a smile. Knowing you don't begrudge the time I consume gives me huge security and appreciation for you. Please help me love others in the same way."

God always has time for you right now.

ANONYMOUS

"Your whole life speaks of your connection to me."

Work willingly at whatever you do, as though you were working for the Lord rather than for people. COLOSSIANS 3:23

If we were to compile a biblical checklist to stay connected with God during our daily business, today's reading could suffice nicely.

Colossians basically sums up how to live like new creations with the Holy Spirit's power. Paul, the book's author, covered everything from our thought life to our sex life to our habits of worship to our habits of behavior. He wrote of greed and anger, old and new natures, peace and gratitude, work and home life. Tying everything together, we're left with the encouragement to invite God into every nook and cranny of life, and not just as a guest, but as our leader.

If we belong to God, then God belongs in every moment of our day. Our connection with him can't be filed away at work, not to be welcomed at home. Nor can we keep a vibrant relationship with him on Sunday from showing itself in the workplace Monday through Friday.

And the area of life we keep to ourselves—our thoughts? That part of us was the first one Paul addressed. Notice it? "Think about the things of heaven, not the things of earth" (3:2). Basically, everything we do and think reflects our connection to our Savior. The more we ponder something, the more deeply it becomes part of us.

All parts of ourselves must align with God's directions if we're to maintain a God-honoring lifestyle. The only way to succeed is to make the Lord's heavenly priorities our own. When we think and pray and believe and live and talk as if we're doing it for God, our connection to him will show in countless ways throughout our days.

TALK TO HIM

"Father, I love being connected with you. Please help me strengthen that connection by keeping you as the motivation for all my efforts."

All my life I have risen regularly at four o'clock and have gone into the woods and talked to God. There He gives me my orders for the day.
GEORGE WASHINGTON CARVER

November 20 1 THESSALONIANS 1:1-10

"Personal attention to others helps you pray specifically for them."

As we pray to our God and Father about you, we think of your faithful work, your loving deeds, and the enduring hope you have because of our Lord Jesus Christ.

1 THESSALONIANS 1:3

Surely this has happened to you . . . you're talking with an old friend one day when suddenly you find yourself listening to an update about something your friend obviously thinks you remember. In reality, you don't have a clue. You feel your face melt into a blank expression, but before you can recover, your friend catches on. Frowning, your friend speaks the obvious: "You have no idea what I'm talking about, do you?"

Your gaffe is so out there that you don't even try to cover it up. "Sorry. Did you tell me about that?"

Your friend sighs and sends you the irritated eyebrow lift you'd expect. "We just talked about this last week."

Uh huh. At one time or another, we've all been caught not paying close attention to what's going on in someone's life.

Among the qualities that made Paul such an effective influence was his attention to the details of other people's lives. He engaged; he tuned in. He remembered what was going on with them from one visit to the next, and his careful attention increased his relationship integrity as they learned to trust his concern.

In addition to being a basic practice of good friendship, tuning in to people also helps us know how to pray for them more effectively. Paul prayed constantly for the Thessalonians, and because he made a point to put their concerns in his memory bank, his conversations with God on their behalf were specific and earnest.

What's going on with the precious people God entrusts you to pray for?

TALK TO HIM

"Father God, thank you for getting my attention about paying attention. Please help me tune in to others so I can bring their specific needs to you."

The greatest gift you can give another is the purity of your attention.

RICHARD MOSS

November 21

"Cheer on my other followers; build on each other's strength."

We have been greatly encouraged in the midst of our troubles and suffering, dear brothers and sisters, because you have remained strong in your faith. 1 THESSALONIANS 3:7

Do you remember pep rallies? Those school events that boosted school spirit and built unity and support for the home team? Reading 1 Thessalonians 3 stirs us as if we've just attended a spiritual pep rally.

Though it's doubtful that the apostle Paul's spiritual education included rallies as we know them, he certainly understood the value of cheering on his fellow believers. God's team goes by various names, including the Kingdom of God and the family of God. And like any other team, we're all working toward the same dream: the promise of eternity with our fearless leader, Jesus.

As we journey toward our goal, we face many opponents. Satan and his forces are, of course, our fiercest enemies. But we also battle fatigue, discouragement, personal weakness, shaky unity, and just plain busyness. Because of all we're up against, we need each other to ensure that we don't get sidelined on our way to the big win, fighting strong as joyful victors instead of merely limping into eternity.

Our encouragement, prayers, examples of faith, and tenacious trust in Jesus impact one another more than we might realize. By following the direction of coaches like Paul and caring for our fellow members of the Kingdom to build them up, we also strengthen the Kingdom as a whole. And the support we give inevitably comes back as encouragement to ourselves, too, because we see our efforts build the team we love and on which we stake our die-hard beliefs.

Be encouraged by Paul's chapter 3 pep rally, and pass along the legacy of Kingdom spirit to the team members you know.

TALK TO HIM

"God, thank you for creating such a magnificent Kingdom and for recruiting me for your team. Please help me stay true to your Spirit and boost others with team cheer."

Build for your team a feeling of oneness, of dependence upon one another and of strength to be derived by unity.

VINCE LOMBARDI

November 22 1 THESSALONIANS 4:13–5:28

"Prepare for my return."

Be on your guard, not asleep. . . . Stay alert and be clearheaded. 1 THESSALONIANS 5:6

You've heard the phrase "Guard your heart" found in Proverbs 4:23 and Philippians 4:7. Well, today's reading also is about guarding ourselves, but this focus is on protecting our minds.

In this first letter from Paul to the Thessalonian church, he shared a lot about preparing for Jesus' return. Much of his focus revolves around keeping a clear head in order to stay prepared for the big day. Why would he choose to steer our thoughts toward our minds?

We need to protect our hearts for sure; the heart is a muscle we certainly can't live without. The more we exercise it, physically and spiritually and emotionally, the stronger it grows. Well, in a way our minds are more vulnerable because they determine how we process all of life, from pain and sadness to joy and hope. We don't know our hearts are feeling anything unless our minds tell us. Our brains sense danger, they hold our memories, they help us understand and empathize, and they filter truth. Perhaps their most vital work is what they do for our spiritual health; when they're open to the Holy Spirit's voice, they let us know about issues we need to address with God.

Our minds hear the Spirit's warnings when temptation lurks; they boost our faith by recalling all the times God has been faithful; they help us to encourage other people by clueing us in to needs; and they alert us to teachings that don't agree with God's Word.

Any one of those elements of the mind's job description is a point of protection or weakness, ensuring our preparedness or our need to step up our readiness for Jesus' return. It's true that a good mind is a terrible thing to waste, but how much more tragic is a good life that's wasted because someone didn't keep his or her mind guarded for God's purposes.

TALK TO HIM

"Thank you, Lord, for the good mind you've given me. Please alert and empower my mind to hold fast to you while I'm still on earth so I'm ready whenever you come back for me."

Change your thoughts, and you will change your world.
REV. NORMAN VINCENT PEALE

November 23

"Patience and endurance are my gifts to you, but they must be nurtured."

May the Lord lead your hearts into a full understanding and expression of the love of God and the patient endurance that comes from Christ. 2 THESSALONIANS 3:5

Another holiday season is upon us! Images of presents and bows and plentiful surprises will start to swirl through your mind soon because this time of year is all about gifts.

Second Thessalonians 3 revolves around gifts as well, although the blessings it speaks of aren't always viewed as such. They're God's gifts of patience and endurance, two somewhat demanding treasures we love to receive but cringe to own.

In verse 5, Paul spelled out his hopes for the Thessalonian believers. But then his thoughts took a turn, and he expanded on the importance of working hard and avoiding laziness. It isn't difficult to tie the concepts of this verse with the rest of the chapter: In order for the Lord to lead our hearts into "the patient endurance that comes from Christ," we can't waste ourselves on idleness.

Patient endurance can't develop in a lazy life. Endurance by definition demands an energy output. It takes effort and patience. And patience . . . well, growing patience is like growing faith. Pray for either one, and you'll be given opportunities aplenty to develop it!

We would love to receive patience and endurance all wrapped up in one neat package. However, just because those gifts require conscientious effort to make them our own doesn't negate their precious value. In fact, we're able to enjoy life much more when we invest in nurturing those blessings. Patience and endurance enrich every moment of every day. They add depth and reveal what's truly important; they help us weather the winds of life; and they grant us the additional gift of being able to enjoy our time on earth more fully.

Work hard at nurturing your patience and endurance. They're gifts sure to give far more in return than they ever cost you.

TALK TO HIM

"Lord, I would love patience right now! But it's through the hard work of enduring that I learn true patience. Thank you for gifts that are richer for the effort required to own them."

Patience is a gift that appears to take, but in reality it is a great giver.

ANONYMOUS

November 24 1 TIMOTHY 1:1-20

"I see the battles you think you can't win, and I want you to believe I can change you."

This is a trustworthy saying, and everyone should accept it: "Christ Jesus came into the world to save sinners"—and I am the worst of them all. 1 TIMOTHY 1:15

Whoever would imagine that the person we have most wronged would be our greatest defender?

Jesus, the One who could condemn us for every wrong we've done and those we've tried to cover up, has seen it all from us. When we understand the depths of our sinfulness and our capability for destructiveness, guilt and shame threaten to capsize us. Then as we come to grips with how undeserving we are of Jesus' acceptance, we become our fiercest judge. Some of us struggle for years to overcome old patterns of sin, including unforgiveness toward ourselves.

It's far easier to focus on the pits where our sins have taken us than on where God is taking us. We hate that we've hurt him so much, we hate that we continue to cause pain, and we hate that we can't seem to move beyond the trap of guilt and failure.

Yet Jesus breaks through our self-imposed torture and argues against us on our behalf. What a wonderful, beautiful Savior we have! In the midst of all we hate about ourselves, the one with every right to hate us looks at us with pure love.

How gracious of God to show his power by loving one of the early Jesus haters into becoming perhaps the greatest missionary the world has known! Paul was a changed man because Jesus' love proved too awesome to reject. Paul had no reason to believe he could undergo such a drastic, 180-degree soul transformation. But he did.

You struggle to believe you can overcome the issues that bind you. But more importantly, God is fully confident he can free you and move you forward with him.

TALK TO HIM

"The power I need lies in you, almighty God, Lord of my life. It's about letting you be Lord, releasing the good and bad to you. Please change me to be like you."

Dear Master, Thine the glory
Of each recovered soul,
Ah! who can tell the story
Of love that made us whole?

HENRY W. BAKER, "REDEEMED, RESTORED, FORGIVEN"

"Take time to grow with me; your training ensures that my church isn't built with toothpicks."

An elder must not be a new believer, because he might become proud, and the devil would cause him to fall. 1 TIMOTHY 3:6

Much depends on what time will tell: the longevity of a relationship, a report from the oncologist, a person's trustworthiness.

And spiritual maturity. The test of time can't be overstated when it comes to readiness for spiritual leadership. Although an old faith can drift from God and a new faith can soar with strength, there's a great deal to be said for a weathered faith that has endured the proving ground of various spiritual seasons.

God doesn't hand us a lifetime of lessons when we first come to him. His intention is for us to grow steadily with him over time, gleaning new insights and strength as we go. He doesn't expect us to conquer every spiritual battle at once, so we're hasty to expect it of ourselves.

Rushing into spiritual leadership can backfire on a young Christian whose relationship with God hasn't been tested in the fires of life. That said, it's important to note Paul's respect for young leaders such as Timothy, made obvious through his encouragement not to "let anyone think less of you because you are young" (4:12). Likewise, Paul pointed out that youth can set a godly example for all believers (see 4:12).

God's church is an eternal family of believers in him, and he cherishes the time we invest in our growth as his children. Our personal faith reflects his glory, drawing others to him, so we're wise to invest in our own training time on behalf of his family.

All who believe in him have a special role in building his church. Apply yourself to developing your spiritual stamina. Neglecting it is like adding a toothpick's strength to a skyscraper's stability.

TALK TO HIM

"Father God, thank you for being patient with my spiritual growth. Please help me to grow steadily, without wasting time, allowing myself to go at the pace you direct. I trust you to open up leadership opportunities when you know the timing and I are a fit."

Time is the wisest counselor.

PERICLES

November 26 1 TIMOTHY 5:1-21

"In caring for my church, remember your family first."

Those who won't care for their relatives, especially those in their own household, have denied the true faith. 1 TIMOTHY 5:8

There is a misconception running through some Christian circles that revolves around ministry priorities. We want to serve; we need to serve; we're gifted by God to do our part. We love him and want our lives to reflect a God-first, others-second, ourselves-last approach. But when "God first" translates into "ministry first," our definitions become jumbled.

Ministry is not God. If we spend more time serving in church or other places than we do caring for our families, service takes over our first, God-given ministry of loving those closest to us. Paul reaffirmed this family-first focus that he wrote earlier in this letter to Timothy: "[An elder] must manage his own family well, having children who respect and obey him. For if a man cannot manage his own household, how can he take care of God's church?" (3:4-5). Just as parents earn their children's respect by investing quality and quantity time with them, all Christians earn the respect of their family members by ministering to their hearts first before heading out to save the rest of the world.

Our time is precious and always limited, so it's common to feel stretched by conflicting responsibilities. Even in the healthiest of families, there undoubtedly will be days when a pressing ministry obligation reduces the attention we can give at home, and loved ones sometimes don't get as much time as needed with each other. However, we can glean from Paul's teaching that those days ought to be the exception instead of the rule.

Our families are our launching pads into life. For all the love and joy, heartache and tears we experience with them, they're small churches in and of themselves. Do a little soul searching today to find out if your faith is the truest kind that wholeheartedly prioritizes your small nucleus of loved ones.

TALK TO HIM

"Father God, thank you for my family. You know the baggage we share and the love we long to give to each other. Please help me to earn their respect and please you by prioritizing them first."

A happy family is but an earlier heaven.

JOHN BOWRING

"If I bless you with money, I also give you a responsibility to keep your heart right about it."

Some people, craving money, have wandered from the true faith and pierced themselves with many sorrows. 1 TIMOTHY 6:10

"Money, money, money . . . MONEY!" Is it the theme song of a reality TV show, mantra of our times, or both?

Cold, hard cash! We love it, even though most of us can't ever seem to afford our best dreams. Money is necessary and good. However, our tendency toward discontent quickly turns a great resource into a trap if we don't learn to manage our desires. Managing money, like yesterday's reading about managing families, has everything to do with managing our priorities.

Paul couldn't end his first letter to his protégé, Timothy, without addressing the wonderful mixed blessing of money and what it reveals about our "true faith," a key phrase he also used in chapter 5 regarding our families. In today's reading, we see that the priority we give to our finances also reveals something about our faith.

We might assume we're not too money hungry. We can't keep up with Mr. Jones's lifestyle, but then again we do have more than Sally Frugality. Yet, let's be heart-and-soul honest about the time we invest thinking about what we would like to own. We're constantly surrounded by wealth and the endless push to work harder to earn more to have the toys to enjoy a better life. It's tough to avoid being consumed by all we're told we can have.

Keeping in mind that your finances are God's resources that he has entrusted to you can help you maintain priorities that honor him and reveal true faith. Enjoy what God loans you, but always remember that he provides so that you can serve him better. If your desires have become slanted toward fulfilling more of your whims than helping others, it's time to reevaluate whether you're using his blessings from a heart of true faith.

TALK TO HIM

"Lord, money is such a perk and such a temptation. Please help me to remember that everything I think of as mine is really yours on loan to me for your purposes."

Money is not required to buy one necessity of the soul.
HENRY DAVID THOREAU

November 28 2 TIMOTHY 1:1-18

"I have given you a precious and unique spiritual heritage."

I know the one in whom I trust, and I am sure that he is able to guard what I have entrusted to him until the day of his return. 2 TIMOTHY 1:12

Happy Thanksgiving! So what if this year the official day for thanks doesn't fall on November 28? Today is as good as any day to thank God for the legacy he gives us.

When we began life on earth, we became part of family history. Unfortunately for many, the years since have been filled with more family pain than joy. Some people dread the holidays, which serve up cruel reminders of what they've endured and still grieve. Picture-perfect portrayals of happy holiday gatherings around tables laden with heartfelt warmth drowned long ago in a gravy boat of lost hopes.

If only you could turn back time and convince God to spare your family from the hurts that twist and tear. But God doesn't change the past.

However, he does offer you a future. And a future is so much better than a past. He invites you to a spiritual legacy of healing, hope, and more love than anyone has ever mourned losing. If you know Jesus as Savior, you're part of a spiritual history that extends back to heal the past while reaching with hope into the eternal future. Your legacy in God's holy family covers it all: your brokenness, grief, confusion, misery, fear, and despair. And that same legacy goes with you beyond your last breath on earth, carrying you straight into the waiting arms of your heavenly Father.

You do have a loving family this holiday season. Jesus, your spiritual brothers and sisters, and most of all, your heavenly Father became your family when you acknowledged your need for Jesus' salvation.

Your history, with all its bruises, will feel uniquely precious to you one day when you meet your Savior. Move that promise to the forefront of your thoughts. Know the One you trust. He guards your heart for himself, and he is elated at the thought of returning for you one day.

TALK TO HIM

"Lord, how I wish for a happy family legacy. Please help me to build on the legacy you graciously share with me."

The family you come from isn't as important as the family you're going to love.

RING LARDNER

"My purity in you will ensure your usability for my work."

If you keep yourself pure, you will be a special utensil for honorable use. Your life will be clean, and you will be ready for the Master to use you for every good work. 2 TIMOTHY 2:21

The right tools make all the difference. Sometimes special circumstances call for extra special tools. You wouldn't reach for paper plates and plastic utensils for an elegant feast when the china and silver sit glistening behind cabinet doors.

Tools make life better, particularly the special ones. But in order for them to work, they typically require maintenance. It's essential to keep those tools clean to make them last long and work well. Cleanliness is one of the first aspects of maintenance for any tool that's going to be fit for its pure purpose. Until someone invents self-cleaning tableware, we're stuck loading the dishwasher or hand cleaning fine china and silver.

God's children are his utensils, and like any other tools, we require maintenance to remain pure and usable for him. Our purity is no easy task since we're inundated daily with the world's messes. Impurity in the media, in our workplaces, and unfortunately in our homes smears layers of filth across our hearts and minds. Quite often the process happens subtly, creeping up on us like dust that collects gradually, tarnishing our ability to shine with Jesus' light.

God's purity in us doesn't happen on its own. It must be guarded and polished our entire lives. But the more pure we keep ourselves, the better we'll last for God's service. The more we put the effort into maintaining our purity, the more we'll shine with Jesus' love through the attitudes, words, and behavior that make us usable for his most special work.

TALK TO HIM

"Thank you, Lord, for creating me as your pure tool. Please clean me up for your special work."

If clearer vision Thou impart,
Grateful and glad my soul shall be;
But yet to have a purer heart
Is more to me, is more to me.

WALTER C. SMITH, "A CLEAN HEART"

November 30 2 TIMOTHY 4:1-22

"Be courageous enough to abide by my unpopular truths."

A time is coming when people will no longer listen to sound and wholesome teaching. They will follow their own desires and will look for teachers who will tell them whatever their itching ears want to hear. 2 TIMOTHY 4:3

What do rationalization, compromise, and tolerance have in common? For starters, they're all good descriptions of attitudes of our times. Even though they embody some valuable virtues, when human beings twist them to fit the moral code of the day, they lose their agreeability with God's definitions of truth.

We can rationalize anything with today's mind-set that claims that what's wrong for one person isn't necessarily wrong for someone else. Then there is compromise, which can be a virtue or a filthy word, depending on the issue and who's fighting on opposing sides. And lastly, there is tolerance; to some it may as well be spelled "d-o-n'-t-t-e-l-l-m-e-I'-m-w-r-o-n-g!"

All three concepts relate in some way to truth, a word that's embraced by some, spat on by others. Is there any truth left, or was it discarded with outdated lingo of past generations? According to human logic, we could rationalize for or against truth's existence to fit our preferences. Fans of compromise might push for some truths, but reject others, just so everyone can get along. And those who want tolerance at all costs forfeit the benefits of absolute truth. Heaven forbid we be required to adjust our behavior to God's commands when he could adjust his expectations to fit our day and age.

God's truth often isn't popular or attractive to everyone. Unless we accept some difficult realities, we will never live God's way. God's goal isn't to make everyone comfy and cozy no matter what lifestyle we choose. His goal is to glorify himself and love us into reflecting his holiness.

Abiding by God's truth takes courage in a world that wants its own changing definition of whatever "truth" works today. However, in the eternal scope of things, God's truth is the only one that truly works.

TALK TO HIM

"Lord, thank you for embodying everything that's true. Please help me be a courageous defender of your ways."

We do not err because truth is difficult to see. It is visible at a glance. We err because this is more comfortable.
ALEKSANDR SOLZHENITSYN

"True faith in me requires the discipline of a humble attitude."

Once we, too, were foolish and disobedient. . . . Our lives were full of evil and envy, and we hated each other. TITUS 3:3

Do you know that old game of matching pairs that belong together? It showed up on school tests and children's TV programs and went something like "A kite string is to a kite as a ladder rung is to a (fill in the blank)" or "Blue is to the sky as yellow is to (pick one: a horse, a tree, a lemon)."

Here's another one: "Love is to hate as humility is to (pick one: timidity, courage, arrogance)." If you guessed arrogance, A+ for you.

We usually think of arrogance and humility as opposites. But arrogance may not be the only quality that interferes with our capability for humility. Titus 2 and 3 show that foolishness, disobedience, evil, envy, and hatred also oppose a humble heart.

Basically, anything that focuses us on ourselves more than on God and others gets in the way of humility. Humility is about having a right perspective of ourselves in God's sight, which means we're secure in who we are in Jesus and freed from the need to prove or draw attention to ourselves. Humility shows wisdom instead of foolishness, favors obedience instead of disobedience, promotes purity instead of evil, encourages happiness for others instead of envy, and calls for love instead of hatred.

Contrary to some beliefs that humility means thinking poorly of oneself or speaking with self-deprecation, humility has it all going on. It knows what—or rather Whom—it is about. It takes pride in its beautiful Savior, Jesus Christ, rather than getting puffed up about its own grandness. It has no need for being "humble and proud of it" because its others-centeredness is too busy thinking outwardly to become wrapped up in its own merits.

Humility is a by-product of a true, vibrant, growing faith in Jesus. Nurturing it requires self-sacrifice, but the healthy relationships, godliness, and joy that it yields are beyond measure.

TALK TO HIM

"Lord, thank you for modeling true humility that puts others first. Please humble me as needed to be like you."

Lord, where we are wrong, make us willing to change;
where we are right, make us easy to live with.
REV. PETER MARSHALL

December 2 PHILEMON 1:1-25

"Who can thank me for your gracious spirit?"

Your love has given me much joy and comfort, my brother, for your kindness has often refreshed the hearts of God's people. PHILEMON 1:7

A cool drink, a gentle breeze, a filling meal, a good book—all are wonderful sources of rejuvenation. But one of the greatest comforts we know comes from the warmth of a caring person's gracious spirit.

Fearing the degradation of slavery and the unknowns awaiting him on his return to Philemon, Onesimus was on the verge of what likely amounted to the most difficult decision of his life. The courage it must have taken to escape was nothing compared to the guts required to return—and not only courage, but character and humility to accept possible punishment and a future of being owned by a fellow human. Onesimus desperately needed the refreshment of his master Philemon's gracious spirit.

Setting the example of grace for Philemon, Paul provided initial refreshment for Onesimus, his new brother in the faith, by writing to encourage Philemon to be a breath of fresh air for Philemon's ex-slave. Philemon had shown kindness to fellow believers in the past, but would his character measure up to what Onesimus showed by returning? More importantly, would it measure up to God's grace?

Paul unabashedly laid out the situation for Philemon, adding a tongue-in-cheek comment about Philemon's debt of gratitude to him. We have every reason to believe Philemon did the godly thing and acted with grace toward Onesimus. We can hope he not only waived all punishment, but also offered Onesimus true, unbegrudging grace that showed in a warm smile and the gift of freedom.

Being a refreshment is about giving others what they need, not necessarily what we feel like offering. No doubt someone needs a touch of your gracious spirit today. Be a breath of fresh air to them with every breath God graciously grants you.

TALK TO HIM

"Thank you, Jesus, for the refreshment you are to my soul. Please help me pass along that grace to others."

Gracious Spirit, dwell with me!
I myself would gracious be;
And with words that help and heal
Would Thy life in mine reveal.

THOMAS T. LYNCH, "GRACIOUS SPIRIT, DWELL WITH ME"

"I send my angels to help you, not to be worshiped by you."

Angels are only servants—spirits sent to care for people who will inherit salvation.

HEBREWS 1:14

Angel pins, angel books, angel sightings . . . angels are everywhere these days. What we really need is some angel clarification. Just who are they, and how are we supposed to view them? They're spiritual beings, so does that mean they're minigods we should worship? The subject of angels could—and does—fill bookstore shelves. Thankfully, clarification is right there in the first chapter of Hebrews.

Angels really are everywhere, and not just these days. They've been around since God created everything. As created beings, they are not gods. God never has called them his children, as he calls Jesus his Son and believers his adopted sons and daughters. Nor has he called them god, much less God with a capital *G*, as he called Jesus. He also never invited an angel to sit in a place of honor next to him, nor is his goal to humble their enemies under them.

An angel's job is to do God's bidding, not to call the shots in his place. Because there's no indication that they're created in his image, as we are, we have no reason to think that most angels resent being his workers instead of his prized heirs. We know from Luke 10:18 that Jesus saw the angel Lucifer, known by us as Satan, "fall from heaven like lightning!" So angels do have some form of will to choose or reject God—again, a sign of a created being and not the perfection of God.

We are not to worship angels, but we are to thank God for them. They're important, though typically unseen, protectors and comforters on God's behalf. We don't fully know how we will relate to them in eternity, but we can look forward to worshiping God with them.

TALK TO HIM

"Father God, thank you for the help of your angels. As your wondrous creations, they inspire me to worship you."

Angels, sing your sweet refrain—
Glory in the highest, glory!
Tell the waiting earth your story
Of the Christ Who came to reign.
Sing—sing that sweet song again,
Earth and sky repeat the story—
Glory in the highest, glory!
On earth peace, good will to men.

GRANT C. TULLAR, "THE ANGELS' SWEET REFRAIN"

December 4 HEBREWS 4:1-16

"Come and rest with me."

God's rest is there for people to enter. HEBREWS 4:6

Two days ago we rediscovered the refreshment of a gracious spirit. Today we soak up the subject of rest. And what better time than the busy holiday season to give ourselves the gift of R & R: refreshment and rest?

Actually, rest was God's idea. He rested after Creation, and he commanded his people to observe Sabbath rest every week. He also planned for them a land of abundance on earth, which would be a restful home for them and their descendants. But that first generation missed his blessings of rest because they didn't have faith to go the distance. Instead, they stopped believing he would get them to his goal. Their generation paid dearly for their disobedient faith, but their tough lesson could spare us from missing the greater rest he offers us.

When Jesus came to earth and died, he ushered in a grander, eternal plan of rest for us, one that was hinted at long before that first Christmas of his birth and was confirmed through his life. "There is a special rest still waiting for the people of God" (verse 9). That special rest is eternal refreshment that God promises to anyone who acknowledges their sin and accepts Jesus as Savior.

The invitation couldn't be more personal. God sent Jesus to provide you the refreshing rest of salvation and the joyful privilege of worshiping him forever. His rest awaits you when he calls you from this earth. He offers you peace, joy, and hope that refresh your heart during this life, while giving you a taste of the eternal rest that awaits you. His ultimate rest is in the future, but today—in this season we celebrate his Son—he wants you to accept his holiday gift of rest for your soul.

TALK TO HIM

"Thank you, Lord, for eternal rest. I will rest in you until I can rest with you."

Before His throne the Lamb will lead thee,
On heav'nly pastures He will feed thee,
Cast off thy burden, come with haste;
Soon will the toil and strife be ended,
The weary way which thou hast wended.
Sweet is the rest which thou shalt taste.

JOHANN S. KUNTH, "A REST REMAINETH FOR THE WEARY"

December 5

"Move with me into deeper hope."

This hope is a strong and trustworthy anchor for our souls. HEBREWS 6:19

Imagine you're captaining a ship at sea. A storm rages, keeping you from pulling safely into harbor. You've battled the elements for hours, and you're weary enough that the temptation to give up churns as fiercely as the weather. Giving up means being dragged back to sea, so your only strategy is to drop anchor and wait out the wind and waves. Your hopes live or die by one anchor; will it go deep enough to hold?

Even the deepest hope is only as powerful as the object in which we put it. That object must be both ready and capable. An anchor well-suited to its boat secures our hope more than a flimsy one on a short line. Similarly, unless people are trustworthy and empowered to keep their promises, all the confident hope in the world won't guarantee they won't disappoint us—or we won't disappoint them.

God is the perfect anchor for our hopes. Not only is he true to his word, but he is motivated and capable to keep his promises. We can count on him to securely hold our deepest needs and longings, and to ensure our safe arrival into an eternity with him. He cares about our soul's security even more than we do.

The writer of Hebrews focused in chapter 6 on moving forward with God: forward into maturity (verses 1 and 3) and into deeper hope in him (verses 9-20). No matter how our circumstances threaten to drown us, we can ride out the storm without being capsized if we've plunged our hopes deeply into God, our anchor.

Hope is not brittle or dull. It's pliable, giving us flexibility to maneuver through life's turbulence, shining through the darkness the best when it's challenged the most. You are far safer anchored in God during turbulent times than sitting in quiet waters without him. Let him take your hopes even deeper today, and experience the peace of riding steadily through the waves.

TALK TO HIM

"Father God, you are my only hope, but you also are the only hope I need. Thank you for being my deep anchor."

When you say a situation or a person is hopeless,
you are slamming the door in the face of God.
REV. CHARLES L. ALLEN

December 6 HEBREWS 10:1-39

"My case against you is closed. Don't reopen it."

"I will never again remember their sins and lawless deeds." HEBREWS 10:17

What triggers guilt in you? A half-truth (a whole lie)? Accidentally overlooking taxable income on your taxes? A pan of gooey brownies with icing . . . recently devoured by you?

The Hebrews author addressed two types of people in chapter 10: those whose guilt sensors could use polishing and those whose sensors run on overdrive. Those who aren't familiar with guilt would benefit from verses 26-31 about the future that awaits people who treat "the blood of the covenant, which made us holy, as if it were common and unholy" (10:29). But the ones whose sensors trip at the slightest provocation need the relief of verses 1-22 about God's guilt-cleansing forgiveness.

Good guilt helps us deal with sin; that's the kind God uses. He intends for guilt to get in and get out—to visit our heart, prompt us to deal with ways we've caused hurt, then leave and never return about the same sin. Bad guilt is from Satan; it hangs on and batters our hearts after we've repented and received God's forgiveness.

God gave his Son's life to free us from ongoing guilt. He chooses not to remember sins we've addressed and received his forgiveness for (verse 17), and he certainly doesn't want us mistakenly thinking we can make it up to him by punishing ourselves for those sins.

If your guilt sensors work on overdrive, they will overheat and give you a feeling of condemnation instead of motivation to move forward in a better way. Continuing to punish yourself is like telling Jesus his death wasn't enough for you. Accept the relief God offers along with his forgiveness. The case is closed; move on.

TALK TO HIM

"Father, sometimes I don't know how to act apart from guilt. Thank you for the eternal opportunity to discover what freedom from guilt feels like."

The feeling of being, or not being, forgiven and loved, is not what matters. . . . If there is a particular sin on your conscience, repent and confess it. If there isn't, tell the despondent devil not to be silly. . . . What the devil loves is that vague cloud of unspecified guilt feeling or unspecified virtue by which he lures us into despair or presumption.

C. S. LEWIS

"Your life will speak as a unique example of faith. What will you refuse to place ahead of it?"

He thought it was better to suffer for the sake of Christ than to own the treasures of Egypt, for he was looking ahead to his great reward. HEBREWS 11:26

What makes a hero? You could name a host of virtuous qualities: courage, honor, strength, tenacity, goodness, selflessness. How about faith? The Bible's great heroes showed faith in God despite incredible odds. What a legacy they've left us who desire to follow in their faith-filled footsteps!

Read Hebrews 11 and listen for the heavenly applause building to a crescendo as verse after verse cheers on the faith of Abel and Enoch; Noah, Abraham, and Sarah; Jacob, Joseph, Moses, Rahab, David, Samuel, and too many prophets to mention. They all made tough decisions to trust God, to keep trusting when life got hot, and to hang on to him for all their worth when circumstances boiled over.

A heroic faith makes sacrifices and keeps going. Anyone can claim faith in God, but the heroic type is proven in the storms that challenge it. Just as we don't know what true hope or true peace look like until they're tested, true faith shows its heroism only in circumstances that require a hero.

Heroes are willing to give up what's of lesser value—even if it's still of value—for what's greater. Our devotion to God will always fit the "greater" category.

Your story of faith is yours alone; it hasn't been done before, and you're the one who received the gift of living it. Undoubtedly, you will have opportunities to prove the depth of your faith. Will you rely on God for strength and encourage those after you to emulate the trust you showed in God no matter what?

Your first and last acts of heroic faith are the same: refusing to put anything ahead of the Lord in your life. Someone coming after you will learn about faith through yours. Will your faith inspire a hero-to-be?

TALK TO HIM

"Lord God, thank you for being faithful to all who show heroic faith in you. Please help me to have the courage to be counted among that group."

Here I stand. I can do no otherwise. God help me.

MARTIN LUTHER

December 8 HEBREWS 12:1-29

"Let my discipline safeguard you."

Watch out that no poisonous root of bitterness grows up to trouble you, corrupting many. HEBREWS 12:15

Wow, it looks like today is a good day for a paradigm shift. Discipline, a blessing? By whose book? We don't often consider discipline as one of life's perks, but that's exactly how God views it when it's from his hand.

One of the most intimate ways God reveals how precious we are to him is by not letting us continue hurtful patterns. Whether we struggle against selfishness, anxiety, fear, anger, or any other vice, we would end up with bitterness choking our spirit if not for God's loving hand of discipline.

How does his discipline work? Well, it has something to do with our heart attitude toward it. Directly following the first thirteen verses that clarify the blessing of discipline, we read about working (or applying discipline) to live at peace, free of bitterness. We can glean a connection between God's discipline and protection from bitterness referred to in verse 15.

Someone who resists the benefit of being chastened by the Lord may very well end up bitter from being unaccustomed to yielding to someone else. Bitterness grows when our hearts focus inward and refuse to move past pain into God's comfort. We might have many genuine, deep causes for bitterness to take root, but if we let it, we face continued emotional, spiritual, and even physical agony beyond our initial hurts. God wants so much more for us than that. He wants healing, but sometimes healing hurts when it requires cleaning so the wound doesn't fester.

A child of God who is committed to growing closer to him will weather his refining process and experience the healing of his Spirit's light within. His Spirit's disciplining work minimizes any room left for bitterness to grow.

Discipline from God is a beautiful gift—painful at first, but offering the potential for immeasurable joy and protection from the bitterness that would threaten to kill that joy. Embrace his discipline for life, and see your life flourish.

TALK TO HIM

"Okay, Lord, I'm a little uneasy about asking for your discipline, but I will trust you with my heart. Thank you for wanting more for me that can grow only through your refinement."

Better a little chiding than a great deal of heartbreak.

WILLIAM SHAKESPEARE

"Don't let anger burn your spirit or anyone else's."

You must all be . . . slow to get angry. Human anger does not produce the righteousness God desires. JAMES 1:19-20

"Watch out! She's gonna blow!" Few emotions drive people away as quickly as anger. Sure, we all get ticked occasionally, like when we have to wait thirty minutes at the dentist, or when a neighbor lets his dog do its duty on our lawn for the umpteenth time. But if we're chronically irate at a loved one who folds the towels differently than we prefer, or at a coworker who forgets to return a pen, or at a spouse who squeezes the toothpaste differently from us, we have an anger problem.

All anger is not wrong. God gets angry at sin, so that kind of anger cannot be sin. We ought to be maddened when people speak against God or encourage injustice. And we certainly should feel anger toward child molesters and murderers and those who mistreat others in need (verse 27).

However, when we let anger get the best of us, we give it control in our hearts that only the Holy Spirit can rightfully handle. James referred to that overpowering rage as "human anger." It wells up and explodes like a volcano, showering a hot lava of words that burn.

Then again, anger isn't always vocal, although James warned repeatedly about controlling our tongue (verse 26, for starters). We can devour someone's heart with a scorching expression or dehydrate someone's spirit with the arid atmosphere of the silent treatment.

Human anger delivers destruction to communication and relational health. Most devastating, wrong anger puts a barrier between us and God and blocks his gracious Spirit from shining through us. God calls his children to more than religious claims (verse 26); his desire is that we will act with the soothing balm of purity and gentleness flowing from a heart that's slow to get angry.

Cool the flames of wrong anger, and open up your horizon to let God's Spirit flow freely through you.

TALK TO HIM

"Lord, I'm sorry for my angry spirit. Please help me to cool its fire so nothing diminishes your Spirit's life in me."

An angry man opens his mouth and shuts up his eyes.

CATO

December 10 JAMES 2:1-13

"A rich faith in me should prompt you to treat others as royalty."

Yes indeed, it is good when you obey the royal law as found in the Scriptures: "Love your neighbor as yourself." JAMES 2:8

Although the United States doesn't have royalty, it does have more than its share of privileged living. To most of the world, American wealth is off the charts.

But in his discussion about favoritism—or on not showing favoritism—James clarified that God gives the financially poor a wealth of faith that develops from a deep understanding of their need for him. A few steps of logic bring us to a powerful conclusion:

Those with a rich faith in God are called his children.
God is the King of the universe.
His children are royal heirs to his Kingdom.
Conclusion: Those who are financially poor but rich in faith in God are wealthy, privileged royalty.

It's no coincidence that James used an unobtrusive word in verse 8 that amplifies this section's theme about rich and poor. It's the word *royal*. James's clarifying use of *royal* deepens the impact of the law that says we're to love others as ourselves. Why? Because the law came from God—King of the universe, Royal of royals. It wasn't a wishful rule from the masses who wanted to be treated well. It was a standard set at the Top. The law couldn't have come from a higher, more privileged place than God's throne room, so it evens the situation for everyone under him—which means everyone, rich and poor.

No matter if we are rich in faith, rich in finances, or somewhere between both, we are to deepen our investment in others by treating them as royalty. That is, after all, how our Lord treats us.

How wonderful to be treated like royalty by the King of kings! May we, his children, take after our Father.

TALK TO HIM

"Father God, thank you for blessing me richly. Please help my faith grow rich as I treat others as your privileged loved ones."

I once was an outcast stranger on earth,
A sinner by choice, an alien by birth,
But I've been adopted, my name's written down,
An heir to a mansion, a robe and a crown.
HARRIET E. BUELL, "A CHILD OF THE KING"

"I created you to live each day with a sense of expectation."

It is by his great mercy that we have been born again, because God raised Jesus Christ from the dead. Now we live with great expectation. 1 PETER 1:3

Joy to the world and fa la la, it's Christmas time again! Only two weeks to go until the big day, and those herald angels are singing once more about this great season of expectation. Isn't it exciting?

God's people have always lived with a sense of expectation, even long before that first Christmas when he sent his tiny Son. God's prophets had spoken of the Messiah for hundreds of years, and the people had waited day after day for God to fulfill their dreams of freedom. Their anticipation was based on generations of prophecies about a King who would rescue them. They were looking for freedom on earth, but God had a bigger surprise in store because his greater purpose through Jesus was to free souls.

Part of what increases the drumroll buildup of our expectations at Christmas is the sense of surprise that goes along with the anticipation. Our expectations now revolve around Jesus' return and our eternity with him—even more to look forward to than the freedom the people hoped for before Jesus came the first time.

Because those who know Jesus as Savior have so much to get excited about, every day of the year holds the thrill of expectation as much as Christmas. God surely has more surprises planned than we can imagine. Go ahead and dream big this holiday season, because your most amazing hopes will only be exceeded as God continues to complete his purposes in your life.

Anticipate today a Merry Christmas and a joyful eternity!

TALK TO HIM

"Father, your gifts are always beyond my expectations, especially when they're filled with surprises. One would think I'd have learned by now to anticipate bigger when it comes to you. My mind simply isn't big enough to wrap around the gifts that you have in store. So I simply send a heartfelt 'thank-you' this Christmas."

Hail, the heavenly Prince of Peace!
Hail, the Sun of Righteousness!
Light and life to all he brings,
Risen with healing in his wings.

CHARLES WESLEY, "HARK! THE HERALD ANGELS SING"

December 12 1 PETER 2:11-25; 3:8–4:19

"Experience my help to suffer well for my glory."

If you are suffering in a manner that pleases God, keep on doing what is right, and trust your lives to the God who created you, for he will never fail you. 1 PETER 4:19

We don't understand pain. In fact, we go to great lengths to avoid it. When our distress is bad enough, it shatters our feeling of control, even if that feeling was misleading all along. Pain has a way of pulling our sense of authority out from under us, leaving us broken, vulnerable, and very often with shaken faith.

We can't control cancer or evil or natural disasters or ridicule for our faith. Even so, there is light within suffering for those who hold on to the one control we never have to give up: what we do with our faith in the midst of it. Although it's a timeless human question why God allows us to hurt—why he actually guarantees it—we can deal with suffering in positive ways.

"Oh really?" we say in frustration. How does someone watch loved ones tortured during genocide or lose a child or endure betrayal, and find anything worthwhile in their agony? The Bible's encouragements to shine God's glory despite inhumane treatment or overwhelming pressures can feel trite in the face of unspeakable atrocities.

The apostle Peter feared pain. He denied Jesus three times before Jesus' crucifixion because he didn't want to suffer for loyalty. However, later on Peter's mature faith changed his attitude toward suffering for Jesus' sake. Suffering filters out fear and the distractions of sin. He wrote, "If you have suffered physically for Christ, you have finished with sin. You won't spend the rest of your lives chasing your own desires, but you will be anxious to do the will of God" (4:1-2).

Life includes heartache. But the very trials that bring us to the brink are opportunities to reflect God's character to magnified degrees. We will suffer here. How we respond to suffering is up to us.

TALK TO HIM

"Lord, I don't understand this pain, but please don't let it go unused for your glory."

Anyone God uses significantly is always deeply wounded. . . . On the last day,
Jesus will look us over not for medals, diplomas, or honors, but for scars.
BRENNAN MANNING

"Find true and freeing stability in me."

They promise freedom, but they themselves are slaves of sin and corruption. 2 PETER 2:19

Okay, today we're going to play a game. It's a short one with a single question, but it does have serious consequences, so choose well: Which would you rather have, a life of unstable freedom or stable slavery?

Freedom and stability go hand in hand. One can't exist without the other. What value is freedom that we can't count on, or very secure bondage, for that matter? One could never choose because both are thoroughly unappealing. Neither situation offers any real peace, and both create constant tension.

Peter's warnings about false teachers tie together the concepts of freedom and stability. It's only through a stable faith that we find freedom, but false teachers act as detriments to an unstable faith.

It's sobering to read verses 18-22 about how much worse off immature believers are when they taste God's freedom, but then lose it by falling for the lures of people who twist God's truth and tempt them back into old habits. Those teachers use empty promises to undermine people's fledgling faith, and once their victims fall for their talk, it's like lust that can't be satisfied. It always needs more of the very things that drive it deeper into slavery.

We're always either stabilizing our freedom in Christ or securing our slavery to sin's obsessions. But we are not without hope, because God's freedom is more powerful than Satan's slavery. He gives us freedom of choice in the matter. Although our growth as Christians is dependent on God's supernatural help to grow his character in us, we do have a responsibility to nurture our own faith.

Remember, your faith is your freedom. Guard it, grow it, and ask God to guide it so it's genuine, gentle, yet gutsy enough to withstand lies that test it.

TALK TO HIM

"Father, thank you for making me free. Please help me to apply your wisdom and stay close to you as a guard for my faith."

Deceit and falsehood I abhor,
But love Thy law, Thy truth revealed;
My steadfast hope is in Thy Word;
Thou art my Refuge and my Shield.

AUTHOR UNKNOWN, "DECEIT AND FALSEHOOD I ABHOR"

December 14 2 PETER 3:1-18

"Imagine if I sent my Son back too soon."

Remember, our Lord's patience gives people time to be saved. 2 PETER 3:15

Oh, how we want to be finished with earthly troubles! We're worn out from heartaches across the world. Our desires to fix them battle our hopes that someone else will save the day because we don't have enough time or inclination. And then there are the hurts that hit much closer: a child who isn't shaping up to our hopes, a financial bottom line that continues to fall, terror that arrives in our mailbox or onboard a plane.

Why doesn't God fix these things? What is he waiting for?

Us. He's waiting for us: those of us who invite others to discover his salvation; those of us who ought to care more for other people's eternity; those of us who don't know him yet. We are the reasons almighty God waits for his last say about sin.

Without minimizing or disrespecting the immensity of pain, our pain here cannot compare with people's future agony if they don't know Jesus as Savior when God sends him back to earth to collect his people.

What appears to be God's lack of mercy is actually mercy so profound that we miss its impact. He cares for the souls next door and a thousand miles away, the old man passed out on the park bench across town and the tiny girl scavenging for garbage in a Third-World gutter. They are why he waits. He wants to offer them so much more. As hard as it is to wait for him, thank the Lord he waits for us.

And in the meantime, let's ask ourselves why we wait to share him with those he is waiting to save.

TALK TO HIM

"Thank you, God, for seeing the world's greater needs beyond today. Please grow my desire to help others find you."

We are waiting, blessèd Savior,
We are watching not in vain
For the cloud that bore Thee upward,
And will bring Thee back again.
Then, among Thy ransomed people,
We shall tread the shining way,
And our eyes behold the splendor
Of the glorious crowning day.

FANNY CROSBY, "WAITING FOR THY COMING"

"Live in my light; you can see much better from there."

If we are living in the light, as God is in the light, then we have fellowship with each other, and the blood of Jesus, his Son, cleanses us from all sin. 1 JOHN 1:7

Temperatures have dropped outside, and cozy evenings come earlier every day as we say good-bye to autumn and prepare to officially welcome winter in a week.

The days are short, but they will soon start to lengthen again. For the next six months, we will see a minute or two more sunshine every day. As cozy as winter can be, we love the rejuvenation and freedom of spring, when we see better, our hopes dare to breathe again, and life appears more optimistic in the light.

But we get to celebrate a different kind of light as we await spring. Christmas is the season of light—Light, actually, because the holiday is about Jesus, the Light of the World. In a dark world, his love lights our hearts, "lightens" our burdens, and illuminates our way back to God. Through his life, we see more clearly the destructive effects of our sin and our need for his commandment to love as he loved.

Jesus shows us how to live in his light by loving one another: "Jesus lived the truth of this commandment [to love one another], and you also are living it. . . . If anyone claims, 'I am living in the light,' but hates a Christian brother or sister, that person is still living in darkness" (2:8-9). When he lights our souls, we experience his eternal spring with love that shines day and night.

Choose this Christmas season to escape the world's darkness and view life from within Jesus' light. You will be amazed at the clarity that takes shape from eyes that see others as he does. It might be dark outside, but the day is dawning in hearts that glow with his love.

TALK TO HIM

"Thank you, Jesus, for lighting my world. Please fill me to bursting with the light of your love for others."

Walk in the light: and thou shalt find
Thy heart made truly His
Who dwells in cloudless light enshrined
In Whom no darkness is.

BERNARD BARTON, "WALK IN THE LIGHT"

December 16 1 JOHN 3:11-24; 4:7-21

"What is the quality of your love?"

As we live in God, our love grows more perfect. So we will not be afraid on the day of judgment, but we can face him with confidence because we live like Jesus here in this world. 1 JOHN 4:17

"His love is brought to full expression in us" (4:12). Our eyes read the words; our minds take in their meaning; but do our hearts feel his love's full expression? We long to be overwhelmed by a greater understanding of God's love for us, to know the "full expression" of that love. And we want to share his love more with others.

God spends our lifetimes showing us the quality of his love. We know he sent his Son to die in our place, but it's a rare occasion when the impact of his sacrifice brings us to our knees, halts our thoughts, or renders us speechless for the wonder of it all.

When we understand his love for us, we realize that top-quality love is free of fear. We lose our anxiety about being rejected, and we release our frantic need to prove ourselves worthy or to hide our unworthiness. God sees it all and loves us perfectly.

It's one amazing phenomenon to really feel his love, but we take a step beyond that when we offer his quality of love to others. Do your loved ones experience freedom from fear of your rejection? Do they have to prove themselves worthy of your love? Do they try to cover up their faults in case you won't accept them? If someone you love were to drop the ball in your relationship, letting you down in a huge way . . . would that person guess that your love would remain?

God's love for you depends on him, not you. If his love is brought to "full expression" in yours, may those you love feel its depth that chooses to love them no matter what.

TALK TO HIM

"Lord, loving well is not easy, at least for me. Thank you for setting a perfect example of love's full expression. Your love not only shows me the way, but gives me the love I need in order to love others."

To love without role, without power plays, is revolution.
RITA MAE BROWN

"I will give you confidence and victory."

We achieve this victory through our faith. . . . We are confident that he hears us whenever we ask for anything that pleases him. 1 JOHN 5:4, 14

Did you ever notice that confident people succeed more than insecure people? It's as if success breeds success. If we could latch on to confidence 24-7, maybe we would be assured of a front-seat ride to victory all the time. If we could do that, we would be supernatural. Unfortunately, life doesn't work quite so smoothly for most of us. We experience our share of bumps and bruises as we try and try again, sometimes winning, other times battling failures that make us question our abilities.

However—and this is a big however—we serve a God who has the corner on confidence and victory. Better still, he invites us to join his guaranteed success and enjoy his gift of confidence the whole way.

However—yes, another however, this time requiring something of us—his confidence is available to us when we ask for things that please him. In other words, as long as we're moving in step with his will and praying submissively for his will, we can know without insecurity that he listens to every word.

Does that sound demanding of him? too limiting? like he has to have everything his way? Putting aside the fact that he's God and he has a right to his way, let's unwrap his possible reasons for placing restrictions on the confidence and victory he gives us.

First off, he isn't a gimmick who caters to our "gimmes" (i.e., "Gimme this; gimme that"). Second, he loves that our true confidence comes from a growing faith in him; as we experience his faithfulness, we base our confidence on him, not on our abilities. And third, he knows that our hard work of trusting him strengthens our spiritual muscles.

Victory is assured in him when we want what he wants, when we join his efforts, and when we hold to our faith—confident that he will be true to himself and to us.

TALK TO HIM

"Almighty God, your very name inspires confidence. Thank you for sharing your might with me."

Victory, yes, victory.
Hallelujah! I am free,
Jesus gives me victory.
Glory, glory, hallelujah!
He is all in all to me.

BARNEY E. WARREN, "VICTORY"

December 18 2 JOHN 1:1-13

"True love means passing it on."

Love means doing what God has commanded us, and he has commanded us to love one another. 2 JOHN 1:6

We've read all year about God's love for us, and we know he showed love's ultimate expression by giving his Son's life for ours. Love doesn't get any better . . . that is, unless it keeps giving.

God isn't involved with us on a temporary basis. By his choice, he expresses his love to us every day and is "in life" with us for keeps. The more we experience his ongoing love, the more we want to love him in return.

But how does one love God? Surely the King of the universe doesn't need our affection. He doesn't need it, but he definitely desires it. And he knows a world of people who do need to feel his love through us. If we truly belong to him, then we're to be examples of his Son's love on earth—many people's first experience of real love.

We know we're loving God well when we not only think it's a good idea to share his love, but when we sacrifice time and energy to offer it because other people need it, not to make ourselves feel holier. God's love inspires us to return the gift, but it doesn't stop at a desire to love only him. His love keeps growing and extending itself, reaching through us to everyone we meet, regardless of whether they welcome it.

God is loving you right now. When you stay close to him so he can keep filling you, you will realize his love far exceeds what your soul can hold. As he overflows your heart, he will bring people your way who need the excess. Will you pass it on and love him by loving those he loves?

TALK TO HIM

"Heavenly Father, I've tried for a long time to pass off a convenient love for the real kind that welcomes the selflessness of loving with someone else's interests above mine. Please help me to show you my love by loving as you do."

There are as many ways of loving as there are people in the world and as there are days in the lives of those people.

MARY CALDERONE

December 19

"Discover my Son's example of godly leading that begins through partnership and following well."

We ourselves should support them so that we can be their partners as they teach the truth.

3 JOHN 1:8

Attend most growing churches for a time, and you're sure to come across some sort of leadership training. Whether through an ongoing Sunday school class, a special seminar, or a stand-alone sermon, we stress the goal of building strong leaders in the church. And while godly leaders are priceless, so are those who follow and partner well. Wouldn't it be something to see training advertised for "Forming Good Followers" or "Practicing Partnership"?

Leading can't happen successfully without followers to train or partners to handle behind-the-scenes ministry upkeep because churches aren't comprised of only one role any more than they're defined by bricks and mortar.

Imagine if a church was made up of only leaders. It would quickly become a cacophony of controllers like Diotrephes, whom the apostle John criticized for wanting his way all the time (among other things). Demetrius, on the other hand, gained John's high approval for the way he had earned everyone's respect. He was the better leader by far because he partnered with others and cared for the church as a whole.

One quality of good leadership is showing sensitivity to the plethora of vital roles within a group. Being a good follower and partner embodies an overlooked aspect of leadership. Jesus wasn't one to call attention to himself. He came to earth, in fact, as a follower of his heavenly Father. And look how he took the lead at showing us how to follow God.

Take the lead and find countless ways to follow well and partner effectively.

TALK TO HIM

"Lord, I love that you find uses for all types of personalities and abilities. Please show me ways to take the lead by following and partnering according to needs."

He that would be a leader must be a bridge.

WELSH PROVERB

December 20 JUDE 1:1-25

"Guard your faith from faulty instincts."

In this way, you will keep yourselves safe in God's love. JUDE 1:21

The saying goes that our greatest strength can be our greatest weakness, and that's true about our instincts. God gave us instincts for survival and common sense. Most importantly, he designed them to sense our need for him. Romans 1:20 says we can see God's invisible qualities by looking at his creation, so our God-given instincts are a gift that leads us to him.

However, because we're faulty humans, our instincts are imperfect. They don't always guide us toward God because our human nature runs from him even when we know we need him. Our hearts are rebellious, we like to have our way, and Satan works to divide our unity with God, so our instincts are hard pressed to serve us well instead of getting us into trouble.

Twice in his book, Jude broached this topic in reference to Satan's workers who scoff at God's truth. He wrote that they "do whatever their instincts tell them, and so they bring about their own destruction" (1:10) and seek "to satisfy their ungodly desires" (1:18). It's clear from the rest of the book that they drag others into destruction with them.

God's children have two forces vying for our attention: our natural instincts and his Holy Spirit. Every moment we follow one or the other. Without God's Spirit guiding us, our instincts eventually lead us into trouble. They do us no favors when we follow them blindly because they're controlled by selfish motives.

Although the Spirit's protection is available to us (whereas those who don't have Jesus' salvation only have their natural instincts to follow), we still have the choice of which voice to heed. They often sound alike—an effective lie typically seems true—so we must learn to discern the difference between the Spirit's warnings and a tempting but twisted untruth.

God's Spirit protects us from opposition to his truth, but we can be our faith's own enemies if we ignore the Spirit to follow human instincts. If your instincts don't lead you toward God, they undoubtedly lead you away from him.

TALK TO HIM

"Lord, I want a life guarded by truth. Please align my instincts with yours."

Our instincts are obviously in conflict. The satisfaction
of one demands the denial of another.
C. S. LEWIS

"Reflect on our history, and look ahead to news of our future."

"I am the First and the Last. I am the living one. I died, but look—I am alive forever and ever!" REVELATION 1:17-18

In this information age, there's no end to our sources of news. Consider the last time you went to a restaurant; you passed newspaper stands alongside the building, racks of classifieds in the breezeway, a giant TV screen over the bar, and the mouths of patrons seated all around you.

From headlines to features and forecasts, news envelops us. It's a rare day when a story doesn't floor us. One bizarre tale after another challenges our sense of belief. If we think we have a corner on shock value, we'd be wrong.

God always has been responsible for the most fantastic headlines. As Alpha and Omega—beginning and end—he has heard all and seen all. As our Almighty, he knows no bounds to the news he will create next. Was his most surprising act sending a baby to save the world? Maybe the true shocker was that the baby was God. Then again, Jesus' miracles were quite amazing, as were the scandal of his murder and the questions surrounding his resurrection. By the time Jesus returned to heaven, stories about him had only begun to circulate. The subsequent growth of his church warranted countless headlines about martyrs, shipwrecks, crowded gatherings, violent windstorms, and fiery tongues.

The churches that received John's letter of Revelation surely thought they had finally heard it all. This book might sound like tabloid fodder to those who don't know God's awesome capabilities. For those who do, Revelation's very personal message makes it extra special. From Creation's first day until the end of earth's existence, our spiritual heritage culminates here.

Perhaps Revelation holds Jesus' best news because it forecasts what is yet to come, the most newsworthy events the world will ever behold. This book is news of your past, present, and future. Your story may surprise you.

TALK TO HIM

"Thank you, Lord, for being news worth waiting for. Please help me to pass it on."

Tell me the story of Jesus,
Write on my heart every word.
Tell me the story most precious,
Sweetest that ever was heard.

FANNY CROSBY, "TELL ME THE STORY OF JESUS"

December 22 REVELATION 2:1-29

"Fire up your godly passion."

"You don't love me or each other as you did at first!" REVELATION 2:4

The weather outside is frightful, but inside your hand warms around a mug of tea that you remove from the microwave. You started drinking it earlier that evening, but then you were distracted by gift wrapping and cookie baking. Before long your tea was tepid, so into the microwave it went for a reheat.

Hot tea or iced tea—both default to lukewarm if left on their own. A hot drink cools at room temperature, and a cold drink becomes lukewarm at best and definitely doesn't reheat without a heat source. This bit of science illustrates a profound spiritual analogy.

Each of us is born with either a lukewarm or a cold default temperature on our passion for God. As we grow through life, that temperature peaks and wanes along with our responses to experiences and how we let circumstances affect our view of the Lord. Many hearts run from his heat source and opt for a lukewarm existence, or they head directly into belief patterns that keep their would-be faith downright chilly toward their Creator.

And then there are the believers whose hearts once warmed with love for their heavenly Father. However, their affection needs constant reheating because life's distractions keep them preoccupied instead of staying close to God's love to keep their spiritual passion fired up. The Ephesian church fell into that category, earning them Jesus' warning in Revelation 2. The warnings continued for the other churches, cautioning them to protect their faith from influences and habits that had crept in and threatened their effectiveness.

Don't let your faith default to lukewarm. If necessary, turn back to him for a spiritual reheat, but keep fanning the flames of the Holy Spirit's fire within you. Your love for him warms you and spreads to warm other souls as well.

TALK TO HIM

"Lord, please fire up my passion for you. Thank you for being my soul's comforting warmth and its torch to pass on to others."

I will walk with Jesus, bless His Name,
And to be like Him I ev'ry day aspire;
For His love is like a heav'nly flame,
And my soul is burning with the fire.

JOHNSON OATMAN JR., "THE FIRE IS BURNING"

"Wear your faith well, fit for the celebration of eternity."

"They will walk with me in white, for they are worthy. All who are victorious will be clothed in white. . . . Buy white garments from me so you will not be shamed by your nakedness."

REVELATION 3:4-5, 18

Have you been to many holiday parties lately? Maybe you've dressed up for a church program or an evening at the theater. Or quite possibly you could be shopping for a New Year's Eve outfit, since the end of the year is right around the corner. Whether you love or hate fancy gatherings, most people would admit to feeling good when they're wearing something grander than everyday clothes. We would look out of place showing up at a black-tie affair sporting dingy jeans and an old T-shirt. Some situations warrant special attention.

Our faith is like our spiritual clothing. We're decked out in it every day, but often it can seem run-of-the-mill to us because it's always there, always taking the wear and tear of daily life. But one day, those who know Jesus will join him in the grandest celebration ever. It's sure to be an occasion to deserve special care to the faith he purchased for us.

Taking care of our faith during this lifetime ensures that it will be gleaming and bright forever, not drab, as if we've dragged it through the muck of sinful habits and the mire of lackadaisical, lukewarm living. Those who care for their faith on earth will wear garments of victory and will have no reason to feel ashamed for being underdressed.

Imagine standing before Jesus in the vibrance of his purity, the purity he gave you by washing your soul clean in his blood. Wear your faith in him well, and enjoy anticipating the era of celebration when the eternal "holy day" arrives and you find yourself dressed well for the event.

TALK TO HIM

"Lord, you look past the outward clothing to see the quality of my clothing of faith in you. May you be pleased by how I'm caring for it so it will wear well into eternity."

Faith is a power suit for the weak, nightclothes for the weary soul, and wedding attire for Jesus' bride, his church.

ANONYMOUS

December 24 REVELATION 4:1-11

"Worship me by working for eternal rewards to offer back to me."

They lay their crowns before the throne. REVELATION 4:10

There are only hours to go until Christmas! Our hopes that rush-hour traffic would thin out as businesses wind down for the week fade among gazillions of commuters moving at a pace we can't seem to relinquish. Slow down? Ha! We simply swap busy workdays for a frenzy of last-minute holiday preparations. The relaxing season portrayed in Christmas carols sounds more like "Ho, ho, ho—boy, I've got so much to do" than "Peace on earth."

Most people don't need help filling the moments. Our motivations for our ambitions vary as calendar seasons and life seasons flow. But through it all, we continue to be driven.

Our workaday ambitions typically carry us through most of the year. In large part, our ambitions determine our lifestyle, how much time we spend with loved ones, and what hobbies we enjoy in the midst of striving for coveted success.

But one of these seasons will be our final one on earth, and someday God's children will receive rewards, or crowns, for how we've lived. Verse 10 shows something amazing about those crowns. We think of them as our prizes, but notice that the twenty-four elders removed theirs and laid them before Jesus' throne. Why?

The crowns that rewarded their godly lives became their worship offerings to God. Such a beautiful picture of how everything leads back to God's glory! Everything they had poured their earthly time, talents, heart, and soul into accomplishing ended up at Jesus' feet, as a way to glorify him.

What a lesson for us with days ahead to fill with ambitions of our choosing! The passions we strive after, the desires we focus on, the faith we defend (see Revelation 3:11) ought to fit well on a crown that eventually we will lay before the Lord.

TALK TO HIM

"Thank you, Lord, for the crown that waits for me. Please help me earn a good one to offer back to you."

Let all that look for, hasten
The coming joyful day,
By earnest consecration,
To walk the narrow way,
By gath'ring in the lost ones,
For whom our Lord did die,
For the crowning day that's coming by and by.

DANIEL W. WHITTLE, "THE CROWNING DAY"

"My future for you could not be better."

"God will wipe every tear from their eyes." REVELATION 7:17

Merry Christmas!

Hopefully yours is merry. But maybe it doesn't inspire celebratory feelings in you; holidays aren't easy for many people. It's possible you would rather skip these twenty-four hours and avoid the added stress of putting on a good face for others while pain sears your soul. Holidays can be alienating times if life has you feeling closed up in a glass box, able to watch others' joy but barred from joining in or feeling a sense of belonging.

Where is God this season? Maybe you feel like he ignored your Christmas request for peace, and you can't help wondering why. Maybe you wonder for the millionth time why it seems God doesn't love you as much as he loves others. You know he saved your soul, but is there something about you that isn't good enough to receive his notice, his care, his rescue, his healing? Why would he let you keep hurting? Is this really all he planned for you? You've heard he loves you, but you honestly don't feel it. Others have come through circumstances as bad or worse, but you're tired of pulling yourself up, sickened by the triteness of someone's "It'll be okay," or worse, "I know just how you feel."

If those ideas resonate with you this season, there isn't room right now for processing dozens of thoughts of God's goodness or harboring hopes of his faithfulness. But do make room for one mighty promise, because it is his precious Christmas gift to you: His plans for you include a time when he will wipe every tear from your eyes.

That time is coming. Jesus is coming. Better still, he's coming for you. Spare yourself a day of trying to understand your pain, and fix in your mind the one thought that your Father does love you. He prizes you, precious child, and his best for you couldn't be better.

TALK TO HIM

"Father God, please give me faith today to believe you love me. That's all I want this Christmas, just to know you're glad you created me."

He has said, and we believe it,
'Tis a promise made of old,
From the trusting and the loving
No good thing will He withhold.

FANNY CROSBY, "GOD'S PROMISE"

December 26 REVELATION 8:1-13

"Your prayers today reach into eternity."

The smoke of the incense, mixed with the prayers of God's holy people, ascended up to God.
REVELATION 8:4

Northwest Arkansas is home to a system of waterways that the Army Corps of Engineers developed in the 1960s when they built a dam that flooded the lowlands. Unbeknownst to most travelers passing through, underneath a few acres of that vast area lay the ruins of an early twentieth-century resort town called Monte Ne.

The town was the brainchild of entrepreneur William "Coin" Harvey, a man who once ran for president and mingled with such well-known people as politician William Jennings Bryan. One of Harvey's plans that never came to fruition at Monte Ne was the building of a structure he called the Pyramid. Harvey intended the Pyramid to serve as a time capsule for storing memorabilia that his era could send into the future. It was his way of influencing future generations. Well, the Pyramid idea died along with many of Harvey's dreams for Monte Ne, but during times of drought the water recedes, and hundreds of people visit the site. In a way, Harvey did realize his dream of leaving a mark on a world he wouldn't live to see.

As Christians, we have a much more profound opportunity to impact future generations. Every time we pray, we send a time capsule into eternity. God never wastes a single prayer of his faithful ones, and verse 4 encourages us with a picture of what happens in his throne room when prayers ascend to him from earth.

Someday when Jesus welcomes his followers to worship him in his throne room, he may reveal to us many answers to prayers we didn't live long enough to see on earth. Your prayers of worship, praise, repentance, thanksgiving, and petition are long lasting—eternal, in fact. Keep in mind the power of each word you send God's way, because he keeps them all forever.

TALK TO HIM

"Yet another amazing quality about you, Lord! That you hold my prayers for eternity provides hope for each today on earth."

Pray, pray till faith grows strong,
And in your heart rings Heaven's song;
Till self shall die in pure desire,
And every thought to Him aspire.
LIZZIE DEARMOND, "PRAY, PRAY"

"I hold many secrets that I long to share with you one day."

I heard a voice from heaven saying, "Keep secret what the seven thunders said, and do not write it down." REVELATION 10:4

Did you catch the secret in verse 4, the one about the seven thunders? Of course you didn't. All of us except John missed that one.

But did you notice the underlying secret? It's for the rest of us. It's the secret of intimacy with God to such a degree that he shares his other mysteries with us. It's the secret of faithfulness, which he longs to reveal to everyone—if only everyone would draw near enough to listen to him.

The apostle John—writer of the Gospel by his name and several other books of the Bible, including Revelation—lived a life that spoke of utter faithfulness to his Master and Lord, Jesus Christ. He called himself the "disciple Jesus loved" (John 13:23; 21:7, 20), leading us to understand that he was in tune with the desires of Jesus' heart. His security in his Savior's love for him grew his faith and deepened his passion for sharing that love with others. And his mature faith earned him the reliability of being the only person God entrusted with at least one eternal secret the rest of us must wait to discover.

In the process of clearing up some of God's mysteries, Revelation creates even more. No one, including John and even Jesus himself, knows the vastness of God the Father's plans (see Mark 13:32). But through this one verse tucked away in Revelation, we can understand that the secret of being entrusted with more secrets lies in living a life in tune with God's heart.

Live a faith that cherishes God's secrets, and be amazed by what he will show you.

TALK TO HIM

"Lord, understanding your ways will take an eternity. But to think that you offer eternity to share your secrets with me boosts my faith. Please mature my faith to be worthy of entrusting with your mysteries."

Sweet secret prayer, comfort divine,
There, O my Lord, I know Thou art mine;
Great Master, there in secret with Thee,
Heaven comes nearer and nearer to me.
CHARLES H. GABRIEL, "SECRET PRAYER"

December 28 REVELATION 11:1-19

"I will have the final word."

"The time of your wrath has come." REVELATION 11:18

What's the most powerful three-word sentence God ever spoke to humans? Try these:

"I love you."
"You are mine."
"It is finished."
"Come to me."
"Peace be still."

Any one of those arguably could be the most meaningful words we've heard from our Lord. They were and still are miraculous.

But two three-word sentences God has yet to speak will top off all the others. One day our heavenly Father will say to his Son and Spirit, "It is time." With those words he will usher in the beginning of the end of evil and death, followed by the creation of a new world for his followers to enjoy with him. Pain and sorrow will never touch that perfect home because God will free his creation from sin. Evil's wrath will shrivel beneath God's when his perfect time finally arrives for him to judge the dead, reward those who fear his name, and destroy all who have caused destruction. It will be a time like no other before and none to follow.

Those three mighty words, a mere eight letters, wrap their impact around the other statements listed above. When it's time, there will be no doubt in our hearts when we hear "I love you" from him. Nor will there exist any sin, pain, discouragement, disillusionment, insecurity, hatred, bitterness, doubt, or anxiety within any of his children's hearts to threaten our intimacy with him. We will experience endless, safe freedom because he will follow his "It is time" with "Victory is mine."

The time is coming, but for now we must wait. One day we will worship him endlessly, but knowing the day is coming inspires us to begin eternal worship today. Worship him for who he is, for being Commander of time and Victor over evil.

His victory is your victory if you know his Son as Savior.

TALK TO HIM

"Heavenly Father, I can hardly wait for you to make things right again and destroy wickedness. But Lord, please help me use the time left to know you better and help others meet you."

To wait is not to sit with folded hands, but to learn to do what we are told.

OSWALD CHAMBERS

"Truth will win in your life."

Then I saw the Lamb standing on Mount Zion. REVELATION 14:1

Are you feeling befuddled in your attempts to sort out Revelation? It's a book to be studied repeatedly because each time, it reveals fresh truth about God and where we stand with him. God could've inspired John with a crystal-clear picture of what's to come, but in his wisdom he laced its events with mystery. Why? Maybe he wants us to dig deep and in the process, experience his truth securing its roots in our hearts.

As widely as Revelation's story reaches—across humanity and the entire spiritual world—its message is personal for each of us. For all its confusing symbolism and prophecies, Revelation can be summed up in one word: *truth.*

Its story builds toward the middle of the book with descriptions of Satan's reign of terror to annihilate everything God created to love. It's a terrifying read, actually, because we know these events will take place someday. The millions who face persecution and death are real souls with real bodies that feel real pain.

But then in the midst of the wearying war for truth, Jesus appears, and instantly the decision is sure. Truth stands. God wins, and along with him, so does each person on his side.

You may have felt the battle for truth in your life. If lies and hurts have battered your spirit and attacked your belief of God's love for you, you need Revelation's reassurance that Jesus died to guard your soul, and he will never lose you. His holy love is securely yours, no matter how stained your life has been.

If you wonder whether Jesus' victory truly includes you, remember that he appears on your horizon to defend you; he will return to hold on to you. Everything and everyone who threatens his truth in your life will face his vengeance.

Truth wins.

For you.

TALK TO HIM

"Thank you, Lord, for the finality of your truth. Thank you for including me in truth's victory."

> *A nonrational, absolutely true intuition perdures that there is something unfathomably big in the universe . . . something that points to Someone who is filled with peace and power, love and undreamed of creativity— Someone who inevitably will reconcile all things to himself.*
>
> BRENNAN MANNING

December 30 REVELATION 19:1-21

"Have you sent your RSVP to a future beyond your dreams?"

"Come! Gather together for the great banquet God has prepared." REVELATION 19:17

One more holiday to go before the January diets begin! Oh joy. By the time January 1 rolls around, many of us feel as though we'll need to be rolled around because we can't move very well after eating so much. Cookies and cakes and pies and hors d'oeuvres, turkey and stuffing and sweet potatoes, office munchies from well-meaning vendors, fruitcake from well-meaning relatives. . . . Can anyone say *overload*?

If we think we'll never see another table loaded with so much sustenance, just wait for the banquet of eternity that believers in Jesus will enjoy. This won't be like anything any human has dreamed of, much less experienced. The banquet is only part of the celebration, which centers around Jesus, the King of kings and Lord of lords. God sent the invitations long ago, and along with them he provided a glimpse of the Guest of Honor's entrance.

Picture it: A vast crowd gathers before the great door of heaven. Praises resound from the believers who await Jesus' arrival, anticipating his unsurpassable glory. The elders and four living beings cry out their worship. And then from his throne God calls, his voice filled with pride as he invites the praise and worship of each one he formed, each one he carried through life, each one he welcomes home.

Sounds of the ocean's roar crashes with thunder. The door opens to a white horse and its rider, Jesus, Faithful and True, the baby born to die, the man who went to the cross for us, the One whose victory is cause for the grand celebration, including a banquet the likes of which no one has enjoyed. Its sustenance provides eternal fulfillment and family unity that will fill us up yet always allow room for more. Jesus' followers will partake in endless fulfillment and offer gifts of worship that know no limit.

You received God's invitation. Have you given him your response?

TALK TO HIM

"Lord, in this holiday season, thank you for the glimpse of what celebrations await with you. Yes, I will be there!"

Feasting, I am feasting,
Feasting with my Lord;
I'm feasting, I am feasting,
On the living Word.

JOHN S. BROWN, "FEASTING WITH MY LORD"

"Your past is gone; enjoy a new year closer to me."

"Look, I am making everything new!" REVELATION 21:5

You made it.

Another year is behind you, another 365 days of growing older and (hopefully) wiser. Above all, another year of creating history with your Lord and Savior. Maybe you began this year feeling far from him. Maybe you hadn't met him yet. Or maybe you thought you knew him, only to discover around day 178 that you needed to accept Jesus' salvation personally and move closer to him.

Today is the end of something, but more importantly, it marks the beginning of something better. One of God's amazing qualities is his habit of always having something new in store—more newness beyond your greatest success, more than the sum of your costliest weaknesses, more than your hugest hurts stole, and more than the deadliest penalty for your sin. He is the God of more, yet his love for you is profoundly simple and pure in its newness.

As you continue with him into next year, commit to discover what more his *new* means in regard to your life. You can count on his thoughts to outshine your own dreams.

New may include some heartache, because heartache often serves as a catalyst for new growth in Christ's grace, new understanding of his heart, and new and healthy habits. But never waste time doubting that new also will mean fresh reasons for joy and unprecedented depths of peace if you stay close to him.

Learn from the past, but then put the past away so you don't trip over it as you keep in step with Jesus through the coming year. End this one well by committing to begin the next one even better. It just may be the year God sends his Son back for his children. Carry the encouragement of that possibility into each new moment, trusting that your God's newness will extend through eternity.

Happy New Year.

TALK TO HIM

"Lord, thank you for this year, and thank you even more for making all things new next year."

New mercies, each returning day,
Hover around us while we pray;
New perils past, new sins forgiven,
New thoughts of God, new hopes of heaven.

JOHN KEBLE, "NEW EVERY MORNING IS THE LOVE"

DAILY SCRIPTURE INDEX

TOPICAL INDEX